NEW SPAIN

NEW SPAIN

THE BIRTH OF MODERN MEXICO

Nicolas Cheetham

LONDON
VICTOR GOLLANCZ LTD
1974

© Nicolas Cheetham 1974

ISBN 0 575 01379 6

PRINTED IN GREAT BRITAIN
BY EBENEZER BAYLIS AND SON LTD
THE TRINITY PRESS, WORCESTER, AND LONDON

ACKNOWLEDGEMENTS

The author wishes to acknowledge the following sources from which he has quoted short passages for the purpose of comment: *Historia General de las Cosas de Nueva España* by Bernardino de Sahagún edited by Miguel Acosta Saignes (Editorial Nueva España, 1946); *Historia Antigua de Mexico* by Francisco Javier Clavijero (Editorial Porrúa, 1945); *The Lords of New Spain* by Alonso de Zorita abridged and translated by Benjamin Keen (Phoenix House, 1965); *The Aztecs under Spanish Rule* by Charles Gibson (Oxford University Press, 1964); *Mexican Mosaic* by Rodney Gallop (Faber, 1939); and *La Conquista Espiritual de Mexico* by Robert Ricard (Editorial Jus, 1947).

CONTENTS

Introduction 11

Part I
MEXICO BEFORE THE SPANIARDS

Chapter
1. The Ancient Civilizations 17
2. The Aztecs and their Neighbours 37

Part II
CONQUEST

3. Gods or Men? 79
4. The Two Worlds Collide 105

Part III
RECOVERY

5. The Spiritual Conquest 133
6. Wolves and Shepherds 159
7. Utopia in Michoacán 184

Part IV
THE VICEROYS AND THEIR WARDS

8. Lords of Two Races 203
9. The Limits of Justice 225

Part V
THE SEARCH FOR FUSION

10. The Frustrations of Learning 263
11. Towards a Nation 287

Maps 316
Glossary 320
Bibliography 323
Index 327

LIST OF ILLUSTRATIONS

'Pyramid of the Sun' at Teotihuacán (*photo: Mexican Government Department of Tourism*) *facing page*	64
Aztec Pyramid at Tenayuca (*photo: National Institute of Anthropology and History, Mexico City*)	64
Pyramid at Xochicalco (*photo: Mexican Embassy, London*)	65
Quetzalcóatl as God of the Winds (*photo: National Institute of Anthropology and History, Mexico City*)	65
Atrio Cross at Tepepulco. 16th century (*photo: National Institute of Anthropology and History, Mexico City*)	65
Hernan Cortés (*photo: Mexican Embassy, London*)	96
Antonio de Mendoza (*photo: Mexican Embassy, London*)	97
Pedro de Gante (*photo: National Institute of Anthropology and History, Mexico City*)	160
Bernardino de Sahagún (*photo: National Institute of Anthropology and History, Mexico City*)	161
Bartolome de las Casas (*photo: National Institute of Anthropology and History, Mexico City*)	192
Vasco de Quiroga (*photo: National Institute of Anthropology and History, Mexico City*)	193
Monastery Church at Huejotzingo. 16th century (*photo: National Institute of Anthropology and History, Mexico City*)	256
Monastery Church at Tecamachalco. 16th century (*photo: National Institute of Anthropology and History, Mexico City*)	257
Monastery Church at Acolman. 16th century (*photo: National Institute of Anthropology and History, Mexico City*)	257
Monastery Church at Actopan. 16th century (*photo: National Institute of Anthropology and History, Mexico City*)	288
Monastery Church at Tepeaca. 16th century (*photo: National Institute of Anthropology and History, Mexico City*)	289

INTRODUCTION

History offers a no more rewarding field of study than the encounter of two civilizations in widely differing stages of development and previously unacquainted with one another. Indeed, at a time when the world faces an indefinite prospect of increasing cultural uniformity, the very rarity of such confrontations in the past makes them appear the more fascinating and dramatic.

The collision between ancient Greece and Persia, the irruption of Alexander and his Macedonians into India, the age-long struggle and interaction between Christians and Moslems and the early contacts between Europeans and the peoples of the Far East, are memorable examples of themes which will always excite the imagination. They have a heroic character which lifts them above the common trend of historical record.

This quality is even more strikingly revealed in the clash which occurred in the early sixteenth century on Mexican soil between the civilization of Mesoamerica (a term roughly comprising modern Mexico and Central America) and that of Renaissance Europe as represented by Spain.

The event itself was unique because those civilizations had grown towards maturity in continents separated by a great ocean and in entire mental as well as geographical isolation one from the other. Neither even suspected that the other existed. No such total ignorance had preceded past conflicts of civilizations on the land mass of Europe and Asia, where the opponents usually possessed at least a hazy notion of each other's existence and where the gulf between each other's modes of thought and levels of technology was not unduly profound. They tended to meet on more or less equal terms and after the initial clash there was no very great obstacle to cultural interchange or, in many cases, to some degree of fusion. In Mesoamerica, on the other hand, there was no pre-disposition for the civilizations to mingle so easily.

The Spaniards conquered Mexico and the adjoining lands because their techniques were superior, their intellect more adaptable and their whole society more flexible and competitive than its Mexican-Indian counterpart, which for all its elaborate brilliance and remarkable cultural achievements was still rooted in the Stone Age.* It had already reached the most advanced stage that a neolithic civilization could attain. Nevertheless, when the dust of the Conquest had settled and the political systems of the Aztecs and the other Indian nations subdued by the Conquistadors were seen to have been shattered beyond repair, it was plain that the new Spanish order would have to take full account of the fact that the surviving masses of these peoples were not barbarians or primitives but the inheritors of two thousand years of civilization and social cohesion. Thus the problem immediately arose of building a European structure on Indian foundations and of grafting European religion, ideas and techniques on the Indian stock. The main purpose of this book is to describe how this work was tackled, and with what measure of success, within the compass of the vital sixteenth century. In the words of an eminent Mexican scholar, Angel Maria Garibay, "Mexico's past is shaped and synthesized in the sixteenth century, the true embryo of the whole subsequent history of the Mexican nation" (*Historia de la Literatura Náhuatl*).

The military epic of the Spanish conquest, under the leadership of Cortés, has often been retold, and it is a story which seldom palls in the retelling. But it is surely incomplete unless equally full and sympathetic treatment is accorded to the much longer and more crucial period during which the vast Stone Age community was transformed and reinvigorated for its future destiny by the infusion of European blood, thought and techniques. There is clearly room for a balanced account of the age of transition from the pre-Columbian to the colonial society. In attempting this task, I have sought to contrast the destructive impact of the conquest on the older civilization with the resilience which enabled the Indians, struggling for survival amid a chaotic upheaval, to assimilate the ways of their conquerors and to adjust them to their own.

This has led me to examine the complex relationship between the conquered peoples and the men of thought and action who

---

* The use in this book of the terms "Stone Age" and "Neolithic" does not imply that pre-Columbian culture was crude and primitive. But it is important to keep in mind that metal-working played a very minor part in Mesoamerican technology before the Spanish conquest. There was no Bronze Age nor Iron Age in ancient Mexico.

founded New Spain. The development of such a theme necessarily embraces a wide variety of incident on a vivid and constantly changing scene. I have paid particular attention to the diffusion of Christianity by the friars and its effects on architecture and the arts, to the reshaping of social, economic and cultural life by the introduction of European ways, to the treatment of the Indian by his new masters and to the restraining influences of the Church and the viceregal government on the behaviour of the Spanish settlers in their new and exotic surroundings.

The early chapters of the book deal with pre-Columbian Mexico and with the Conquest itself. Although the pre-Columbian field has been thoroughly explored by scholars and more general writers, no analysis of the process of fusion of the two cultures would make sense unless preceded by a broad picture of the Indian scene and of the evolution of the strange society which the Spaniards discovered. As for the Conquest, I have been less concerned with its purely military aspects than with the reactions of the principal Spanish and Mexican participants in its glories and horrors, and especially with the behaviour of the latter when faced with an overwhelming and totally unforseen upheaval and its incalculable consequences.

In choosing the title of this book, I have of course been aware that the limits of "New Spain", as the term was understood in the sixteenth century, were not the same as those of modern Mexico. Roughly speaking, New Spain comprised the whole of the central heartland of Mexico from the Gulf to the Pacific, and of the south as far as the isthmus of Tehuantepec. The present states of Chiapas, Tabasco, Campeche and Yucatán were not regarded as belonging to New Spain. Nor, for purposes of formal nomenclature, were the north-west and north-east, areas of shifting frontiers and spasmodic colonial advance over huge thinly populated regions. These were known as Nueva Galicia and Nuevo León respectively, but for all practical purposes they can be considered as extensions of the Viceroyalty of New Spain which had its seat in Mexico City.

The expression "New Spain" was first used by Hernán Cortés in concluding his Second Letter from Mexican soil to the King-Emperor Charles V, dated October 30, 1520. He informed his sovereign that in as much as he had been able to form an opinion, the country which he had conquered bore a striking resemblance to Spain, in its fertility, size, cold climate and many other aspects. He had therefore judged that the most suitable name that he could bestow on it was New Spain of the Ocean Sea, and he entreated the monarch to confirm his choice. After a long delay the imperial sanction was received.

Part I
MEXICO BEFORE THE SPANIARDS

Chapter 1

THE ANCIENT CIVILIZATIONS

MAN IS NOT indigenous to the American continent. According to the anthropologists, the first human inhabitants of the New World crossed the Bering Strait from north-eastern Siberia some tens of thousands of years ago. Thus the ancestors of all American Indians were distant cousins of the future Chinese and Mongols. Subsequently wave after wave of migrants filtered slowly downwards through North and Central America, and thence to Tierra del Fuego in the far South, adapting themselves at each stage of their long journey to an extraordinary variety of climates. As one millennium succeeded another, they eked out a primitive existence as hunters, fishers and food gatherers, in the apparently endless stagnation of the Old Stone Age. As Father José de Acosta, a Jesuit who published in 1590 his *Historia Natural y Moral de las Indias*, picturesquely but correctly puts it:

> the ancient and first inhabitants of the provinces which we call New Spain were very barbarous dwellers in the wilderness, who subsisted by hunting alone . . . They neither sowed nor cultivated the land, nor did they live in communities . . . They dwelt in the clefts and most rugged places in the mountains, living bestially, without polity, totally naked.

Early Spanish writers, being almost invariably clerics, were not particularly interested in the origins and racial connexions, Mongolian or otherwise, of the Indian peoples of Mesoamerica. They were much more closely concerned to establish that the Indians were descended, like other folk, from Adam and Noah. For once this was taken for granted there was no theological obstacle to their conversion to the Christian faith and to their participation in the benefits to be gained in this world and the next by rational and Christian human beings. Emphatically they were not to be considered as sub-human creatures who could be exploited without trouble to the exploiter's conscience, as so many Europeans were only too prone to assume at the time.

Nevertheless the same Father Acosta, a man of deep learning and of an enquiring mind, was puzzled by the problem of how the Americas had come to be populated at all. After carefully examining such passages in classical writers, in the Scriptures and in the Fathers of the Church as seemed to him to be relevant to the subject, and drawing on his own lengthy experience of the New World, he firmly rejects the theory that the original inhabitants reached that continent from across the oceans. On the contrary, he concludes that they arrived by land a few thousand years ago, and conjectures that this was made possible by some continuity between America and either Europe or Asia as yet undiscovered by geographers. He adds that in his opinion the first dwellers in America must have been rude and savage, or that if they had brought with them any civilized customs from their homelands they had forgotten them, and the result had been "una barbariedad infinita en el Nuevo Mundo".

Apart from its theological basis, Acosta's explanation of the origin of man in America is logical and sensible. In refusing to believe that the Indian civilizations of America were at any time influenced by contacts with another continent he was anticipating modern conclusions. He agrees in fact with serious scholars and scientists of our own time who cannot accept the attractive but thinly supported arguments of the so-called Diffusionists in favour of the contrary thesis. In default of further evidence, we must be satisfied that the ancient civilizations of America were developed by the Indians themselves, the remote descendants of primitive wanderers from Asia, without assistance from outside.

By the third millennium B.C. a revolution had occurred in the life of the nomadic groups occupying the high plateau of Central Mexico. They had already begun to form small but settled communities, to cultivate maize and other plants and to make pottery. Some authorities maintain that these early ceramics reproduce basic designs of Asian ancestry which penetrated into Mexico from the eastern side of North America. The now barren central plateau was at that period fertile, well watered and forested, and the temperate climate favoured a swift cultural advance. It is therefore surprising to find that whereas this advance began in the central highlands it developed much faster when it spread to the coast of the Gulf of Mexico. There, in very different conditions, it gave birth to the archaic civilization known as Olmec.

"Olmeca" means "inhabitant of Olmán", that is to say the land of the rubber tree, from which the Spanish word hule is derived. This tree is typical of the lush vegetation of the coastal strip, five hundred miles in length but averaging only fifty miles in width, which stretches from the mouth of the river Pánuco in the north to that of the Grijalva in the southern state of Tabasco. In this unpromising environment of slow, sinuous rivers, matted swamps and dense tropical jungles the peoples whom we call the Olmecs waged a brilliantly successful struggle against nature. By 1200 B.C. they had so well diversified their economic activity and organized their social system as to be able to project their influence over a much wider area. A distinctively Olmec style of life both recoiled upon the plateau and spread rapidly southwards. Such expansion was greatly accelerated at the end of the first millennium and Olmec culture reached its apogee between about 800 and 200 B.C.

The Olmecs were the first to develop that sense of social discipline which was so striking a feature of all Mesoamerican communities and which, when it was destroyed by the Conquest, the Spaniards found such difficulty in restoring. This no doubt sprang from the need for a careful regulation of economic life in the tropics, at a time when stone tools were man's only weapon against the jungle. But the Olmecs managed to obtain a plentiful yield from their subsistence agriculture, and their diet was abundantly supplemented by game and fish. The jungle dominated not only their material existence but also the evolution of their religious ideas. These centred around the cult of the jaguar, the dreaded and omnipresent beast which obsessed the Olmec imagination and served as the totem or ancestral symbol of the whole race. In the words of Ignacio Bernal, "the concept of associating man with an animal seems to be basic in Mesoamerican thinking" (*Mexico Before Cortés: Art, History, Legend*). A superior class of magicians or shamans seems to have interpreted the cult to the people, and to have directed all social and economic activity. As it gradually became refined and intellectualized, the shamans emerged as a full-fledged hierarchy of priests conducting an elaborate religious ceremonial and presiding over a rigidly controlled and stratified society of peasants, artisans and traders. So far as can be ascertained, this society was essentially pacific; at least no warlike traits are apparent.

To judge from the numerous archaeological sites already explored or awaiting exploration, the Olmec lands were prosperous and densely populated. As depicted by their own artists the Olmecs were plump and stocky folk, with slanting eyes, thick lips and necks and endearing chubby features. They often had deformed, pear-shaped heads and artificially serrated teeth. Normally both sexes wore scanty clothing but painted or tattooed their bodies. They made lavish use of ear and nose rings, bracelets and similar adornments. On ceremonial occasions they sported turbans and plumes, or magical masks in the form of jaguars, serpents and fabulous birds. We have no idea of the character of the endless and colourful festivities held in honour of the jaguar totem and other divinities of nature, but the celebrations certainly included an early version of the ritual ball game which was part of the Olmec legacy to all later Mesoamerican cultures. It was played with a solid rubber ball which the players struck with rubber knee and elbow pads. It also seems to have ended with the ritual decapitation of one or more members of the losing team. There is little evidence, however, of the extent to which human sacrifice was practised in the Olmec religion.

The Olmecs excelled as craftsmen. They produced a great variety of ceramic vessels and of realistic or fantastic figurines representing men, animals and combinations of human and animal forms. Their favourite medium, however, was stone. In their treatment of hard and semi-precious materials such as jade, quartz, serpentine and diorite they approached perfection. Even more impressive, if less delicate, was their monumental sculpture. This took two principal forms, the shallow bas-relief in which the human figure is seen in profile, and the colossal basalt heads with bulbous negroid features which decorated the great ceremonial centres such as La Venta and Tres Zapotes. We cannot guess what magico-religious purpose was fulfilled by these massive geometric shapes. The ceremonial centres themselves, though spacious and symmetrically planned, were constructed of earth and wood and the stone altars and columns which are found among them served only as embellishments. Nothing existed in the way of a true architectural style. In view of the Olmec preoccupation with fine stonework, it is a remarkable fact that the material itself had to be transported from a distance of sixty miles, most probably by water, for southern Vera Cruz and Tabasco are notably deficient in stone.

There is much substance in the claim that the Olmec culture was the source or substratum of all future civilized development in Mesoamerica. In the early period before 800 B.C. its influence can be traced at Tlatilco, in the Valley of Mexico, and many other sites on the central tableland. Later it expanded across the isthmus of Tehuantepec into Chiapas and the borders of what is now Guatemala, and penetrated to the Pacific coast by way of Morelos and Guerrero. Oaxaca also became an important focus of Olmec expansion in its final stage. Typically Olmec sculpture can still be seen in place on the great ridge of Monte Albán which soars above Oaxaca city. What is more exciting and significant is the discovery on that site that its occupants had worked out a system of numeration and employed a very early form of writing. Other glyphs found at La Venta and Tres Zapotes provide unmistakable evidence that the Olmecs, in the last centuries of their era, had invented the calendar. Two of these can be read as recording the years 31 B.C. and A.D. 162 respectively. It also appears that they had started to make astronomical observations. By this time the Olmecs were on the point of disappearing from history, or rather pre-history, as mysteriously as they had entered it. But before they finally vanished they bequeathed to their successors the principal elements of the classical cultures of Mexico which grew up simultaneously in the first millennium of the Christian era.

The most important of these were the Maya, the Zapotec and that of Teotihuacán. It is well to keep in mind that they were all three flourishing a thousand years before the Spaniards burst upon the scene, and that their previous existence was to all intents and purposes ignored not only by the invaders from Europe but even by the Aztecs, the last representatives of Mesoamerican civilization. They had perished centuries before the Aztecs, a small barbarian tribe, arrived in the Valley of Mexico and made a fresh start, relearning and elaborating in their own fashion the traditions and refinements of the legendary past.

Before reviewing the other classical cultures we should take a look at that which arose at Teotihuacán, because it combined features peculiar to the central plateau with others imported from the Olmec region, as typified by the finds at Tlatilco. The archaic society of the Valley of Mexico, a landscape of reedy lakes and huge forested mountains, was less sophisticated and inventive than that of the Gulf, but in spite of its rusticity it made some notable advances. At Cuicuilco in the Federal District, half submerged by a lava flow, stands the earliest known example of the pyramid, a type of structure which has come to be associated closely with Mexico as with Egypt. The Cuicuilco monument is not in fact a real pyramid but is shaped like a cone, seventy feet high and topped by a platform which originally supported a small temple with a thatch roof. It was surrounded by a pattern of lesser ceremonial buildings, and a similar though not so inspiring layout was recently discovered, in 1967, during the clearance of land for the Olympic village. Dozens of similar sites probably lie buried below the lava of the district and the suburbs of the capital, but they were eclipsed in the early classical period by the grandiose conceptions of Teotihuacán, the first real city in America and the precursor of Aztec Tenochtitlán.

The city, together with the surrounding villages, formed a community of possibly three hundred thousand people. It stands to reason that the civilization of this immense place was not confined to one narrow corner of the Valley, about thirty miles north-east of Mexico City, but radiated over most of what came to be known as Anáhuac, that is to say the lake basin and the plain of Tlaxcala and Puebla to the east, the plain being divided from the Valley by the high mountain chain which includes the volcanos Popocatépetl and Ixtaccíhuatl. This cultural diffusion is indeed confirmed by excavations still continuing at Cholula and other sites. They have revealed, as might have been expected, the existence of other flourishing centres with the same characteristics as Teotihuacán. We can also safely assume that in ancient times the whole region was tremendously fertile and populous. Finally the archaeological evidence proves that social and economic cohesion was maintained for the best part of a thousand years by a theocratic government.

The early Mesoamerican civilizations matured, by modern standards, with incomprehensible slowness. Scholars have therefore been accustomed to divide these long vistas of time into periods corresponding to phases of cultural progress. Teotihuacán has been allotted at least four of these, beginning about 100 B.C. and ending not later than A.D. 800, throughout which the same system, controlled by the ruler-priests, continued to prevail.

Apart from a few so far unreadable hieroglyphs, the Teotihuacános developed no form of writing, so our knowledge of them rests entirely on what the archaeologists find. All that the Aztecs and the Spaniards were aware of was an enormous area—about forty square miles—of scrub-covered mounds, some of them very large. It was the Aztecs who named the place Teotihuacán, which means "home of the gods" in the Náhuatl language. The Spaniards were likewise totally ignorant of what lay under the surface, nor did they much care. After the first excavations by Mexican archaeologists, purely arbitrary names were given to the city's two most prominent structures, the so-called pyramids of the Sun and Moon, the first of which rivals in bulk the great pyramid of Gizeh in Egypt. The exact religious purpose of these huge buildings remains obscure, but it is obvious that the whole monumental section of the city, which contains the temples and their precincts and is traversed by a ceremonial avenue one and a half miles long, was designed on an elaborate astronomical plan. Whether or not this arrangement stemmed directly from the Olmecs, it is a fact that the precise mathematical siting of monuments in conformity with the demands of a solar cult was practised quite independently and in much earlier periods by neolithic peoples in other continents. The residential quarters of the city, too, conformed to a regular, rectangular pattern.

The Teotihuacán civilization attained its apex between A.D. 200 and 500. With the passing of centuries the principal edifices were frequently remodelled, as if the architects were determined to improve on their predecessors' efforts. For instance the famous sculptured frieze of feathered serpents and other monsters symbolizing the deities of nature which adorn the temple of Quetzalcóatl were buried under a plain new pyramid devoid of decoration. No doubt some religious impulse dictated this urge for renewal. Many of the delicate frescoes which embellished temples and dwellings have survived almost intact, but their exterior covering of gaily coloured stucco has perished. Thus, like ruined Greek temples which also lost their colour, they give a misleading impression of austerity. The craftsmen of Teotihuacán excelled in luxury products, fine ceramics, jewellery and stone masks inlaid with mosaic, but they also turned out in the mass clay figurines and more banal objects which were exported to other centres of classical culture, such as Zapotec, Oaxaca and the Maya country, as well as to the less advanced areas to the west and north. In return, the products of the other civilized regions flowed into Teotihuacán.

The stability of this civilization was not demonstrably shaken by inner convulsions or outside pressures during the whole of its thousand year span. Unaccustomed as we are to the leisurely rhythms of Stone Age society, we regard its durability and apparent lack of disturbance as almost incredible. Such prolonged calm can only have been due to the preservation of an easy balance between population and the means of subsistence. Resistance to change did not imply stagnation but the acceptance of a way of life which satisfied man's spiritual and material needs and to which no alternative was simply conceivable. We find it hard to imagine why this busy and lively society, so obviously endowed with intellectual and artistic ability, failed to invent the wheel and the plough and, to develop metal-working. But these advances were never achieved by any of the Mesoamerican peoples in the classical and post-classical periods. All reached a high but strictly neolithic stage of development and evolved no further. So far as Teotihuacán is concerned, it would not be too fanciful to claim that its nameless folk were living in a golden age.

The Teotihuacanos were not warlike. Trade, not war, was the distinguishing feature of the classical era. There is no evidence of habitual strife between communities in their own sphere and they enjoyed an extraordinary immunity against attack by barbarians from the north. Either their prestige was so awe-inspiring as to deter aggression or, for obscure climatic reasons, the outer tribes were not on the move. Eventually, however, the barriers were breached, the nomads poured in and Teotihuacán itself was burned and abandoned. The whole fabric of its civilization suddenly dissolved. Exactly why this catastrophe occurred is anybody's guess. Perhaps the population at last outran the food supply: it is significant that Tlaloc, the god of rain and agriculture, occupied first place in the local pantheon. Alternatively the theocracy had become uncreative and oppressive and its foundations were fatally sapped by social disorders. It must be assumed that some kind of internal decay preceded the disaster. In any case this was so complete that the great city was erased from human memory, giving place to insubstantial myths about gods and giants.

Far to the southward, the Old Empire of the Mayas was, roughly speaking, contemporary with Teotihuacán. It originated in the Petén, the tropical plain in northern Guatemala and British Honduras. Thence it spread rapidly west into Chiapas, across the Usumacinta river, south across the Motagua river into the Republic of Honduras and north into Yucatán, Campeche and Quintana Roo. The foundation of its numerous cities can be accurately dated because scholars have unravelled the Mayan calendar and can read the date glyphs inscribed on the stone stelae which the Mayas erected in order to mark the end of each twenty-year period. Unfortunately the date of the earliest stelae is disputed. Some archaeologists, basing themselves on the evidence of the glyphs discovered in the Olmec area, put the foundation of Uaxactún in the Petén as far back as the first century A.D. Others are sure that the beginnings of Uaxactún and the neighbouring Tikal cannot be traced earlier than A.D. 330. But there is general agreement that, except in Yucatán, the Old Empire had collapsed so utterly by the end of the ninth century that the cities must have been voluntarily abandoned. This conclusion is deduced from the total lack of new monuments and inscriptions on the old sites after that point. The cities vanished as mysteriously as they had arisen, and were engulfed in the jungle.

There has been much speculation about the cause of this sudden decline, which followed a period of great brilliance. The most reasonable explanation is that after five hundred years the tropical soil had been exhausted by primitive methods of cultivation and would no longer support the population of the cities. It is calculated that some of these must have contained fifty to two hundred thousand inhabitants, who could not be fed indefinitely by burning the forest, working the soil to exhaustion and then passing on to another piece of forest. In short, the fate of Teotihuacán was repeated. The Old Mayan Empire fell because its economy, and perhaps its social organization as well, had become top-heavy.

However that may be, the catastrophe was not the end of the Mayas. After deserting their original homeland they migrated northwards to the outlying regions of the Yucatán peninsula, where they reinforced the population of the existing cities and founded others. The result was a renaissance of Mayan culture which lasted from the tenth century, the great age of Chichén-Itzá and Uxmal, till about a century before the Spanish conquest. It was partly due to a fusion of these northern Mayas with a smaller but influential stream of migrants from central Mexico. This period is known as the New Empire. Internal dissension and wars between the cities eventually destroyed it and the Spaniards only completed the process.

The Old Empire was not a centralized state but a loose confederation of cities with a common culture and internal organization. Their relations with each other have been compared with those of the ancient Greek or mediaeval Italian city-states but seem to have been less quarrelsome. Each was governed by a hereditary chieftain called the Halach Uinic, who was assisted in the event of war by an elected Nacom, or Commander-in-Chief. But the real power appears to have rested not so much with the nobles and warriors but with the astronomer-priests, a caste of intellectuals who enjoyed special privileges. They were the community's experts in divination, religious directors and, above all, mathematicians, dedicated to the study of the heavenly bodies and the working out of the most sophisticated chronological and calendrical systems. (They habitually used two calendars, one solar and one purely religious, for fixing dates.) On a descending social scale were grouped the soldiers, traders and craftsmen, the cultivators and finally the slaves. Although hostilities did from time to time occur, society was essentially pacific.

The Mayas recorded their calculations in manuscripts made from tree fibres, using a mainly ideographic writing. Of the innumerable documents which must have constituted the libraries of their temple-observatories, only three have survived Spanish bonfires and earlier vicissitudes. Luckily they have sufficed, together with the wealth of inscriptions found on the excavated sites, for an understanding of Mayan mathematics, although the significance of most of the recorded glyphs still remains hidden. Notably the Mayas were the first Meso-american people to grasp the importance of zero and to have a sign for it. We also possess a few Mayan manuscripts written in Latin characters after the Conquest, which give a very interesting if fragmentary picture of historical events. There are plenty of references in the Spanish writers of the sixteenth century who dealt with Mayan affairs to "books" of "characters", "letters" and "figures" preserving the annals and traditions of the various tribes. Most probably these were pictographic manuscripts like those of central Mexico. They were jealously guarded by the Indians but sometimes used as the basis of transcriptions in Latin letters. But both originals and transcriptions soon became lamentably rare.

Thanks to the sculpture, painting and writing of the Mayas we know a lot about their religion. In comparison with the simple nature divinities worshipped at Teotihuacán, their pantheon was vastly complicated. They conceived of a shadowy creator or supreme being, but he had little connexion with mundane affairs. The heavens above the earth and the nether regions beneath it were divided respectively into thirteen and nine superimposed worlds, each presided over by a separate god. There were gods and goddesses of the sky and the underworld, of the sun, moon and stars, of night and day, wind and rain, war and death and many others. Some were benevolent, others hostile to man. The Mayans believed in a future life, which could be one of pleasure or of pain. Naturally this host of dieties needed propitiation in the form of fasting, sacrifices and elaborate ceremonies enlivened by music and dancing. Human sacrifice, which was sparingly practised at Teotihuacán, was a common feature of Mayan religion, especially in the New Empire, and was frequently followed by ritual cannibalism. It could be the fate of captives after a victory, or of slaves, women or children selected for immolation at the festival of a particular god.

The cities of the Old Empire, clustering thickly throughout the forests of the Petén, presented an appearance that was at once perfectly ordered and flamboyant to a fantastic degree. Fray Diego de Landa, Bishop of Yucatán in the mid-sixteenth century, who combined a pitiless zeal in the persecution of the Mayan religion with a deep interest in Indian culture, wrote with regretful admiration, in his *Relación de la Cosas de Yucatán*, of the beauty and stateliness of those which he saw in their decadence. If they could have been observed by European eyes at their apogee, they would have appeared strange and extravagant beyond belief, more exotic even than the Aztec Tenochtitlán which made its conquerors gasp with wonder. The buildings—pyramids and temples, palaces, observatories and ball-courts—profusely decorated with sculpture and formal carvings and gleaming with white or coloured stucco, were arranged in planned groups at varying distances from each other. At Copán one group is seven miles away from the principal plaza. Mayan architects were versatile, at least by neolithic standards; they surpassed their contemporaries in central Mexico in both the design and the decoration of their stone buildings. They invented the corbelled arch and some of their patios and colonnades have an almost modern air about them. Simplicity of line contrasts with a baroque extravagance of ornament. Each city exhibits its own variations from the common style, which reaches the height of delicacy and sophistication at Palenque. Here the unique discovery was made of an elaborately carved sarcophagus containing the body of a great dignitary. This lies in an underground tomb-chamber surmounted by a pyramid and temple and approached by a staircase which descends steeply through the interior of the structure. It can be dated to the seventh century A.D. As even the best-known Mayan sites have been only partially explored, there is no knowing what surprises future digs may have in store.

The perimeters of the cities, and the spaces between the groups of monumental buildings, were covered by the thatched houses of the people, resembling the cottages of modern Yucatán. Each urban complex was set among gardens and fields stretching out towards the jungle horizon. But no community was really isolated from its neighbours, with which it was easily linked by water or along raised causeways. In the Petén the rivers carried most of the traffic. In Yucatán, on the other hand, there are no rivers, since the water everywhere underlies a thin crust of rock: thus the causeway was the natural means of communication. We may thus imagine a constant coming and going between the cities, in conditions of security and order. In the background were the deep rain forests, the haunt of the jaguar and the tapir, the howler monkey and the brilliantly plumed quetzal bird.

The chief inhabitants of the cities lived up to their exotic environment. It would be hard to imagine more bizarre specimens of the human race than those portrayed on the stelae and bas reliefs, and more especially in the series of wall paintings at Bonampak, in the jungle of southern Chiapas. It is thought that these latter must commemorate a famous victory, for the central scenes represent a spirited battle and the triumph of the chieftain over a troop of dejected captives. Others depict in various attitudes, ceremonious or relaxed, great personages in full warlike panoply and courtly attire, also a host of lesser fry —soldiers, musicians, dancers and attendants—and even a few noble ladies. The whole effect is remarkably unstylized and naturalistic. Here, we feel, are the Mayas as they were in real life, fat, brown and sleek, hooknosed and with artificially flattened skulls. Gorgeously as they are dressed and ornamented, the height of riotous fantasy is attained in their towering feathered head-dresses, grinning animal masks and swelling turbans such as any sultan might envy. The glyphs and the paintings are liberally labelled and doubtless hold the clue to the true nature of the occasion, but they have so far proved undecipherable.

Besides the Bonampak murals (the originals of which are unfortunately deteriorating fast) our best impression of what the Mayas looked like is derived from the innumerable clay figures unearthed from an immense cemetery in the island of Jaina. This lies off the western coast of the Yucatán peninsula, that is to say at the opposite end of the Mayan area. These little masterpieces of sculpture portray in the most lively and faithful manner all types of Mayan society from the highest to the most lowly, in very realistic postures, and provide an admirable foil in the queer pageantry of Bonampak.

The second flowering of the Maya culture in Yucatán can only be understood in relation to developments on the Mexican plateau after the fall of Teotihuacán, but before these are described mention must be made of the third important centre of civilization in the classical period, that of the Zapotecs, which died away at roughly the same time as Teotihuacán and the Old Empire of the Mayas. Unlike the latter it was limited to a small territory in the valley of Oaxaca and the surrounding hill country, a region of luminous beauty with an almost Mediterranean climate. The Zapotec community received its first stimulus from the Olmecs and was later susceptible to influences from the more extensive cultures to the north and south, but it was never absorbed into either of these spheres. For many hundreds of years it preserved a vitality and distinction of its own. Like all Mesoamerican societies it was a theocracy, self-sufficient and unamenable to change. The rulers practised astronomy and the art of writing, but once more their hieroglyphs provide no clue to the course of their history.

The political and religious capital of this little state was the imposing acropolis of Monte Albán. Here the monumental buildings, with their singular purity of line and absence of heavy decoration, are marvellously adjusted to the natural environment. Eschewing the colossal, the architecture triumphs by sheer elegance and sense of proportion. A peculiar feature of this culture was an almost exaggerated reverence for the dead; Zapotec magnates were buried in richly frescoed tombs pierced in the rock of the sacred hill and furnished with splendid funerary urns representing the deceased in their full ceremonial array. The craftsmen modelled beautifully in clay, but curiously enough produced no figure sculpture in stone. As with the other classical cultures, the creative period lasted for many hundreds of years. But shortly after A.D. 800 the same mysterious law of decline overtook the Zapotecs as it did the Teotihuacanos and the Mayas of the Old Empire. No more monuments were built and the Zapotecs themselves were squeezed into the corners of their own land by the invasion of the Mixtecs, a dour race from the mountain massifs immediately to the north.

These people occupied Monte Albán and even took over the Zapotec tombs for their own dead chieftains. They were no great intellectuals—for instance they had little bent for astronomy—but like most Indian nations they had their outstanding talents. One of these was for working in metals, especially gold, and in other precious materials such as jade and rock crystal. Their artificers also experimented with copper, but not to the point of breaking out of the Stone Age. Their second and surprising contribution to culture consists of the lively pictographic manuscripts on which they recorded genealogies and certain events in their history. A few of these have survived the general massacre of pre-Columbian writings and can be interpreted.

In central Mexico the fall of Teotihuacán was followed by a long period of obscurity and confusion, a sort of dark age of which it is hard to give any coherent account. Some regions, like the Valley of Mexico, suffered a sharp cultural relapse. The barbarian invaders who sacked the city lack even a name. These nomads, who had for long haunted the fringes of the settled country, presumably formed the vanguard of the Nahua-speaking tribes which dominated the highlands of Anáhuac in the subsequent Toltec and Aztec periods and whose descendants live there today. Presumably, too, they fused with the existing inhabitants and thus acquired a measure of civilized habits. This process can be detected at various sites in the Valley, but it was no revival of past glories. Teotihuacán itself was gradually deserted and forgotten.

Outside the confines of the Valley the classical civilization did not end so abruptly. It certainly persisted at Cholula, eighty miles south-east of Teotihuacán, where archaeology has revealed an unique record of continuous human occupation from archaic times until now. While in classical times it obviously played a lesser role than Teotihuacán, fresh traces of the culture common to both are constantly coming to light there and in the surrounding district. Apart from these discoveries, Cholula once boasted the bulkiest pyramid ever constructed in Mexico, ancient Egypt or anywhere else. Rebuilt time after time, it was finally ruined when the Spaniards destroyed Cholula's temples and now resembles a steep amorphous hill, with a church perched on the top. Traditionally the pyramid was crowned by the temple of Quetzalcóatl, by origin the nature god whom we have already observed at Teotihuacán represented as the feathered serpent. But whether he is conceived as a god, a legendary hero or an historical personage—or merely used as a peg on which to hang the most improbable fictions—he broods inescapably over the Mexican scene, and wherever he crops up he poses a new puzzle.

In particular he dominates Xochicalco, a site where the old culture lasted apparently unscathed for two or three centuries after the end of the classical age. Indeed it served as a link between the latter and the short-lived kingdom of the Toltecs, the first of the Nahua peoples to leave their mark on Mexican history. Xochicalco is also an acropolis, a smaller version of Monte Albán, commanding the plain of Morelos and looking northwards to the Ajusco range which hides the Valley of Mexico itself. The main temple is decorated with a superb frieze of feathered serpents in low relief, a motif which of course recalls Teotihuacán, and we know from Toltec traditions chronicled by Aztec writers after the Conquest that Xochicalco was in fact famed for its cult of Quetzalcóatl. So far so good; the heritage of Teotihuacán is established; but it is baffling to notice at the same time that the human figures of richly attired priests which alternate with the monsters on the frieze are executed in unmistakably Mayan style. So are many of the glyphs carved on the same building. Thus the connexion of Xochicalco with the Mayas is plainly revealed, but how their influence came to be clearly stamped on this lonely stronghold, so distant from the Mayan homeland, is inexplicable. We shall soon see, however, that in due course Quetzalcóatl made his way to the Maya area.

Elements from Xochicalco and the Maya country are combined in the architecture of El Tajín, a very substantial city in the coastal region of central Vera Cruz. Little is known of the people who built it. Their antecedents may have been Olmec, and they were certainly the ancestors of the Totonacs, the first Indians whom Cortés encountered when he landed in Mexico and whose language was related to the Mayan. Among the buildings excavated are a seven-storied pyramid with niches instead of wall panels on each storey and an immense ball court. The whole site is laid out on a majestic scale quite reminiscent of the Mayas, but has been only partially explored. In general, one suspects that much remains for archaeology to search out in order to add to our inadequate knowledge of this transitional period. Is it not likely that other populous and sophisticated places of the type of Xochicalco and El Tajín are still awaiting discovery?

The void left in central Mexico by the destruction of Teotihuacán was filled in the tenth century by the Nahua speaking Toltecs, who came from the north-west. There was something about these people that appealed most insistently to the imagination of their contemporaries and of all successive generations down to the Spanish conquest. Their prestige remained so high that well after their supremacy had been swept away by fresh hordes of barbarians a good claim to Toltec ancestry was dearly prized by the invaders' chieftains.

They were invariably represented by the Indian annalists who wrote shortly after the Conquest as the first inhabitants of Mexico, and this version of native history was uncritically accepted by contemporary Spanish writers. Even Fray Bernardino de Sahagún, the learned Franciscan who devoted a lifetime to the study of Indian languages, manners and traditions, states briefly in the prologue to his vast work *Historia General de las Cosas de Nueva España*, that the Toltecs built their capital, Tula, a thousand years before his own time. Their successors gave them credit not so much for their military prowess, which was undoubted, as for their preeminence in all the arts of government and civilized living.

The Toltecs must certainly have possessed remarkable qualities, and more especially that of rapidly assimilating such remains of the former classical civilization as they found in their new domain. Moreover they were in touch with declining examples of the old culture at places like Xochicalco. Sahagún's favourite adjectives for the Toltecs are "pulidos" and "curiosos", and he adds in parenthesis "like those in Flanders today". Thus he follows the native chroniclers in regarding them primarily as skilled and ingenious artificers and builders; indeed that is exactly the significance of the word "tolteca" in Náhuatl. He goes on to describe their excellence as architects, painters and carpenters, workers in precious stones and metals, weavers in textiles and in the feathers of exotic birds. On a higher plane, he praises their accomplishments in medicine and music. Under the heading of "natural astrology" he attributes to them the invention of the calendar and the pursuit of all kinds of astronomical research. They were in addition "good men and addicted to virtue"; they recognized the existence of a supreme god and his consort who reigned over the twelve heavens and the earth, but worshipped principally Quetzalcóatl, whose priest was a high personage, leader of the people, bearing the same name.

The above is obviously a succinct and impressionist picture of the classical culture, as viewed by those whose memory did not go further back than the Toltecs. As a matter of historical fact, the latter's achievements were more modest. They arrived in the mid-tenth century, but by the beginning of the thirteenth they had already been broken and dispersed. It so happens that the fortunes of the tribe were bound up with the careers of two or three outstanding individuals. The first of these was Mixcóatl, the chieftain who led them into Anáhuac and established their first capital at Culhuacán, now a small village on the southern fringe of Mexico City. For a time he prospered, and extended his rule over the neighbouring mountains into Morelos. Naturally it took in Xochicalco, which seems to have been preserved intact, together with its worship of Quetzalcóatl. Then Mixcóatl was murdered by a usurping brother. Luckily his posthumous son, Topiltzin, was secretly entrusted to the care of the priests at Xochicalco, who brought him up in the service of their own deity. When he grew up he duly challenged the usurper and killed him. Having thus vindicated his claim to the kingdom, he decided to found a new capital at Tula in the present State of Hidalgo, to the north-west of the Valley of Mexico and nearer the frontier between the settled zone and the nomad barbarism from beyond. He made the cult of Quetzalcóatl the official religion of the Toltec people and, as the high priest of the god, adopted his name as well. We are now confronted with the historical Quetzalcóatl, and with a new and intriguing problem.

The foundation of Tula is dated to A.D. 980, and Topiltzin-Quetzalcóatl is recorded as having reigned there for nineteen years, a time of peace and abundance. According to the legends the royal treasury overflowed with riches and the land regularly produced bumper harvests. Meanwhile the king was busily promoting the mild cult of Quetzalcóatl as the official religion. Sahagún says that he used to tell his subjects that "there was one lord and god only and that was Quetzalcóatl, and that he wanted only snakes and butterflies offered in sacrifice". But the Toltecs were still barbarians and fighting men at heart. As such they preferred the bloody rites of their traditional war god Tezcatlipoca, and in time the opposition grew too strong for the reformer. Accompanied by a large band of followers, he went into exile and never again returned to Tula.

Topiltzin is next located at Cholula, which had of course worshipped Quetzalcóatl since classical times. Finally he turns up on the coast where he vanishes as a historical figure and myth takes over. The chroniclers say that he sailed off to Yucatán, but not before predicting his eventual return from the east in a particular year—designated as One Reed—of the cyclic calendar of ancient Mexico. A similar designation recurred every fifty-two years and by a truly ominous coincidence it was to do so in the very year when Cortés disembarked on the same gulf coast. In sixteenth-century accounts of the Conquest this tradition, and another which attributed to Quetzalcóatl a fair skin and a beard, were naturally given enormous prominence by both Indian and Spanish writers. Since then they have regularly served as the explanation of Moctezuma's apparent inaction and fatalism in the year of the Spanish invasion, when faced with the prospect of the god-man Quetzalcóatl, in the shape of Cortés, returning to claim his own.

Yet another story makes Topiltzin-Quetzalcóatl the leader of a Toltec expedition which landed in Yucatán and, after subduing the local Mayas, founded the city of Chichén-Itzá. While there is obvious difficulty in accepting Topiltzin himself in this new warlike role, the historical and stylistic evidence for central Mexican influence, if not supremacy, in the New Empire of the Mayas is established beyond question. There are astonishing resemblances between the architecture of Chichén-Itzá and that of Tula, and in general the New Empire cities are a happy blend of Toltec and Mayan elements. The Mayas actually called the Toltec leader Kukulcán, which is a literal translation of Quetzalcóatl.

The fortunes of the Toltec adventurers in Yucatán are not easy to follow, but it looks as if their incursions began in the early eleventh century and were spread over a considerable period. For a while they formed the dominant minority in the peninsula, but since they were never very numerous they inevitably lost their identity and were absorbed in the Mayan mass. But for the next two hundred years their ascendancy was wholly invigorating. Yucatán blossomed with resplendent cities and must have supported a vast and thriving population. Chichén-Itzá and Uxmál grew to an immense size. Together with another Toltec foundation, Mayapán, they formed a league which kept the peace till 1194, when a ruinous civil war put an end to the unity and prosperity of the region. Under the leadership of Mayapán a gradual cultural decadence set in. This was accelerated after the destruction of Mayapán itself in 1441 by a general revolt against its overbearing rule. When the Spaniards landed eighty years later, the imposing fabric of the Maya-Toltec world had utterly collapsed and its territory was parcelled out between a dozen squalidly warring tribes.

The Toltec kingdom of Tula outlasted the secession of Topiltzin for another two centuries, its end rather neatly coinciding with the break-up of the Maya-Toltec league of Mayapán. The site of Tula was only cleared in the early nineteen-forties. Until its impressive monuments had been revealed scholars had become quite confused by trying to locate the Toltecs at Teotihuacán. The new discoveries only proved the validity of the old traditions, as well as Sahagún's clear statements that Tula lay, as it does, close to a river, that in his time remains of ancient buildings could be traced on the spot and that ancient pottery and precious stones were to be found among the ruins.

The city as now excavated reflects the military character of the Toltec monarchy. Its architecture and sculpture are massive and awesome, an assertive and flamboyant tribute to the warrior qualities of the nation. They lack the refinement conferred on the Toltec style by Mayan craftsmen in Yucatán. Nevertheless they are superb in a kind of brutal way, and must have dazzled the barbarians who succeeded to the Toltec heritage.

For all its confident strength Tula was unable to stand up for long against renewed nomad pressures from the north. By the mid-twelfth century these had become irresistible. The last effective ruler, Huemac, is said to have reigned for seventy years. Evidently he put up a brave front against the invaders, but he was eventually forced to abandon his capital and to fall back on the Valley of Mexico. After his death the Toltec realm dissolved into a number of small domains which were progressively eaten up by the newcomers. Tula itself was destroyed in 1224 and Sahagún compares its fate with that of Troy. The Aztec empire, last of a long line of Mesoamerican civilizations, was destined to emerge from the ensuing chaos.

Chapter 2

THE AZTECS AND THEIR NEIGHBOURS

THE TRIBES WHICH flooded into the rich lands of Anáhuac, ringed with forests and lakes, as well as those which remained to roam the high sierras and barren plateaus of the vast Mexican north-west, were all lumped together by subsequent writers as Chichimecs. The meaning of this term is uncertain, but it was applied to a very broad variety of nomads and semi-nomads. Sahagún, for instance, distinguishes several sorts of Chichimecs. One of these, he says, was entirely primitive and nomadic, lived by hunting and food gathering alone and built no permanent habitations. After referring appreciatively to their skill in cutting precious stones and in dressing feathers and skins, he rather casually mentions their addiction to the root called peyotl and to certain mushrooms which made them drunk on festal occasions. These habits, as still practised by their descendants, have attracted an inordinate amount of interest in our time.

The same writer seeks to establish a connexion between the less primitive types of Chichimecs and certain large ethnic groups which existed in his day and have survived to our own —Nahuas, Otomis and Huaxtecs—each with its own language and distinct physical characteristics. It is true that one important section of the Chichimecs was already related by a common origin to the Nahua-speaking Toltecs whom they displaced, and from whom they had picked up some civilized traits. Again according to Sahagún, these tribesmen had already emerged from a state of pure nomadism, lived in simple houses and raised crops of maize. In fact the remains of considerable settlements of rough stone buildings at La Quemada in Zacatecas and other sites in the north indicate that before they began to migrate southwards on a large scale they had for long tried, however clumsily, to imitate the achievements of their kinsmen in the settled lands.

At a later date, when the Aztec power was at its height, a Chichimec origin was nothing to be ashamed of, especially if there was also a Toltec connexion in the background. The

Chichimec kings of Texcoco, who eventually became the somewhat reluctant associates of Aztec imperialism, regarded the Aztec emperors, their partners and overlords, as comparative upstarts. Years after the Conquest their descendant, Don Fernando de Alva Ixtlilxóchitl, whose Chichimec blood was mixed with that of Spanish hidalgos wrote (in Spanish) a history of the Chichimecs (*Historia de la Nación Chichimeca*), tracing the ancestry of the dynasty back to Xolotl, the chieftain who led the invasion of the Valley of Mexico. Xolotl settled at Tenayuca, now a suburb of Mexico City and the site of the only remaining Aztec pyramid. But he was only one of innumerable petty rulers, each intent on carving out a piece of territory for himself and his war-band. When the dust of the great Chichimec migration had subsided, Anáhuac was seen to be split up among a multitude of quarrelsome little lordships, any one of which might eventually come out on top.

The Chichimecs mixed easily enough with the older inhabitants of Anáhuac, and in the course of fusion Náhuatl was established as the dominant language of the area comprising the Valley of Mexico and the present states of Puebla, Tlaxcala, Hidalgo and Morelos. But it was not the only one in use. For example in the valley of Toluca, which lies immediately to the west of that of Mexico, an entirely different tongue, Matlatzinca, prevailed. This was in turn related to Otomi, the idiom of the ancient mysterious folk of that name who occupied, and still occupy, a wide arc of territory to the north of Mexico City, extending through six states from Michoacán to Vera Cruz. They call themselves the "Nyam-Nyu". According to Rodney Gallop (*Mexican Mosaic*), their language "is monosyllabic, with five different vowel intonations, and in sound has a marked though superficial resemblance to Chinese".

The Otomis had tilled their soil for countless centuries before the Chichimecs appeared. Indeed they represented the original peasant substream of the Teotihuacán and Toltec eras. They are visibly distinct from the Nahuas in their ethnic characteristics as well as in their language. In ancient times they were derided for their rusticity and drunken habits. Slow, rough and clumsy are the epithets bestowed on them by Spanish writers, and it is true that they failed to develop culturally like other Indian peoples. Although they never asserted themselves politically they were known as tough fighters; one Spanish friar, Sahagún, comments that they were like the Germans (tudescos) "who die and do not run away" (*Historia General de las Cosas de Nueva España*). Another, Motoliniá, describes them as good material for conversion to the true religion (*Historia de Los Indios de la Nueva España*). Patient, shy and sensitive, they have a strikingly oriental appearance and their little old men in particular, with their wispy hair and slit eyes, recall the Confucian sages of Chinese paintings. No doubt their nature has always been moulded by the parched and rocky environment of the Mezquital, the forbidding country behind Tula which produces nothing but spiky desert plants and looks something like the trans-Atlas region of Morocco.

To the north-west of Anáhuac another nation, the Huaxtecs, held the rugged sierra and the approaches to the Gulf of Mexico. An isolated branch of the Maya family, they contributed little to Mesoamerican culture but were not subjugated by the Nahuas until the last century of Aztec ascendancy. Their habitat, which was calculated to discourage any inroads, is a region of inaccessibly steep mountain ridges plunging with dizzy suddenness into the narrowest and most terrifying of gorges. The harsh climate of the uplands alternates with the lushest vegetation in the clefts three thousand feet below. These tropical recesses produced fruits and spices which were much coveted by the Aztecs when they began to hanker after luxuries, and despite the natural difficulties the Huaxtec lands were eventually invaded and brought under Aztec control.

In the opposite direction, to the west, the Nahua tribes never succeeded in penetrating into the vast jumbled country lying between Anáhuac and the Pacific ocean, which roughly corresponds with the state of Michoacán. This consists mainly of a densely wooded mountain massif studded with the cones of a thousand volcanos, normally extinct but liable from time to time to spring to life in a spectacular eruption. This seismic but highly fertile land was the home of the Tarascans, a race sharply distinguished from its Otomi Nahua neighbours both by its language, which belongs to an entirely separate group, and by its physical traits. The men are unusually tall for Indians, with slim figures and handsome clear-cut features. The Tarascans, or Purépecha as they still call themselves, were an archaic people, the legacy of some long-forgotten migration washed up among the Michoacán sierras, which had grown up undisturbed in its own isolated domain and was only marginally affected by the classical cultures. They were the Arcadians of Mexico. Secure in their fastnesses, they repulsed every attempt by the Nahuas to spread westwards.

To the south the austere ridges of the Mixteca Alta barred the way to Oaxaca, while the eastern Sierra Madre, rising to 18,000 feet in the highest peak in Mexico, Citlaltepetl (Mountain of the Stars), formed a natural barrier between Anáhuac and the coastline Totonacs. In the event neither of these obstacles availed to stem the advance of Aztec imperialism, but when the Aztecs came to surmount them they found themselves in alien and hostile country. Like all the Nahuas, they were at home only on the cool tablelands.

Such was the setting, remarkable for its diversity of peoples and languages, in which the Aztecs created their empire. At the start, however, they were the most humble and inconspicuous of all the Nahuas. They took their name from Aztlán, the fabulous northern island from which, according to their chronicles, they originally set off on their travels, but they were more usually known as "Mexica", a term of uncertain origin by which their memory has been perpetuated. After they had been swept into the Valley of Mexico, on the crest of the Chichimec tide, the best part of a century went by without their finding a settled abode. The early codices depict them as uncouth tribesmen dressed in skins and carrying bows, and they cannot have numbered more than a few thousand people all told. At that time there was fierce competition for land in the valley, where many small city or rather village states, governed by petty rulers, were striving to widen their territory. In these overcrowded conditions the Aztecs were invariably foiled by their stronger rivals in their attempts to found a permanent home. They were condemned to trek forlornly from one temporary resting place to another, and subsisted by farming themselves out as mercenaries in the wars between the contending groups. Since they were good fighters their services were much in demand and they were saved from extinction.

Besides a knack for self-preservation, they also possessed a wonderful sense of social discipline, of loyalty and faith in their own destiny. All authority was vested in four leaders, priests of the tribal god Huitzilopochtli, "humming-bird on the left-hand", the symbol of the all-conquering sun. Although the Aztecs subsequently absorbed their neighbours' gods in dozens and incorporated them in one huge and confusing pantheon, Huitzilopochtli was their own special and exacting patron. Whenever the ruling priests announced their decisions, it was in the god's name.

Huitzilopochtli's prescience was severely put to the test in the year Two Reed (A.D. 1325), when the Aztecs' fortunes had sunk to their lowest ebb. A few years previously they had managed to establish themselves at Chapultepec (Grasshoppers' Hill), a strategic position overlooking the great lake of Texcoco, and later to earn fame at every turn in Mexican history from Moctezuma to Maximilian. But once again they proved too weak to hold their own. Two more powerful communities in the neighbourhood, the Culhúas of Culhuacán, who claimed Toltec origin, and the Tepanecs of Azcapotzalco, combined to throw them out. Many were killed and the remnant found refuge in the marshes fringing the lake. At this gloomy moment the priest Cuauhcóatl (Eagle-Snake) came forward with a fresh utterance from the god directing the Mexicans to settle permanently in those very marshes, at the exact point where they would find an eagle perching on a tenochtli (prickly-pear) and gripping a snake in its beak.

Their new habitat, consisting of a few cramped islets surrounded by swamps, resembled that chosen by the ancestors of the Venetians when they sought in the lagoons of the Po estuary a refuge from the barbarians who infested the mainland. It presented a similar challenge to human endeavour, and one which was as promptly answered. It is hardly surprising that when the Spaniards first beheld the marvellous city of Tenochtitlán–Mexico they instantly likened it to Venice. But from the first moment there were compensations for the Aztecs. In the first place no one envied them their home. Secondly they did not have to bother about food. The lake teemed with fish and waterfowl, and they soon picked up from earlier dwellers by the waterside the peculiar technique of making chinampas, or floating gardens, supply the lack of solid fields. Soil was simply dredged from the lake, piled on wicker rafts and planted with maize, beans, chiles and other staple Indian crops. In the course of time the rafts became anchored by vegetation to the shallow lake bottom and the gardens ceased to float. Gradually they became firm enough to support modest buildings.

Less than two hundred years elapsed between the founding and the extinction of Aztec Tenochtitlán, and long before the end the obscure lake village had been replaced by a glittering stone-built metropolis of several hundred thousand inhabitants, itself the nucleus of a region containing a dozen satellite townships and the capital of an empire in full expansion throughout Mesoamerica.

The speed of this development was unprecedented by Stone Age standards and contrasted strangely with the almost imperceptible evolution of the preceding classical era. It cannot be attributed to sudden advances in the economic and technical basis of society, which remained essentially the same as in classical times. The explanation must rather be sought in the character of the Aztecs themselves, which was moulded by the struggle for survival among the busily competitive clans of the Valley. Like all Mesoamericans, their thoughts and behaviour were tightly determined by their all-pervasive and fatalistic religion and by elaborate social codes to which every individual unquestioningly conformed. They were dominated by the supernatural to an extent incomprehensible to the devout Catholics who conquered them. At the same time they were pre-eminent among their Indian contemporaries in their resourcefulness and dynamism, their restless nervous energy and the calculated ruthlessness with which they pursued their practical aims. Moreover they were extremely adaptable and quick to assimilate the traits of more polished Indian peoples. But when they first settled by the shore of Lake Texcoco they were little better than lively savages, and it remains a wonder that they should have succeeded in working out a complex and sophisticated way of life in so short a time.

Once installed in their new home, the Aztecs continued to exploit for their own benefit the current wars and intrigues between local dynasts. These early conflicts were waged within a very small space, the kernel of the future Aztec dominion, on the western side of the Valley, and the three principalities which disputed the leadership in this territory—Culhuacán, Azcapotzalco and Tenayuca—are now all contained within the area of greater Mexico City. Their feuds resembled those of the little cities of the early age of Greece or Rome, but on an even more insignificant scale. The Culhúas and the Chichimecs of Tenayuca were in turn overrun by the Tepanecs of Azcapotzalco, a mixed group which included a strong Matlatzinca (i.e. non-Nahua) element from across the mountains to the west. These Tepanecs were led by a wily and aggressive monarch named Tezozomoc, who devoted his reign of sixty years to the systematic subjection of other centres of power in the Valley and outside. The Aztecs were shrewd enough to attach themselves to his banner and to serve as his vassals in a long series of successful campaigns. It was an admirable training for their own future aggrandizement.

The Culhúas were the first to succumb, and shortly afterwards the Chichimecs, dislodged from Tenayuca, took refuge at Texcoco, on the eastern side of the lake of that name. The Aztecs took part in both these operations and it was a sign of their increasing importance in the affairs of Anáhuac that they saw fit at this time to change their manner of government. In 1376 they chose a king to rule over them, one Acamapichtli. He was the first of a line which lasted, in the same family, until the Spanish invasion.

It is interesting that this personage based his claim to kingship at least partially on a presumed relationship with the chiefs of the very Culhúas whom the Aztecs had recently combined with their neighbours to crush. The Mexican parvenu sought to establish a connexion, however tenuously based, between his people and the vanished but glamorous Toltecs, and from then on the Aztecs, only too conscious of their native crudity, eagerly sucked in all the elements they could possibly digest of their predecessors' culture, of their art, architecture, religion and historical traditions. In the future they were to take pride in being known as Culhúas, and that is how they were described by the local Indians in southern Mexico when Cortés, on the way to his eventual landing at Vera Cruz, first enquired who the overlords of the country might be. Furthermore, the Hill of the Stars above Culhuacán was peculiarly holy among the high places of the Valley. On its summit the sacred fire was rekindled at the beginning of each fifty-two-year cycle of the calendar which the Aztecs, like the Toltecs, inherited from classical times.

So long as Tezozomoc remained alive, the Aztecs were firmly

restricted by him to their role of useful instruments. Their independent energies and ambitions found no outlet until the old tyrant's death in 1426. The situation then changed rapidly. The Tepanec realm fell apart and the Aztecs, under their brilliant sovereign Itzcóatl (1427–40), succeeded to the political leadership of Anáhuac. His power was based on a triple alliance with the King of Texcoco across the lake and the ruler of Tlacopán (Tacuba), a very minor principality on the mainland bordering the watery capital of Tenochtitlán. These two potentates were to play a strictly secondary, though not negligible, part in the subsequent development of the Aztec state. From the accession of Itzcóatl history allotted to the Aztecs less than a century of independent existence. It turned out to be an epoch of feverish expansion and daemonic activity in all spheres of life and the pace of social and cultural advance was unparalleled in Mesoamerica.

Itzcóatl and his four successors who reigned throughout the fifteenth century—Moctezuma I Ilhuicamina, Axayácatl, Tizoc and Ahuitzotl—were outstandingly able men. They all pursued a course of systematic and determined aggression. In seventy years, besides tightening their grip on Anáhuac, they created an empire which included (see Map 2) the Huaxteca, the whole coast of the Gulf of Mexico down to the isthmus, the Mixtec and Zapotec lands and a long line of military and trading colonies stretching southwards to Guatemala and the Pacific seaboard. To the west, however, Axayácatl (1468–81), was sharply checked when he tried to encroach on the Tarascan kingdom and the attempt was not repeated.

There were also some curious territorial anomalies within Anáhuac itself. Beyond the mountains to the east of the Valley three important Nahua cities, Tlaxcala, Cholula and Huejotzingo, managed to maintain their independence from the Aztec empire. Cholula, a large and pacific commercial community, was in practice content to accept Aztec hegemony, but Tlaxcala remained truculently hostile, and even little Huetjotzingo occasionally ventured to raid the Valley of Mexico. Tlaxcala was a republic governed by a council of four chieftains who were required to reach unanimous decisions: its Nahua warriors were superb fighters and could if necessary enlist the aid of thousands of their equally fierce Otomi dependents. The Aztecs' failure, or as we shall see, their reluctance to smash Tlaxcala, was to prove a lethal flaw in their defences when they came to face the Spanish threat.

It may well be thought surprising that a simple tribe which had only recently emerged from the hunting and fishing stage should have so soon become capable of the sustained effort necessary for ordering the administration and economy of an empire of perhaps ten million people. But the Aztecs were not only good soldiers but first-class organizers as well. Indeed it was only by developing a complex system of government that they imposed and maintained their authority over their own Nahua-speaking neighbours and the bizarre collection of alien peoples whom they subjugated by their carefully planned conquests. Nevertheless there was much more substance in their achievement than just a brutally efficient imperialism. At a time when the Mayas, the last survivors of the classical age, were finally dissolving into barbarism, it was the Aztecs who brought about a very real though short-lived renaissance of Mesoamerican culture. This revival of the half-forgotten classical traditions among the Nahua folk was mainly due to their innate vigour and sense of purpose. Economic conditions also happened to favour the rapid development of a civilized society within the bounds set by the neolithic way of life.

Anáhuac itself was a populous and richly productive region, abounding in villages and small townships. The land was worked by a free peasantry who in normal years provided the increasing population, and in particular the huge city of Tenochtitlán, with an ample supply of basic foodstuffs. Meanwhile the tribute of the provinces and the plunder from the freshly conquered borderlands filled the imperial storehouses and overflowed into the luxury market. Gold and precious stones, exotic ornaments, feather head-dresses and cloaks, brightly-woven textiles, tropical fruits and spices, fish from the Gulf, transformed the previously austere style of living of the Aztec rulers. The new prosperity soon affected all classes of society, and was fostered not merely by exploitation but by lively trading within and outside the Aztec realm. The commercial spirit was never lacking in Mesoamerican civilization: despite natural difficulties and strict official regulation commodities were exchanged in bulk over long distances and communications were remarkably rapid. Such long-range trade was the monopoly of an exclusive caste or corporation of merchants known as the Pochteca. Their function was to operate the caravans which carried the products of Mexican craftsmen beyond the empire's boundaries and brought back the luxury goods for which there was an insatiable demand.

This activity is a good example of the odd mixture of sophisticated organization and primitive simplicity which characterized the whole of the Aztec economy. Money was not used in Mesoamerica and wealth was obtained solely by the exchange and accumulation of commodities, including of course precious stones and metals. Since there were no draught animals and no vehicles—for the wheel always eluded the inventive powers of the American Indian—the sole means of transport consisted of the backs of human beings. Everything, magnates in litters, live wild animals for the emperor's zoo, heavy building materials, endless bales of cotton cloth (the standard units of taxation) was carried by porters at their own ambling pace, or hauled for short distances. The trails, however, were well trodden and well policed, so that traffic moved with surprising ease for many hundreds of miles over the most formidable obstacles that geography could devise. Travel was if anything less arduous than in contemporary Europe. Again, although the plough had not been invented and agricultural implements were limited to the digging-stick and a rudimentary spade, the soil was intensively and efficiently cultivated. Similarly, the most delicate work of the sculptors and craftsmen was mainly accomplished with stone tools. Metallurgy, apart from the exquisite products of the gold and silversmiths, was not developed for industrial purposes, although axes and ornaments of copper were in common use. Such skills as existed in handling metals were derived from the Mixtecs and other sources in the south.

The modern mind has no particular difficulty in grasping how it was that in spite of its technological backwardness the Aztec economy satisfied the nation's requirements and created a secure basis for prosperity and civilized living. In an environment of plenty it was inevitable that rapid cultural advances would be achieved, and that provided Mesoamerican society remained undisturbed and isolated from the rest of the world, it could well continue to flourish, as in past ages, without bronze, iron, the wheel, the plough, domestic animals and overseas fruits and crops. No economic problems, even in a neolithic setting, catch us on altogether unfamiliar ground. But when we turn to consider the social and religious system which prevailed in the Aztec empire on the eve of the conquest we enter a strange field which is not readily understood in all its variety and complexity. The very abundance of the remains and records of the period have enabled scholars to subject every facet of ancient Mexican life to the closest scrutiny, and new data are continually emerging from the soil of Mexico itself. Consequently the picture we possess of the immediate pre-Columbian scene is in many respects precise and clear. We think we know the facts with reasonable accuracy and we watch with fascination the movements of the individual actors. Only too often, however, we fail to interpret to our own satisfaction the motives of Indian behaviour and despair of adapting our sympathies to the mental and psychological climate of the age. This is especially baffling when we are looking at events which took place less than five hundred years ago and with personalities who were not semi-mythical but contemporaries of the early Tudors.

The structure of Aztec society in 1500 was majestic, elaborate and hierarchical. Many of its features were derived from models of the half-forgotten classical and Toltec eras: others were contributed by the Nahua people and by the Aztecs themselves, once an insignificant minority among the Nahuas. At the apex of the pyramid stood the emperor, whose title in Nahuatl was Uei Tlatoani (literally "the high one who speaks"). From 1376, when the Aztecs first adopted the institution of monarchy, sovereignty resided in the same family, though it was not necessarily transmitted from father to son, the actual choice being made by an electoral council of about a hundred high dignitaries. The president of this body, and the emperor's deputy in all civil and military affairs, was called, queerly enough, the Cihuacóatl or Serpent-Woman. This office was also dynastic in character, for the Serpent-Women were all descended from the brother of Moctezuma I (1440–69). The Cihuacóatl wielded very wide powers, especially at times of crisis, and we shall see him take a leading part at various stages in the final agony of the empire. It is as if the head of the house of Orléans or Condé had been the hereditary vice-king of France.

In the two sub-kingdoms, Texcoco and Tlacopán, which occupied territories in the Valley of Mexico and shared with the Aztec monarchy the advantages of the latter's conquests, the rulers exercised a highly honorific but politically limited sovereignty. While Tlacopán always remained insignificant, a glorified suburb of Tenochtitlán, Texcoco enjoyed enormous prestige as the seat of Nezahualcoyotl, the philosopher-king who reigned there for the best part of the fifteenth century and was treated by the Aztec emperors with extraordinary deference. As the representative of the Chichimec dynasty which traced its descent back to Xolotl, he had a better-established lineage than his Aztec neighbours who were obliged to rely on a dubious claim to Toltec origin. In his domain the kingship was handed down from father to son. Texcoco and Tlacopán each received a due share of the provincial tribute and were in many respects integrated into the empire. Their institutions scarcely differed from those of their Aztec overlords. Nevertheless Texcoco retained a sense of separate identity which asserted itself as soon as Tenochtitlán displayed any sign of weakness.

The ruling class of the empire comprised three parallel hierarchies, civil, military and religious. It was mainly but not exclusively recruited from the magnates or higher lords (tetecuhtin, singular tecuhtli) and the minor noblemen (pipiltin, singular pilli). As military commanders or high officials these persons formed an aristocracy of service. Rank depended essentially on merit and not on the hereditary ownership of land or any other kind of wealth. On the contrary, the emperor was the sole fount of the honours and material rewards which were lavishly meted out by his court to successful servants of the state. It was impossible for a nobleman to inherit the riches and social position of his father and reside idly on his private estate. Although he belonged by right of birth to the caste of the nobility, he was expected to qualify anew by his own deserts for his possessions and privileges. Moreover the nobility was constantly renewed from below by the promotion to its ranks of promising commoners. The social system, while establishing in theory a rigid distinction between classes, was in practice flexible enough to enable any young man, the son of a free citizen, to be enrolled among the lords at the emperor's behest, provided that he distinguished himself in battle or gave proof of administrative talent. Alternatively he could graduate by way of a religious college to the priesthood.

It may seem perverse to associate bureaucracy with a Stone Age society. Nevertheless the Aztecs evolved a highly developed bureaucratic and judicial system. As their state grew more complex, so the officials proliferated, nicely graded in their ranks and functions. The centre of government was the great palace in the main square of Tenochtitlán, where the emperor himself dealt with the daily business of his capital and realm, assisted by the principal Secretary of State, entitled the Uei Calpixqui, and the High Steward or Petlacalcatl. These great officials were assisted by a multitude of scribes, messengers and slaves. They were the most important members of a sort of inner cabinet, called the Tlatocan, which advised the monarch and was presided over either by him personally or by the Cihuacóatl. The Uei Calpixqui governed the city of Tenochtitlán, and as if that office were not sufficiently arduous, he was also made responsible for the collection of revenue from the whole empire. His authority was delegated for this purpose to a corps of subordinate calpixque working in the provinces, whose arrogance and harshness in exacting the tribute caused bitter grievance. As soon as the commodities of which the tribute was composed reached the capital the Petlacalcatl took them over and saw to their storage or disposal. Since the Aztecs had a passion for writing things down, careful tallies were kept of State property and, together with administrative acts, recorded in a developed form of pictographic script on paper made from the bark of the ámatl or wild fig tree. But of these huge archives nothing is extant; they perished in the flames which consumed Tenochtitlán.

The country towns of Anáhuac were governed by tetecuhtin appointed by the emperor and usually endowed with estates in the district. Further away, the subject nations and tribes were allowed a measure of self-government: their traditional chiefs and magistrates were confirmed in their authority provided that they kept their people in order and submitted to the demands of the calpixque. Any tendency to recalcitrance on the part of local populations was sternly quelled by the Aztec garrisons stationed at strategic points along the supply routes, or if necessary by forces despatched from the capital. The burden of exploitation weighed heavily on the more civilized of the conquered peoples, and especially on the rich but effete Totonacs of the Gulf coast. From time to time, indeed, their exasperation came to a head in revolts, but these were of no avail when matched against the efficient apparatus of repression.

The administration of justice was no less elaborately organized than that of civil affairs. Like the senior officials, the judges were appointed to their charges by the emperor or by the Cihuacóatl, who seems to have enjoyed supreme jurisdiction in criminal matters. In general they were drawn from the noble class, but we also hear of commoners being promoted to judicial office. Judges were treated with the highest respect and in return were expected to observe exacting standards of duty and personal behaviour. The country was covered by a network of tribunals ranging from those of first instance to an appeal court of twelve judges presided over by the King of Texcoco. In the lower courts proceedings opened every day at dawn and unless the case was sent up to a higher tribunal judgments were promptly delivered and executed. Great care was taken to avoid legal delays and discrimination against humbler litigants. So far as sentences were concerned, the law was extremely severe. Torture was not used to extract evidence, and nothing was to shock the Indians more deeply than its habitual employment by the Spaniards, but the code prescribed the most drastic punishments for violations of that strict discipline on which Aztec society depended for its cohesion. Imprisonment was not considered a suitable penalty for any kind of crime, while petty offences, such as thefts, were punished by fines or loss of civil rights, that is by the reduction of the offender to slavery until he had made restitution. But murder, adultery, banditry and drunkenness were all punishable by death inflicted in various unpleasant ways, including public stoning. Mutilation was also practised; slanderers, for instance, could have their lips and ears cut off. On the whole, however, Aztec justice was in practice no more cruel and arbitrary, and certainly more expeditious and impartial, than the contemporary European system based on custom or the portentous heritage of Roman law as interpreted by the jurists of Bologna.

The Aztecs won and held their empire by proficiency in war, in which they outclassed all other Indian nations. They extended it by planned aggression and assertion of the initiative. While no expansion took place during the reign of Moctezuma II Xocoyotzin (1502–19), there is no reason why it should not have been resumed under a fresh ruler if the Spanish assault had not put an end to the Aztec state. The Tarascan kingdom, for example, which had successfully resisted Axayácatl, offered a possible field for new conquests. Although Mesoamerica contained no rivals capable of a counter-attack, Aztec hegemony depended at all times on a strong military establishment ready to squash attempts at dissidence. Consequently all free citizens were required to serve as soldiers.

From the age of fifteen or even earlier a youth received instruction in arms at a college known as the telpochcalli, or "house of young men", where the education was mainly military but also included training in various civic and communal activities. After a while he was tested in real combat, and if he showed the necessary skill and courage he was destined for a permanent military life. Otherwise he was returned to civilian status with no obligation but to obey the call to arms when an emergency arose. But once he became a professional warrior the highest commands were brought within his reach, even if he began his career as a commoner. The successful fighting man could also look forward to rewards in the form of lands and other material possessions while he rose in fame and rank. The military hierarchy grew more complicated as the simple concept of the Aztec tribe in arms, according to which every able-bodied man turned out for war under the leaders of the clans composing the tribe, evolved into something of the nature of a standing army.

In an important campaign the army was led by the Tlacatecatl, or Commander-in-Chief, in person. He was chosen from among the close relatives of the emperor, as also was the Tlacochcálcatl, or adjutant-general, whose task was to keep the army supplied. This was a difficult task when the war had to be waged a hundred or more miles away from the Valley of Mexico and, in the absence of carts and transport animals, all weapons and food had to be carried across the sierras by the combatants themselves or stocked in advance at convenient points. The soldiers were grouped in basic units of twenty, which were multiplied as necessary into companies, regiments and larger bodies. They wielded a variety of arms, bows, slings and spears, and for work at close quarters wooden clubs studded with obsidian blades with a deadly cutting edge. For defensive purposes they carried small wooden shields and protected their bodies with close-fitting suits of padded cotton. Such equipment was of course miserably inadequate when it came to be pitted against weapons of steel, plate armour, charging horses and artillery. It was, however, perfectly effective for the ends of Mesoamerican warfare, when the main purpose of a battle was not the infliction of casualties on the enemy but his reduction to obedience by an overawing show of force and, above all, the capture of as many unwounded prisoners as possible. In Aztec hostilities the carnage came after the battle, when the captives were sacrificed to feed the gods.

The leading warriors were distinguished by the brilliance of their insignia of rank—necklaces, bracelets, knee-ornaments and towering head-dresses of feathers. Conspicuous too, were the members of the two Aztec military orders, whom we call the Eagle and Jaguar Knights. The former, who were dedicated to the service of Huitzilopochtli, the sun-god, wore wooden helmets shaped to resemble the head of the god's living emblem, the eagle. Similarly the latter, as devotees of the ancient Toltec war-god Tezcatlipoca, were dressed from top to toe in jaguar-skins. The outward likeness, however fortuitous, between the Eagles and Jaguars and their own Knights of Santiago or Calatrava, naturally appealed to the Spaniards of the Conquest, and was emphasized in modern times when the shrines of the Aztec orders, surrounded by the warriors' living quarters, were unearthed at Malinalco in the Matlatzinca country, between Toluca and Cuernavaca.

In its secular aspect the Mexican state was an autocracy, but not in the sense of the state being subject to the arbitrary will or caprice of the monarch. The emperor was revered as a semi-divine personage, but his freedom of action was circumscribed by the need to conform strictly with the precise obligations imposed on him by Aztec social and religious traditions. It would not have occurred to the Uei Tlatoani to overstep, for personal motives, the bounds of his predestined role. Nor was it practicable for him to follow his own inclinations against the consensus of his spiritual and political advisers. On the other hand there is no record of the Aztecs turning against their ruler until Moctezuma II became a puppet in Spanish hands and was for that reason repudiated by his people. The Aztec upper class, the tetecuhtin and pipiltin who manned the higher grades of the civil and military hierarchies, were absolutely loyal to the sovereign; it was unthinkable that a subject belonging to the aristocracy of service should harbour treasonable thoughts and independent ambitions.

At the same time it was taken for granted that the emperor, as well as the whole secular establishment, had no *raison d'être* except to serve the will of the gods as interpreted by the third and most important hierarchy of all, the priesthood. In common with all its predecessors in Mesoamerica, Aztec society, including the apparatus of government, was theocratically inspired and controlled. The state had no life without the church. Any analysis of the priestly establishment is therefore inseparable from a consideration of religious beliefs and some understanding of the all-pervasive religious atmosphere which every Mexican of whatever class breathed from birth to death. Religion, in all its peculiar and exotic manifestations with which Europeans, from the time of Cortés to the present day, have found it so hard to feel sympathy, was the major influence on social and cultural activities. Thus, before an attempt is made to depict the religious scene, we must examine the conditions in which the mass of the population, in which the ruling class had its roots, lived and worked in Anáhuac.

At the end of the fifteenth century the Nahua-speaking inhabitants of the region were in the process of being welded into a homogeneous nation. Their origins were of course diverse. The substratum of the population was descended from the peasant cultivators of the Teotihuacán era and even earlier times. In the course of seven centuries their stock had become fused with the two waves of barbarian settlers who overran the country in the pre-Toltec and post-Toltec periods respectively, and unity had been imposed by a common language, Náhuatl, and by Aztec leadership. Naturally the Aztecs themselves were at first few in number and had been for many decades confined to their lakeside city and its immediate environment. But as the surrounding communities were merged into a centralized state the distinction between Aztecs and non-Aztecs was blurred and local loyalties grew gradually weaker. The man of Chalco or Cuauhtitlán became conscious of a wider identity, especially when he began to profit from the spoils of empire. However, the parochial spirit was not easily extinguished and was apt to flare up at moments of stress. An extreme example of its persistence was the survival of Tlatelolco, Tenochtitlán's twin city, as an independent entity, though its great market-place was only two miles or so distant from the plaza of the major capital. This anomaly was terminated in 1473, when the last ruler of Tlatelolco met a violent death at the hands of the emperor Axayácatl.

Thus the macehual or commoner, the basic human unit of the Nahua peoples, inherited social traditions of great antiquity. He was a free man, not a serf, with his rights and obligations carefully laid down by immemorial custom and enforced by law. Every Aztec citizen was a member of a communal group, the Calpulli. Strictly speaking, this institution may be traced back to the primitive organization of the tribe in its nomadic state, but a similar communal system prevailed throughout Anáhuac as a whole. Its character was essentially territorial, but in the cramped conditions of Tenochtitlán its primary function of allotting plots of land to its members for cultivation had to give way to a municipal system which divided the city into urban parishes or quarters in which the Calpullec, or head of the group, acted as a sort of mayor. But in the rural districts it was his duty to preside, with the aid of a council of village elders, over the distribution of lands. The actual ownership and disposal of the land were vested in the village commune; what the individual farmer received was the right to work his plot for his lifetime, to enjoy its produce and to hand down the right intact to his son. If he failed to work it properly, however, he forfeited his security of tenure. Moreover, the commune had the power to order the redistribution of lands to its members when required by circumstances, such as the rise or fall of population and an increase or decrease in the total area available. When the Mexican Revolution of the twentieth century resuscitated the commune, or ejido, as the basis of agricultural development, it took this ancient system as its model.

The great majority of the macehualtin remained farmers for life, but as already explained opportunities existed for the young men of talent to enter the warrior class through the rigours of the telpochcalli, or the priesthood by means of an even more arduous form of training. Those who failed to improve their status were liable to taxation, as assessed by the calpullec and his council, and to various forms of compulsory labour.

The rich merchants (pochteca), who were beginning to

develop into an influential middle class, were not permitted to own or work land. Nor, by definition, were the artisans (tolteca), who were dedicated to their ancestral skills and tightly organized in craftsmen's guilds. On the other hand, the central authority freely granted agricultural estates to members of the nobility in order to reward their services and to maintain them in a state suitable to their rank. Large tracts of land, particularly in newly conquered districts, were also set aside for the imperial family and for the temples. The relation in which such estates stood to the rural communes, and the extent that they may have been worked by communal farmers, and in what conditions, are questions which remain obscure. In many cases labour was no doubt provided by a class of free but landless labourers (tlalmaitl), under a rudimentary tenant system, or less frequently by slaves.

Slavery among the Aztecs was a rather haphazard institution. An individual (man or woman) could become a slave (tlacotli) in two principal ways, by incurring a legal penalty or by a voluntary act. In the former case servitude took the place of imprisonment in our own society and could be terminated when restitution had been made; alternatively a slave could regain freedom through ransom and through emancipation by his master or by imperial decree. In the second case a man could voluntarily surrender his liberty in order to discharge a debt or simply because he was too feckless to face the obligations of life as a free person. The master was strictly required to treat his slaves humanely and they were automatically released on his death. Their children were born free and were entitled to own and accumulate movable property. In short their existence was more tolerable and hopeful than the lot of the much more numerous slaves in the Greek and Roman world and infinitely less miserable than that of the negroes shipped to America. For one category of unfortunates, however, slavery in ancient Mexico reserved a more horrible fate. These were hopeless and recalcitrant evil-doers who were available for purchase as sacrificial victims by persons unable to provide themselves with prisoners of war for the purpose.

There are no particularly puzzling features in the preceding sketch of the institutions and material condition of Mexico in the last stage of Aztec rule. In general the picture is of a disciplined society becoming more flexible as it adapts itself to the expansion of the empire and to the political and social consequences of its own development. Although it is vain to speculate as to how far and in what direction this development would have proceeded had it been left undisturbed, we can be sure that it would have remained inhibited by the apparent incapacity for technological advance which affected all the peoples of pre-Columbian America, by contrast with those living on the land mass of Europe and Asia. In the latter's case progress was no doubt quickened by the comparative ease of movement and communication between the races of the twin continents. But in America such mobility, and the accompanying exchange of ideas and intentions, were restricted to a much greater extent by climate and geography, and there was of course no human contact with other parts of the world. Nevertheless, when the stimulus was eventually received from outside, the American Indians proved themselves perfectly responsive to technological innovations.

After the first appalling shocks they also absorbed readily enough the strange concepts from overseas which broke through their own closed system of cosmological and religious beliefs. This did not differ in any essential respect from the system which had begun to take shape in Olmec times and was inherited by the Aztecs from the classical cultures, a blend of pure intellectualism with the rankest superstition. For long centuries it had obsessed and imprisoned the lively Indian mind, and under the Aztecs it had increased in complexity while losing much of its refinement. We do not find in Tenochtitlán the same philosophic interest in mathematics and astronomy as inspired the Mayan ruler-priests. The necessary calculations continued to be made, but for ritual and calendrical purposes only.

When first confronted with Mexican religion, we are tempted to regard it as polytheism run wild, an ugly and confusing proliferation of outlandish deities with obscure attributes and overlapping functions. We cannot, however, follow the example of the Spaniards and simply lump them together as instruments of the devil. It is better to start by looking at the cosmic myth which underlay the relationship of man and the universe to the host of supernatural beings; it also provides a clue to the concept of fixed and inescapable destiny which governed all Mexican thought.

The Mexicans held a cyclic view of the universe, according to which the world and men had five times been created and four times destroyed. The successive ages were known as "suns", and they believed that each of the preceding suns had perished in a vast natural cataclysm. They themselves were living in the fifth age, which was doomed to annihilation by earthquakes. Nothing could avert the endless alternation of catastrophe and renewal. Each era had a major deity as its creator or patron— Tezcatlipoca, Quetzalcóatl, Tlaloc, Chalchihuitlicue (the water goddess) and finally the sun-god, Huitzilopochtli or Tonatiuh.

While the fifth sun still shone, the sky, the earth and the elements were the domain of a bizarre assemblage of god and goddesses. Some watched over specific activities of the living and the shadowy existence of the dead. Together with the great primordial gods of Mesoamerica like Tlaloc, Quetzalcóatl and Xiuhtecutli (the Lord of Fire), the Aztec pantheon housed the numerous nature and fertility deities of the old settled population of Anáhuac, the tribal symbols of the barbarian immigrants and the uncouth divinities of the neighbouring peoples of non-Nahua origin. The priesthood made little attempt to reduce this celestial jumble to an ordered hierarchy, and allowed popular religion to flourish in all its diversity. While the capital was dominated by the bloody official cult of Huitzilopochtli, it was balanced in the countryside by the tipsy jollifications held in honour of the harvest godlets who went by the name of Centzon Tochtli, or the Four Hundred Rabbits.

The priests did postulate the existence of a creator god, Ometecuhtli (Lord of Duality), from whom all the other gods sprang and who in some mysterious way determined the destiny of both gods and men. In turn the gods created the heavenly bodies and the earth with its inhabitants. But the priests were not so much interested in a system of theology as in the problem of aiding the gods to fulfil their function of keeping the universe intact and in motion pending its eventual disappearance at the end of the fifth sun. It was here that humble humanity was held to exercise a crucial influence in the scheme of things. Indeed religion revolved around the central idea that the efficacy of a god's function (especially when the god personified a heavenly body or a force of nature) depended on the constant stimulus of human sacrifice. The shedding of human blood was considered necessary to save the world from extinction: hence it was of far greater significance than the purely propitiatory sacrifice of animals, and less frequently of men, which was resorted to in the ancient civilizations of Asia and Europe.

In fact human sacrifice had always been a feature of Mesoamerican religion, even in the peaceful societies of the classical period, but on a limited scale. The practice seems to have grown with the invasion of central Mexico by northern barbarians. We have already seen how vainly the historic Quetzalcóatl reacted against it before his exile from Tula. Under the Aztecs it developed to a truly horrifying extent. The prisoners of war taken in the conquests of the fifteenth century provided a rich supply of victims for Huitzilopochtli; a pictographic manuscript preserved in the Bibliothèque Nationale of Paris records that no less than twenty thousand captives from the southern cities were immolated in a single day in 1487 by the emperor Ahuitzotl to celebrate the reconstruction of the great temple which the god of war and of the sun shared with Tlaloc, god of rain. Twenty years earlier there had been a similar mass slaughter at the same shrine of prisoners from the Huaxteca. The further the boundaries were pushed, the more insatiable the god's appetite became, or the more it cost in human lives to keep the sun on its course. In the words of Dr. George Vaillant, "sacrifice led to war and war back to sacrifice" (*Aztecs of Mexico*).

When no war was being waged and the supply of captives had consequently dried up, the Aztecs had recourse to the so-called "Flowery War" (Xochiyaoyotl). According to the post-Conquest chronicler Ixtlilxóchitl, the three component states of the empire—Tenochtitlán, Texcoco and Tlacopán—arranged with the republic of Tlaxcala and the independent cities of Cholula and Huejotzingo to stage a series of ceremonial battles, the sole aim of which was to furnish prisoners for sacrifice. These combats had no political purpose; they were ritual tournaments in which the participating warriors, apart from displaying their prowess, faced the prospect of what they themselves regarded as a highly honourable fate. Whether they fell in battle or were kept for the altar, they believed that their destination was a special paradise reserved for the devotees of the sun-god.

It is curious that while the Mexicans and the Tlaxcalans disliked each other intensely, the Aztec emperors never made a serious effort to subjugate the republic. The traditional enmity boiled over when the Tlaxcalans allied themselves with the Spaniards against Tenochtitlán and contributed tens of thousands of auxiliaries to Cortés's army. Indeed Cortés could not have won through without Tlaxcalan support. We can only suppose that a struggle *à l'outrance* between the two quasi-military rivals was averted by their mutual preoccupation with the purely religious aspects of war. One could not do without the other as a source of prisoners. On the other hand the Tlaxcalans would not have been easily crushed, for they and their Otomi subjects were very numerous and warlike.

Sacrificial rites took many forms, being generally adjusted to the character of the god to whom the victims were offered. Children were drowned to appease Tlaloc the rain-god; in honour of the harvest goddess Xilonen, women were decapitated as they danced. The fire-god's victims were thrown into the blaze and retrieved half-cooked to have their hearts torn out. Those dedicated to Xipe Totec, the fertility god of the savage mountain tribes between Oaxaca and the Pacific, were pierced with spears and arrows; they were then flayed and the priests donned their tightly-fitting skins. By contrast with these grisly performances, the prisoner who personified Tezcatlipoca was treated for a whole year with honours due to the god himself, feasted and provided with beautiful girls, until it was time for him too to lose his heart on the sacrificial stone. This was set up in front of the god's shrine, a small building which crowned the platform of the temple pyramid.

At a mass immolation the priests, caked in drying blood, worked overtime. Endless files of prisoners would ascend the steps; each would be stretched on the stone and have his heart deftly removed with an obsidian knife. It was placed in the dedicatory dish, while the corpse was hurled down the pyramid steps. On certain festivals suitable parts would be cut up by attendants to be ceremonially eaten. Alternatively, warriors captured were armed with toy weapons, tethered to a stone and required to fight to their death against Aztec soldiers in full battle panoply.

The frequent and elaborate ceremonies which culminated in human sacrifice were of course not all blood and horror. They moved to their climax in an atmosphere of intense devotion amid music and dancing, incense and flowers. All who took part in them were conditioned to assume that the death of those offered to the gods was necessary and desirable, because the taking of individual lives ensured the survival of the natural order, including the perpetuation of life itself. Nevertheless it would be wrong to imagine that the victims all perished in a mood of religious exaltation or even of stoic acceptance. Even if this were true of the warriors, the most ardent apologist of the Aztec way of life cannot honestly believe that the wretched slave, as he stumbled towards his fate half-stupefied by the liquor of the maguey (octli) or by hashish (yauhtli), was immune from the ordinary human feelings of terror and despair. Nor can one reasonably fail to conclude that the Aztec preoccupation with human sacrifice had reached a thoroughly unhealthy pitch, quite incompatible in the long run with a sane society. It horrified the toughest of the Conquistadors, and they, if often callous and prone to excesses of their own, were not usually hypocrites. We therefore need not be afraid of being thought naive if we confess that it shocks us as well, although we try to study it objectively as an anthropological curiosity.

The domination of the supernatural in Mexican thought led inevitably to the emergence of an ecclesiastical organization. This irresistibly reminded the Spanish friars, however reluctant they might be to admit it, of their own Church. Sahagún's description of the Mexican hierarchy is especially interesting because it stresses the moral and spiritual qualities demanded of the priests, irrespective of the grim rites which they were accustomed to perform.

> They chose [he writes] as high priests (*sumos pontifices*) those who were perfect in all the customs, rites and doctrines of the ministers of idols. These were two in number, one was called Quetzalcóatl Totec Tlamacazqui, and served Huitzilopochtli; the other, who served Tlaloc, was called Quetzalcóatl Tlaloc Tlamacazqui. These two high priests were equal in estate and honour. No matter if their parents had been humble and poor; the reason for which they were chosen was that they faithfully carried out all the exercises and teachings of the calmecac [seminary or religious school —Sahagún renders it by "monasterio"] and lived chastely. They had to be virtuous, humble and peaceable, steady and

reasonable, not frivolous but grave and austere, sober in their habits, loving, compassionate and friendly to all, pious and god-fearing.

He then lists three subordinate grades of clergy and translates their Náhuatl equivalents by "acolyte", "deacon" and "priest". Sahagún was of course reproducing the statements of the Indian notables whom he consulted about the details of their former religion, but he had no doubt that they reflected the truth.

The Aztec church abounded in dignitaries with resounding titles. Under the two paragons mentioned by Sahagún the principal officer was the Mexícatl Teohuatzin or Chancellor, whose functions included the control of education. Religious instruction was imparted in the Calmecac, where boys were sent off at an early age. Candidates for the priesthood were drawn from all classes of free citizens, but the Calmecac also prepared the sons of nobles for a secular career. According to Sahagún the training was harsh (*aspera*), full of fasts, vigils and bodily penances: piety, courtesy and self-control were the virtues drummed into the future rulers. Nor was their literary education neglected; they studied the hymns and sacred texts in the priests' archives, together with the rudiments of astronomy and numbers. The discipline of the telpochcalli, where the sons of lesser folk received their military and civic training, was much less austere. There was plenty of dancing and singing, and girls were brought in for the amusement of the older pupils.

When the novices graduated from the monastery-schools and became full-fledged priests (tlamacaxque), they were dedicated for life to their profession and continued to be bound by the same strict standards of discipline, poverty and celibacy. The élite among them were chosen to direct the calmecacs and to fill important posts in the Church hierarchy. Although intellectual life as we understand it did not flourish in the Aztec world, they were the nearest approach to an educated class, acting as keepers of the nation's conscience and of the traditions handed down from tribal days by word of mouth or in pictograms. They alone were capable of working out the mathematical calculations required for arranging rituals according to the religious and solar calendars; with so many gods to be honoured at the appropriate season, the difficulty was to find enough days for their celebration. But the priests' most significant function was to steer the actions of the rulers in conformity with the divine will and the correct interpretation of the destined course of future events. Here great skill in divination was required. No emperor would take a crucial decision without calling on his priestly advisers for guidance and predictions, and these acquired supreme importance when the sovereign, like Moctezuma II, was uncommonly superstitious by nature.

Many tlamacaxquis were employed in the routine tasks of managing Church property and supplying the temples with the means necessary for their upkeep. Each had its full programme of festivals demanding a lavish outlay of resources in kind. Other priests officiated at sacrifices and ceremonies, or organized the grand spectacles which crowned the religious year, filling the enormous central square of Tenochtitlán with fantastic pageants of dancing and music.

The Aztecs managed to combine harmoniously in their religion moral high-mindedness with the most perverse inhumanity. Only the extreme determinism of their thinking can explain this apparent paradox. There was no element of hypocrisy in it, nor was there any question, as there was in Christianity, of the contradictions being simply due to failure to live up to an ideal. The Mexicans assumed that the survival of the divine and natural orders depended to a vital extent on a certain type of human action. On the basis of that principle the practices of their religion became consistent with its philosophy and perfectly logical.

On the popular level predestination was of course unquestioned. A man was born under a certain sign, the course of his life was inevitably settled by the date of his birth, and his day-to-day decisions, no less than the affairs of state, were shaped by the judgment of experts in the supernatural. These were in the main reputable members of the priesthood. They knew the intricacies of the calendar, which days were counted lucky or unlucky and why, and which god happened to be in the ascendant. They could be relied upon to offer disinterested advice on the right moment to launch a trading enterprise or arrange a marriage, and to give correct interpretations of omens and dreams. Nevertheless people were apt to behave as if fatalism was not absolute, and applied to sorcerers to divert the destined trend of events by magical means. Although the abuse of divinatory skills was heavily punished, the magician flourished, and the distinction between the proven expert in astrology and the unscrupulous practitioner of witchcraft was often thin. In medicine, too, the physician merged easily with the wizard, the "brujo" as he is called in modern Mexico.

It is fair to ask whether the universal preoccupation with fate and the supernatural did not stifle the people's energies and talents. Could they not have developed more freely without this incubus? The answer is that Stone Age thought in Mesoamerica was in its essential nature theocratic and fatalist. It could not have taken any other direction. It was incapable of altering its character by any process of internal change, for there was nothing to set such a process in motion. Society did not carry with it the seeds of its own evolution. Moreover its whole fabric, the product of two thousand years of self-contained civilization, was liable to dissolve at the first sharp blow to its mental framework. In fact the only alternatives to its survival in much the same state were a relapse into unrelieved barbarism and a radical transformation brought about by a clash with an alien culture. The chances of a spontaneous breakaway from theocentrism towards some sort of humanism were nil.

If Mexican civilization at the turn of the sixteenth century was static, this certainly does not imply that it was stagnant or decadent. The impression it made on the Conquistadors was one of immense liveliness and vigour. They were astounded by its brilliance and refinement but only moderately puzzled by its incapacity for technical advance. As for Aztec power, it was clearly not on the decline, and had perhaps not yet reached its zenith. It is true that during the reign of Moctezuma II there were revolts among the subject peoples and even rumblings of resentment in the cities of the Valley. But all these movements had been put down by the efficient Aztec armies, and there was no possible threat from outside the empire. Still less was there any sign of social strife or decay within the Aztec community.

The symbol of Aztec greatness was the resplendent city of Tenochtitlán, capital of the empire and, more significantly, the heart of the last pre-Columbian culture of Mesoamerica. This culture was not created by the Náhuatl-speaking people of Anáhuac but inherited by them from their classical predecessors in Teotihuacán and elsewhere. It had survived the extinction of Teotihuacán and, four centuries later, the downfall of the Toltecs. It had twice declined to a low level under the impact of nomadic tribes, including the Nahuas themselves, and twice strongly revived as the settled population reasserted its influence and civilized the invaders. The final period of fusion between the settled and the nomadic elements ("Toltecs" and "Chichimecs") coincided with the rise of Aztec power. When the process was complete the civilization which emerged from it differed in no essential feature from that of the classical era. Its religion and social structures, political organization and economy, craftsmanship, art and architecture had their roots in the remote past of Teotihuacán, Monte Albán and the Mayan cities.

The inhabitants of Anáhuac were proud of their culture, but ignorant of its origins. Their earliest traditions did not go back beyond the Toltecs, although some sites, like Cholula, had been continuously occupied by civilized folk since the earliest times. The Aztecs themselves, a small barbarian group with no past glories to remember, lived intensely in the present, exploiting to the full the practical bent which so exactly counter-balanced their philosophy of fatalism. While they conquered, administered and amassed wealth, they almost effortlessly acquired the polish of their more sophisticated neighbours and subjects. Their realm contained vast reserves of material resources and human skills, all of which flowed into the centre and contributed to the most remarkable of their achievements, the creation of Tenochtitlán.

When the Spaniards first caught sight of the city, they were taken aback by its beauty and acclaimed it as one of the world's greatest wonders. Bernal Díaz, the old soldier whose eye-witness record of the Conquest has an uncanny photographic quality about it, says that such things had never been seen nor dreamed, and in another passage he mentions that his astonishment was shared by fellow-soldiers who had seen the great Italian cities and Constantinople. The invaders were duly struck by the monuments and the natural environment of lake and mountain, but what seems to have impressed them most deeply was the cleanliness, order and discipline. As an example of civilized planning, neolithic Tenochtitlán is hard to beat.

The city—or rather the twin cities of Tenochtitlán and Tlatelolco—formed an island rather less than one and a half miles square in the salt waters of Lake Texcoco. It was protected on the east side against flooding by a dyke ten miles

'Pyramid of the Sun' at Teotihuacán

Aztec Pyramid at Tenayuca

Pyramid at Xochicalco

Quetzalcóatl as God
of the Winds

Atrio Cross at Tepepulco.
16th century

long, and linked to the mainland on the north, west and south sides by broad causeways. These carried the heaviest traffic into the city, while lighter goods were transported in canoes and flat-bottomed barges. Fresh water was brought in by two aqueducts, the shorter of which was fed by springs from the hill of Chapultepec. These great public works were executed in the mid-fifteenth century, when the city was rapidly expanding, and are connected with the name of Moctezuma I.

The three causeways terminated in the main square, the modern Zócalo, around which the city was laid out on a strictly rectangular grid, being divided into four administrative districts. Its thoroughfares were canals bordered by footways of beaten earth and crossed by numerous wooden bridges. Thus it was as easy to move about by water as on foot; there was a harbour for canoes in the Zócalo itself. The system of water transport within the city was one of the few features of Aztec Tenochtitlán which lasted through the colonial period, and the principal southern canal was still bringing boats into the centre in the early years of the twentieth century. Apart from its geometrical design, the likeness of the Aztec city to Venice was extraordinarily close. The Mexicans, however, could have given their Venetian counterparts a lesson or two in civic behaviour. The streets of Tenochtitlán were swept clean every day by squads under the control of the district authorities; it was forbidden to dump rubbish in the canals, and night-soil was collected for use as manure in the Chinese manner. In their personal habits, too, the Mexicans were scrupulously clean, resorting regularly to the temazcalli or steam bath. The result of this respect for the simple rules of health was a remarkable immunity from infectious diseases, which only disappeared when the Spaniards imported the familiar plagues of Europe and Asia.

The houses lining the canals were for the most part one-storied and plainly constructed; they presented a blank, windowless façade to the passer-by. In the outskirts cottages of wattle and thatch were to be found dotted among the "floating" gardens of which the primitive settlement had been composed. These soon gave way to dwellings of white or colour-washed adobe (sun-dried brick), and as the traveller approached the centre of the city he would come upon grander edifices of stone and wood. Even the imperial palaces, however, did not exceed two stories. The outer door of a typical house would lead into a courtyard with rooms opening off it, or to a series of similar courtyards. The interior walls were sometimes decorated with frescoes, while the flat roofs and the patios themselves were ablaze with flowers. Gaily embroidered curtains hung over the doors. Furnishings, however, were restricted to wooden chests and stools, beds and rugs of matting and utensils of stone and plain or polychrome pottery.

Bernal Díaz has left a fascinating account (*Historia Verdadera de la Conquista de la Nueva España*) of the palace where he was lodged in the satellite township of Ixtapalapa, at the end of the southern causeway. He admires the finely worked stone and the fragrant woods of which it was built, the spacious courts and the apartments lined with cotton tapestries, the sweet water pool of stone and painted stucco, teeming with water birds, the garden with its roses, sweet-smelling shrubs and diversity of fruits, and the canal which led from the lake straight into the precincts. "Now," he sadly ends, "it is all cast down and lost; nothing is left."

The general aspect of the capital resembled, except for the regularity of its town-plan, some old-fashioned city of Morocco, or indeed of the southern Spain which had been wrested from the Moslems only a quarter of a century before Mexico was overrun. In Tenochtitlán steep pyramidal temples (teocallis) took the place of the square minarets rising above a similar monotonous expanse of roof-tops. The tallest of these were the double temple of Huitzilopochtli and Tlaloc in the Zócalo and that which dominated the plaza of Tlatelolco. Both were about a hundred feet high. We have no accurate count of the others, but there must have been several dozen, large and small, in the city itself, besides a great many more in the environs. Of this forest of shrines only one, at Tenayuca on the mainland, survives above ground. The thickest concentration of religious buildings was to be found in the central square, enclosed by a wall known as the coatepantli or snake-hedge. They included the drum-shaped sanctuary of Quetzalcóatl in his aspect of god of winds, and a nightmarish structure called the tzompantli or skull-rack, on which were displayed the mouldering crania of the sacrificial victims.

It must be admitted that by contrast with the monumental architecture of the Mayas or even the Toltecs the Aztec teocallis were rather dull. They were nothing like as grandiose as the Teotihuacán pyramids and they lacked the distinction of the classical age. If Díaz had seen Chichén-Itzá and Uxmal at their zenith he might have been moved to eloquence surpassing his famous comparison of the temples and towers of Tenochtitlán with the dream-like enchantment of those mediaeval romances which were the Spaniards' favourite reading. In reality, however, the city was a vision of fantastic splendour, dwarfing in sheer scale anything to be found in renaissance Europe. According to a sober calculation it contained, together with its lakeside suburbs and adjoining towns, upwards of a million people. Such a spectacle had no rival in the contemporary world, except possibly in Cathay.

Each of the last three Aztec rulers built himself a new palace adjoining the sacred enclosure. Moctezuma's stood next to the double temple, on a site more than two hundred yards square. Besides the emperor's living quarters and the apartments devoted to state ceremonies and his private pleasures, this Mexican Versailles housed the central administration, the higher courts of justice and the storehouses of the treasury. Here too, according to Bernal Díaz, were workshops where skilled artisans supplied the needs of the court, gardens and ponds, cages for wild beasts and even a snake-pit. During the short period of peace that followed Cortés's arrival in Tenochtitlán, various parties of Spaniards were escorted through the palace, but in those tense moments there was no opportunity to make a complete and coherent record of its wonders. In writing to the King-Emperor Charles V, Cortés confesses that it was too marvellous for description, adding bluntly that there was nothing like it in Spain. Had he ever seen the Alcázar at Granada, he might have found the appropriate comparison.

Another sight which vastly intrigued the Spaniards during those halcyon days before the storm was the immense market-place of Tlatelolco, where produce from the whole empire changed hands. According to Cortés, there was room in it for sixty thousand people, and it was twice the size of the town of Salamanca. It reminded Díaz of his birthplace, Medina del Campo, site of the mediaeval fair which was frequented by merchants from all over Europe. Cortés's estimate of its extent was doubtless exaggerated, and it is a little disconcerting to find Díaz also referring to Salamanca when he goes on to say that the temple enclosure adjacent to the Tlatelolco market was larger than the principal plaza of the Spanish city. But allowing for a slight confusion in the conquerors' minds, it is clear that the scene was hugely impressive, and again indicative of the generous scale on which all Mexican events were staged. The square was surrounded by arcades and divided into tiny lanes or sections for the display of a particular type of goods, order being maintained by constables and three permanent magistrates. Of all the features of ancient Mexico the tianguis (market) has changed least since pre-Columbian times, and just as it aroused among the first Spaniards nostalgic memories of their home country, an Aztec of that time would scarcely feel out of place on a market-day in modern Cholula, when the plaza buzzes with the soft Náhuatl speech of the peasants from the villages around.

As has been shown, Aztec civilization was mainly derivative, drawing its inspiration from the distant past. It was therefore apt to fall short of classical standards, especially in the fine arts. Our appreciation of its quality has also suffered because its visible relics are so disappointingly few. An enormous quantity of works of art perished in the plundering and annihilation of Tenochtitlán and the subsequent systematic destruction of religious monuments. Thousands more still lie hidden in the rubble underlying the foundations of the modern city. The great monolithic statues preserved in the National Museum are only a pitiful remnant of the mass of free-standing sculpture which formerly adorned the teocallis. Grotesque and lumpish, they have little aesthetic appeal, but they convey only too well the sense of dread and horror of the unseen powers which filled the Mexican mind. Remains of the many friezes in bas-relief which encircled the temples are unfortunately even more fragmentary, but it is unlikely that any Aztec work ever rivalled the delicate mastery of the art of low-relief achieved by the sculptors of Mayan Palenque. But the Aztec artists also worked in a more naturalistic style: this produced the splendid head of an Eagle Knight in the National Museum, and many charming figures of animals, birds and reptiles. The temples, palaces and houses of the nobles were likewise lavishly decorated with frescoes, all of which have been obliterated. One would not expect the painters to have attempted anything like the realism of the Bonampak murals. Their style was probably either rigid and conventional, or naive as in the pictographic manuscripts.

The Aztec goldsmiths absorbed and developed the skills of their Mixtec neighbours. To judge from the scores of references in Spanish writers there must have been an extraordinary profusion of gold objects for display and daily use. With rare exceptions they were swept into Spanish melting-pots. The lapidaries' art fared better, and a great number of exquisite small carvings in hard and semi-precious stones have come down to us. Lastly there still linger in European museums a few pathetic survivals from the original treasures despatched by Cortés to Madrid after his first encounter with Moctezuma, here a turquoise and jade mask, there a skull in rock-crystal or a high feathered head-dress which the emperor himself may once have worn.

The most advanced stage of culture in Anáhuac was reached at Texcoco in the reigns of its tlatoani Nezahualcóyotl and his son Nezahualpilli. It will be recalled how the former prince restored the fortunes of the Chichimec dynasty after narrowly escaping with his life from the tyrant Tezozomoc. He ruled from 1428 to 1472 and his son succeeded him until his death in 1516. Neither attempted to dispute the political supremacy built up by the Aztec monarchy across the lake. They were content to enjoy a subordinate though honorific position in the empire and were consequently free to cultivate the arts of peace at home while the Aztec sovereigns were busy pushing back the frontiers. Texcocan contingents, however, served with the Aztec armies, and the Chichimec kings received their fair share of the tribute.

During most of this period there was no serious disharmony between Texcoco and Tenochtitlán, and the rulers married into each other's families. So far as administration and revenues were concerned, Texcoco remained a self-governing unit. The emperor Moctezuma I treated his ally and contemporary Nezahualcóyotl with peculiar respect, turning to him for advice, as to an elder statesman, on all critical occasions. It was Nezahualcóyotl who designed, at his request, the long embankment which guarded the Aztec capital against inundation from the lake. As already mentioned, Nezahualcóyotl acted as supreme judge of appeal for the whole empire. He enjoyed an immense reputation for wisdom and learning, while his court surpassed that of Tenochtitlán in its lavish magnificence and the refinement of its manners.

We are indebted for our detailed acquaintance with the life and times of this rich personality to his descendant Ixtlilxóchitl (Don Fernando de Alva), himself a product of Indo-Spanish cultural fusion. In his *Relaciones* and *Historia Chichimeca* this chronicler, who was a thoroughly sophisticated writer, was at pains to depict his ancestry as every whit as distinguished as that of any princely family in the Spanish realm. Fortunately Nezahualcóyotl was an ideal hero for his theme. In the first place, he lived in a setting of almost sultanic extravagance. His palace enclosure at Texcoco measured a thousand by eight hundred yards. Not far away, at Texcotzingo, he caused a whole hillside to be converted into a pleasure-park complete with groves and terraced walks, pools and cascades, pavilions and statuary. If Ixtlilxóchitl's description is to be trusted, it must have resembled a great garden of the Italian renaissance, or perhaps the "Garden of Perfect Brightness" near Peking, where the Manchu emperors luxuriated in mysterious seclusion. Mexican potentates had a passion for out-of-door pursuits —hunting, bathing, the collecting of rare animals, birds and fish, and the planting of trees and shrubs. Moctezuma I, for his part, after his conquests in the tierra caliente of Morelos, planted an arboretum at Oaxtepec; the site can still be identified by its lush vegetation and fine trees. Texcotzingo, however, is now a steep and dusty wilderness with no trace of its former glories except a few fragments of masonry and stone water channels.

In true Oriental fashion the princes of Anáhuac maintained enormous harems. The Spanish historian Oviedo records that Moctezuma II kept four thousand women, and that they disported themselves in over a hundred heated baths, after the manner of the Moors. Ixtlilxóchitl explores in even greater detail the feats of polygamy accomplished by the Texcocan royal house and the general Arabian Nights atmosphere of court life. Nezahualcóyotl, he says, had 118 sons and daughters, and Nezahualpilli no less than 144. Of all this progeny, however, only the sons of the one principal wife were eligible as candidates for the succession. In Texcoco the son of a lesser wife or concubine could not aspire to the throne save in the absence of a legitimate heir. This situation obviously encouraged intrigues in the seraglio. Nezahualcóyotl allowed his sole legitimate son to be put to death for plotting rebellion on the strength of a denunciation from a concubine trying to push her own son to the fore. As for Nezahualpilli, he sentenced his heir to death on suspicion of pursuing an affair with his own favourite, whereas in fact they had done nothing more reprehensible than exchange the verses which each had composed.

Despite the drama in his own family the old King was not prepared to tolerate truculence or laxity of morals among his subjects. He was celebrated for his severity as a lawgiver and also for his concern with the condition of the poor. But for us the most interesting aspect of his powerful and versatile personality is his traditional reputation as an intellectual and a philosopher. When due allowance has been made for the fact that the Texcocan chroniclers who wrote after the Conquest were for the most part members of his family, they are not just telling romantic tales; their statements clearly rest on a solid basis of fact. The tradition is neatly summed up in the words of an eighteenth century scholar, the Jesuit Clavijero, who wrote:

> His enlightenment and love for his subjects were an inspiration to his court, which came to be regarded as the fatherland of the arts and the centre of civilization. Texcoco was the city where the Mexican tongue was spoken with the greatest purity and perfection, where the best craftsmen were to be found and where there was the greatest abundance of poets, orators and historians. Thence the Mexicans and other peoples derived their laws, so that it can be said that Texcoco was the Athens, and Nezahualcóyotl the Solon of Anáhuac. (*Historia Antigua de Mexico*)

Without treating too seriously the resounding classical parallels so dear to writers of the Age of Reason, but which are difficult for students of ancient Mexico to resist, we have to conclude from the near-contemporary evidence that innovations quite untypical of the Mesoamerican past were taking shape at Texcoco under the King's inspired guidance. Nezahualcóyotl governed his domains through four councils of state. One of these was the supreme court of justice; two others dealt with military and fiscal affairs. The fourth and most interesting Ixtlilxóchitl calls the council of "music", using the word in the Greek sense of culture in general. W. H. Prescott, who was fascinated by the whole subject of Texcoco, describes it more prosily as a "board of education" (*History of the Conquest of Mexico*). Its function was to promote the arts and sciences, the study of astronomy and natural phenomena and the compilation of historical records. It also encouraged various forms of literary composition. Poems and set-pieces of rhetoric were ceremonially recited on regular occasions before an audience which included all three sovereigns of the empire, and the winners of these competitions, as well as outstanding artists and inventors, received generous rewards.

The Aztec period surpassed its Mesoamerican predecessors in one important respect: it was alone in producing a genuine literary culture, and it was at Texcoco that literacy in the Náhuatl language was most finely developed. Strictly speaking, of course, it is incorrect to speak of literature when there are no letters, for Náhuatl did not possess an alphabet. It is unlikely that the hieroglyphs of the classical period registered anything but dates (which can in fact be read), astronomical calculations, religious formulae and perhaps names of persons and simple events. But later the art of picture writing, which seems to have originated in the Mixtec area, was practised throughout Anahuac. It proved a useful, if clumsy, medium for recording tribal history, legal and official decisions and details of ritual, and for drawing up lists of property and tribute. A vast mass of purely factual material was accumulated in the two centuries before the Conquest, every aspect of communal life being meticulously documented. Pictographic writing was not, however, suitable for the transmission of abstract ideas, and in the final stage of Aztec civilization it was in the process of being superseded by a system combining simple symbols or ideograms with a phonetic syllabary. It is possible that this would in time have developed into a real alphabet capable of expressing all the nuances of the rich and supple Náhuatl tongue. As things were, the elaborate compositions in verse and rhythmical prose characteristic of Náhuatl literature had to be learned by heart and handed down orally, with some mnemonic help from the manuscripts, from generation to generation. Their style was extremely ornate, metaphorical and repetitive.

A great and growing body of literature in Náhuatl undoubtedly came into existence during the century before the

Conquest. Books too, of a clumsy and archaic character, but nevertheless real books, were gradually supplementing the resources of the human mind. In the ensuing catastrophe poets and annalists, patrons, scribes and manuscripts alike perished, and texts were no longer committed to memory in calmecacs and telpochcallis and at court. But considerable fragments of pre-Conquest literature were fortunately written down in Latin characters in early colonial times. Sahagún and others, both Spaniards and Indians, took them down from the lips of those Mexicans who could remember the old songs and narratives, or still possessed some of the old books. As soon as native writers had mastered the Latin alphabet they began to compile anthologies of ancient compositions, bringing together in haphazard fashion annals, epics and sagas, lyric and dramatic poems, didactic and rhetorical discourses, stories and fables. 1528 is the earliest date registered for a collection of this kind.

Modern research has revealed a wide variety of literary forms, more especially in poetry. Song, as well as music and dancing, had an irresistible attraction for the people of Anáhuac. Sahagún has preserved a series of formal hymns to the gods, reflecting in their archaic diction the religious experience of a remote and primitive past; it is thought that he took them down about 1547 from old men who had spent their youth under paganism. In his and other collections the numerous passages surviving from epics suggest that a whole cycle of long poems covered the exploits of divine, mythical and historic personages, among whom Quetzalcóatl is of course prominent, while incidents in their careers were also celebrated in mimes or dramatic dialogues. All such compositions have the impersonal character suited to public recitation and collective performance, but a more individual flavour can be detected in the different classes of lyric poems which are contained in the Náhuatl manuscript known as *Cantares Mexicanos*.* They are the nearest approach to secular literature that can be found among a people so deeply imbued with religion as the Mexicans, and may be assumed to be typical of those current in courtly and aristocratic circles.

In those poems the language is clear, the phrases short and lapidary, the images simple but striking. Among the various categories the Yaocuicatl (war-songs), Teuccuicatl (songs of the

* Quoted extensively by Angel Maria Garibay, *Historia de la Literatura Náhuatl*

princes) and Cuauhcuicatl (songs of the Eagle-Knights) speak for themselves. Curiously enough there is no distinct group of love poems. The Xochicuicatl (flower-songs), however, celebrate the joys of life and especially the intense love of colourful nature felt by all Mexicans, while the opposite tendency, a pervasive melancholy, is represented by the Icnocuicatl (songs of sadness). An extreme form of the latter, the Miccuicatl (songs of death), is preoccupied with death as the ultimate reality, the supreme enigma. Such was the delicately pessimistic and epicurean spirit which prevailed at the courts of the princes, at Tenochtitlán and Chalco, at Tlaxcala and Huejotzingo, and above all at Texcoco during the reigns of Nezahualcóyotl and Nezahualpilli. The world, it suggests, is on the whole a sad place and there will be no pleasure in the shadowy hereafter. The delights of human existence are as transitory as the fugitive beauties of nature and men must enjoy them to the full while they still have a chance to do so. These are the commonplaces of European and Asian poetry, but they are a far cry, it seems, from the doctrines of discipline and abnegation which were drummed into the youth of Anáhuac. In these poems a new emphasis is emerging on man as an individual whose tastes and personal attitudes matter in themselves and who is not just a cog in the religious and social wheel.

The names of some of these poets have come down to us—Aquiyauhtzin of Huejotzingo, Chichicuepon of Chalco, Motenehuatzin of Tlaxcala, Yohyontzin of Texcoco, and twenty or thirty more. It would be a mistake to regard these princes and nobles as a band of *esprits forts*. Whatever groping advance they may have been making towards intellectual independence did not in the least weaken the traditional fabric. By the standards of Anáhuac, there was no more unconventional figure than Nezahualcóyotl himself. He was famous as poet and orator, and his restless and curious temperament earned him a reputation for pursuing knowledge for its own sake. By his institution of the council of "music" he was plainly endeavouring to bring out and develop the innate talents of his people. The Texcocan chronicles of the colonial period go further and credit him with a bent for speculative theology. They say that he built a temple in honour of an unknown but supreme creator god called Tloque Nahuaque, whose worship did not even require an image. As good Christians, these writers were naturally concerned with presenting the king's personality in the best possible light. There is no reason to suppose that he in fact rejected any of the beliefs and practices of contemporary polytheism, but there is surely some substance in the tradition that he was in private feeling his way towards a more refined conception of religious truth.

The civilization of Anáhuac ranks as one of man's most brilliant creations. When overtaken by disaster from outside it was in full vigour and no sign was apparent of any internal menace to its stability. Its native strength was derived from two factors. The first was a material affluence which, though unevenly spread, enhanced the well-being of the whole population. The second was a disciplined and harmonious social system which offered equal opportunities to free men, and, on the whole, a just and reasonable distribution of burdens and rewards. Mexican society contained remarkably few outcasts and misfits. But the same inner self-sufficiency as protected it against change from within, and against any development incompatible with the traditions of Mesoamerican culture, was revealed as a deadly source of weakness when it was disturbed by intruders from an alien hemisphere. The Mexicans lived in a closed world where stability had been preserved at the expense of intellectual flexibility and technical advance. Once its defences had been breached, they were bound to crumble as if struck by the giant earthquake which, as pretold by the Aztec astrologers, was destined to destroy the fifth age of mankind.

Part II
CONQUEST

Chapter 3

GODS OR MEN?

ON 2ND JANUARY, 1492, Granada, the last bastion of Moorish power in the Iberian peninsula, surrendered to Ferdinand and Isabella, the Catholic Kings, sovereigns of Aragon and Castile. After eight centuries of intermittent struggle the Moslem presence was finally extinguished and the abounding energies which had been concentrated on the expulsion of the Moors from Spain were obliged to seek new outlets.

The obvious field for the deployment of Spanish power was the Mediterranean. It was open to the Catholic Kings to carry the anti-Moslem crusade into North Africa or to attack the western flank of the Turks who, having swept inexorably through the Balkans, were threatening the Danubian basin. A more pressing task, however, was to assert Spanish supremacy in the Western Mediterranean and, in particular, to frustrate French efforts to take over the Kingdom of Naples and to establish political ascendancy in Italy as a whole. Over the next twenty years the French challenge was decisively repelled, while the Moors were hemmed in by a line of enclaves and fortresses along the North African coast and the Spanish fleet came to grips with the Turks in the Ionian Sea. Ferdinand and Isabella no doubt foresaw that as soon as Granada was taken Spain would expand to the west and south. What they could not have envisaged was that in the coming century she would become not only the dominant power in Europe but also the owner of an enormous realm beyond the confines of the known world.

It is true that the Spaniards had been watching with jealous attention the progress of their Portuguese neighbours in finding a way round Africa towards the fabulous riches of the East Indies. By 1492 the Portuguese had not yet achieved that aim, but each voyage was taking them nearer their goal and meanwhile they were trading profitably with the west coast of Africa. Spain was clearly behindhand in the race for the Indies. Nevertheless a Genoese adventurer called Columbus had succeeded in interesting Queen Isabella in the possibilities of reaching the

Indies by sailing due west across the Atlantic instead of south and then east. Seven months after the fall of Granada he set off on his first voyage of discovery and on 12th October his little ships made a landfall in the Bahamas.

Whatever degree of scepticism may have prevailed at the Castilian court about the eventual result of Columbus's early discoveries, Queen Isabella and her advisers immediately took diplomatic steps to obtain legal possession of all lands which Spanish navigators might come upon in the western hemisphere. They had no difficulty in securing from the Borgia Pope Alexander VI, another Spaniard, the vast territorial rights which they were demanding, but the Bulls in which these concessions were set out were very naturally challenged by the Portuguese. In the event it did not take the rivals long to reach a sensible compromise by direct negotiation. The Treaty of Tordesillas, which they concluded in 1494, delimited the spheres of influence reserved to each power. It obliged Spain to abate the extreme claims which the Pope had been only too eager to satisfy, and to accept a settlement guaranteeing to the Portuguese their southerly route to the Orient (by which Vasco de Gama was to reach India four years later), as well as their future dominions in Brazil. All the remaining regions within the enormous area under dispute were allocated to Spain.

Unfortunately it soon became clear enough that Columbus had discovered neither the golden East, nor the near approaches to it, nor a strait which would give the Spaniards a quicker access to India than the long passage round the Cape of Good Hope. What he did find was an infinity of islands, large and small, and in the course of his third voyage in 1498 he landed on the South American mainland near the mouth of the Orinoco. Admittedly the coasts and islands of the Spanish Main were beautiful and frequently fertile. The first Spanish settlers in Hispaniola (Santo Domingo and Haiti) found conditions excellent for agriculture and stock-rearing, but these occupations involved hard work and earned only moderate rewards. Encouraged by reports from Columbus himself, the colonists arrived with the fixed idea that since the East was well-known to abound in gold, and the newly discovered lands were assumed to be the gateway to the East, gold in huge quantities was waiting there for them to amass with no particular effort. But they were soon disappointed, for the supply of gold turned out to be strictly limited. No enormous fortunes were to be had for the asking and mining proved in general a more precarious and scarcely more lucrative business than farming.

It was therefore not surprising that in the early years Spaniards tended to regard Hispaniola as a springboard for further exploration rather than as a land of settlement. After ten years the colonists numbered only three hundred. From 1499 to 1502 several navigators skirted the southern shores of the Caribbean from Panama to Trinidad and mapped the South American coast as far as the Equator and even beyond. Large reinforcements of colonists reached Hispaniola in the following years and Puerto Rico, Jamaica and Cuba were successively occupied between 1509 and 1511. An ambitious attempt was made at the same time to found colonies on both sides of the isthmus of Panama. These ventures met with appalling disasters; the original conquistadors nearly all perished in conflict with the Indians or at each other's hands. Nevertheless they resulted in two significant achievements, the discovery of the Pacific by Balboa and the establishment by 1517 of a permanent colony at Nombre de Dios on the mainland, which became known as the Tierra Firme.

With the exception of the landing of Ponce de León in Florida, all expeditions at this period were directed towards the south, across the open Caribbean. Whether the adventurers were seeking gold, or lands, or a strait which would guide their caravels swiftly to Asia, it did not apparently occur to them to sail due west from Cuba across the bare hundred miles of sea separating that island from the Yucatán peninsula. No rumour had reached them of the existence of a great land mass lying immediately to the west, still less of a rich and civilized empire inhabited by an entirely different type of Indian from those whom they had encountered in the islands or on the fringe of South America. It is difficult to account for their initial reluctance to sail westwards, but so far as we know no Spanish sailor had penetrated before 1517 into the stormy and shark-infested waters of the Gulf of Mexico.

Strange as it may seem, there was no contact between the native inhabitants of the Caribbean islands and those of the Mexican mainland. If a canoe from Yucatán had occasionally been carried by wind and current to Cuba, or a similar craft from Cuba to Yucatán, the castaways rarely if ever survived to return to their own people. The Arawaks and Caribs of the islands, and the Mayas and other nations of the mainland opposite, belonged to two very distinct branches of the American race; nor was there any linguistic affinity between the two groups. The Arawak and Carib languages both originated in South America and the Conquest interrupted the process by which the Caribs were supplanting the Arawaks throughout what is now known as the Caribbean area. Culturally the peoples of the islands had remained on a far lower level than that attained by the nations of Yucatán and Central Mexico. Left to themselves, they had failed to develop the essential characteristics of a civilized society, and they were equally incapable of withstanding or of adapting themselves to the shattering intrusion from Europe.

Inevitably enough, the settlers regarded them as an inferior race of humanity. Their frequent and desperate revolts were pitilessly quelled, and although they tried to take to the bush in order to avoid their conquerors, they were rounded up and put to work in the fields and mines. In the words of Salvador de Madariaga, "the plight of the native during the first years of the Spanish conquest was tragic beyond words". It is true that Church and State soon intervened to protect the Indians and safeguard their basic human rights. The Dominican Order in particular, with the formidable Las Casas in the van, campaigned unceasingly against the excesses of the colonists. The Spanish Crown, for its part, endeavoured as early as 1511 to define by legislation the relationship between settlers and Indians. In that year the Laws of Burgos gave provisional sanction to the system of repartimiento, or allotment, under which the Indians were required to work for Spanish masters in return for pay, shelter and religious instruction. There was at no time any question of the formal enslavement of the conquered, as had so often been the case in the Moorish wars, but despite the good intentions of the government and the passionate protests of the friars the repartimiento in the islands degenerated into something scarcely distinguishable in practice from slavery. Furthermore the Arawaks and Caribs did not possess the physical and moral strength to resist their fate. War, ill-treatment and deadly epidemics sapped their will to survive and so reduced their numbers that they eventually died out altogether and were replaced by imported negroes.

As we shall see later, the introduction into Mexico of the repartimiento, there known as the encomienda, or trust, did not produce the same fatal results. The Indian of the mainland, fortified by centuries of civilized life, was altogether a tougher, more self-reliant and adaptable human being than the type with which the Spaniards were familiar in the Caribbean, and it is a credit to their intelligence that they lost no time in grasping this essential distinction.

The first expedition to cross the strait to Yucatán sailed from Cuba in February 1517, under the command of Francisco Hernández de Córdoba. According to Bernal Díaz, who took part in it, the purpose of this venture was vague in the extreme, "to seek and discover new lands in which to employ our persons". It is significant that Hernández and his men rejected the urgings of Diego Velázquez, Governor of Cuba, that they should help finance the expedition by slave-raiding in a group of islands between Cuba and Honduras. Indeed they replied indignantly that the enslavement of free men was contrary to the commandments of God and of the King.

With this snub to the Governor, they set off "at random towards the west, ignorant of the prevailing tides, currents and winds" and after tossing about for twenty-one days reached the tip of the Yucatán peninsula. Close to the shore they were astonished to find a town, certainly a small town by Mayan standards but in a quite different class from the primitive Carib villages to which they were accustomed. Deeply impressed by the stone-built houses and temples, they nicknamed it "Gran Cairo", as if it reminded them of the Moslem world which some of them had no doubt glimpsed before they came to America. As for the Mayan inhabitants, the Spaniards noticed that the men were decently dressed in cotton shirts (camisetas) and breech-cloths, unlike the Cuban Indians "who went about with their sexual parts exposed", and concluded that they were a more rational species of man (hombres de mas razón).

They were disappointed, however, when these men of reason laid an ambush for them and a nasty skirmish ensued. Leaving the "Gran Cairo", they sailed along the northern and western coasts of Yucatán, but wherever they landed they were fiercely attacked and forced to flee to their ships. The Maya, although sunk in political confusion and cultural decadence, were perfectly capable of defending themselves. Their reaction to the intruders was to kill as many of them as possible. Nor were they deterred from joining battle by any suspicion of the kind which Moctezuma and his advisers were later to entertain, that it might be useless, and even impious, to resist the invaders because they were probably of divine origin. They simply charged in disciplined battalions and at Champotón they routed Hernández de Córdoba with the loss of over fifty soldiers. This defeat was so grave that the expedition had no choice but to return with all speed to Cuba. The pilots, however, insisted on taking a longer route home across the mouth of the Gulf of Mexico. This brought the ships to the southern extremity of Florida, where the exhausted adventurers had to fight another battle with local Indians before limping back to Havana. "Oh," exclaims Díaz, "what a laborious thing it is to discover new lands, in the way in which we ventured forth."

Undismayed by this setback, Velázquez lost no time in fitting out another expedition for the following year and appointed his kinsman, Juan de Grijalva, to lead it. Serving under him was Pedro de Alvarado, one of the heroes of the future Conquest. To act as interpreters he took with him two Indians who had been abducted by Hernández from Yucatán and had picked up a little Spanish in the interval; they had also been baptized and were known as Julián and Melchor, or more familiarly Julianillo and Melchorejo. At first Grijalva's voyage pursued much the same course as his predecessor's. When he landed, this time on the island of Cozumel, the Indians avoided contact, but he picked up a girl from Jamaica who happened to be the only survivor of a party of fishermen cast up on the island two years previously: the rest had been sacrificed at once. As she spoke Mayan and the Spaniards were able to converse with her in her own language they took her along to help with the interpreting. On the cliffs of the mainland opposite they caught sight of another and bigger Mayan town. This was Tulúm, founded under the old Mayan Empire as far back as 564. In 1518 it was in decline and probably half-deserted, but they nevertheless judged it to be of the same size as Seville.

Grijalva next touched at Champotón, the scene of Hernandez's discomfiture, where the Indians were waiting in arms for him. Their missiles flew like hail or locusts, and the Spaniards were lucky to embark after losing only seven men. They continued to follow the coast westwards and it dawned on them that Yucatán was not, as their pilot had assumed, an island. Soon they arrived at the mouth of the great river of Tabasco, to which they gave their captain's name. There the inhabitants were more friendly; supplies were provided and gifts exchanged. Moreover they indicated that still further to the west was to be found a country full of gold. They kept on repeating the words "Culhúa" and "Mexico". Although the Spaniards had no idea of what that was meant to convey, the truth was that they had reached the verge of Moctezuma's empire. It will be recalled that the Aztecs preferred to be called Culhúas because their emperors liked to trace their descent from the Toltec princes of Culhuacán. Grijalva was of course also unaware that he was about to cross the language frontier, beyond which Mayan ceased to be understood and Náhuatl became the *lingua franca*. He would no longer be able to rely on Julianillo and Melchorejo, or on the girl from Jamaica.

So it was a thoroughly mystified Grijalva who pursued his voyage northwards along the shores of the Gulf, from the neighbourhood of Coatzacoalcos as far as the Pánuco river. The mountains of the eastern Sierra Madre were soon discerned, topped by the snowy symmetrical cone of Citlaltépetl. The ships' course was at the same time being tracked by the inhabitants of the coastal strip, who were Moctezuma's tributaries, and by the resident Aztec officials and garrisons. We may be sure that these extraordinary apparitions were promptly reported to the emperor. Indeed Moctezuma subsequently told Cortés that he had been kept informed of both the previous expeditions. In the case of Hernández de Córdoba, it is likely enough that the news of the Spanish rout at Champotón was picked up, perhaps by a party of pochteca, and duly relayed to Tenochtitlán, but if so it was hardly calculated to impress the ruler with the godlike qualities of the invaders.

Grijalva's men, however, landed at several points in Aztec territory and until they reached Pánuco, at the northern extremity of the empire, their reception by Moctezuma's subjects was uniformly amicable and even deferential. Díaz was convinced that their arrival was not unexpected and that the emperor's subordinates had been instructed to treat them with honour. All their wants were attended to and they were presented with gold objects valued at sixteen thousand pesos. Mutual explanations were impossible without interpreters, but

Indian scribes were busy making pictographic records of the meetings for the emperor's eye. The reports and pictures which he received caused deep alarm, which persisted after the Spanish vessels had vanished over the horizon. Obviously, he thought, they would return, and when in the next year, 1519, Cortés followed Grijálva, his most gloomy forebodings were justified.

The encounters of 1518 are fully described by Díaz and other Spaniards but more sketchily treated by native chroniclers of the Conquest. In general, Indian writers were less interested in giving a factual account of what happened at the time than in recalling the omens and portents which heralded the invasion and the emperor's reactions to them. In the memory of Mexicans who had lately been through the ordeal of the Conquest the events themselves, and the actions of the chief participants in the drama, became deeply tinged with the legendary and the supernatural. This tendency reflects the naturally superstitious mentality of the Aztecs as well as the agonies undergone by Moctezuma and his advisers while they awaited the inevitable third coming of the strangers.

Sahagún gives an elaborate list of the omens which alarmed the Mexicans during the last ten years of Moctezuma's reign and led him to expect that something untoward was about to occur. These wonders—comets, pillars of flame, sudden conflagrations and floods, thunderbolts, waterspouts, two-headed men and a bird with a mirror in its head—have a familiar ring; there is nothing specifically Mesoamerican about them. Portents of the same general character are reported in plenty by the sedate historians of classical antiquity. The Romans were almost as keen in divination as the Aztecs. Cicero wrote a treatise about it and according to the Oxford Classical Dictionary portents were "considered precursors of social, political and dynastic changes". It was precisely a crisis of that kind that Moctezuma dreaded. Apart from his preoccupation with the supernatural, he had not had an easy reign, and the prospect of a new and imponderable addition to the burdens of empire was bound to fill him with dismay.

One suspects that if the omens had not been followed by a national catastrophe they would have been rapidly forgotten. As it was they remained firmly fixed in the Indian mind. The fuss which the emperor made about them is recorded in much detail by Don Hernando Alvarado Tezozomoc in his *Crónica Mexicana*, a work written in Spanish towards the end of the sixteenth century. Although it was composed some eighty years after the Conquest, it no doubt accurately represents the tradition current among Mexicans of the former governing class, especially as its author was a grandson of Moctezuma and a descendant of the imperial family on both sides. Born not long after the Conquest, he was still alive in 1609 and had apparently been employed for many years as a "nahuatlato", or official interpreter, by the viceregal government.

Tezozomoc records that Moctezuma was unable to extract from his experts in divination any clear indication of what the omens might signify. The most they would say was that a "great mystery" was impending. But the emperor immediately linked this vague statement with an argument which he had had some years previously with King Nezahualpilli. On the advice of his soothsayers, the Texcocan monarch had warned Moctezuma that the signs were that his empire would shortly be overthrown, adding that he, Nezahualpilli, would not live to see the disaster. When Moctezuma retorted that his own seers had foretold nothing of the kind, the two rulers decided to put the matter to the test by playing a series of ball-games, which Nezahualpilli won by three to two (a little unlikely, one would think, since he was the emperor's great-uncle). It looks as if this picturesque tale may reflect the latent jealousy which existed between Tenochtitlán and Texcoco and exploded with fatal consequences after Nezahualpilli's death. This wily old epicurean was not incapable of implanting uneasiness in Moctezuma's impressionable mind for political purposes of his own.

Tezozomoc's history then follows the popular story, according to which the first news about the Spanish ships was brought to Tenochtitlán from the coast by a commoner (macéhual) who spoke of "mountains" floating on the water. Moctezuma sent high officials to investigate, and from that point there are obvious connexions between this traditional Aztec account and Díaz's narrative of Cortés's arrival. The former provides enjoyable touches about Moctezuma's emissaries climbing a tree and watching the Spaniards as they fished from a small boat; the newcomers wore rather dirty coloured jackets, and on their heads kerchiefs, caps or large round sun-hats. In the popular version the successive appearances of Grijalva and Cortés, and the shock which struck the emperor's entourage on each occasion, have been merged into one event. We must, however, assume that the interval between the two expeditions was filled by anxious and inconclusive consultations in the grand council of the Aztec empire and between the emperor and his magico-religious advisers. By the time that Cortés was sighted off the Vera Cruz coast, at Easter 1519, Moctezuma must already have been highly upset, not only by omens but by facts.

Sahagún's record of the Conquest, as taken down from his own Indian sources, does not, like Tezozomoc's version, ignore the Grijalva episode, which it tries to distinguish from the occurrences of the following year. It also gives the names of the imperial calpixque and local personalities who greeted the Spaniards and reported their impressions of them to the emperor. It stresses that Moctezuma gave strict orders for a special watch to be kept from the coast for the reappearance of the strangers. Finally it states baldly that the Mexican notables assumed that the Spanish leader must be Quetzalcóatl, and also that they managed to convey to the Spaniards (despite the lack of a common language) that the lord of Mexico was called Moctezuma. This account would ring entirely true if it were not for the fact that two of the Mexican notables named Tentitl and Cuitlalpitoc are mentioned by Díaz as having been involved with Cortés. It therefore seems that the distinction between the events resulting from the arrival of each separate expedition had become blurred in the native memory by the time that the first Indian post-Conquest records came to be compiled.

While Moctezuma was worrying whether he should identify Grijalva's battered adventurers in their dirty jackets with Quetzalcóatl's divine retinue, Pedro de Alvarado and others among Grijalva's followers who later accompanied Cortés were unable to enlighten their new leader about the political realities of the exciting new country which they had discovered. They had indeed picked up a young Indian in the region south of Vera Cruz and subsequently christened him Francisco, but the most he could do was to convey to them by signs that it was the priests of the "Culhúa" who had sacrificed the victims whose remains they had found on the islets in Vera Cruz bay. But Alvarado was still no further towards knowing who these

Culhúa were. Cortés, on the other hand, was supremely lucky in finding the two interpreters he needed, a man and a woman, whose characters, talents and personal histories were quite remarkable. Chance brought them together, under Cortés's control, at exactly the right moment, before the expedition had yet reached Moctezuma's dominions, and neither could have been effective without the other.

Jerónimo de Aguilar had been a member of the ill-fated colony in Darien (Tierra Firme) and one of a party of fifteen men and two women who were first wrecked on a reef and then cast on the Yucatán shore from the ship's boat. Both the women died of drudgery and all the men but two on the altar stone. The survivors managed to keep up their end in different ways. Aguilar's comrade, a seaman named Gonzalo Guerrero, solved the problem by going native and enthusiastically identifying himself with the part. He was one of the very few Spaniards on record as having so acted, whereas the sixteenth century is full of Indians who turned themselves into something very like Spaniards. He gained some renown as a warrior in the Mayan tribal squabbles; moreover he married and become the father of three sons, the first known mestizos in Mexican history. His skin was tattooed, his ears and lips were pierced for ornaments and he had apparently no desire to go back to his own people.

Aguilar, however, never gave up hope of rescue. He was a devout man, a clerk in holy orders, and when found by Cortés he was still carrying a tattered book of Hours wrapped in a cloth. For eight years he had served Indian masters with changing fortunes. Cortés owed his discovery of him to his own quick intelligence. He had been told that Hernández de Córdoba had been puzzled by the Indians repeating the words "Castilán, Castilán", and rightly concluded that a Spaniard must not be far away. Hence he was able to trace Aguilar and induce his master to give him up, while Aguilar failed for no lack of trying to persuade Guerrero to come away too.

Aguilar proved his worth while Cortés was punishing the Tabascans and reducing them to a more tractable frame of mind. At that stage he received from the Tabascan chieftain with whom he made peace the gift of Doña Marina, a Mexican tecuhtli's daughter disposed of a slave in Maya country. Whether she is regarded as the heroine of the Conquest, or as the symbol of the betrayal of her compatriots to the aliens, she was an exceptional woman, and she and Aguilar understood one another very well. Together they forged, in Díaz's phrase, "gran principio para nuestra conquista", an instrument worth many fighting men. As soon as the expedition made contact with Náhuatl-speaking folk Cortés was enabled to communicate with them, because Aguilar was bilingual in Spanish and Maya and Marina was equally so in Maya and Náhuatl. Before long, of course, there would be no further need for this clumsy though reliable system, for Aguilar soon learned Náhuatl and Marina became proficient in Spanish. From then on the language barrier was surmounted with surprising ease from both sides.

Thus, when Cortés arrived off San Juan de Ulúa on Easter Thursday of 1519, Marina had certainly prepared him to the best of her ability for what to expect. She had given him some idea of the character and importance of the Aztec empire, but she would not have been able to tell him about internal conditions and personalities. The Indians came out in canoes to greet him as if they had been expecting him daily, and he was informed that Moctezuma's representatives were near at hand. When he met these envoys, however, he was not impressed, for their behaviour was calculated neither to overawe Cortés with the majesty of the empire nor to lead him to suppose that the honours due to a god were being offered to him. They seemed to be acting for a master who did not know his own mind.

Although Moctezuma had been given plenty of time between the two expeditions to ponder and consult about the right way to handle the strangers, he had got no nearer to solving the problem. He had not made up his mind if they were normal men or possessed supernatural qualities, and, in the latter case, if they were most likely to be the forerunners of the god-king Quetzalcóatl, returning at last to claim Anáhuac as his own. Moctezuma's hesitations seem to have been more deeply rooted in his own personality than in the psychology of his people as a whole. To judge from their future attitudes, other Aztec magnates, including the short-lived emperors Cuitláhuac and Cuauhtémoc, to say nothing of the rulers of Texcoco or Tlaxcala, were by no means as worried as Moctezuma undoubtedly was by speculations about the divine attributes of the Spaniards. The Aztecs were not primitives, but heirs and participants in a sophisticated culture. At the same time there were two contradictory sides to their character; when confronted with unforeseen situations their ruthlessly practical and aggressive drive in mundane affairs was blunted by their preoccupation with the supernatural and their fixed belief in a determined order of things.

According to Madariaga (in *Hernán Cortés, Conqueror of Mexico*), Moctezuma was an extreme example of subordination to religious fatalism, "the archpriest of a magic religion dealing with events as expediently as he and his colleagues in the service of the gods thought fit". "Like all primitives," says another distinguished authority, Mr. J. Manchip White, "he was not an individual: he could only think, feel and function in and through the tribe, he was embedded in the tribal body, incapable of thinking and acting outside its frame of reference" (*Cortés and the Downfall of the Aztec Empire*). For the latter writer "Moctezuma and the Aztecs ... were already overwrought and half-demoralized before the ships of Cortés were sighted. Their demoralization was complete when the person of Cortés seemed to fulfil all the prophecies concerning the physical appearance of the man destined to overthrow the Aztec Empire."

There is much force in these views, but one cannot help thinking that their authors have gone too far in stressing the stultifying influence of magic and superstition on the Aztecs' capacity for independent judgment and action at the critical moment. In general their reaction smacked of human perplexity rather than of holy dread. If they had been blessed with a ruler of a more decisive nature to give them a lead, there would have been less talk in modern times of tribal numbness or collective paralysis in the face of peril.

All early authorities agree that Moctezuma was unusually devoted to his religious duties and addicted to magical practice. At the same time he had proved a shrewd and competent ruler in difficult times. He was neither a weakling nor a puppet of his own priests. When only a young man, in his father Ahuitzotl's reign, he was already serving as tlacochcálcatl, or organizer-in-chief of the armies, and he was later chosen emperor out of sixteen candidates. His own reign had been disturbed by unrest among the southern tributaries, which he had firmly and successfully suppressed. Nearer home he had probably been guilty of a political mistake in the matter of the Texcocan succession. At the death of the old king Nezahualpilli in 1516 he had used his influence to promote Cacama, one of Nezahualpilli's numerous sons, to the throne at the expense of his brother Ixtlilxóchitl, who would have been a more popular choice among the Texcocans. His intervention produced a serious outbreak of disaffection at the heart of Anáhuac which, though soon stifled, upset the delicate balance of shared leadership in the empire. Quite apart from supernatural worries, Moctezuma had ample cause for disquiet over the purely political effects of the irruption into his territories, at that particular juncture, of a body of outlandish warriors whose exploits on the southern borders of his realm might easily have become known to him.

Thus, while Cortés's landing caused dismay, but no surprise, in Tenochtitlán, it is curious that Moctezuma sent no great dignitary of the empire to meet him. It is also strange that he omitted to despatch any armed force to the neighbourhood of Vera Cruz, a precaution which would have presented no particular difficulty, for thanks to the efficiency of the Aztec military system, a sizeable army could be assembled at a few days' notice at any point in Mexican territory. The emperor, however, did neither of these things. Instead, as soon as he was informed by express runners that the ships had arrived, he decided to put to the test his own mounting supposition that the lord Quetzalcóatl had returned, in fulfilment of the ancient myth, to reign for the second time in Tula. It was a possibility that he personally contemplated with pride and terror, bewilderment and fascination.

The traditional native accounts of the first transactions which passed between Moctezuma's envoys and the Spaniards, as given by Tezozomoc and (at much greater length and with much circumstantial and convincing detail) by Sahagún, are not altogether easy to reconcile with the down-to-earth narrative in which, some decades after the events, the eye-witness Díaz set down his recollections of what Madariaga calls a "real comedy of errors". The personalities involved on the Mexican side do not show up very clearly. The emperor seems to have left the preliminary arrangements for the reception and provisioning of the newcomers to his local governor, Tentitl, and to Pinotl, the chief of his calpixque in the region. Also to the fore was a not entirely comprehensible character called Cuitlalpitoc, who was assumed by the Spaniards to be an important personage and amused them by his physical resemblance to Nicolás de Ovando, the former governor of the

Indies, and they nicknamed him "Ovandillo". He figures, however, in Sahagún as the mere servant of a calpixqui, and Tezozomoc as a slave who was brought along for the sole reason that the presumed gods from the east might wish to have him sacrificed and eat him. In any case the Mexican officials were instructed to offer their guests whatever nourishment, including human flesh, they might desire. The officials observed with interest that the Spaniards, who had been living for many weeks on dried meat and mouldy ship's biscuit, partook with pleasure of the delicious spicy Mexican dishes set before them, but rejected any suggestion of sacrificial meats with anger and disgust.

But the crucial mission was entrusted to five commissioners from Tenochtitlán. They brought with them nothing less than the precious insignia of Quetzalcóatl himself, the very vestments and adornments which the high priest would wear when impersonating the god on the most solemn religious occasions. In Moctezuma's view, no more certain trial of Cortés's identity could have been devised. If, as he was driven to believe, the Spanish leader was really Quetzalcóatl, surely, when presented with his own glorious apparel, he would stand forth in all his majesty, manifest himself as the god and receive back at Moctezuma's hands the kingdom which the Uei Tlatoani and his forebears had been holding for him, so to speak, in trust.

It is a little disconcerting to find that the commissioners also carried in their baggage the insignia appropriate to Tezatlipoca and Tlaloc. The former, of course, was equally a deity of the Toltecs, and in fact Quetzalcóatl's rival, while Tlaloc, the ancient nature-god, had been worshipped in Anáhuac long before Toltecs and Aztecs were heard of. It may be significant that Cortés was evidently not expected to assume the mantle of the Aztec tribal war-god Huitzilopochtli.

Sahagún provides a wonderfully detailed catalogue of these treasures. Chief among the adornments of Quetzalcóatl was the fantastic head-dress which he wore as the Plumed Serpent, consisting of a turquoise mosaic mask shaped like a snake's head and surmounted by a lofty crown of quetzal feathers, while the stuff which covered his breast and shoulders was sewn thick with gems. Other attributes of the same god included shields richly decorated or inlaid with gold, mother-of-pearl and turquoise; a jaguar-skin "mitre" from which hung a huge feather cape and a "bishop's staff", also inlaid with turquoise and tipped with a serpent's head. All the garments glittered and gleamed with golden discs and priceless pieces of jade.

Cortés received these and other rich presents on board his ship, "smiling and with good grace" and at the same time indicating that more gold would be welcome, but whether or not the Aztec envoys had been expecting an epiphany, it did not take place. He allowed himself to be dressed in some of the finery, but he soon resumed his Castilian cap and doublet. In return he treated the Mexicans to a number of mystifying and sometimes alarming experiences. They were first required to witness high mass sung by Fray de Olmedo, the expedition's chaplain. Then Cortés got to work on their imaginations. Having tied them up, presumably to prevent them from panicking, he ordered his guns to be discharged, using a specially strong charge of powder in order to make the loudest possible noise. His horsemen exercised their terrifying "hornless deer" over the nearby dunes, while huge Spanish hounds, so different from the little dogs which the Mexicans were accustomed to fatten for their tables, gambolled and bayed around them. They were encouraged to have their scribes record these demonstrations to the best of their ability.

At one stage in the proceedings Cortés took his guests aside and sought to impress on them, for their master's benefit, that he had come to their land by command of the King-Emperor Charles, the greatest sovereign in the world and therefore superior to their ruler of Anáhuac, and that he desired to pay the latter a visit. Some of this discourse must have filtered into their minds through the channel of double interpretation, for Díaz records that Tentitl was nettled and snapped back that Cortés was presuming a lot if he thought he could so easily gain access to Moctezuma. It looks as if he himself was satisfied that Cortés was not Quetzalcóatl or any other god, and on that note he hurried back with the other envoys to Tenochtitlán.

We shall never know how they went about explaining their experiences to Moctezuma. But they could be relied upon to give him an honest account of what they had seen and heard and to express their opinions sincerely and manfully. That was what the men of the tecuhtli class were trained to do. Most probably they reported that so far as they could judge the strangers' leader bore no resemblance in his aspect and general conduct to Quetzalcóatl, either in the latter's capacity as Ehécatl, the wind-god, or in that of the legendary author of peace, plenty and culture in ancient Anáhuac. He had exhibited none of the qualities and tastes of the deities whose insignia he had been invited to assume. On the contrary, he and his followers had behaved like men, strange and unaccountable, but recognizably human. The great majority of them were white and full-bearded but a few—for the Spaniards had brought a few negroes with them—were black and curly-haired. Cortés had acted when he so wished in a friendly and hospitable manner, but at other times had shown himself violent and greedily acquisitive. As for his men, their rough and uninhibited manner contrasted poorly with the polished gravity of demeanour which came naturally to all educated Mexicans.

At the same time, the envoys no doubt continued, there were disquieting signs that the strangers possessed, if not superhuman characteristics, at least very formidable and highly magical powers. Moreover these mostly related to the waging of war. Most alarming of all, Cortés had repeatedly spoken of his intention to bring his company to Tenochtitlán, for purposes which plainly boded no good for the empire. Fortunately, however, they were not numerous.

Sahagún's narrative provides at this point some useful clues to the working of the emperor's mind. When the envoys had finished speaking, he became extremely sad. He sent them home and retired into his private rooms, where he stayed for a long time "muy pensativo y afligido". Finally he summoned the members of his council and explained to them how matters stood. Addressing them with his usual persuasive eloquence, he called on them to find a way of preventing his enemies from carrying out their design of destroying him. If Sahagún's source is to be believed, the emperor was by no means paralysed with dread, but doing his best to adapt himself to a new situation. Steeped as he was in a magico-religious atmosphere and in the legendary traditions of his race, and innately disposed to seek supernatural explanations of extraordinary events, he seems to have gone at least half-way to convincing himself that he had been selected by the divine will to preside over the lord Quetzalcóatl's return. And whatever consequences that might entail for him personally, it was bound to usher in a golden age for his people. But when he saw that the crude reality was quite otherwise, and threatened unpredictable damage to his people and himself, he was appalled. Now at last he understood the meaning of those disagreeable omens, and the mystical construction which he had placed on the coming of the strangers was shattered. At once he jumped to the opposite conclusion: divorced from their connexion with the Quetzalcóatl myth, the strangers have become "enemies" to be thwarted.

Again following Sahagún, we find that the council's conclusion was that the Spaniards should at all costs be deterred from reaching the capital, and that if possible they should be destroyed where they were. But in order to carry out this eminently prudent aim the Aztec notables did not, in accordance with the pragmatic bent of the national character, take the obvious course of launching the full levy of the empire against the strangers. They decided that a more effective way of getting rid of them would be to nullify the magical powers which they undoubtedly wielded with superior magic of their own, after which it would be easy to wipe them out. Unfortunately, we read, these counter-enchantments turned out a complete failure.

Díaz comes to the rescue here and shows that this affair of sorcerers was not just a fairy-tale. He says that when Tentitl returned from Tenochtitlán after the conference he brought with him a magnate ("Quintalbor"—a name which has an utterly non-Náhuatl ring) who physically resembled Cortés in a remarkable way, and it is clear that this person was produced for some magical purpose. He also indicates that the deputation proceeded to perform a number of rites the import of which the Spaniards failed to understand. But it also brought vastly valuable gifts, and among them two huge gold and silver calendrical disks of the sun and moon respectively. These may have had some magical purpose or they may have simply been intended as bribes; in the latter case they were counter-productive as they merely strengthened Cortés's determination not to be deterred from marching up-country. He calculated that he would not be obliged to face an equally inflexible determination to keep him out.

When Moctezuma learned that his sorcerers' mission had been a failure, and that Cortés was still aiming to meet him face to face, he took no action except to give orders that the Spaniards should continue to be given food and presents.

Nevertheless Aztec officials were soon withdrawn from the vicinity of the camp and supplies also ceased. It was as if the emperor was now trying out a policy of no contact and no co-operation, in the faint hope that the strangers might still go away of their own accord. As regards the future, he could not decide what to do and his advisers gave him no help. He again betrayed deep anguish of mind, and this time his distress spread to the whole population, who began to suspect that something sinister was about to happen. Moctezuma was moved to "hide in a cave", or even to commit suicide. But eventually he confined himself to changing his residence from one palace to another, and by the time Cortés began his march from the coast he had recovered his nerve and was again trying to influence the course of events. If he momentarily resigned himself to apathy and despair, the mood could not have lasted for long.

The Aztecs' earliest reactions to their experience of Europeans can be partly, but by no means fully, understood in terms of tribal psychology and determinist superstition. Certainly too much reliance should not be placed, as by some modern writers, on their belief in the return of Quetzalcóatl, and in other vague prophecies of national disaster, as the clue to their alleged defeatism and lack of will to stand up to the Spaniards. As the story of the Conquest unrolls, the other-worldly factors which bulked so large in Moctezuma's mind and in near-contemporary chronicles give place to the familiar interplay of power politics and personal ambitions which is common to all races at a reasonably advanced stage of development. It must again be stressed that the Indians of Anáhuac, despite their Stone Age technology and spiritual inhibitions, were no primitives but enjoyed their own kind of sophisticated culture. And so far as human relations on the broadest scale were concerned their minds were as active and supple as any in the Old World.

Even before the Spaniards began to move up to the plateau the political factor was already assuming primary importance. The Quetzalcóatl myth had been exploded, and the problem for the Aztecs and other native peoples was not whether the Spaniards were divine, but what they intended to do among them and if they proposed to stay, how their relations with the empire and its dependants would develop.

It is true that the word "teotl", or as Díaz renders it "teul", was being employed to denote an European and that "teotl" meant "god" in Náhuatl, the *lingua franca* of the empire. Such common use of that word, however, did not mean that the Indians regarded the Spaniards as gods within the same category as their own deities, and as beings outside and above the framework of human nature. It was soon apparent that the strangers were subject to disease and death, and to the normal human motives and reactions. If some of their exploits seemed superhuman, their behaviour was rarely godlike, and the relations which they were beginning to establish, individually and collectively, with the Indians, were relations between two kinds of men, not between men and gods. In Indian eyes they figured as men with a difference, superior in many respects, disposing of more effective types of magic, and perhaps irresistible, but still essentially men. They nicknamed the golden-haired Alvarado "Tonatiuh" (the sun) without identifying him with the sun-god, while Cortés, the most formidable of all the teules, they called "Malintzin" (hispanicized as Malinche), which is simply the Spanish name of his Indian lady-interpreter, Marina, with the Náhuatl honorific suffix—tzin tacked on to it.

Before leaving the coast the Spaniards spent some weeks of the summer of 1519 among the Totonacs of Cempoala. This was an instructive period, for it provided them with their first experience of peaceful Indian ways and their leader with his first insight into the political realities of the Aztec world. The Totonacs were a friendly and easy-going people and worked busily to conciliate and assist their unusual guests. Their chief, the famous "fat cacique", inspired the Spaniards with a kind of humorous affection and was treated by them rather like a mascot, while they obtained from him all they desired by way of lodging, food and service.

Cempoala was a rich and populous town where the Spaniards were brought face to face with the facts of Indian life in a luxuriant tropical setting. They violently disapproved of some of their hosts' habits, which included a marked addiction to sodomy, and were revolted by the evidence of idolatry, human sacrifice and ritual cannibalism which they saw around them. The priests, they noted, wore black mantles and long capes, "like canons", or shorter ones, "like Dominicans"; their hair, clotted with blood, hung down to their waists and they stank abominably of a mixture of sulphur and decaying flesh. As soon as they felt secure enough to give effect to their indignation they did so in a form which was to be repeated countless times in future years throughout the conquered lands. The idols were hurled down the steps of the principal pyramid and smashed to pieces at the bottom; the shrine was purified and whitewashed, an altar and cross erected and mass said. The Indians were exhorted to abjure their unpleasant practices and embrace the true faith. On this first occasion such action could naturally be little more than symbolic, for apart from the usual difficulties of interpretation (Spanish into Náhuatl and Náhuatl into Totonac) the sole cleric with the expedition, Father de Olmedo, was hardly in a position to attempt the conversion of the whole Totonac people. Nevertheless a start was made and although the Totonac notables protested in horror they did not dare to resist. No doubt they counted upon lapsing into their old ways as soon as the Spaniards had moved on.

Another precedent was set by the treatment of the eight noble girls presented by the chief to Cortés. Before distributing them among his captains he had them ceremonially baptized, and like Marina they received Spanish Christian names and the title of Doña. This was a sign that while they were not to count as the Spaniards' legal wives, and the friar was not required to perform a marriage ceremony, the soldiers were expected to regard them with deference as Christian subjects of the King-Emperor.

While these preliminary skirmishes between the two cultures were in progress, Cortés was looking far beyond the immediate horizon. He had soon been made aware that the Totonacs found Aztec overlordship, which had been imposed on them in the reign of the first Moctezuma, increasingly onerous and were hoping for a chance of using the teules to shake it off. The issue was precipitated by the arrival in Cempoala of a party of five Aztec calpixque, who proceeded about their business with their customary efficiency and arrogance, utterly ignoring the Spaniards' presence and behaving as if their own capital had never been convulsed by a crisis caused by those very strangers. Cortés thought this opportunity too good to waste. He had the emperor's officers seized on the spot and clapped in the stocks; moreover he followed up this personal humiliation of the master-race by ordering the Totonac chiefs to cease thenceforth from paying tribute or any kind of obedience to Moctezuma.

This act immensely enhanced the Spaniards' prestige among the people of the coast. Indeed, in Díaz's recollection, it was only from that moment that the name of teules stuck to them. The Totonacs, who had formerly cringed before the calpixque, now clamoured to have them sacrificed, but Cortés promptly removed them from danger. Two of them he sent back at once to the emperor, with a message claiming credit for their rescue, while the others, after a short sojourn on board a Spanish ship, were quietly released. Thus Cortés achieved two successes at one stroke; he ensured that the Totonacs would stand by him and not resume their allegiance to Moctezuma, if only for fear of the punishment which they would inevitably incur by again changing sides; and at the same time he indicated to the emperor that he had no wish to incur his enmity. He acquired useful allies and left Moctezuma guessing.

If the downfall of the Aztecs could be ascribed to any single cause, it would not be their fatalism, nor their lack of mental agility, nor even their inferiority in war, but the skill with which Cortés exploited the differences and discontents within the empire and over a period of two years progressively detached subjects and allies from their loyalty to Tenochtitlán. The process started in Cempoala and was later accelerated until the heart of the empire was effectively isolated and alienated from the rest. The case of Tlaxcala, towards which the Spaniards directed their march in August 1519, was however exceptional, because that republic was Tenochtitlán's traditional enemy and needed little encouragement to join in active hostilities against the Aztecs.

We cannot quite satisfactorily account for this ancestral antipathy. The artificial requirements of a "flowery war" waged between the two states for the sole purpose of providing captives to feed the gods provide no convincing explanation, since a half-religious, half-chivalrous exercise of this kind would be unlikely to generate hatred between kindred peoples. On the side of the Tlaxcalans it grew, in all probability, from the simple fact that they were becoming more closely hemmed in by Aztec territory, were kept deliberately short of staple commodities by blockade methods and cut off, in particular, from trading with the tropical coastlands. They found life a perpetual and irksome struggle against pressures from the Aztecs and their vassals. Whether the Aztecs would have been capable of dealing them a knock-out blow, or merely abstained from doing so for reasons of the "flowery war", it is impossible to tell. When Cortés asked Maxixcatzin, one of the four equal-ranking heads of the quadripartite republic, how it was that Tlaxcala had managed to survive repeated aggressions, he confessed that they had often had a painful fight of it. But, he added, they had usually enjoyed in these combats the support of Huejotzingo, a neighbouring semi-independent community, and such was the disaffection latent in Moctezuma's empire that they could always count not only on a warning of impending attack but also on a half-hearted performance in the fighting by the Aztecs' allies. Either the "flowery war" was not mentioned in this conversation, or the Spaniard did not grasp Maxixcatzin's point.

In writing to Charles V about the republic Cortés compared its constitution to those of Venice, Genoa and Pisa. Evidently he was struck by the fact that it had no monarch but was ruled by the four clan-chiefs in council. In their religion and other institutions the Nahua-speaking Tlaxcalans were practically indistinguishable from their enemies in the Valley of Mexico. Like the latter they had come in with the great Chichimec migration and had fused with the settled population which had been there throughout the age of Teotihuacán, and indeed in more remote "Olmec" times. Their territory comprised the little modern State still called Tlaxcala and much larger parts of the States of Pueblo, Hidalgo and Mexico. It was a populous, fertile country bordered by hillier regions which contained large concentrations of Otomi folk, preserving their own language and customs but fighting under the banners of the republic.

Paradoxically enough, it was the ingrained dislike and suspicion which the Tlaxcalans felt for the Aztecs that nearly put an end to Cortés's venture. The Cempoalans were quite right in suggesting to him that he would find a valuable ally in Tlaxcala, but when he applied for passage through its territory he was rebuffed. The Tlaxcalans could not believe that he was not combining with Moctezuma against them. They knew that he had been in close touch with emissaries of the Aztec power and had received lavish presents from the emperor. Not unnaturally they tended to view these less as propitiatory offerings for a Quetzalcóatl than as an incentive to the queer-looking teules to attack them in the rear. In point of fact Cortés's attitude towards them was purely opportunist and his intention was to use them for his own designs as and when that might become possible.

Despite their mistrust of the Spaniards the Tlaxcalan elders found much difficulty in deciding to challenge them in battle. Once their resolution was taken they deployed their full warlike effort and in three successive engagements came within an ace of wiping out the invaders. It nearly happened that Tenochtitlám was saved—although the respite might not have lasted for many years—by the exertions of its arch-enemy. Each battle ended in a Spanish victory, but by an ominously narrow margin. Cortés's soldiers were disheartened and began to demand a retreat to the coast. The Tlaxcalans, however, were in much worse shape and their villages were being cruelly ravaged. The Council therefore changed its mind and decided to accept the overtures for peace which Cortés had never ceased to hold out.

After this near shave it was lucky for Cortés that the diplomatic situation turned so soon and so easily in his favour. Before the fighting was over a resplendent Aztec embassy, headed by six important lords, arrived in his camp and witnessed the last stage of Tlaxcalan military discomfiture. It brought more rich presents and even the promise of a regular tribute to the teules so long as they remained in the country, but on condition that they agreed not to march deeper into Anáhuac. Cortés accepted the gifts, but without entering into any undertaking in return, and professed to regard the offer of tribute as a sign that Moctezuma had accepted the suzerainty of his own Emperor Charles. The envoys were still present while the negotiations with Tlaxcala were in progress, and Cortés duly enjoyed the spectacle of the grandees of both states hurling recriminations and accusations of treachery at each other's heads. The Mexicans also attended the grand finale of the peace talks, when the chief magistrates of Tlaxcala came out from the city in solemn procession to beg the Spanish army to enter and be its guest, and when Cortés made his triumphal entry they went in with him. Before they were dismissed they were obliged to watch the development of what it had been their mission to prevent, namely the conclusion of a firm alliance between Tlaxcala and Castille.

It took Cortés precisely three weeks to establish relations of confidence and natural friendship with the Tlaxcalan chiefs, which suggests that given favourable circumstances the barriers of communication and understanding between men of such differing backgrounds were by no means insuperable. Nevertheless, in the light of the mixture of awe, repulsion and distrust with which the Spaniards had originally been regarded, of the bitter fighting and destruction which preceded the reconciliation and of the tragic outcome of Cortés's future incursion into the Aztec lands, it was remarkable that matters should have been arranged so smoothly. The ordinary people, too, welcomed the Spaniards with the same enthusiasm as their leaders had shown, associating them with a sudden release from the strains and threats with which generations of them had grown up. The warmth of this sentiment, which appears to have been quite spontaneous, at first surprised the Spaniards, who suspected that some treachery was afoot, but when they understood that there was nothing to fear, it was gladly reciprocated.

Indeed a degree of fraternization quickly developed which was not again achieved in the long history of Hispano-Indian relations, and the episode therefore possesses great psychological interest. It would be unrealistic to imagine that it could ever have become a precedent, for the evil example set by the subjection and illtreatment of the Caribbean natives had sunk into the Spanish soul. But in the early days of the conquest of Mexico the Spaniards were frankly fascinated by the civilization which they had discovered and for which they could only find parallels in the Old World. Their leader himself represented Tlaxcala as larger and more populous than Granada at the time of the latter's capture, and its inhabitants as in many respects more orderly and civilized than the Moors of Spain and Barbary. Cortés may have been intentionally exaggerating in order to excite his sovereign's interest, but the fact remains that he and his soldiers were amazed by the culture as well as by the mettle of their late adversaries: their first impulse on getting to know a Nahua people was to establish with them a frank and honourable relationship from which the concept of equality was, at least in the initial contacts, by no means lacking.

In this happy state of affairs the army's chaplain wisely dissuaded Cortés from offending his hosts by attacking their religion. Conversion, the friar thought, would follow more easily and appropriately at a later stage, after the Spanish presence had been consolidated. In that forecast he proved strikingly right, for in future years the Tlaxcalans were to turn out model Christians, and the city's original church of San Francisco is the oldest still standing on the mainland of the Americas. For the time being Cortés had to content himself with releasing captives from the cages where they were being kept for sacrifice and with taking over a pyramid for the erection of a Christian altar. There, as in Cempoala, was celebrated the baptism of the girls whom the heads of the republic insisted on bestowing upon the Spanish captains. Cortés would not take one for himself, but Pedro de Alvarado was rewarded with the daughter of the magistrate Xicoténcatl, whose son, the younger Xicoténcatl, had led the Tlaxcalan army in the recent battles. The lady, who was known as Doñá Luisa, became the mother of another Don Pedro and of a daughter called Doña Leonor. The latter married Don Francisco de la Cueva, a cousin of the Duke of Albuquerque, and Díaz relates that they had "four or five sons, all very fine caballeros". Thus the blood of the magnates of Tlaxcala was transfused into the nobility of Spain. It is only ironic that the process should have been initiated by Alvarado, that great slaughterer of Indians, high and low.

Chapter 4

THE TWO WORLDS COLLIDE

CORTÉS SPENT THOSE days in eliciting information about Tenochtitlán and its rulers from the Tlaxcalan notables. The latter, while stimulated by the prospect of humbling the Aztecs at the side of their new allies, the teules, were uneasy because Cortés was apparently intending to plunge without delay into the Valley of Mexico with his Spaniards unsupported by any considerable contingent of Tlaxcalans. Xicoténcatl and Maxixcatzin advised him to think twice. The Aztecs, they argued, were both deceitful and extremely strong, and no doubt they also hinted that if the Spaniards had with difficulty avoided succumbing to the Tlaxcalans, the risk of their being overwhelmed by the greatly more numerous Mexicans, if they went ahead unaided, was only too real. The leaders of the republic had no wish to lose their allies before the alliance had even started to prove its worth, and they were alarmed that Moctezuma, suddenly changing his tactics, had sent another embassy actually inviting the Spaniards to visit his capital, or as the Tlaxcalans viewed the situation, to stick their heads into the trap. Finally, they were disturbed by Cortés's decision to take Mexican advice and pass through Cholula, a city even larger than Tlaxcala and a faithful adherent of the Aztec empire. They themselves would have preferred him to pause at Huejotzingo, a smaller town a few miles nearer the passes leading to the Valley of Mexico. Huejotzingo was well disposed to Tlaxcala and by no means subservient to Moctezuma.

Cortés was not unduly swayed by these fears and counsels. He was grateful for Tlaxcalan friendship, and keenly sensible of the advantage of having gained a secure base for his enterprise. But he had no intention of leading the host of Tlaxcala to the assault of Tenochtitlán. The grand design which he was revolving in his mind was to win an immense new realm, the wealth and grandeur of which he was only beginning to appreciate, intact for the Crown of Spain. He had no precise idea by what tactics this purpose could most easily be attained, but he was supremely audacious and had complete confidence in his own powers of improvisation. He already knew of the political cracks in the stately structure of Aztec dominion, and had detected signs of irresolution in the conduct of the ruler. He was convinced that these weaknesses could be profitably exploited. But he was also sure that although it would be fatal to shrink from fighting if there was no alternative to the use of arms, as in the case of Tlaxcala, it would be much more sensible to see how far he could get by diplomacy and guile. He was prepared to be devious and if necessary ruthless, but he had no preference for destruction and bloodshed. He wanted the prize, if possible, undamaged. Consequently, although he allowed Tlaxcalan warriors in their tens of thousands to escort his force across the plain to Cholula, he dismissed them, all but five thousand, as soon as he reached the city and was in touch with its authorities. It was no part of his plan to help them to wipe off old scores against the Cholulans.

In the event the Cholulans brought destruction on themselves. Just as the Tlaxcalans had warned Cortés, they had concerted with Moctezuma's agents a well prepared scheme to entrap and annihilate the Spaniards. The so-called "massacre" which ensued, and in which three thousand Cholulan warriors fell in five hours of hard fighting, has been represented by many writers as a cold-blooded atrocity, an act of sheer terrorism against defenceless or near-defenceless people. So it was condemned by the great Dominican Bartolomé de las Casas, aflame with anger with his countrymen for the cruelties inflicted by them on the Indians. Sahagún's informants, too, insisted that the Cholulans were cut down unarmed. On the other hand Franciscan friars no less sympathetic to the Indians than Las Casas later investigated the episode on the spot, which Las Casas never did, and acquitted Cortés of an act of gratuitous frightfulness. Moreover, the circumstantial and unrhetorical accounts of the affair by Cortés and Díaz have the ring of truth for the objective reader and it would be absurd to reject them as fabrications. It was neither in Cortés's character nor in his interest to order a pointless killing. What he did was to react with the utmost sternness against a deadly threat to his safety. Had there been no plot he would have been content with a formal recognition by Cholula of Spanish suzerainty and marched on.

The planning of the operation which was to have wiped out

the Spaniards did credit to the organizers. The aim was for the Cholulans first to involve the enemy in street-fighting, thus neutralizing the effect of his cavalry and guns. Barricades were built, pits dug to bring down the horses, stones and other missiles heaped on the flat roofs. Once the Spaniards were engaged, an Aztec corps which had been hurried over the mountains and was lurking in the ravines on the city's outskirts would intervene and finish the job. Nevertheless the plan miscarried; its details were disclosed to Marina, and Cortés was given time to forestall it with a stratagem of his own. The bulk of the Cholulans were caught within the boundaries of the Spanish camp and cut down. Later the fighting spread through the city and the Tlaxcalans eagerly came to the Spaniards' aid. As for the Aztecs, they failed to support their allies and melted back into the mountains.

But as soon as the battle was over, Cholula was treated with leniency. The Tlaxcalans were forced to stop looting and to release their prisoners. The government of the city was entrusted to the brother of its former ruler, who had been killed in the fighting, assisted by other notables who had not been implicated in the plot. Such inhabitants as had fled into the countryside were ordered to return and the markets for which Cholula was famous were re-opened. Not only was commercial activity restored, but the Spaniards interfered hardly at all with the religious life of the city, which contained over three hundred shrines as well as the huge pyramid sacred to Quetzalcóatl. Cortés, between whom and their tutelary god the priests saw no connexion, again accepted the advice of the friar Olmedo not to press Christianity on the Indians before they were ready for it: as in Tlaxcala, only one of the temples was appropriated and a Cross raised over it.

Moctezuma's first and, as it transpired, only attempt to dispose of the Spaniards by non-magical means had signally failed. Furthermore, he knew that Cortés was well aware that it was the Aztecs rather than the Cholulans who were responsible. Cortés, for his part, could entertain no further illusions about the emperor, who had tried to destroy him once and might at any time try again. Nevertheless he determined to go on to Tenochtitlán. He was leaving behind him a friendly Cempoala, a friendly Tlaxcala and a Cholula severely chastened but no longer hostile: in other words his line of retreat to the coast was reasonably secure. Ahead of him the risks were immense, the possibilities incalculable, but the prizes seemingly unlimited. Quite coolly he chose to advance without an army of Indian allies in support. He began by sending home the Cempoalan contingent which had accompanied him as far as Cholula, and from Tlaxcala he would only accept a thousand men to act as porters and servants. His only effective strength was the tiny band of four hundred and fifty Spaniards.

Chiefly he would have to rely on his own quick intelligence and adaptability to new and surprising situations. For all the exotic surroundings of the adventure, however, the atmosphere of his relations with Moctezuma had come to resemble that which was apt to prevail in the familiar Europe of Machiavelli and the Renaissance Popes, where violence and treachery were the order of the day, and power struggles were waged amid the forms of chivalry, but with a notable absence of scruple and humanity. The Cholula incident might have been paralleled in a hundred encounters of the Italian wars in which many of Cortés's soldiers had served. Thus in his messages to the emperor, whose envoys had never left his camp, he alternated between elaborate professions of amity and scarcely veiled threats, conscious that the longer he kept Moctezuma guessing about his intentions the more insecure he was making him feel. No doubt he enjoyed the game of bluff at which he was such an adept. But ostensibly he was going to Tenochtitlán as the emperor's friend and guest, albeit self-invited.

If it is right to define Cortés's ambition as the delivery of the Aztec empire, so far as possible unscathed, into the hands of his sovereign, he well-nigh achieved it in the six months during which, with Moctezuma as his prisoner, he was quartered in Tenochtitlán and, without causing any violent revolution, exercised the real authority in Anáhuac. But once the four hundred and fifty had climbed the pass into the Valley and had been swallowed up in the great city by the lakeside, there was no good reason, apart from the nervous fatalism of Moctezuma and the chronic indecision of the Aztec leadership as a whole, why they should ever have emerged again. They could have been crushed at any moment by sheer weight of numbers. In considering why the leaders never moved we are hampered by having no idea of the course which their deliberations took. It is conceivable that the emperor himself, although he had sanctioned the Cholula plot, subsequently insisted that the Spaniards, while not divine, were the mysterious men from the east who, according to the prophecies in which he believed, were destined one day to rule the land, and that as had been proved at Tlaxcala and Cholula, they were irresistible. It was therefore his wish that his subjects should pay them honour and obedience. But other members of the imperial family and of the council may well have assumed a vigorously hostile attitude to the Spaniards and advocated their destruction. We only know that Cuitláhuac, Moctezuma's brother, was in favour of preventing them, by force or persuasion, from reaching Tenochtitlán, while Cacama, king of Texcoco, advised admitting them to the capital. We are not told why that was his view, but he quite probably thought that as soon as they were bottled up in the city a second attempt should be made to get rid of them.

There appears to have been an abortive plan to ambush the Spaniards on their march through the mountains, and desperate appeals were addressed to Cortés by last-minute deputations of increasing importance and magnificence not to proceed any further. When these failed Moctezuma came out along the southern lake causeway to greet him. The emperor did not behave like a man in a panic. He was perfectly composed, dignified and affable, and his whole comportment during the short period of freedom which was left to him, as attested by numerous Spanish eye-witnesses, was incompatible with the state of a man suffering from nervous exhaustion. Moreover he gave very little away in his talks with Cortés. At their second meeting he explained that ever since he had heard of the two previous expeditions he had been anxious to satisfy himself about the nature of the beings whose arrival from the east had been predicted by his ancestors. Now he was sure that they were of flesh and bone and "mucha razón". He added that he himself did not claim to be a supernatural being. At the same time he did not hurry to place his empire in Cortés's hands, and continued to administer it as if the Spanish irruption was totally irrelevant. He politely brushed aside Cortés's attempts to interest him in the Christian religion. Meanwhile the Spaniards, cooped up in the palace of Moctezuma's father Axayácatl, had lost their power of influencing events in the world outside.

That was the moment when the Aztecs could easily have seized the initiative, and Cortés was clearly afraid that this was about to happen. Even before he entered Tenochtitlán he had heard that one Cuauhpópoca, the Aztec governor of the coastal region north of Vera Cruz, had killed two Spaniards and despatched their heads to his master. Now Tlaxcalan messengers brought the news that his own commander on the coast, Escalante, whom he had left to guard the newly founded Spanish settlement, had been ambushed and killed. He concluded that both acts had been committed by Moctezuma's authority. His own Tlaxcalan attendants warned him that a treacherous stroke was being prepared in Tenochtitlán, and he himself noticed that whereas the emperor remained smiling and courteous as ever, the demeanour of his subjects was turning from deference to cold hostility. Obviously they had only to cut off supplies and the Spaniards would be at their mercy; they could not for one moment have hoped to break out of the city along the narrow causeway and win their way into open country. Their sole chance of survival would have been to receive a safe-conduct from Moctezuma.

Whatever action was impending on the Aztec side, it is reasonable to suppose that in an atmosphere of increasing tension it could not have been delayed much longer, and that the eventual conquest of Mexico by Spain would have taken a different course. But the order was never given and Cortés, always one step ahead, anticipated it by making the emperor his prisoner. The Aztec nation looked on in helpless bewilderment while this neatest of reversals of fortune was accomplished. Without firing a shot Cortés was transformed from a captain of a band of adventurers in the tightest of spots into the *de facto* ruler of an enormous and smoothly functioning realm. In its boldness and cynicism the coup was a masterpiece of Renaissance statecraft, an inspired and brilliantly successful gamble.

Nevertheless the seizure of Moctezuma killed any prospect of a friendly and fruitful relationship developing between Spaniards and Aztecs. The free and easy atmosphere which had prevailed at Tlaxcala could not be re-created at Tenochtitlán. The longer Cortés was seen to be usurping authority, as if he were the all-powerful vizier of a puppet monarch, the deeper grew the resentment and suspicion felt for the intruders, more especially among the ruling and priestly castes. Outwardly nothing had changed in the life of the capital; Moctezuma was not kept segregated from his subjects; the business of administration was conducted as usual and the religious ceremonies and rituals punctiliously observed, although the Spaniards were itching to interfere with them. But Cortés was behaving as if the machinery and resources of the empire had been placed unconditionally at his disposal. He was sending out small expeditions to explore the remoter provinces and search for gold, and it was significant that these regions were already tending to repudiate Aztec rule to the extent that they were prepared to welcome the Spanish parties but not the Aztec officials and warriors whom the emperor had ordered to accompany them. It was a bitter blow for the dignitaries of the empire.

They were also shocked to see their emperor so passive and pliant as regards Spanish demands. A glaring example was his surrender of Cuauhpópoca, who on his own orders had attacked Cortés's rearguard on the coast, to be burnt in public at the stake. Nor was there any limit to the strangers' appetite for treasure, which Moctezuma docilely hastened to gratify. His predicament appeared to cause him no sense of humiliation or personal outrage. He even found pleasure in playing gambling games with the Spanish captains, and when two brigantines built by Spanish carpenters were launched on the lake, he enjoyed the novel sensation of sailing in one of them to a favourite hunting ground. His mood was not dull apathy but a serene resignation to his fate, a state of mind which Madariaga, following Díaz, explains as due to "religious prepossession", or submission to what he assumed to be the behests of Huitzilopochtli. In other words, he had found consolation in making the will of the gods the excuse for the inadequacies of his own temperament, for his inborn inability to grasp the nettle when confronted with events outside the scope of his experience and imagination. We will probably never find a more convincing interpretation of his disinclination to act, or even to respond to the feelings of his subjects with whom he had never lost touch in his very loose captivity.

The magnates of his empire, led by his nephew Cacama, king of Texcoco, and by his own brother Cuitláhuac, were in no doubt that the situation was intolerable. They were not deterred by any religious obsessions from advocating war as the only solution. Cacama estimated that he could dispose of the Spaniards in four days. But the princes were unable to keep their conspiracy secret. Worst of all, they struck no spark of encouragement from the emperor, who calmly arranged for Cacama and the other chief conspirators to be arrested by trickery and handed over to Cortés, who promptly clapped them in irons. It is only fair to add that Cacama had been warned by both Cortés and Moctezuma that they were aware of his plot, and that he would be well-advised to drop it. Cortés still hoped to conciliate the princely and noble class and wished to avoid inflicting unnecessary harm on its members. Only those guilty of actual assaults on his men were likely to meet an unpleasant end.

But the ease with which dissidence was stifled on this occasion made him over-confident and impatient to proceed with the two steps of capital importance which in his judgment would align Anáhuac with the other realms subject to the Hapsburgs. The first of these consisted of the formal renunciation of sovereignty by Moctezuma and a declaration of allegiance to Charles V; it would also involve the recognition of Cortés himself as his master's representative with full powers of government. The second was the introduction of Christianity into the country.

There was no difficulty in inducing Moctezuma to summon the Aztec notables and to announce to them his intention to hand over power to the unknown potentate across the ocean, justifying his decision by the need to conform with the will of the gods and to fulfil the ancient prophecies. The actual ceremony, a brilliant but melancholy affair, was attended by most, but by no means all, of the notables; one close relative of the emperor, the governor of Tula, would have nothing to do with the transaction and stayed in his province. Its significance was only too clear to those present, although the importance to Cortés of the legitimization of his conquests before a Spanish notary would have escaped them. They now understood that their tribute, as well as their obedience, was due to the white lord who had supplanted the Uei Tlatoani. There is only one slight hint of a reservation in the speech attributed to Moctezuma on the occasion by Díaz, when he is made to say that "as time goes by we shall see whether we get a better answer from our gods".

In their attack on the religion of the Aztecs, the Spaniards faced a far more obstinate problem when dealing with Moctezuma. However weak and vacillating he had appeared in secular matters, it never occurred to the principal devotee of Huitzilopochtli that his political submissiveness might lead to the substitution of the Christian god for Huitzilopochtli and the whole Mexican pantheon. In his own case it was quite unthinkable that he could be persuaded to countenance a threat to the religion which sustained the whole social and intellectual framework of Mexican civilization. Consequently he had never yielded an inch to Cortés's insistent suggestions that as a preliminary to adopting the Christian religion he should use his powers to suppress the bloodier rites of his own. The Spaniards, for their part, were irritated and genuinely appalled as they watched the customary human sacrifices being performed in all their horror at the solemn succession of Aztec festivals. This time the influence of the friar, Olmedo, was not exercised to restrain them from striking prematurely; probably he did not know what was in Cortés's mind, or Cortés, although he had been contemplating action for some time, struck on the spur of the moment.

His character was compounded of imagination and cool calculation. But it also contained an odd streak of militant fanaticism, which impelled him at that moment to profane, in a particularly brutal and challenging manner, the twin shrines of Huitzilopochtli and Tlaloc. The scene is described without emotion in his despatch to Charles V, and more graphically by his fellow Conquistador Andrés de Tapia, one of the small party which mounted the great pyramid in the central square, wrecked the images in their dark, foetid chapels and hurled them down the hundred steps of the teocalli. Tapia wrote that he would never forget the spectacle of his leader seizing an iron crowbar and splitting the gold mask of one of the huge idols, the stone surface of which was overlaid inches thick with stinking dried blood.

It is an extraordinary tribute to the discipline of the people of Tenochtitlán that they did not instantly rush to exterminate the desecrators. Some days passed in ominous stillness while the priests reasoned with Moctezuma, and the Spaniards, after cleansing the shrines of their filth and stench, set up altars in them with images of the Virgin and Saint Christopher. Then Orteguilla, the Spanish boy who acted as page to Moctezuma, reported that he had been conferring at length with his priests and principal officers. The boy had acquired a good knowledge of Náhuatl, but this time the gist of the discussion was—small wonder—beyond him. The result, however, was that Moctezuma became convinced that the Spaniards, by their violent and sacrilegious behaviour, had forfeited the favour of the gods, and that destiny no longer required the Aztecs to submit to them. On the contrary, it was now the emperor's duty to demand that they should leave Anáhuac altogether and take to their ships, and to make war on them if they refused. So at his next interview with Cortés he told him crisply, and in his most confident and imperial style, to get out or be killed. When Cortés asked for time to have his ships made sea-worthy, he agreed to stay his hand, whereupon Cortés countered by casually announcing that when he left he would of course take Moctezuma to Europe with him. But he knew only too well that he had again placed himself in a most precarious position. Half his soldiers were ranging the provinces, exploring and collecting gold; the sooner he could join up with them the better, whether or not he really contemplated abandoning his whole enterprise and sailing away.

The situation changed yet again when Moctezuma impassively laid before Cortés a painted roll of cloth depicting the arrival of no less than eighteen Spanish vessels at Vera Cruz. This was the powerful force under Pánfilo de Narváez, whom Velázquez, the governor of Cuba, had deputed to supersede Cortés and bring him to book for having flouted his authority in setting out from Cuba in the preceding year. Realizing at once the hostile purpose of the expedition, Cortés hurriedly devised a new plan. He resolved to leave for the coast and tackle Narváez with all the men he could muster, while Alvarado with a small garrison stayed behind in the palace of Axayácatl to guard Moctezuma, Cuitláhuac and the other princely conspirators. Meanwhile, without Cortés's knowledge, the emperor was already in touch with Narváez through his own vigilant officers on the coast. Undeterred by the grisly fate of Cuauhpópoca, these men continued to serve their master's interests with devotion. Using as interpreters three of Cortés's soldiers whom Narváez had chanced to pick up, they ascertained the nature of Narváez's mission and his great superiority over Cortés in men and weapons. Those facts they reported to the emperor, together with an assurance that Narváez had come to deliver him from captivity, and they in return conveyed to Narváez an offer of Moctezuma's help in apprehending the rebel Cortés. Despite the shocks to which it had been subjected, the Aztec administrative machine was still functioning efficiently. Moreover Moctezuma himself was holding his own in the battle of wits; when released from his obsession with the predestined victory of the Spaniards, the Indian was fully the equal of the European in dissimulation and intrigue.

The Conquest may conveniently be divided into three phases. The first or preparatory period ended with the entry of the Spaniards into Tenochtitlán. During the second, also of six months' duration, Cortés gained and then lost the mastery of Anáhuac. The final and catastrophic phase, which lasted from May 1520 till August 1521, witnessed successively the defeat of Narváez and the integration of his much larger force with Cortés's own; the latter's re-entry into the city and his expulsion with disastrous losses on the "Noche Triste"; and the consequent organization of the campaign which led to the destruction of Tenochtitlán and the crushing of all Aztec resistance. It is not the purpose of this book to explore the details of these convulsions, except insofar as they affected the relationship of Spaniards and Indians in the first years of the formation of New Spain. And the nature of that relationship, being extremely complex, is by no means susceptible of simple definition. It varied from one region of Anáhuac to another and was influenced by a host of factors beside the crude military facts of the Conquest. To a striking extent it was shaped by the efforts of individuals, and not only individuals belonging to the conquering race. Without playing down the appalling horrors which accompanied the fall of the Aztec capital, it would be unrealistic to envisage the Mexican scene, when Cortés had done his work, as one in which only triumphing Spaniards and crushed Indians faced each other across a landscape of universal ruin and desolation. The truth is that wide regions remained unscathed and that for a great part, if not the majority, of the Aztecs' kinsmen their downfall was a source of satisfaction rather than one of outrage or even regret.

In the final phase of the Conquest Anáhuac turned decisively against the hegemony of Tenochtitlán. It is not easy to understand how it came about that within a few months from the end of June 1520 when the Spanish army, decimated and shattered, barely managed to escape from the city and seek refuge in Tlaxcala, the Aztecs' hold on their empire had been broken beyond repair, especially as so much of it was composed of peoples racially and culturally indistinguishable from the Aztecs themselves. Surely it would have been more natural if all the Indian communities which, so to speak, had been sitting on the fence and waiting to see what the outcome of the crucial struggle between Spaniards and Aztecs would be, had reacted by making their peace with the latter and helping to finish off Cortés, who to all appearances was in his last agony. In fact, however, exactly the opposite happened. The Indian communities came over in increasing numbers to Cortés and in a very short time the reconstituted Spanish force was spear-heading a vast coalition of native allies intent on striking the fatal blow at Tenochtitlán.

Quite apart from the undoubted religious and cultural unity of Anáhuac, there were no obvious social or economic weaknesses presaging the early disintegration of the empire. Its peoples were disciplined, prosperous, law-abiding and held together by the cement of an age-old theocratic and communal system. Clearly however, as Cortés sensed soon after he landed, internal political tensions, and the jealousy felt by many communities towards the upstart Mexicans, were much more serious than might have been deduced from the outward show of strength presented by the empire under Moctezuma II and his immediate predecessors. Indeed it looks as if the widespread resentment with the high-handed and extortionate features of the Aztec régime may have been approaching explosion point. But this is only conjecture. It is doubtful whether an explosion would have occurred so soon had it not been for the totally undreamed of incursion of strangers from another continent. Otherwise the Aztec hegemony could well have been prolonged for decades and terminated by a mere shift of power among the indigenous peoples, and without any kind of cataclysm. In any event it is instructive to follow the process of alienation. Evidently the fiercer the hostility which developed towards the Spaniards among the Aztecs, the stronger the tendency became on the part of other powerful communities to detach themselves from the empire's cause and combine against it.

In Tenochtitlán the shock caused by the desecration of the great teocalli was turned to fury by Alvarado's massacre of the unarmed Aztec nobles as they performed a ritual ballet in the temple precinct at the festival called Toxcatl. Blockaded and hourly expecting an assault, Alvarado lost his head and tried to forestall it in the same way as Cortés had acted at Cholula. He failed to see that his blundering brutality would only inflame the populace and provoke the attacks which he wished to avoid. These, however, were not pressed home. The Aztecs, with sound military instinct, waited until Cortés, with over a thousand Spaniards and two thousand Tlaxcalan auxiliaries, arrived by forced marches to relieve Alvarado and was bottled up with him in the centre of the city. They then launched their grand onslaught and in six days' fighting very nearly succeeded in destroying him altogether. Moctezuma's contribution to the victory was to advise Cortés to release Cuitláhuac, in the hope of starting a parley, a gesture which he must have known would be unavailing. The Aztec electoral council promptly proclaimed Cuitláhuac emperor and a few days afterwards Moctezuma was dead, killed by the missiles of his own people as, prodded by the Spaniards, he pleaded with them for peace from the roof of Axayácatl's palace.

After the calamity of the "Noche Triste" Cortés retired to a secure base at Tlaxcala, and his victory at Otumba, on the way to that city, over a pursuing Aztec army commanded by the Cihuacóatl helped to salve his prestige. At that moment the younger Xicoténcatl, who could not forgive himself for having been worsted in battle by the Spaniards, tried to persuade the elders of the Tlaxcalan republic to change their policy and align themselves with the Aztecs. He was, however, disowned by his father and the other chiefs, and they proceeded to help Cortés to mount small operations against neighbouring townships which had offended or injured the Spaniards in one way or another. Cortés affected to treat them as rebels against the King-Emperor and exceptionally allowed his men to make slaves of their inhabitants and sell them at a profit. But in most cases there was no need for severity. The local communities were only too keen to join what they regarded, despite its recent defeats, as the winning side, and Cortés's main activity in the autumn of 1520 was therefore political, being devoted to bringing the whole country east of the great volcanos into an anti-Aztec alliance. He pursued this aim with an inspired and systematic thoroughness which almost suggests that he had at his elbow a shrewd native adviser, bitterly hostile to Tenochtitlán and adept at exploiting tribal jealousies and traditional rancours. He could already count on the support of Huejotzingo, Tlaxcala's ally, and of Cholula which he had himself purged of its Aztec sympathizers. In an effort to prevent the secession of the well-populated Nahua country between Huejotzingo and the Mixtec highlands to the south, Cuauhtémoc, who had now succeeded Cuitláhuac as emperor (the latter had died of an epidemic of smallpox brought to Mexico, with devastating results, by a negro in Narváez's army), hurriedly reinforced the Aztec garrisons in the region. But as usual the Aztecs moved too late. Cortés sent small forces of Spaniards and Tlaxcalans which helped the inhabitants to expel the Aztecs, and in a short time the resources, human and material, of the whole of eastern Anáhuac were at his disposal. He had become the lord of half the Aztec empire. In Díaz's opinion, this was the crucial period of the Conquest. As he put it, the peoples "gave obedience to His Majesty". Deputations of Indians poured in from all directions to beg Cortés to settle disputes about lands and properties, and especially about the succession to the numerous chieftainships which were becoming vacant as a result of the epidemic. Outside the Valley of Mexico and the adjoining districts to the west and south, Aztec supremacy had been completely repudiated by the people and their leaders.

The next step was to invade the Valley itself. Whether by his own sure instinct or on intelligent advice, he made straight for Texcoco and established himself there in the New Year of 1521. He had long known that political loyalties in Texcoco were divided and that if he could turn that situation to his advantage a large part of the Valley would be his without a fight. The union between Tenochtitlán and Texcoco, on which the stability of the Aztec empire was founded, had lasted for nearly a century. At the beginning of that period Mexicans and Texcocans had combined to destroy the Tepanec kingdom, and during the whole of the fifteenth century the two cities had expanded and flourished in harmony. Those were the palmy days when Nezahualcóyotl and Nezahualpilli reigned in Texcoco and acted as fatherly advisers to a whole line of Aztec monarchs from Itzcóatl to Moctezuma II. But the sympathy between the two cities had waned since the death of Nezahualpilli in 1516. Much resentment was caused in Texcoco by Moctezuma's clumsy intervention in the competition for the succession between two of the king's sons, Cacama and Ixtlilxóchitl. The emperor's support gave the throne to Cacama, but the powerful faction which favoured his rival was only cowed by a display of Aztec armed force and remained a source of discontent. Thus at the time of their greatest need the Aztecs were unable to rely on any effective co-operation from their associates on the other side of the lake.

The part played by Texcoco in what became virtually a suicidal civil war in Anáhuac is described by the historian Ixtlilxóchitl (Don Fernando de Alva) in his *Relación de la Venida de los Españoles y Principio de la Ley Evangélica*. This writer was in fact a mestizo—and an excellent example of the mixed culture which flourished for a time in the sixteenth century—but he was prouder of his descent from the kings of Texcoco than of his Spanish blood. The purpose of the *Relación* was to exalt the exploits of his namesake the prince in the war and the value of his contribution to the defeat of the Aztecs, while complaining bitterly of the ingratitude of the viceregal government at the end of the century towards the surviving members of the house of Texcoco, as a result of which they were living in penury and neglect. Many of his assertions are exaggerated or tendentious. He claims that among the Indian allies the Texcocan contingent bore the heaviest burden of the fighting, that their effort transcended even that of the Tlaxcalans and that Ixtlilxóchitl rescued Cortés from many a desperate situation and acted as his principal Indian adviser throughout the campaign. Nevertheless, when its obvious exaggerations are discounted, the *Relación* throws much light on the character of the war and on conditions in Texcoco while Cortés was using it as his base.

The unfortunate Cacama, whom we left as a prisoner in Cortés's hands, disappeared in the slaughter of the "Noche

Triste". The vacant throne was then disputed between two further sons of Nezahualpilli, Cuicuitzcatl and Cohuanococh. After Cacama's arrest Cortés confidently promoted the former to the kingship and had him baptised as Don Carlos. This did not save him, however, from being put to death, together with a number of his supporters, by his ruthless brother Cohuanococh, who thus assumed the leadership of the pro-Aztec party. When Cortés marched into Texcoco, Cohuanococh fled to Tenochtitlán with his adherents and as much treasure as he could remove in a hurry. In his place Cortés elevated yet another brother, one Tecocoltzin (the supply of Texcocan princes in the running for the succession is bewilderingly inexhaustible) and christened him Don Fernando. The historian Ixtlilxóchitl records that this Don Fernando was "a very noble man, tall and very white, indeed as white as any Spaniard could be", and that "he knew the Castilian language". He must have been a fast learner, for he soon died, probably from the same fatal wave of smallpox, and was succeeded in his turn by a Don Carlos Ahuaxpitzactzin. Most confusingly, Díaz does not mention Tecocoltzin and calls Ahuaxpitzactzin Don Fernando, but Ixtlilxóchitl (the historian) says that he only lasted for "a very few days" and that the leadership then passed to his own namesake the prince "because he was so valiant". It does not seem as if Ixtlilxóchitl was at first formally installed as king. But there is no doubt that he excelled as a warrior and the organizer of the Texcocan forces which fought for Cortés, and this is confirmed by Díaz who twice acknowledges his bravery and energy.

This involved story illustrates how sharply Indian sympathies and loyalties were divided in the chaotic period of the war in the Valley of Mexico. In this vast conflict virtually the whole fighting force of Anáhuac was marshalled on one side or the other. It is impossible to estimate with any accuracy just how many warriors were engaged. Ixtlilxóchitl put the total number of combatants at six hundred thousand. This is certainly a heavy exaggeration, but allowing for the historian's tendency to inflate the figures and for the great wastage of lives which occurred throughout the campaign, it would not be too fanciful to assume that two hundred thousand men were arrayed on each side at one time or another. The allies held the advantage because their gaps could always be filled by reinforcements, whereas the Aztecs were gradually encircled and finally pressed back into the overcrowded island fortress of Tenochtitlán. The Spaniards also received reinforcements as fresh detachments arrived from the Caribbean. At Christmas 1520 they numbered five hundred and eighty, not many more than the original army with which Cortés had landed, and they had grown to over nine hundred in May 1521, when the assault on Tenochtitlán began. This compact little force gave direction and coherence to the alliance, but every operation which it undertook was played out amidst the swirl and confusion of murderous encounters between tens of thousands of native warriors. There is no doubt that the ferocity of these battles and the consequent destruction of life were unprecedented in Mexican warfare. Customary and religious restraints broke down and were replaced by a savage urge to kill and wreck. Díaz, in an illuminating passage, describes how his comrades had to intervene in order to mitigate the cruelty of their Indian allies. The Spaniards, he says, were content with putting the enemy to flight and subsequently with looking for "a piece of loot or a nice Indian girl". It was their Indian "friends" who were so intent on massacre. He also stresses that they had no scruples about eating the flesh of their victims. In his opinion meat and plunder were the motives which attracted such hosts of "friends" to the war; just as in the Italian campaigns the armies were followed by "crows and hawks and other birds of prey", so the Indians in their thousands swarmed in the wake of Cortés's advance.

For all their disagreeable habits the allies fought courageously if not heroically. As might have been expected the Tlaxcalans, under their chieftain Chichimecatecuhtli, made the most valuable contribution to victory. The only notable absentee from their ranks was the young Xicoténcatl, who still could not stomach the prospect of a Spanish triumph, and absconded from the army. He was caught and hanged by Cortés's orders, despite a plea for mercy from Alvarado, who respected the Tlaxcalan's panache and knightly qualities, so similar to his own. Together with the contingents from Huejotla, Cholula, Huaquechollan, Tepeaca and other districts of eastern Anáhuac, the Tlaxcalans probably mustered a hundred thousand men. They provided a large force for the spring campaign which preceded the actual siege of the city, and thirty thousand more marched into Texcoco in April, escorting the porters who carried Cortés's pre-fabricated brigantines. These had been built in sections on Tlaxcalan territory and were transported forty miles or more to the lakeside. Bernal Díaz portrays their discipline as excellent, as they paraded to shouts of "Castilla! Castilla!" and "Tlaxcala! Tlaxcala!", but Ixtlilxóchitl the historian, in his zeal to establish that Texcoco was more helpful to Cortés than Tlaxcala, decries their exploits and accuses them of wholesale looting, including the "sack and ruin" of the splendid Texcocan royal palaces with their treasuries, library and archives. There was clearly no love lost between the two cities, and the mestizo historian, writing at least two generations after the Conquest, inherited his full share of the ancient grudge.

On the west side of the volcanos the only effective allies of the Spaniards were the men of Chalco and the Texcocan "vassals" raised by the prince Ixtlilxóchitl, but they were very numerous and at that stage of the war their support was decisive. The communities lying to the north, west and south of Tenochtitlán were in the main loyal to the Aztec connexion, but in Cortés's spring operations they were subdued or overawed one by one. Cuauhtémoc made no serious effort to rescue them, and they in turn proved incapable of combining to help in the defence of his capital. Around the lakeside towns, and on the precipitous spurs of the mountains enclosing the central Valley, scores of fierce battles were fought, but since the allies were in overwhelming strength and their opponents lacked direction and co-ordination, the issue of these struggles was always the same. One township after another compounded with Cortés and by the end of April the island city of Tenochtitlán—Tlatelolco, packed with Aztec warriors, stood isolated from its former sympathizers and dependants. Its enemies guarded the approaches to it by land, and the Spanish brigantines, launched from the Texcocan shore, were in control of the lake.

Cortés had some right to expect that Cuauhtémoc too, seeing the rest of Anáhuac leagued with the Spaniards against him, would recognize the futility of resistance and submit to the King-Emperor's authority. He himself was impatient for a peaceful settlement, for his own men, irked by losses and fatigue, were on the point of revolt. When he undertook the reconquest of Tenochtitlán, he certainly did not envisage that this could not be accomplished without the virtual destruction of the city and vast loss of life on both sides. But the Aztecs, who had so often shrunk from pitting themselves against the Spaniards while they held the balance of advantage, refused implacably to negotiate when their situation had become desperate. They were collectively imbued with a strange determination to court national suicide, although, if they had been in a mood for clear calculation, they might have reckoned that a prompt submission would have put them on the same basis, so far as their relations with the Spaniards were concerned, as the Tlaxcalans and Texcocans. The clue to their fanatical intransigence may be sought not so much in their hatred for the teules as in their alienation from the other peoples of Anáhuac, in the schism suddenly sundering them from the kindred tribes among which they had made themselves supreme. It must have seemed to them that every man's hand was again turned against the Mexicans, that they were back where they had been two centuries before, a lone tribal group struggling for bare existence within a ring of hostile neighbours.

Incredibly enough, the siege lasted for three and a half months. The Aztecs' ferocious courage, combined with Cuauhtémoc's tactical resourcefulness, took a dangerous toll of the Spaniards and caused Cortés many anxious moments. But in the event the Mexicans could neither hold off the enemy nor break out themselves. Defections from Cortés's Indian allies were repaired by fresh drafts, whereas the Aztecs could expect no reinforcements, and the warriors who survived the battles were perishing from sheer exhaustion. Economically they were in a hopeless position. No food supplies from outside were reaching the hundreds of thousands of fighters and non-combatants penned into the ever-shrinking perimeter, among the rubble and the piles of decaying corpses. In the end there was nothing left to eat except scraps of vegetation and animalculae from the lake, and as for human flesh, the Aztecs only ate the captives whom they had sacrificed, according to immemorial custom, to their gods. They were also deprived of fresh water, for the Spaniards had cut the aqueducts and the lake water was so brackish as to be almost undrinkable. The besiegers were also suffering from lack of provisions, since the passage of the armies had disrupted the agricultural life of the Valley. Nevertheless the Spaniards, says Díaz, always had plenty of maize pancakes (tortillas), the staple food of the Indian population; otherwise they had to fall back on herbs and the fruit of the nopal cactus. Such shortages were endurable so long as it was clear that a successful end to the struggle could not long be delayed.

The cost of the siege in human lives is impossible to estimate with any accuracy. Ixtlilxóchitl puts the loss of Mexican fighting men alone at 240,000 and although so high a figure is suspicious it would not be surprising if the total mortality among both warriors and non-combatants on the Aztec side had reached a quarter of a million. On the other side the Indian allies also lost very heavily. Ixtlilxóchitl claims that thirty thousand Texcocans died, and if the Tlaxcalans and other peoples suffered to a like extent the total allied loss through war and sickness might well have amounted to eighty or a hundred thousand men during the siege and the preceding campaigns. Butchery on that scale was of course unparalleled in Mesoamerican warfare, and it appalled the Spaniards themselves. Díaz commented that he had read of the destruction of Jerusalem but doubted whether the slaughter on that occasion could have been so widespread, so great were the hosts of Indians drawn into the holocaust from all over the country. The allies wasted little compassion on the Aztecs in their downfall. No matter whether they had been their associates or their enemies in pre-Conquest days, they massacred and despoiled them as ruthlessly as if they had never shared with them a common language and civilization. It seems that in upsetting the political balance of Anáhuac the Spanish irruption had sparked off a fatal and savage recrudescence of tribal savagery, and the Mexicans certainly paid a terrible toll for their bare century of supremacy over the other tribes of the region. Although they had at times been proved guilty of arrogance and brutality, they never deserved so dreadful a punishment.

Tenochtitlán, once by far the most populous city in America and Europe too, had been reduced to a chaotic and noisome wreck. The ghastly stench which overlay the ruins drove out the conquering armies and Cortés readily agreed to the first request he received from his prisoner Cuauhtémoc after the emperor's surrender, which was to allow the Mexican survivors to pass over unharmed to the mainland. But there was never any question of leaving the site desolate. Cortés instantly resolved to rebuild the devastated capital, to bring back the Indian population and to reserve certain quarters for settlement by Spaniards under their own forms of municipal government. This colossal task could not have been accomplished without the recruitment and more or less willing co-operation of a vast Indian labour force, and these shocked and bewildered people could only be collected, supplied and organized for the work by the efforts of their surviving leaders. Remarkably enough, both the authority of the Aztec chieftains and the habit of communal discipline were unimpaired by the catastrophe. Nor did it then occur to the Spaniards that the new Indian subjects of the King of Spain could in future be governed in any other way but through their own traditional rulers. Although they had for weeks past been obliged to watch the gruesome immolation of dozens of their fellow-countrymen, by Cuauhtémoc's orders, on the altars of Huitzilopochtli, they spared the lives of the emperor and his magnates. They were kept under supervision but treated with respect. Moreover they were assured that under the dispensation they would have a position which would be both honorific and responsible. As heads of their communities, they would enjoy prestige and hold property. Meanwhile Cortés kept Cuauhtémoc, together with the kings of Texcoco and Tacuba, in his own entourage at Coyoacán, which he had chosen as the temporary seat of government. Other royalties and notables of the tlatoque class were taken under safe guard to Texcoco, and particular care was taken to see that the numerous children of Moctezuma were properly looked after. In the towns which had taken the Spanish side, and to which the warriors were now returning, depleted in numbers but laden with plunder, the former rulers were for the time being left undisturbed.

Under Spanish direction the Indian authorities restored the water channels from the mainland to the city, buried the dead and began to restore the causeways and bridges. The whole work of clearance, reconstruction and repopulation was put in charge of the Cihuacóatl, Tlacotzin. This personage, whose predecessor had been killed the year before when leading the Aztec army at the battle of Otumba, must have possessed unusual ability and tact, for he somehow succeeded in winning the Spaniards' confidence and satisfying their demands as well as in restoring to some extent the shattered social and economic life of his own people. Three years afterwards Cortés reported to his sovereign that thanks to the endeavours of Tlacotzin—now baptized as Don Juan Velázquez—thirty thousand Indian households under their own governors had been established in the city and that their numbers were increasing all the time. Merchants and craftsmen, he added, were engaged in their old occupations and Spanish plants were growing in native gardens.

The Franciscan friar Toribio de Benavente ("Motolinía"), who in subsequent years did so much to help and protect the Indians, included the rebuilding of Tenochtitlán in his list of ten "plagues" which afflicted Mexico in the immediate post-Conquest period. Without pay and at a time of acute agricultural scarcity, huge drafts of masons and carriers toiled among the rubble. A great many died in accidents, or of undernourishment and fatigue. So many were at work that the broad streets of the city became impassable; up to four hundred men could be seen hauling a single great block of stone. The Spaniards vied with each other in putting up showy houses, some of which later collapsed from faulty construction. Others were built on the ground-plan of former Aztec palaces including that of Cortés which had as many patios "as the labyrinth of Crete". By 1523 the proud owners were already installed and exchanging splendid entertainments. But the most arduous task of all was the demolition of the enormous teocallis which still towered over the scene, and it was many years before the last of these monuments, with its statues and bas-reliefs, had been levelled and converted into the walls and flagstones of the new city.

Yet these swarms of impressed toilers seemed to be fired by a genuine collective enthusiasm. The friar records that they sang as they worked and that the chanting did not cease day or night. In modern times the very idea of a mass corvée is repulsive, but in the Aztec world it was an essential feature of the social system. All commoners (macehualtin) were accustomed to being called up in rotational drafts for compulsory labour service, which was not regarded as servitude but as an honourable contribution to the welfare of the community.

Thus the performance of their task, fraught as it was with danger and hardship, was capable of giving them satisfaction or even inspiring them with fervour, especially if they were spurred on by their own national leaders. Cortés himself decided to exempt them from the payment of tribute until the process of rebuilding and repeopling was sufficiently advanced.

For three years after the Conquest Cortés remained master of the former Aztec empire and began to extend his power into the surrounding lands which had not previously acknowledged Aztec rule. His authority over the Spaniards was confirmed in October 1522, when he was appointed Governor and Captain-General of New Spain, although it was to some extent circumscribed by the strong and often anarchic individualism of his countrymen and by the presence of royal treasury officials jealously watching his every movement. But the prestige which he enjoyed among the Indians was absolute. Princes and people regarded him quite simply as their sovereign, who had inherited something of the magical glamour which had formerly emanated from the Uei Tlatoani. Thus an unique opportunity, not to recur in the three-hundred-year history of the colony, was given to one man to shape its future and to define the relations between the two races which thenceforth were to share the country.

By the standards of the age Cortés's conception of the lines on which Mexico should develop was surprisingly enlightened. It compared favourably with the conditions then prevailing in the parts of Spain recently conquered from the Moors. There, after the siege of Malaga, Ferdinand the Catholic had branded the whole infidel population of the city into slavery. In the former kingdom of Granada the Moslems were converted by the threat of the sword. In Mexico, on the other hand, slavery was not in general countenanced by Cortés and became less common under his administration than in Aztec times, while the task of conversion was entrusted to the pacific and compassionate members of the Orders of Mendicant Friars. It was envisaged that the Indians should govern themselves, under the overall authority of the Crown, and for some years they were not even disarmed. Indeed this would have hardly been a practicable task when there were still only a thousand or two Spaniards in the whole country. Nevertheless it is noteworthy that armed Indians, drawn not only from the allies but from the conquered Aztecs, formed the bulk of the expeditions which proceeded under Cortés's orders to subdue for the Crown huge provinces stretching from Panuco to Guatemala, from Coatzacoalcos to the Pacific seaboard of Colima.

Yet, for all the vision and practical wisdom which marked his personal administration, Cortés was no more exempt than the general run of overseas Spaniards of the time from the craving for gold, lands and Indians tied to the working of those lands for the benefit of Spaniards. After the first needs of the Crown had been satisfied he helped himself to the lion's share of the spoils and staked out enormous claims to properties with allocations of Indians to exploit them. Moreover the concern which he felt for safeguarding the native population against naked oppression by the conquerors was strictly subject to the principle that the latter must rank as the undisputed and privileged masters of New Spain, while the interests of the former masters and their dependants, while not overlooked, must be subordinated to Spanish exigencies. Once that principle had been established, there would be room for the two races in New Spain (though no one could see how they would interact and intermingle), and for a convergence of their interests. But in the harsh circumstances of the times it was impossible to achieve a balance, and it was equally impossible for Cortés, or any other Spaniard in authority, to face his problems in any but a pragmatic spirit. Cortés's own attitude was dictated by a little philosophy and much common sense.

His zeal for the conversion of the Indians to the Catholic faith was utterly sincere, and it was surely deep reflection that made him so urgently importune the King to send more and more friars to Mexico, thus ensuring that the Indians would find protectors as conscientious in saving them from human exploitation as from the grip of idolatry. But from time to time his better judgment was overridden. A particularly ugly example of this was his decision, under pressure from the King's Treasurer and his own soldiers, to apply torture by fire to Cuauhtémoc and the King of Tacuba in a vain attempt to force them to reveal the whereabouts of the bulk of Moctezuma's treasure, all trace of which had been lost after the Spaniards' flight from Tenochtitlán in 1520. It is but small palliation of his conduct that the two potentates were put to the question in legal form, and that such treatment was no different from that which might be meted out to exalted prisoners in contemporary Europe. Worse outrages and extortions were being sporadically inflicted on Indians up and down the country by individual Spaniards in defiance of Cortés's orders, but these excesses were kept in check and were not typical of his three year period of near-autocratic authority. It was only after October 1524 when he disappeared from Mexico on a totally uncalled-for adventure in the Gulf of Honduras, that Anáhuac and the surrounding lands were plunged into confusion and misrule.

Part III
RECOVERY

Chapter 5

THE SPIRITUAL CONQUEST

THROUGHOUT THE SIXTEENTH century the friar and the Conquistador confront one another on the Mexican stage. The latter, with his superhuman exploits and extravagant inhumanities, is apt to usurp the limelight, diverting attention from the shabby and barefooted ascetic in the background. But as the drama develops, the friar emerges as its true hero. When the original conquest and the immediately subsequent phase of expansion have run their course, and the first generation of flamboyant men of action has receded into history, the Conquistador, far from bestriding the continent like an arrogant colossus, is revealed as an unheroic figure, absorbed in a humdrum and often sordid struggle for possessions and privileges, dependent on the favours of a viceregal government. Reduced to the stature of a mere colonial landlord, and an insecure one at that, he moves in an environment of peace; very soon his privileges can no longer be justified by any military requirement. Apart from frontier scuffles with the Chichimecs outside the widening jurisdiction of the colony, and an occasional clash with English or other European corsairs on the coast, he has no fighting to do. Indeed Mexico was remarkably free of military activity between the Conquest and the interminable independence campaigns of the early nineteenth century. It suffered from many plagues, but war was not one of them. For this unusual state of affairs the friars can largely claim the credit and it will be well to examine the antecedents of those remarkable men who, in response to Cortés's urgings, left their country and devoted their lives to the welfare of the Indian peoples.

The Lutheran tradition which used to prevail, and still influences the popular mind, in English-speaking countries, portrayed the monks and friars of the Renaissance period as decadent, lazy and unenlightened. But the prejudiced view is pretty wide of the mark when applied to Spain, and in the case of the Mendicant friars—Franciscans, Dominicans and Augustinians—in that country it has no foundation at all.

When Ferdinand and Isabella set out to transform the

Spanish feudal kingdoms into an unified, closely knit and authoritarian monarchy, the Church was subjected to the same severe discipline as all other institutions of the realm, while leading prelates became the most effective instruments of the centralized state. In spite of the Spanish Church's position on the frontier of Christendom, its establishment had tended to grow fat and lazy in late mediaeval times, just as in other countries of Western Europe. But in the two decades before the conquest of Granada it underwent a thorough-going reform at the hands of the Catholic kings. Shorn of its independent powers and privileges, and of a large proportion of its revenues, it was firmly harnessed to the promotion of the royal policies.

Organizational reform was accompanied by a vigorous revival of spiritual and intellectual activity, which more especially stimulated the work of the Mendicant friars. In the case of the Franciscans, the spur was applied in no uncertain fashion by a member of their own Order who also happened to be Queen Isabella's most influential adviser and the most formidable cleric and statesman in the Iberian Peninsula, Archbishop Ximenes de Cisneros. Famous for his personal rectitude and austerity, the unrelenting scourge of Moslems and heretics, later Cardinal, Grand Inquisitor and Regent of Spain, Ximenes was also an energetic patron of the new learning and the founder of the great university of Alcalá de Henares, with its chairs of philosophy, ancient languages, medicine and scriptural studies. Such was the mould in which the Spanish Franciscan of 1500 were required to cast themselves, with the important reservation that politics were no concern of the Order as such, but only of prominent members of its hierarchy who chanced to have been called to high office in the state.

The reformed friar, however, was expected to figure at the same time as missionary, scholar, ascetic and practical man of the world. Although a member of a religious community, he was destined and trained for work in the world, for preaching, teaching and looking after the sick and the poor. No more strenuous and exacting profession could have been imagined, and there were no material rewards for a life of unremitting labour and dedication, often in harsh surroundings. Most of the Franciscans engaged on missionary work, and notably in Mexico, belonged to the branch of the Order known as the Observants, a term derived from their exact adherence to the strict rule of St Francis. In the sixteenth century it drew into its ranks the very best type of Spaniard, men of exceptional ability, of unflagging strength of purpose and extraordinary qualities of mental and physical endurance. A high proportion of them had received the best education which Renaissance Spain could provide, graduating from the universities of Salamanca or Alcalá. Many, too, were the sons of noblemen or hidalgos. Man for man, the friar far surpassed the contemporary Conquistador or settler in character and intellect, and was more than capable of standing up to him in the interest of his Church, his Order and of the Indians committed to his charge.

Cortés's petition that friars should be entrusted with the conversion of the Indians was favourably received by the King and immediately acted upon. Charles V recommended it with enthusiasm to the newly elected Flemish Pope Hadrian VI, who as Cardinal Hadrian had acted as his Regent in Spain; and the Pope responded, nine months after the surrender of Tenochtitlán, by addressing to Charles the Bull *Exponi nobis fecisti*, by which the Franciscans and other Mendicant Orders were authorized to begin their work in Mexico. As it turned out, the Franciscans, Dominicans and Augustinians divided the mission among them. Later, and after the conversion had been accomplished, they were joined by other friars, such as Carmelites and Mercedarians, and by the Jesuits, but only the three Orders which reached Mexico in the first twelve years after the Conquest decisively influenced the minds and modified the material life of the Indian population. The Franciscans arrived in 1524, the Dominicans two years later and the Augustinians in 1533.

The three-year gap between the Conquest and the arrival of the first organized body of friars was partially filled by a few individuals, and by one of quite uncommon stature. First came Bartolomé de Olmedo, the cautious Mercedarian friar who, as chaplain to the army, shared its more harrowing experiences. He had to use all his tact and authority to dissuade Cortés and the rasher among his captains from premature onslaughts on the native religion. He was certainly a wise and humane person and we should like to know more about him. He did his best to sustain the soldiers' morale and, with the very inadequate means at his disposal, to instil the rudiments of Christian morality and doctrine into the Indian allies. While thundering away against idolatry, human sacrifice and sodomy, he sensibly attempted no mass conversions, but confined himself to baptising the ladies who had become the unofficial wives of Spaniards and a few Indian grandees in Tlaxcala and Texcoco. He died, worn out, in 1524. In addition to him, we have the names of one other Mercedarian and of two Franciscans, as well as that of a secular priest, Juan Diaz. But these were shadowy figures and left no mark on the country.

They were also all Spaniards, and in the event it was a non-Spaniard who first made it his life's work to give the younger generation of Indians, literally or spiritually orphaned by the war, an all-round Christian education and to introduce them to European ideas, arts and techniques. If Peter of Ghent had not chosen to bury himself in Mexico for the last fifty years of his life, he would no doubt have achieved a lasting reputation for himself in Europe, for by his birth, intellect and abilities he was a brilliant example of Renaissance culture. Without the powerful strains of humility and idealism in his character, he could have aspired to the most important offices in Church or State, but he preferred to quit Europe altogether and to place his enormous talents and influence at the disposal of a subject race in an unknown continent.

The circumstances of Peter's birth are not entirely clear, but it is reasonably certain that he was born in a village near Ghent in or around 1480, and that he was a bastard of the House of Hapsburg. Ixtlilxóchitl calls him "primo" (cousin) of Charles V, but this word does not necessarily denote an exact relationship. Most probably he was the son of the young Archduke Maximilian, heir to the Holy Roman Empire and grandfather of Charles, who would thus have been his nephew. In 1480 Maximilian had recently married Mary of Burgundy, heiress of the Netherlands; he was engaged in defending the Low Countries against the encroachments of France and in asserting his authority over the independent-minded burghers of the Dutch and Flemish cities. The House of Austria had already embarked on the series of dynastic unions which eventually extended its power throughout the old and new worlds, but sixteen years were still to elapse before the negotiation of the marriages which made the Hapsburgs heirs to the Spanish monarchy. Thus when Peter was growing up there was no close connexion between his homeland and Spain, and the Indies were yet undiscovered. Nor did his parentage on his father's side make him a German. He was born and bred a Fleming, and a Fleming he remained until, already in his early forties, he opted for a new life and mission in Mexico. Up to that time he was known as Peter van der Moere or Petrus de Mura.

The Low Countries in the late fifteenth century were Europe's busiest cross-roads. Apart from their obvious political importance, the provinces which the Hapsburgs inherited from the Dukes of Burgundy were extremely rich, and their great but unruly trading cities rivalled those of Italy. The ducal court, with its predominantly French culture, had outshone that of France itself. Flanders was pre-eminent in music and had produced a brilliant school of painters. Its towns abounded in masterpieces of late Gothic architecture. Academic education of the more conventional kind was dispensed by the University of Louvain, where Pope Hadrian studied and taught, while a whole series of more popular pious foundations, in which strict and sometimes mystical devotion was combined with the active pursuit of learning, sprang up in the Netherlands to suit those who wished to work and pray in common without joining any of the normal religious orders. A very high standard of scholarship and educational technique was developed in these institutions, and especially among the so-called Brothers of the Common Life at Deventer, from whom Erasmus himself received his early intellectual training.

It was in this atmosphere that the young Peter was brought up. Perplexingly little is known of his early life; it is not even certain whether he was in fact trained by the Brothers. But we can assume that his antecedents assured him the best education available, and the whole course of his activities in Mexico reflects the principles on which the Brothers' teaching was based. Though eminently fitted by his inherited advantages and very real talents for a career in the imperial service or as an ecclesiastic, he deliberately chose the arduous existence of a Franciscan lay brother at Ghent. Nevertheless his connexion with his Hapsburg relatives remained intimate and, as we shall see, the views and requests of the obscure lay brother were treated with attention and respect by Charles V and Philip II until the end of his long life. He died in Mexico in 1572.

The very promptitude with which Peter was authorized to set out for Mexico suggests that he was in high favour with the

King and the Pope. Within a year of the fall of Tenochtitlán he was pressing for permission to cross the Atlantic. We may guess that at Charles's court in Flanders he was given the opportunity of reading Cortés's first two despatches (carrying the story of the Conquest down to the period when Cortés was planning his final campaign against the capital), and that they so strongly excited his imagination that he was impatient to leave for the New World even before it was known that Cortés had succeeded. What is certain is that he was immediately given every facility to proceed with his venture. He followed the King to Spain in 1522 and eventually sailed for Mexico in May 1523. He was accompanied by two senior Flemish friars called Johan van Auwera and Johan Dekkers, both men of the highest learning and distinction.

The country into which the three Flemings were suddenly projected under such mysteriously favourable auspices was the Anáhuac subject to the personal authority of Cortés, whose powers were still largely delegated to the traditional Indian rulers, particularly in the cities allied to the Spaniards in the recent war. At that moment Mexico-Tenochtitlán was nothing but an immense building site, but Texcoco, despite damage and looting, was a thriving Indian community of perhaps a hundred and fifty thousand people governed by its own prince Ixtlilxóchitl. It had also become a place of refuge for eminent Indians from across the lake. It preserved reasonably intact the features of pre-Conquest society, with the important qualification that the native religion had become discredited and its priests had been largely deprived of their authority and functions. There was no more suitable centre in which the friars could get to know the Indians, gain their confidence and begin their work of filling the religious vacuum and introducing the Indians to European culture. They therefore settled down quietly in Texcoco. It would have been impossible for them to pursue their aims while residing among the Spaniards, or attached to Cortés's headquarters in Coyoacán and Mexico City. Of Peter's personal relations with Cortés we know nothing, but we can be sure that the Captain-General, who was well disposed to friars in general, would neither have wished nor thought it politic to thwart him in any way. Indeed in the following year he persuaded Peter's two companions to join his ill-omened expedition to Honduras where, along with many leading Indians and Spaniards, they uselessly forfeited their lives.

Peter, however, stayed on for three years in Texcoco. During this period he learned Náhuatl perfectly, a feat which was the more remarkable because, though fluent in Flemish, French and Latin, he was at first less proficient in Spanish and therefore not capable of taking full advantage of the services of Indian and Spanish interpreters. Apart from his linguistic talent, the king's uncle found that he possessed the most extraordinary gift for understanding the minds of the Indians and for leading them into new ways and beliefs without scaring and offending them. Realizing that it was essential not to cause further shock to nerves already torn by the ordeal of the Conquest, he attempted no public evangelism, but moved unobtrusively among the principal Indians and their families within the four walls of their houses. When the time was ripe he began gently to catechize them. One of his most willing pupils was Ixtlilxóchitl himself.

Naturally the King's intense interest in the conversion of his new subjects did not stop short of sponsoring what was essentially an individual enterprise by a kinsman. As a result of Pope Hadrian's Bull, the first official mission, consisting entirely of Spanish Franciscans of the Observant branch, was formed in the course of 1523. Its members were very carefully chosen for their piety, initiative and intelligence, as well as for their experience of missionary work among the Spanish Moslems. The party was limited to twelve friars only, for the Pope and the King, besides setting greater store on quality than on numbers, were anxious to proclaim the importance of the occasion by establishing a parallel between the mission and those of the Twelve Apostles and the original twelve followers of St Francis. The leader was Fray Martín de Valencia, a former Provincial of his Order in Extremadura, the country from which Cortés and many other well-known Conquistadors had sprung. A simple but curiously moving black and white mural in the monastery of Huejotzingo, which the friars began to build in 1525, depicts the Twelve on their knees, each labelled with his name.

In contrast to the discreet activities of Peter of Ghent, the arrival of the Twelve was stage-managed by Cortés with the object of making the biggest possible impression on the Indians.

The motives for which he determined to focus attention on the friars' pacific mission and to inculcate universal respect for them are easily understandable. Like the King, he ardently believed that it was his duty to bring Christianity to the Indians and that conversion would win them every kind of benefit in this world and the next. It was the only abiding and convincing justification of the Conquest, of the accompanying subordination of one race to another and of the enrichment of the Spanish state and Spanish individuals at the Indians' expense. Moreover the attachment of the Indians to the friars would provide a powerful guarantee of internal stability.

He therefore directed that the Franciscans should be received with ceremony and reverence in all the towns which they would pass through on the journey from Vera Cruz, where they landed on May 13th, 1524. All Spaniards were instructed to give the right example by kneeling to the friars and kissing their hands and habits. In order to play their part the friars had only to act sincerely and naturally. To the stupefaction of the natives they walked barefoot, instead of riding like the Spanish colonists or reposing in litters like Indian lords, all the way from the coast to the Valley of Mexico, through the stifling jungles and over the dusty tableland. As Díaz noticed, their habits were torn and they themselves were thin and "very yellow". When they stopped at Tlaxcala the Indians watched them in amazement, repeating the word "motolinía" (poor man). On learning what it meant one of the Twelve, Fray Toribio de Benavente, adopted it as his own for the whole of his long and deservedly famous career in the service of the Indian folk.

There is some doubt as to where the dramatic reception which Cortés had prepared for the friars actually took place. Díaz, an eyewitness, says "near Mexico", the historian Ixtlilxóchitl "three leagues from Texcoco", adding a mass of local details which give a ring of truth to his account. He records that besides the principal Spaniards Cortés had lined up an imposing array of Indian magnates, including Cuauhtémoc and the prince Ixtlilxóchitl, "with much rejoicing and dances". Cortés was the first to dismount and kneel before Fray Martín de Valencia, whereupon all the Spaniards and Indians sank to their knees as well. It was remarked that whenever he spoke with the friars, he did so cap in hand. Peter of Ghent was of course present; one suspects that he had something to do with organizing the dances. He had already arranged that the friars should be lodged and suitably entertained in the palace of Nezahualcóyotl. He had converted one of the rooms into a small chapel where the friars celebrated vespers, and the next day, the feast of St Anthony of Padua, mass was sung with much pomp.

The festivities ended with the baptism of Ixtlilxóchitl, his brother and a whole bevy of the descendants of Nezahualcóyotl whom Peter had prepared for the occasion. Thereafter they sported names like Don Pedro Tetlahuehuezquititzin, Don Juan Cuauchloictactin and Don Francisco Mochiuhquecholtzomatzin. The sole discordant note was struck by the prince's mother, an Aztec princess. Being "somewhat hardened in idolatry", she at first flatly refused baptism. Telling her son that he was a fool so lightly to reject the gods and laws of his ancestors, she took refuge in one of Texcoco's many temples. Only when Ixtlilxóchitl lost his temper and threatened to burn her alive if she remained obdurate did she consent to emerge and be christened as Doña Maria Tlacochuatzin. Then he set the temple on fire and demolished it.

This occasion reveals that so long as Cortés controlled New Spain relations between the Spaniards and the Indian upper class were marked by a certain mutual respect; in such a climate a real understanding might have been reached between the races at that level. It is also clear that (although an underground pagan movement would be unearthed in future years at Texcoco) the Indian notables were quite ready to abandon the old religion which had proved so impotent to uphold the supremacy of its Aztec devotees. As for the docile Indian masses, they were equally lacking in fanaticism. They could be relied upon to follow in the steps of their traditional leaders, especially as the influence of the priestly establishment, so powerful and pervasive in pre-Conquest days and seemingly capable of putting up an obstinate resistance to Christianity, had evaporated with surprising rapidity, leaving a spiritual and to some extent a social vacuum which demanded to be filled from outside. The impatience of Cortés to launch the friars, still pitifully few in number, upon a campaign of mass conversion suggests that he had appraised the situation correctly. In the event the care which he took to stage a demonstrative welcome for them, and to exalt them in the eyes of the whole population, was brilliantly justified. It could not at the moment be foreseen that the success which the friars were about to make of their mission would be constantly and gravely hampered by civil confusion, and by the cupidity and violence of the Spanish colonists.

Despite Cortés's urgent appeals few friars arrived in the early years to reinforce the Twelve. Thus the first four Franciscan monasteries, situated at Texcoco, Tlaxcala, Huejotzingo and the new Mexico City, at first housed only three or four friars each. Peter of Ghent moved into the latter foundation in 1526 and proceeded to set up the boys' school which he personally directed for the next forty years, in virtual independence and freedom from supervision by constituted authority. Not even his own Order presumed or desired to interfere with his radical plans for educating the Indians. Ostensibly he held no rank, for he remained a lay brother and steadily refused to be ordained priest, but since everyone in New Spain was fully aware that he was a relative of the mighty King-Emperor and frequently exercised his privilege of corresponding privately and directly with the monarch, he wielded vast influence in the colony and equalled in prestige any Viceroy or Archbishop. Fearless and uncompromising in the defence of his Indians' interests, he was scrupulously modest and respectful towards his many superiors. Nevertheless it was the head of the hierarchy who exclaimed years afterwards, with a mixture of humour and irritation, "I am not the Archbishop of Mexico; it is Fray Pedro de Gante".*

The school was attached to a chapel, San José de los Naturales, which as its name implied was intended solely for use by the Indians of the capital. For the purpose of elementary education, the boys were divided into the sons of nobles and those of commoners, though this distinction was not always observed in the case of the more intelligent pupils. In general the former, who were regarded as potential candidates for higher studies, boarded at the school, while the latter lived at home and attended daily classes. The primary instruction was the same—reading, writing, numbers, singing and of course the catechism. The curriculum did not include the Spanish

---

* Mendieta, quoted by John McAndrew, *The Open-Air Churches of Sixteenth Century Mexico.*

language. Fray Pedro and his assistants taught entirely in Náhuatl, no mean intellectual feat in itself. At the same time Náhuatl was rendered in the Latin alphabet. This truly startling innovation was grasped without too much difficulty by children who had not yet been grounded in their own clumsy system of writing, and once it had taken root it led to a new outburst of literary activity in the native language.

Fray Pedro took much trouble to develop the natural talents of the Indians and adapt them to Christian beliefs. More especially he encouraged their addiction to singing and dancing at religious festivals. The great courtyard of the chapel formed the stage on which pageants and mimes involving hundreds of performers, both adults and children, re-enacted scenes derived from the Bible and Christian doctrine. He was the first to introduce the Indians to the folk music and musical instruments of mediaeval Europe, with the result that to this day Mexican popular music owes more to themes inherited from that source than to the native tradition with its very restricted range of musical resources.

With a similar object in view the primary school was before long eclipsed in importance by its adjunct, a technical college where the pupils were taught to earn their living by practising European crafts. The sons of the famed tolteca of Tenochtitlán took up the new trades with enthusiasm and showed remarkable proficiency. The school turned out thousands of skilled masons and carpenters, blacksmiths, shoemakers and tailors, all capable of supplying the Spanish colonists, too proud or lazy to work with their hands, with the goods to which they were accustomed. On a somewhat higher plane it produced real artists specializing in painting, sculpture and ornamental carving for the newly built churches and cloisters. Of the increasing number of sixteenth-century murals which have emerged in recent years from under layers of whitewash, it is hard to tell which are the work of Indian or European masters, for their style is predominantly European. On the other hand an unmistakably Indian touch may be recognized in the countless examples of stone carving of the same period. Apart from their Christian motifs they are in direct line of descent from the vanished reliefs of the Aztec teocallis. According to a younger contemporary (incidentally a mestizo), Fray Diego de Valadés, the secret of Fray Pedro's success as an educator lay in his own versatility:

"he taught the Indians all the arts; for he was the master of all of them".*

The Franciscans had the field to themselves for the first four years after their arrival, for of the twelve Dominicans who followed them in 1526 five died within a year and another four were shipped back ill to Spain. They did not start effective work till 1528. The first Augustinian party of seven reached Mexico in 1533, by which time the total number of friars in the country did not exceed a hundred. Yet, according to Fray Martín de Valencia, the Franciscans alone had already baptized 1,200,000 people. Progress had been slow at first. The few friars available were worked to death and insufficiently acquainted with the native languages, while the Indians themselves, although not hostile, were found to be shy, apathetic and reluctant to offer themselves for instruction. They often fled to the woods and caves to avoid the preachers. Then suddenly their attitude changed, the urge for baptism became infectious and at the peak period of conversions in the mid-thirties mass christenings of up to 15,000 a day were being recorded. After due allowance has been made for exaggeration by missionary writers, there is no doubt that there was an unprecedented rush into the Church. The friars had no need to seek converts; they were overwhelmed by them. In the experience of the Spaniards whose whole missionary effort had in the past been directed towards singularly intractable Moslems and Jews, this was a most unusual phenomenon. Indeed, ever since Charlemagne's forcible conversion of the Saxons, the sword had been the most effective weapon of the mediaeval proselytizer. In Mexico its place was taken by persuasion and example.

As soon as the friars' message, which consisted of the Catholic faith reduced to its most simple tenets, began to penetrate the language barrier, the Indians quickly realized that they could come to no harm by welcoming it. They recognized the friars' motives as essentially unselfish and humane. Moreover the profession and practice of the new religion, especially when linked with communal activities of a useful or festive character, filled the psychological void left by the collapse of the old cults. For those who had fought on the losing side it helped to heal

* Nicolás León, *Fray Diego de Valadés*, quoted by Robert Ricard in *La Conquista Espiritual de Mexico*.

the wounds of the Conquest. But an even more potent factor in impelling the Indians to find refuge in the Church was the protection the friars afforded against the savage outbreaks of oppression and exploitation of the native peoples which occurred in the late twenties and early thirties, after Cortés's restraining hand had been removed and before the royal and ecclesiastical authority over New Spain had been securely established. Although such protection was often unavailing, the Indians knew that they had powerful defenders working tirelessly on their behalf.

In such conditions it is easy to be sceptical about the sincerity and depth of the acceptance of Christian beliefs by the Indians. Even in modern times the assumption is current that Indian Christianity in Mexico is and has always been a superficial veneer, a cover for passive indifference or for an obstinate adherence to ancient rites and superstitions. It gained much credence for political reasons when the Mexican Revolution of the twentieth century took a militantly anti-Catholic form, and was swallowed whole by D. H. Lawrence and other foreign writers. But this view certainly stems either from sheer prejudice or from a serious misconception of sixteenth-century realities. The friars knew perfectly well that immemorial practices and habits of mind would not be eradicated in a generation or two. Sahagún himself admitted frankly that sacrifice—not of men but of animals—was still rife after a few decades, that pagan images, secreted in Christian shrines and country hideouts, were still commonly worshipped and that many Indians, while going through the motions of conformity, were untouched by any genuine feeling for the new faith. In much the same way as survivals of paganism persisted throughout the Dark and Middle Ages in Europe, popular customs and folklore in Mexico indefinitely retained a strong flavour from the pre-Columbian cults. In the more inaccessible regions surrounding the core of Anáhuac (but not excluding Otomi villages almost within sight of Mexico City) minor idolatry and the rites of the local sorcerers continue to co-exist with very real Christian devotion. It would not be hard to find plenty of parallels in Eastern Europe and the Balkans.

The question of the extent to which Christianity was sinking into the Indian soul was a subject of lively debate among the friars and between clerics and laymen. The latter, who liked to maintain for selfish reasons that the Indians were an inferior type of humanity, were naturally the most sceptical, while the friars who had spent their whole lives among the Indians argued vehemently that although their converts could not be expected to master theological subtleties and were tiresomely prone to backsliding, they had firmly grasped the essentials of the faith. All in all no more pious, enthusiastic and well-behaved Catholics could be found in His Majesty's dominions.

By the mid-century there was no trace of organized paganism left in Anáhuac. The vast and pompous hierarchy which had administered the official religion—and no religion was more institutional than the Aztec—had utterly disappeared. Every teocalli had been demolished. The generation which had grown up since 1521 was familiar with the outward evidences of Christianity and could have preserved only the haziest notion of the ancient myths. Since the extinction of the calmecacs and telpochcallis the only doctrine they had heard was the Christian. But how much of this had they assimilated? And what was going on behind those impassive Indian faces which only lit up at festivals?

Only the friars were qualified to interpret the Indians' thought and feelings. Long years of isolation in the remote countryside, combined with an intimate knowledge of native languages and customs, gave them an unique insight into the character of their converts. Baptism was not just a casual and perfunctory rite. It was preceded and followed by exhaustive preparation, until the friars were satisfied that the neophytes had absorbed the necessary minimum of doctrine and moral training. The faith was dinned into them by endless catechizing and sermonizing in their own tongues. This work alone imposed an almost unbelievable burden on the friars, who totalled about five hundred in 1550. It must be remembered that they were at the time building their churches and monasteries and familiarizing the Indians with European techniques and agricultural novelties. But Náhuatl, the most common speech of New Spain, had to be studied thoroughly by all who aspired to preach, instruct and hear confessions. For reasons of policy the Indians were not taught Spanish, which the friars considered unsuitable for the propagation of Christianity, and the offices of the Church were of course recited in Latin. Náhuatl was at least comparatively easy to pronounce—more than could be said for the majority of the fearsome languages of ancient Mexico. As a general rule the three Orders, in dividing the country between them for the purpose of evangelization, expected their members to become fluent in whatever tongues happened to be spoken in the regions allotted to each. Thus a Dominican would specialize in Zapotec or Mixtec but would have no need to study Tarascan, as Michoacán was divided between Franciscans and Augustinians. It was quite usual for an individual friar to be able to preach and write in two or three languages besides Náhuatl, and the historian Mendieta mentions one (probably the famous Franciscan scholar Fray Andrés de Olmos) who could do this in ten. But it was the Augustinians who were the greatest polyglots of all, because ten languages were in fact current in their mission territory—Náhuatl, Otomi, Tarascan, Huaxtec, Matlatzinca, Totonac, Mixtec, Chichimec, Tlapanec and Ocuiltec. Most of the friars were well-educated men but they also possessed an amazing flexibility of mind. As they studied their Latin, Greek and Hebrew at Salamanca, they could hardly have imagined that they would shortly be wrestling with anything so exotic as Chontal, Popoloca or Zoque.

So high a standard of linguistic ability resulted in the production of quantities of books in the native languages for use as aids in learning the languages themselves and in diffusing knowledge of Christianity. They comprised grammars and dictionaries, "doctrines" (manuals for teaching the catechism), sermons, selections from the New Testament, Lives of the Saints and other edifying works. The first "doctrine" in Náhuatl, composed by Pedro de Gante and one of his Flemish collaborators, was originally published in Antwerp and was reprinted twice in Mexico. The purpose of all this literature was strictly practical. Copies of the books in print or manuscript were in continuous use, passing from monastery to monastery and from hand to hand. Consequently few have survived. Nevertheless it has been estimated from references to them in other works, that a minimum of 109 books of this category were circulating in New Spain between 1524 and 1572.

The friars' greatest difficulty was to make the concepts of Catholic dogma intelligible in the native tongues without departing from the narrow orthodoxy of expression demanded by the Church of the Counter-Reformation. At first they allowed themselves considerable latitude in interpreting Christian ideas to the Indians, but after the Council of Trent (1547) they occasionally fell foul of the Inquisition and were obliged to withdraw their writings from circulation. When handing the book to the printer, it became safer to leave in Spanish or Latin the words conveying the more delicate theological ideas. What the friars actually said to the Indians when preaching to them in the huge monastery courtyards was beyond the reach of the Holy Office.

The expansion of the mission system and the division of the country between the Orders were carried out without much friction. In the central Valley and adjoining Morelos the monasteries of the three were intermingled without any recognizable pattern. Further afield the Franciscans established a monopoly of the Tlaxcala–Cholula region, of Michoacán (with the exception of a small but important group of Augustinian houses), of the whole of the vast territory of Jalisco down to the Pacific and of the hitherto untamed north-west. It was they, rather than the colonists and miners, who gradually pacified the savage Chichimecs and extended the settled frontier. It was a dangerous life and not a few of them were martyred in the process. They also gained exclusive rights in Yucatán. The Dominicans took the south as their province, that is to say the Mixtec–Zapotec country as far as the isthmus of Tehuantepec with a further extension through Chiapas to Guatemala. The Augustinians chose the north-east, a region of tangled highlands inhabited chiefly by Otomis and Huaxtecs. By 1560 there were perhaps a hundred monasteries with eight hundred friars in New Spain, and at the end of the century up to fifteen hundred friars in three hundred or more houses.

One is tempted to regard this great monastic network as a kind of ecclesiastical republic, a state within a state, or at least a Mendicant theocracy subsisting alongside and in semi-independence from the colonial administration headed by the Viceroy and the Audiencia. There is much truth in this view in respect of the first thirty years after the Conquest, in which the friars, having successfully vindicated their cause against attack by selfish interests, were granted full freedom to put their aims into practice under a generally sympathetic government. Paradoxically the wider expansion of the system in subsequent years coincided with the weakening of the friars' influence in the affairs of New Spain, the assertion of authority by the episcopate and a more critical attitude towards the Orders adopted by the Court of Madrid. Philip II was less well disposed to the friars than his father Charles V, and they too shed much of the practical idealism which had inspired their earlier work.

The ideal of a Christian commonwealth in which Indian communities would lead a non-hispanicized social and economic existence, pursuing their own separate development under the friars' guidance and protection, originated in the radical Dominican theory propounded by Vitoria and Las Casas that the only possible justification of the Spanish presence in the Indies was the conversion of their inhabitants. It was of course incompatible with the exploitation of New Spain as a source of precious metals for financing the Hapsburg hegemony in Europe. Yet the Spanish Crown felt, or professed to feel, no contradiction in treating the Indians simultaneously as souls to be saved and carefully tended and as labour units regimented by right of conquest to serve Spanish material needs. The King's advisers in Spain were not necessarily hypocrites if they calculated that the best way of ensuring that his Indian subjects remained docile and industrious was to commit them to the friars' care. What could never become a reality was a situation in which the Orders could assume civil as well as spiritual responsibility for their converts. Such a state of affairs came near to being achieved in isolated instances through the efforts of certain exceptional men, but in normal circumstances the friars found themselves competing with the Administration and with landholders, both Spanish and native, for the Indians' obedience and services. And as the Indian population was rapidly reduced by devastating epidemics of diseases brought from Europe, this competition became fierce.

In any case New Spain was such an immense country that no amount of royal favour and papal privilege could make it possible for the Mendicants to cover the whole ground effectively. Inevitably there were gaps in the chains of religious houses and there were areas into which they never penetrated at all. The wilder regions, such as Guerrero, discouraged both evangelization and other forms of Spanish control. But even in the more thickly-populated and economically exploitable parts the Spanish authorities, lay and clerical, found the native communities inconveniently dispersed. Outside the big cities of the Valley and the Puebla plateau the Indians lived in a multitude of large and small villages. As the population shrank and the Spaniards grew hungrier for labour a strong effort was made to concentrate them in new medium-sized towns where they could be more easily supervised and directed. Here the interests of friars and laymen happened to coincide. This process, which was considerably accelerated in the later years of the century, came to be known as "congregación". In many cases old towns were simply abandoned and rebuilt on neighbouring but more accessible sites, but not given new names.

The effect of this policy was to create hundreds of new settlements, each carefully planned on a rectangular grid system recalling that of Aztec Tenochtitlán, with its central plaza and municipal buildings. They long remained strictly Indian towns administered and policed by Indian governors; no Spaniards were permitted to reside in them. Nevertheless for purposes of labour service and payment of tribute their inhabitants were subject to coercive superintendence by Spanish officials (corregidores), appointed by the central authority, and by individual Spanish landholders (encomenderos). The working of the institutions called corregimiento and encomienda will be examined in later chapters, but it will at once be obvious that the duties and exactions imposed by them on the Indians were bound to conflict with the friars' concept of how their lives should be ordered, and to give rise to violent disagreements between friars and colonists.

The Mendicants were calculated to emerge victorious from such clashes because they enjoyed, as well as powerful patronage, the trust and affection of the Indians. They were also an element of stability among the changes of the secular world. Very often their monastery was the focal point of the Indian town, which it dominated architecturally and psychologically. Where the site was the same as in pre-Conquest times the huge barrel-vaulted church with its cloister and dependencies usually stood on the foundations of the principal teocalli. Soaring above the flat roofs of the Indian houses, its massive battlemented walls might give the impression of a castle. So might the crenellations surrounding the forecourt where the Indians gathered for preaching or festivities. The outward appearance of the monasteries has led observers to assume that they were in fact designed to serve as fortresses in case the local

Spaniards were obliged to defend themselves against a native uprising. There is no evidence, however, that any such consideration ever entered the minds of the builders. Not only were the sites and layout of the buildings unsuited to the tactical requirements of a besieged garrison, but in the sixteenth century there would have been no garrison to defend them. As already explained, no Spaniards except the friars lived in the Indian towns, while the friars were without exception unarmed. Moreover their establishments in the settled parts of Mexico did not need to be defended against Indian attacks, and it did not occur to them that such a danger might arise. In short the monastery was a fortress in the spiritual sense only and had no military purpose whatsoever. The frowning battlements were purely decorative.

In order to prevent the Indians from slipping back into their old ways the Mendicants found it necessary to regulate their economic and social activities according to fixed patterns replacing but to a broad extent resembling those of the pre-Conquest age. So far as this traditional life could be reconciled with the practice of Christianity the friars tried to preserve it uncontaminated by unsettling influences from without. The former agrarian system under which the peasants' land was held communally and allotted in plots to individual farmers was maintained essentially intact, though the time which the peasant could devote to his own needs was heavily encroached upon by the labour which he was compelled to contribute to the development of the lands appropriated by the missions themselves, as well as those worked for the local encomendero and for the dwindling but still privileged Indian upper class. But these commitments, which in a period of steeply-falling population impinged more harshly on the rural communities than the corresponding corvées under the old régime, were greatly alleviated by the benevolent tutelage exercised by the friars and the benefits introduced by them in the shape of new arts and crafts, new crops and methods of cultivation and hitherto undreamed-of domestic animals.

While absorbing these innovations the working community was virtually put to school, and its scanty leisure was occupied in learning by rote the routines of worship of the new religion and in the elaborate celebration of feasts. The ceremonies, processions and dances improvised by the friars were intentionally made as brilliant and melodious as possible, orgies of colour and of the blended strains of native and European music, but not (if the friars could help it) exceeding the bounds of decorum. Above all idleness could not be permitted, because it led to social indiscipline (never tolerated in pre-Columbian times), moral apathy and drunkenness, a failing punishable by death under the old order. Penalties for misconduct inflicted by the friars included, besides religious penances, whippings and temporary confinement in the monastery lock-up, but were markedly less severe than those to which the macehualtin had previously been exposed. Yet both civil authorities and friars were worried by the increasing addiction of the Indians to pulque, a depressing proof of the stresses caused by the crash of a civilization.

Indian sexuality, which had been kept severely within bounds by Aztec law and custom, was considered a less serious problem than drunkenness. As a concession to the friars' ideas of outward decency men were required to discard the traditional maxtlatl or breech-cloth and substitute for it cotton trousers reaching to the knee. Polygamy, however, proved awkward to deal with. Among the common people one wife was the general rule, but every Mexican of standing aspired to several secondary wives or concubines, if he could afford them, and important persons might collect upwards of two hundred. Father Motolinía comments that such an establishment resembled a textile factory rather than a seraglio; it was maintained less for pleasure than for profit. At first the notables objected strongly to restricting themselves to one wife, especially as they could point to plenty of lay Spaniards living openly with more than one Indian woman. Then there was the difficulty of selecting which of the women in his household the Indian could have as his wife in Christian marriage. Was the selection to be left to him, or was he required to choose the lady who happened to be his first or legitimate wife according to pre-Conquest custom and ceremonial? And what was to become of the dozens of women whom a man of consequence was obliged to discard? Perhaps the latter problem was the easiest to solve because Motolinía also mentions that the more affluent Mexicans in the Aztec period had grabbed so many women for themselves that there were not enough to go round among the poorer citizens. But in the event, polygamy died quickly, and there was as great a rush by young people for marriage with the rites of the Church as there had been for baptism.

The influence of a monastery radiated from the town where it was situated as far as the outlying villages which could be reached within a few days on foot. Here the friars built small chapels with rooms attached known as "visitas". These were not permanently occupied but sheltered friars when they went periodically on tour in the course of their pastoral work. Until the last fifteen years of the century, when the Church began to encourage an increase in the secular clergy and to impose restrictions on the friars, there was virtually no parochial system in the European sense. Where there were no friars there were no priests, except for an occasional secular installed by the holder of an encomienda.

The thorough-going paternalism which inspired the Mendicants' relations with the Indians is not an attitude which commends itself to the modern mind. But it is all too easy to blame them for having treated their charges like children, fostered their tendency to servility and retarded their natural development. In the circumstances of the times, and granted that the friars' supreme object was conversion, no other approach was open to them. Even if they had not made up their minds straight away that paternalism was the right policy, it would have been forced upon them by the character of the Indians themselves. Early Mendicant writings insist on the childish aspect of their natures, on their exaggerated docility, submissiveness and dependence on the initiative of others. Timorous and reserved, says Motolinía, they seem born to obey, and their mild impassivity is strange and irritating to the Spaniards whose temperament is great-hearted and lively as fire. The outstanding virtue common to friars and natives was patience, to which may be added a high degree of humility and tolerance.

The Christian discipline imposed on the Indians was on the whole less onerous and certainly more humane than the tight curbs of pre-Columbian society. It was welcomed, not resented. When the old controls were dropped, the Indians were much disconcerted, but Christian training restored their confidence and gave them a fresh sense of direction. Wary and hesitant at first, they soon took to their new routines with enthusiasm, singing as they wrecked their stepped pyramids and erected in their place churches looking like rustic versions of King's College chapel. They did not grudge their labour expended in the friars' service because it was so amply reciprocated by the prodigious, salutary and disinterested labours of the friars on their behalf. They appreciated, though they did not always fully understand, their benefactors' sense of dedication and choice of poverty for its own sake, that they were, in contemporary language, "tan desinteresados al oro y plata" (so disinterested in gold and silver). They noticed that if the Mendicants made profits out of the monastery lands, for example from the sale of silk or sugar, they were given to the poor or ploughed back instead of being used to improve their own sparse standard of life.

The work of a few devoted men can still have an almost magical effect on a Mexican community condemned to social decadence and neglect, as the author had occasion to observe in a huge disorderly slum parish on the edge of Mexico City which three foreign Benedictines with the minimum of resources had succeeded in rescuing from crime and squalor. As regards early colonial Mexico there is an enormous wealth of evidence, not only from clerical sources, that the Indians were deeply attached to their friars. Their great fear was that chance might deprive them of their protection. Many stories are told of the lengths to which they would go to prevent friars from being transferred by their superiors from one district to another. Cases are quoted of Mendicants being kidnapped and sequestered by villagers desperate at the thought of losing them. The Indians even took it ill when their favourites, the Franciscans, were replaced in a monastery by another Order, as a result of some internal arrangement, and boycotted their successors, and they were especially incensed when the friars of any Order were superseded by a secular priest.

The friars' affection for their protégés was also genuine. They loved them for their simple virtues, for the spontaneity and naive enthusiasm of their acceptance of Christianity. They were delighted by the excellence of their artistry and the speed with which they picked up technical skills. They had no doubt that in sheer intellectual capacity Indians were the equal of Europeans and that their most gifted pupils therefore deserved a higher education in the humanities. They of course fiercely rebutted the theory, so popular among the lay Spaniards, that

Indians did not count as fully moral and rational beings, and were overjoyed when it was condemned in two Bulls issued by Pope Paul III in 1537.

Thus the Mendicants' attitude towards the natives was rooted in a deep respect for their personality as Indians; respect for their language, way of life and culture. They believed that the latter could be modified to suit the new Christian dispensation without altering its essential Indian character. Although the eradication of paganism in itself involved a measure of integration of the two cultures, in all other respects the friars aimed at strict apartheid for the Indians, a policy of separate development all along the line. The Indians were to be kept segregated from the Spaniards both physically, so far as this might be practicable, and culturally. Only the highest social caste was to be encouraged to learn Spanish and mix socially with Spaniards. Within the boundaries of the native communities the friars would organize the necessary institutions and services —schools, hospitals, roads, aqueducts, workshops—to make them self-sufficient.

The success of such a policy of course implied that the authority of the friars should be absolute, lasting and capable of resisting pressures from outside. The first condition was virtually fulfilled, for the Indians were pathetically dependent on their protectors and never thought of kicking against their tutelage. But the other two were irreconcilable with the development of colonial Mexico. For economic and demographic reasons, a vast section of the country's labour force could not be expected to remain indefinitely insulated or even semi-isolated behind the barriers of clerical reservations. The Mendicants' early triumphs in blunting the grosser forms of exploiting the Indians were wholly admirable, but they only retarded the process by which the mass of Indian labour was forced or attracted away from service in the communities controlled by friars. Monasteries slowly lost their spiritual and social influence as they became simply employers of labour competing with other private employers. Another important factor eroding the ideal of separate development was the rapid increase in the proportion of people of mixed race, the mestizos who were eventually to emerge as the largest element in the population of Mexico.

An equally fatal flaw in the friars' experiment of building

cities of God among the Mexican Indians was that they had no clear conception of where their endeavours should lead after the miracle of the conversion and the prodigious expenditure of effort of the next fifty years. What place did they intend their Indians to occupy in the New Spain of the future? They taught them to be better farmers and craftsmen and to develop their gifts for music and the arts, but they failed to prepare them for any wider functions in civil life. We shall see later how the plans for giving higher education to the talented few broke down after a brilliant start. And the vacillation with which the friars approached the question whether Indians were fit to become friars and priests was even more significant.

It is obvious that objections would be raised on political grounds to the training of Indians for civil advancement in the colony, but once the Pope had recognized their moral and intellectual equality with other Christian peoples there was at least no logical or religious impediment to their entering the ranks of the clergy as seculars or Mendicants. Yet the Mendicants themselves shied away from the idea. They seem to have felt that there was a basic instability in the Indian character which disqualified their wards from admission to the priesthood. Rather surprisingly Sahagún, that unfailing champion of Indian interests and culture, mentions their addiction to drink and women alone as an unsurmountable obstacle. More generally the friars, with their own terrifyingly high standards, regarded the Indians as deficient in the necessary authority, initiative and sustained energy. Nor did they consider that the natives' faith, however enthusiastic, was proof against heretical influences and hangovers from idolatry. From the Orders' own point of view it was safer to keep spiritual authority in European hands. They were also affected by the steady hostility of lay Spaniards, including the increasingly important element of Creoles born in Mexico, to any step likely to give an Indian, by virtue of his spiritual position, a measure of immunity from subordination to the whites. Moreover the prospect of a Spaniard receiving the Sacraments from a native was repugnant. The same prejudice was directed against mestizos.

In high circles opinions on the subject wavered. The first Viceroy, Antonio de Mendoza, cautiously declared that it would be premature to bring Indians into the priesthood, however learned and virtuous they might be, until their nation as a whole had attained the same level of civilization as Spain. The second Archbishop, Montúfar, who though a Dominican himself often clashed with his fellow friars, held a fully liberal view and indeed began to ordain Indians and mestizos. But he was promptly disowned by the government at Madrid, as well as by his own Church in Mexico, and obliged to stop doing so. At about the same time Fray Jacobo Daciano, a Franciscan of Danish or as some said Eastern European origin, and a famous theologian, caused a scandal by proclaiming that the Mexican Church had been founded on utterly wrong principles because it would not admit native priests. An equally erudite member of his Order, Fray Juan de Gaona, was hurriedly called in to refute him in public, a task which he performed to the satisfaction of the shocked Spaniards. Subsequently the ordination of Indians and mestizos was expressly forbidden both by royal command and by the friars' own rules. It was not until the following century that these prohibitions were relaxed, especially in favour of mestizos. Even pure-blooded Indians were occasionally ordained, and in 1679 the first Indian bishop, Don Nicolás del Puerto, was elevated to the see of Oaxaca.

Meanwhile a combination of prejudice and scruple allowed pathetically few non-Spaniards to slip through the net. Motolinía mentions that as early as 1527 three or four young Indians were given the habit of St Francis. But they lacked perseverance in their vocation and the friars, evidently much discouraged, did not repeat the experiment. The same writer tells a touching story of a Tarascan chieftain, Don Juan de Turécato or Tarécuato, who freed his slaves, gave away his property and set a perfect example of saintliness. But although he persisted in his attempts to be received into an Order, walking to and fro between Michoacán and Mexico City to press his petition, he was constantly rebuffed and the most he was accorded was a grudging permission to live with the friars and wear a habit similar to theirs. Indeed the monasteries were housing numerous Indians known as "donados" (dedicated), who followed a religious routine and helped the friars with their chores, but were not allowed to take their vows. However, another notable from Michoacán, Don Pablo, grandson of the last Tarascan king Sintzicha Tanguaxan, is the first Indian known to have been ordained priest.

Even the revered Vasco de Quiroga, first Bishop of Michoacán, was rebuked for ordaining mestizo youths. Nevertheless the prejudice against mestizos was less easy to sustain, especially when the Spanish father (and sometimes the Indian mother) was a person of consequence. Juan de Tovar, son of a conquistador and a lady from the prolific royal family of Texcoco, was ordained at a very early age and became secretary of the cathedral Chapter in Mexico City. An immensely erudite historian and linguist, whose eloquence in Náhuatl earned him the title of the "Mexican Cicero", he was admitted to the Jesuit Order in middle life. Another distinguished mestizo writer was the Franciscan Diego de Valadés, whose mother probably came from Tlaxcala. Trained by Pedro de Gante, he worked for some years in his native country before making his mark in Europe, where he was the first Mexican to publish a book (*Rhetorica Christiana*—Perugia, 1579). Primarily a treatise on rhetoric composed in impeccable Latin, it is peculiar in drawing by way of illustration on the author's experiences in the conversion of the Indians, "in which," he says, "I took not only a part but a leading part" (*quibus ipsi non modo interfuimus sed et praefuimus*). The careers of these two outstanding representatives of a mixed culture dimly suggest what fruitful results might have been achieved if the barriers to Indian and mestizo preferment could have effectively been broken down.

Chapter 6

WOLVES AND SHEPHERDS

THE MENDICANTS' EARLY successes were the more remarkable because they were achieved in the teeth of mounting commotion and strife among the Spaniards themselves. The relinquishment of power by Cortés in October 1524 ushered in a period of near-anarchy which was only terminated six years later when the royal government at last took matters firmly in hand. The Indians derived no advantage from the general confusion.

So long as he was on the spot, Cortés's authority over the Indians of Anáhuac was absolute. But with the Spaniards this was far from being the case, though after the Conquest they numbered less than two thousand as against several millions of Indians. Not even a bare majority of his countrymen could be counted as loyal supporters of Cortés. The stalwarts of his original expedition had been drastically trimmed by war and disease, and the bulk of the soldiers now consisted of later arrivals from the Caribbean islands, men who were influenced by the jealous resentment against him fostered by his rival Diego Velázquez, Governor of Cuba. Added to these was a stream of immigrants who began to reach New Spain when the fighting was over and whose sole motive was to grab the largest possible share in the pickings of the new colony.

The common ambition of all these colonists was to have communities of Indians officially allotted to them under the system of encomienda. It should be kept in mind that an encomienda was not a landed estate, but the grant to an individual Spaniard of the right to use the services of Indians within a specified area, and to collect tribute from them, for the duration of the allotment. Although this institution had depopulated and ruined the Spanish Antilles, it was still regarded by overseas Spaniards as the indispensable short cut to affluence and leisure. And in New Spain fresh supplies of Indians were apparently to be had for the asking.

Representing the original band of Conquistadors, Bernal Díaz had a very precise idea of how the pueblos of New Spain should be distributed. One fifth, he thought, should be reserved for the King, another fifth for the support of churches, hospitals and monasteries, while the remaining three-fifths should be made available to Cortés and other true Conquistadors. He went on to say that while there were plenty of Indians to go round for all the immigrants the original conquerors should have priority, and he indignantly complained that Cortés, in meting out encomiendas, had favoured men who had not gone through the toils of the Conquest, his own needy relatives and connexions of great men.

Certainly Cortés was in no position to resist the local clamour for encomiendas, and he began immediately to assign them, thus imposing fresh burdens on peasants already obliged to provide for their own communal needs and those of their own lords. Yet he knew well that he had no formal authority to do anything of the kind. Also his experience in the Antilles had made him fully aware of the havoc which the system could wreak if not subjected to the strictest of controls. Lastly, his introduction of the encomienda into New Spain coincided most awkwardly with the Crown's decision to abolish it altogether. By this resolution the King and the Council of the Indies hoped to put an end to the controversy which had raged for over ten years between the enemies of the encomienda, led by the Dominicans, and its partisans among the colonists in the Antilles and their friends at Court. At the time it appeared to be a brilliant personal victory for Bartolomé de las Casas, once an encomendero himself, later a Dominican and since 1516 officially designated as "Protector of the Indians".

In the circumstances it is hardly surprising that Cortés found difficulty in justifying his conduct to his sovereign. The tone of the letter, dated May 15th, 1522, in which he sought the King's approval for his actions was unusually hesitant and embarrassed. He explained that his original view had been that it would be wrong to require the inhabitants of New Spain, for whose capacities he had a high regard, to serve the Spaniards in the same way as the far less civilized Indians of the islands. Consequently, since the Spaniards in Mexico would not normally be able to support themselves without such Indian service, he had thought of recommending that they should instead be subsidized by the royal exchequer. On reflection, however, it had occurred to him that it would be

V. P. F. Pedro Gante. Lego de la Provincia de Flandes, uno de los primer
Operarios Evangelicos, emviado por el Señ.r D.n Carlos V. (su muy cercano p[arien]-
te) à esta Nueva España, donde enseñò à millares de Niños la Doctrina Chri[stia]-
na, y à los mancebos la Musica, à tocar instrumentos, y los oficios de P[into]-
res, Esculptores, Herreros, y Carpinteros. Edificò mas de cien Yglesias, y la
[Capi]lla de S.S. Jose primer Parroqu[i]a de [Indios]

Pedro de Gante

Bernardino de Sahagún

unreasonable to expect this great expense to be borne by the Crown, and he had therefore concluded that there was really no alternative to what he called "depositing" groups of Indians with the Spaniards, subject to proper safeguards. He had thus acted accordingly, convinced that his decision would promote the interests of both Spaniards and Indians. He took care to add that the most important "deposits" had been reserved for the Crown.

This argument was received with marked disfavour. Cortés was sharply commanded to revoke all the encomiendas already granted. The terms of the royal instruction, which took another year to arrive, were remarkable for their liberalism. Cortés was told that the reduction of the natives to anything resembling a servile condition would contravene the principle of the papal authority accorded to the King for the purpose of converting the Indians. His Majesty's Indian vassals in New Spain were to be treated in no way differently from his vassals in Old Spain, that is as free men with exactly similar obligations to the Crown. Provided that the Indians gave up their heathen practices and submitted to the royal power, there should be free intercourse between them and the Spaniards. Lands and sites for cities should be selected and distributed among the colonists without infringing Indian rights.

These directions were not written with the tongue in the cheek. They were framed by men who not only sincerely believed in the religious principle underlying the Spanish right to rule over subject territories but were also determined to avoid the dreadful mistakes which had ruined the valuable islands discovered by Columbus and turned them into a squalid liability. Now that an infinitely richer realm had fallen into Spanish hands, the King's government was bent on organizing it on sound and humane lines. So far as ideas were concerned, Spanish colonial policy at the time was worthy of the age of enlightenment which produced Erasmus, Luis Vives and Thomas More. It was not the fault of the policy makers that their intentions were continually nullified by obstinate realities across the ocean.

Cortés's reply to the King's rebuke was to explain boldly but respectfully why, in his opinion, His Majesty's orders were incapable of execution and to present a reasoned defence of his adoption of the encomienda system. His confidence was increased by the knowledge that it was already a *fait accompli* which no instruction unsupported by force would now be able to undo. He pointed out that as there were no means of subsistence available to the colonists which were not based on Indian service they would be destitute without them and obliged to quit the country. New Spain would consequently lose its only defenders and become untenable. The souls of the Indians would be abandoned to the devil. It was an illusion to imagine that Spaniards and Indians could live together, in some kind of free and uncontrolled association. That would only expose the natives to unrestrained violence and exploitation; nor would they be immune from their conquerors' vices. On the other hand such chaos could be avoided if the relations between the two communities were rigidly defined and carefully regulated. In ensuring political stability and social order, the encomienda was the necessary civil counterpart of the friars' campaign of conversion. Furthermore, it would build up economic prosperity and guarantee a steady revenue for his Caesarean Majesty from the tax collected from the encomenderos. In a separate letter Cortés became bolder still and recommended that rights to labour and tribute should be made inheritable. At about that time he annexed for his own use four vast encomiendas in the Valley of Mexico alone, embracing many thousands of Indians at Chalco, Texcoco, Otumba and Coyoacán.

One would not expect Cortés's arguments to be disinterested, but they were persuasive and contained a core of common sense. The ordinances which he issued in 1524 for the administration of encomiendas show a very real concern for the protection of the Indians as well as prescribing a strict code of duties for the encomenderos themselves. The latter's authority over the Indians assigned to them was hedged about with restrictions. They were forbidden to make slaves of Indians in encomienda, to send them to the mines and to exact gold from them. The Indians were to receive wages and their periods of labour for their encomendero were to alternate with rest periods during which they were free to work for their own village community or on their own plots. Their actual working hours were to be from sunrise to sunset, with one hour's rest at midday. The encomendero was required to build a house and live near, but not within, the Indian community, to send for his wife to Spain, if he had one there, within eighteen months, or else to marry locally without delay. Among many obligations of a religious nature the encomendero was enjoined to build a church and, when there were no friars in the neighbourhood, to maintain a priest at his own expense for the benefit and instruction of the Indians assigned to him. Finally, the encomendero was obliged to keep arms in readiness, and if he had more than five hundred Indians in encomienda, a horse.

The King and the Council of the Indies, although lacking precise ideas of their own for the government of New Spain, could not fail to take alarm at the independent airs assumed by their Governor and Captain-General. He seemed to them to be bent on establishing a personal rule based on his almost hypnotic authority over the Indians, and so far as the Spaniards were concerned, on a kind of simplified feudal system within which he himself controlled the distribution of grants and favours to the encomenderos. But in a Renaissance monarchy there was no room for any autocrat but the King, and in Spain the monarchy had succeeded in doing away with all real powers not deriving from its own centralized rule. While Cortés's arguments for the retention of the encomienda might well deserve consideration, he could not be allowed to dictate policy, much less to flout royal orders by the classic Spanish device of "Obedezco pero no Cumplo" (I obey but do not carry out).

The Crown accordingly resolved, after much hesitation, to appoint a special commissioner, known as a juez de residencia, to investigate the Governor's actions on the spot and to take over his functions during the period of enquiry. Its choice fell on a high legal dignitary, Luis Ponce de León. But in October 1524, when Cortés set out for Honduras at the head of an impressive Indo-Spanish array, he did not know what form the royal reaction would take. He may not have thought that he was running a serious risk of suspension, with consequent damage to his personal prestige. He presumably reckoned on strengthening his position in Spain and Mexico by a swift and spectacular campaign of conquest in Central America. The object of the expedition was more probably to acquire new territories and treasures than merely to reduce to order his rebellious subordinate Cristóbel de Olíd, who had presumed to strike out as an independent conqueror in Honduras in much the same manner as he himself had behaved in cutting loose from Diego Velásquez.

In the event Cortés won no fresh triumphs but ruined his prospects of ruling New Spain in undisturbed authority as the King's deputy. His departure from Mexico resulted in a sharp deterioration in the relations between the two races. Nor was the vacuum left by his eighteen months' absence filled by a worthy substitute from Spain. The despatch of the juez de residencia was held up by the dilatory processes of Spanish bureaucracy; it took over a year to frame Ponce de León's instructions and ship him off to New Spain, so that his eventual arrival almost exactly coincided with the return, in May 1526, of an exhausted and frustrated Cortés.

Whatever the motive of the Honduran adventure, it went seriously wrong. It began as a ceremonial progress through southern Mexico, with Cortés receiving the homage of Indian chieftains and recently settled Spaniards. He travelled in unusual state with a retinue of personal retainers, pages and musicians, cooks, jugglers and falconers. He even took with him the two Flemish Franciscans, Johan van Auwera and Johan Dekkers (a former professor of theology at the Sorbonne and once confessor to the Emperor himself), who had come out with Pedro de Gante. The Spanish force, several hundred strong and including 130 horsemen, was led by Gonzalo de Sandoval and other experienced captains. But it was vastly outnumbered by a host of carefully picked Indian warriors, many of whom were armed with Spanish swords and lances. This was the last occasion in history when the levy of Anáhuac marched under its own monarchs, or rather ex-monarchs, for Cortés had insisted that the last Aztec emperor, Cuauhtémoc, should accompany him, along with the pre-conquest kings of Tacuba and Texcoco, Tetlepanquetzal and Cohuanococh. The Cihuacóatl, Don Juan Velázquez, came too; so did Temilotzin the tlacatecatl or Aztec titular Commander-in-Chief, with many other Mexican notables and some Tarascans from Michoacán. As might have been expected Ixtlilxóchitl, the brother of Cohuanococh, commanded the Texcocan contingent in the field.

It is hard to determine the actual number of native warriors. Díaz puts the Mexicans at over three thousand, "not counting many others in the service of the chieftains", while the historian Ixtlilxóchitl, always lavish with his figures, claims that his namesake held a review and chose twenty thousand fighting men for the campaign. The total Indian force can safely be estimated at ten thousand and might have been much larger. At all events it was a resplendent array. The princes and dignitaries were treated by their followers with all the elaborate forms of respect to which they had been entitled in the days of Moctezuma, for the ancient hierarchy was still, at least nominally, in existence.

The trouble started when the army plunged into the interminable morasses, forests and mountains between the Gulfs of Campeche and Honduras. Little armed resistance was encountered but the natural obstacles nearly swallowed up the whole expedition without trace. Floundering waist deep in water and hacking at the tangled jungles, both Indians and Spaniards died rapidly. The valuable horses were lost; maize was scarce and the large herd of pigs provided as a reserve of food for the Spaniards was soon eaten up. Morale sank and Cortés was at a loss how to extricate himself. When his worries were slightly past their height he detected, or thought he detected, a conspiracy against him among the Aztec leaders. An Indian informer accused them of plotting to wipe out the Spanish component of the expedition. Having subsequently disposed of the Spaniards in Honduras, the Indian army would make its way back to Mexico and raise the signal for a general uprising which would restore native rule in Anáhuac and the adjacent lands. Cortés was taking no chances; deaf to all denials or excuses, he pounced on Cuauhtémoc and Tetlepanquetzal and caused them to be hanged without delay. One or two minor notables apparently suffered the same fate, but the majority were spared. If a revolt was intended, certainly none took place.

The facts of this mysterious tragedy will always remain obscure. There is no reason to suspect Cortés of a deliberate intention of removing Cuauhtémoc from Mexico in order to do away with him in a remote place. He may have thought it a wise precaution to take the deposed emperor and the two minor kings with him, though it seems highly unlikely that if left behind in Mexico they would have attempted a forlorn bid for power, especially as Indian feeling had turned decidedly against the Aztecs in the war of the Conquest. Considerations of prestige as well as of security no doubt moved Cortés to include the whole galaxy of Indian lords (but none, it appears, from Tlaxcala) in his train.

A treacherous attack on the ex-rulers was probably far from his mind until he found himself in a really precarious plight, by which time, surrounded by a native force much larger than his band of Spaniards, he had become prone to suspicions and was ready to listen to the denunciations of the informer, one Coxtemexi. The lengthy confabulations in which Cuauhtémoc and the other Indian grandees habitually discussed the situation among themselves in a language he did not understand, made him nervous and irritable.

Cuauhtémoc, for his part, cannot altogether be absolved from the charge of plotting, or at least of contemplating a breakaway. Cortés reported to Charles V that he was convinced of his guilt. Díaz, however, representing the opinion of the Spanish soldiery, regarded him as innocent and emphatically condemned Cortés for acting unjustly. But even if there had been no serious conspiracy, it would indeed have been strange had the Indian lords not weighed the pros and cons of revolt in their private deliberations and speculated rashly about its possible outcome. This would have provided sufficient material for an unscrupulous informer.

Following this line of thought, Ixtlilxóchitl records a romantic but not implausible dialogue round the camp fire between the emperor and his fellow tlatoque. They are musing in a half-melancholy, half-ironical vein about their general predicament, the changes of fortune which had overtaken them and their fanciful claims to share in any conquests resulting from the present expedition, while Temilotzin the tlacatécatl, while blaming their fall on their pride and mutual discord, seeks to console them by reminding them of the blessings of Christianity which they have received from the "children of the sun". They then sing songs and exchange harangues, stories and jokes until Cortés sends Coxtemexi, who figures as his confidential spy, to find out what all the chatter is about. Misled by his report, or choosing to interpret it in a more sinister light than was necessary, Cortés has the two rulers seized and executed. Some doubt surrounds the death of the third, Cohuanococh of Texcoco, but he certainly did not long survive the episode.

Ixtlilxóchitl produces a typical heroic story of how he too was strung up but was cut down while still alive when the prince Ixtlilxóchitl, too late to stop the other hangings, hurried up and intervened with Cortés to save him. But subsequently, the historian adds, he died of his injuries.

Before they were executed the rulers, as newly converted Christians, were permitted or required to make their confessions to a friar, using Doña Marina as interpreter. Very probably it was the learned Flemish doctor of the Sorbonne who was called upon to attend them in their last moments. Both he and his colleague were to succumb to the hardships of the journey. Of the Indian magnates very few besides Ixtlilxóchitl struggled back to Mexico. Another notable casualty was the Cihuacóatl, upon whom Díaz, disregarding the perhaps mythical Coxtemexi, pins the denunciation of the alleged plot. This may have been the truth or simply a good guess, for Don Juan Velázquez had proved a faithful agent of Spanish power since the Conquest.

When the expedition finally reached Honduras its futility became obvious. It proved to have been undertaken for no useful purpose whatsoever. The rebellious Olíd had already been arrested and beheaded by officers loyal to Cortés, and no personal advantage accrued to him from his intervention in the affairs of a province which, as the course of colonial history was to establish, lay outside the periphery of Mexican politics. Suffering from a sense of anti-climax, he hung irresolutely about in Honduras until reluctantly convinced by news from Mexico that his proper place was there and not in Central America.

A ship's captain brought him a message from the lawyer Zuazo, a principal officer of the Spanish municipality in Mexico City, giving him an alarming account of how New Spain had gone to pieces in his absence; in fact most Spaniards believed a rumour that he and his army had perished and were behaving as if he no longer existed. Cortés bestirred himself to the extent of more than once going on shipboard, but when severe storms drove him back he still lingered in Honduras, apparently unwilling to face a reappearance in Mexico with a record of failure behind him. He continued to play with plans for exploring and subjugating the Nicaraguan hinterland in competition with other Spanish adventurers. At last his partisans in New Spain, still trusting that he was alive, became desperate and despatched a Franciscan friar, one Diego Altamirano, to him in Honduras with a pressing summons to return immediately if he hoped to restore his position. After conferring with the messenger he embarked and sailed to Vera Cruz with a brief stay at Havana.

The Governor's return evoked mixed sentiments among the Spaniards, who with few exceptions had been indulging in an orgy of selfish faction and greed. But there was no doubt about the warmth of his reception by the Indians. The fact that a few months previously he had done to death three of their sacred traditional rulers, in circumstances which reflected no credit on himself, in no way discouraged a vast outpouring of popular joy. Nor did this fail to have a sobering effect on the ambitions of the anti-Cortés party among his own countrymen. All along his route from the coast to the city enthusiastic crowds gathered to demonstrate their loyalty and affections. In faithful Tlaxcala and Texcoco the native leaders greeted him with feasts and ceremonial rejoicings. The Indians of half-rebuilt Tenochtitlán gave him the most spectacular welcome of all. The magnates put on their most gorgeous dresses and ornaments, the lake was as full of canoes packed with warriors in battle array as it had been in the days of Cuauhtémoc, there was dancing in the streets and the doors of the houses were illuminated. Then it was the turn of the emissaries from the non-Nahua provinces to bring presents and proclaim their devotion. Some of these, notably the Zapotec and Mije areas to the south, had until recently risen in arms. But in spite of the sorry state of affairs prevailing in Anáhuac itself, no such movement had taken place there.

Unfortunately the rot had spread too far for Cortés to arrest it by his mere presence. Almost immediately after his return his authority was suspended by the arrival of the juez de residencia, Ponce de León. Another four years of indiscipline, intrigue and rank tyranny were to go by before New Spain received some form of coherent and responsible government, and a curb was applied to the Spanish propensity for destructive individualism. Meanwhile the only consistent defenders of the Indians were bishops and friars, and in the atmosphere of disorder their protection was less effective than if it had been backed up by the civil power.

Such government as existed was exercised by four royal treasury officials (treasurer, accountant, agent and inspector) appointed after the Conquest to look after the King's financial interests and, incidentally, to watch the conduct of the Captain-General and report to Spain behind his back. Cortés regarded all four with well-deserved suspicion. He was aware that they were intriguing against each other as well as against him, and when he left for the south he made an arrangement which looks as if it had been devised on purpose to plunge New Spain into chaos, in the expectation that he himself, after a short and victorious progress, would reappear and put matters right.

He began by leaving the administration in the hands of Estrada, the treasurer, and Albórnoz, the accountant, while taking with him the agent Salazar, and the inspector, Chirinos. He had not gone far, however, when he changed his mind and sent the second pair back to the capital with instructions fated to cause the maximum possible mischief. They were that if Albórnoz and Estrada were found to be working harmoniously together the other two should simply associate themselves with them in the government, but if they proved to be on bad terms, they should supersede them. Inevitably they used the discretion given them to oust Albórnoz and Estrada, and even to consign them to prison for a while. Salazar, who was a stronger character than Chirinos, then became the leading figure in the colony. He remained so, exercising a capricious and incompetent dictatorship, until early in 1526, a few months before Cortés's return. At that juncture one of the latter's Spanish servants arrived secretly from Honduras at the Franciscan monastery in Mexico City, where the Governor's principal adherents had prudently taken refuge, and revealed that Cortés was not only alive, whereas Salazar had proclaimed him officially dead, but intending to resume his government. This bombshell was sufficient immediately to unseat Salazar and Chirinos and restore the other pair to nominal authority.

It did not in fact matter who claimed to be in power in the capital. The settlers were thoroughly out of hand, feuding with each other, slave-raiding and extracting the last ounce of tribute and service from the Indians entrusted to them. No attempt was made to enforce restraints on the encomenderos, especially those to whom new grants had been made by the royal officials, more cynical than Cortés had ever been in ignoring the policy of the home government. The newcomers, who had neither fought against the Indians nor formed feelings of respect for them as had many of the original conquerors, were guilty of every kind of brutality. Native artists who decorated the post-conquest codices drew mainly on the experiences of this period when they depicted their wretched compatriots as chained, burned, torn by enormous hunting dogs and dragged behind the Spaniards' horses. Of course not all encomenderos behaved like savages, but in the absence of law and order cruelties were undoubtedly widespread and flagrant. The Indian overseers (calpixque) who worked the encomiendas on behalf of absent Spaniards often outdid their masters in ferocity.

It is astonishing that the rule of officials trained in the strict school of the Catholic Kings should have been so inept, and that their personal conduct should have been so scandalous. All the principles they had learned in the administration at home seem to have evaporated in the disturbing atmosphere of the colony. Reports of the growing chaos and misrule reached the Council of the Indies just as the latter was beginning to doubt the wisdom of its policy of wholesale rejection of the encomienda system. Even its enlightened president García de Loaisa, General of the Dominicans and successor to Cortés's old enemy Fonseca, had been forced to think again by Cortés's arguments and other evidence of the settlers' united opposition to the Crown's orders. Any hope that the juez de residencia might be able to produce a solution of the problem, which he had been ordered to examine carefully, was dispelled by Ponce de León's death shortly after his arrival in Mexico. The same fate soon overtook his successor, a doddering old lawyer called Aguilar.

Eventually the treasurer Estrada, from whom no salutary measures or advice could be expected, assumed office as temporary governor. He at once quarrelled with Cortés and peremptorily banished him from the capital. Acting with perfect dignity and determined to avoid an armed clash between his own followers and Estrada's, the Conquistador withdrew by stages to Tlaxcala, always a stronghold of his supporters. There both colonists and Indian lords reaffirmed their loyalty to him; they even besought him to declare himself King of New Spain. But that was going too far, and he sternly scotched any suspicion that he might be meditating high treason. In fact he had already decided to press his interests in person at Court and in the spring of 1528 duly left for Spain. A number of eminent Indians, including sons of Moctezuma and of the former heads of the Tlaxcalan republic, crossed the Atlantic with him.

The Crown's solution for the troubles of New Spain was the appointment of an Audiencia. Here the Council of the Indies made a right decision in principle but a disastrously bad one in practice. An Audiencia was an administrative and judicial body consisting of a President and a small number of members, normally lawyers, known as oidores. It might be thought that so essentially respectable an institution could have been safely relied upon to give Mexico a sensible and responsible government, but this was not to be so, for the persons chosen to compose the Audiencia proved even more unsuitable for the task they were intended to carry out than the lamentable quartet who had taken over from Cortés.

As President the Council designated Beltrán Nuño de Guzmán. The selection of this sinister and sanguinary adventurer can only be explained by the fact that he happened to be the most active and vocal representative of the settler opposition to Cortés at a time when the latter was in bad odour with the Crown owing to his casual treatment of its instructions and to the persistent campaign of denigration waged against him by the royal officials and the hostile faction among the colonists. What is certain is that the Council failed to examine with proper care whether he had other and genuine qualifications for restoring tranquillity in Mexico.

A native of Guadalajara, Nuño de Guzmán came to the Indies after the conquest of Mexico. With no reputation beyond that of a skilful lawyer, he managed somehow to be appointed directly from Spain to the governorship of Pánuco. The inhabitants of this maritime province to the north of Vera Cruz had originally offered fierce resistance to Cortés and his lieutenants. Subsequently Cortés had shown great diplomatic skill in thwarting the efforts of Francisco de Garay, the governor of Jamaica, to filch it from his jurisdiction, but while he was away in Honduras Nuño de Guzmán slipped in unchallenged. Fairly or unfairly, the Indians of Pánuco had acquired a bad name for ferocity and vice, for which, says Díaz, they were punished two or three times with blood and fire, but their worst punishment was to have Nuño de Guzmán foisted on them as governor, for he enslaved them all and sold them in the Caribbean islands. Indeed he exchanged his career as a jurisconsult for that of a slave-trader on the grand scale. The natives of Pánuco were branded and shipped off by the ten thousand to that graveyard of Indian labour, the Antilles.

The Spanish Crown had always carefully specified in its ordinances that Indians held in encomienda should neither be treated nor disposed of as slaves. On the other hand it was perfectly legitimate to enslave and sell Indian subjects of the Crown taken in rebellion as well as Chichimecs from beyond the frontiers captured in war. No distinctions of this kind bothered Nuño de Guzmán, and during the period of anarchy in New Spain many colonists, aware that there were never enough rebels or Chichimecs to satisfy the demand for labour in the mines and porterage on the interminable Mexican trails —both grinding forms of servitude—plunged eagerly into the lucrative business of slave-trading. They impressed Indians illegally on the encomiendas and elsewhere. They also bought them up in substantial numbers from their own Indian lords. Such transactions were indeed also legal so long as it could be established that the individuals purchased were already slaves in their own communities. But the native magnates, accustomed as they were to the various traditional forms of personal slavery and no less averse than the settlers to making a profit from barter in human beings, cheerfully sold off their defenceless underlings. When they declared that a man was already a slave, to all intents and purposes he was one and no questions were asked. It was soon discovered that awkward demands from Spaniards for gold and tribute could be fobbed off by a timely offer of slaves.

When Nuño de Guzmán assumed authority in New Spain he stimulated these malpractices by handing out or selling official licences to buy slaves. He also arranged on different pretexts for quantities of Indians to be drafted from Anáhuac into the Pánuco province, where they promptly met the same fate as the Huaxtecs of that already depopulated region.

Of the four oidores accompanying Nuño de Guzmán, two died at once of pneumonia, to which Spaniards arriving on the high plateau of Anáhuac were peculiarly susceptible. The other two, Matienzo and Delgadillo, were the creatures of their President, who also made an intimate crony of the factor Salazar, the worst member of the previous régime. This camarilla was supreme in New Spain for two years (1529–30) before the Crown woke up and ousted it. Apparently unaware of the character of the men it had appointed, the Council of the Indies proceeded to supply the Audiencia with detailed and conscientious instructions. The President was told to summon to his aid the newly installed Bishops of Mexico and Tlaxcala and the heads of the Franciscan and Dominican Orders. Lawyers and ecclesiastics were to consult together and take measures for the diffusion of the Catholic religion, the equitable treatment of the Indians and the proper allocation of land and labour. The Council had by now relaxed its opposition to the award of encomiendas in perpetuity to the extent of agreeing that the original conquerors might receive grants of this kind.

These instructions were followed by a stream of admirably conceived regulations for the purpose of restricting slavery, preventing overwork on roads and plantations, stopping the relegation of free Indians to the mines and generally protecting them from exploitation. But the Council's good intentions were doomed to frustration during the period of Guzmán's Audiencia, for it was his policy to exploit the Indians to the utmost degree, while promoting the interests of the new settlers at the expense of those of Cortés and the old conquerors. Far from confirming the latter in the enjoyment of their encomiendas, he deprived them arbitrarily of their Indians and reallocated them to his own followers. How these abused their trust is well illustrated by the case of the royal inspector Chirinos, another relic of the post-Cortesian régime who profited from toadying to Guzmán. Rewarded with the populous encomienda of Tepeaca, he hired out his Indians as carriers supplying the mines, working them so unmercifully that three thousand of them were said to have dropped dead on the roads from exhaustion. Contemporary critics of the colonists seem to have been particularly horrified by this malpractice, against which the authorities in Spain tried doggedly, and in the end not altogether unsuccessfully, to legislate. It was also persistently denounced by the friars. Father Motolinía, that unfailing champion of the oppressed, pointedly inserts in his *History of the Indians of New Spain* an edifying story of how on three separate occasions a puma or jaguar was seen to leap on a Spanish overseer who was in the habit of cruelly driving and belabouring his porters, and to devour him while leaving the Indians unharmed.

New Spain was full of dispossessed and resentful veterans, but without Cortés they had no leader around whom they could rally. When Pedro de Alvarado passed through Mexico from Spain on his way to take up his governorship in Guatemala, Guzmán, suspecting that he might assume that role, had him detained and finally thrown into prison. Scandals and feuds multiplied between the two factions of Spaniards, and some petty despots even indulged in private wars. They had no scruples about arming Indians to fight for them, a state of affairs which much alarmed the Council of the Indians, since the conquered were not officially permitted to carry European weapons. They were even more strictly forbidden to ride horses, only the lords of Tlaxcala and a few other high personages being exempt from that prohibition.

Writing of the trials which the friars had to face throughout those troubled times, Father Motolinía listed what he considered to have been the ten principal plagues afflicting Anáhuac as a result of the Conquest. The first three—the bloody campaigns, the destructive epidemic of smallpox and the accompanying famine—derived from the initial Spanish impact. Three more, which he carefully distinguished one from another, were all connected with the colonists' hunger for gold, "the calf adored in place of God". They were the wanton sacrifice of life in the mines, the enslavement of free Indians to work in them when the supply of slaves was exhausted, and the impressment and ill-treatment of the carriers taking supplies to the mines and bringing out the mineral, "especially at the mines of Oaxyecac, where for half a league around and along a vast stretch of road a man could hardly walk without treading on dead men and bones". In much the same category were the brutal behaviour of overseers on the encomiendas and the wasteful consumption of labour in the rebuilding of the capital, although in the same breath Motolinía admits that the Indians went about the latter task with enthusiasm. But the last and most pernicious of the plagues, in his opinion, was the strife between the Spaniards themselves, because it threatened to lose Mexico altogether for Christendom. He draws a vivid picture of the friars stopping the fights by throwing themselves between the volleys and the charges of horse. The Indians, he says, were watching the Spaniards cut each other's throats (as the conquerors of Peru were doing on a much vaster scale) and awaiting a chance to rise against them. Unlike other writers of the time, he believed that the conspiracy of the kings against Cortés was genuine and had indeed been hatched before the expedition left for Honduras.

Motolinía was in the forefront of the friars' struggle to defend the Indians against the excesses which he describes. Immersed as they were in the enormous enterprise of conversion, the few Franciscans and Dominicans working in New Spain at the time were unable to ward off the plagues from the native population as a whole, although they very often succeeded in providing safe havens for their converts in areas where they were firmly established and where the new monasteries stood like great islands of security amid the surrounding turmoil.

Motolinía's exact observance of his vows of poverty and austerity, if not perhaps of humility, was matched by his fearlessness and stubborn adherence to principle. As early as 1525 we find him, as Guardian of the monastery of his Order in Mexico City, next to Pedro de Gante's school, stiffly rebutting the agent Salazar's charges that Fray Martín de Valencia and himself were guilty of encroaching, in defence of Indian rights, on the civil and criminal jurisdiction of the municipal authorities. He pointed out that the friars' intervention on behalf of the Indians was fully justified by papal pronouncements and produced the relevant Bulls and letters. The Franciscan historian Mendieta says that when the royal officials and the municipal council (Cabildo) refused to take the apostolic injunction seriously, Motolinía fell on his knees before a crucifix and cursed them roundly in God's name for disregarding the mandates of Holy Church. In private he would argue patiently with the Spaniards who objected to his partiality for the Indians that unless the friars shielded them from violence while instructing them in the faith, and ensured that the tribute demanded of them was not too onerous, there would soon be no Indians left to serve the Spaniards. The preservation of the Indians was not only a religious duty but a vital economic necessity if the colony was to survive at all.

The incident in the cabildo initiated a bitter controversy between the Franciscans and the colonial authorities which lasted for five years and ended in a clear victory for the former.

As we shall see, the most striking confrontations were staged in Mexico City, but Motolinía again played a leading part in a clash which occurred in Huejotzingo in the first year of Guzmán's Audiencia. He was then acting as Guardian of the earliest and finest of the monasteries outside the capital, situated in a district which had consistently taken the Spanish side in the wars of the Conquest.

At Huejotzingo the local encomendero happened to be Cortés. That in itself was sufficient reason why the Audiencia would have taken it into its head to extort from the Indian community a much heavier tribute than that which it had previously paid to Cortés's majordomo. The Indians were being obliged to deliver large quantities of food and other supplies daily to Mexico City for the President, his oidores and his interpreter, a shady creature who had been fortunate to escape the gallows in Spain. The lords of Huejotzingo complained to Zumárraga, the newly appointed Bishop of Mexico, that over a hundred carriers had already died in transporting these burdens across the icy pass, 14,500 feet high, between Huejotzingo and the Valley. They protested that their people could not continue to meet such intolerable demands.

Without disclosing who had given him the information, Zumárraga called on Guzmán to forgo the additional tribute. The president, however, lost his temper, told the bishop he had no business to interfere and threatened him, if he persisted, with the fate of the Bishop of Zamora in Spain, who had been hanged from the battlements of his own city for having joined the rebellion of the Comuneros against the Crown. Later, having ascertained that it was the lords of Huejotzingo who had approached Zumárraga, he sent an officer to arrest them. But when they took refuge in the monastery, together with their families and movable property, Motolinía bravely refused to give them up; one of his friars preached a scorching sermon against the Audiencia and he himself adjured the officer, under pain of excommunication, to return to the capital, cease to meddle with native affairs and refrain from carrying out the Audiencia's orders.

It is not clear whether the Audiencia attempted to enforce its commands. At all events Motolinía emerged unscathed from the battle (which had sensational repercussions in Mexico City) and later survived a wild charge of having participated in a conspiracy of friars to overthrow the government by inciting the Indians to rebellion and to establish in its place a kind of Indian Christian commonwealth professing allegiance to the King-Emperor. Whether or not some of the fathers had been indulging in an Utopian dream, the accusation was so patently absurd that it was allowed to lapse. To the intense irritation of the Audiencia the friars' stand, as exemplified by the events of Huejotzingo, was fully supported and encouraged by the bishops of Tlaxcala and Mexico. This is not surprising, for both were friars and men of outstanding qualities.

The choice of Fray Julián Garcés, a Dominican, for Tlaxcala and of Fray Juan de Zumárraga, a Franciscan, for Mexico reflected the idealism and humanity which inspired the Council of the Indies when Loaisa was its president and the influence of Las Casas prevailed at Court. The appointment of Garcés dated from 1526 and he was the first to take up residence in New Spain. He lived until 1542, by which time the seat of his diocese had been transferred to the new Spanish city of Puebla de los Angeles a few miles away across the plain. Very soon after his arrival he had his first taste of the bitter dissensions dividing the Spanish laymen of the colony when he found himself unsuccessfully mediating between Cortés and the treasurer Estrada. In his relations with the Indians, however, he was immediately and wholly successful. Tact and an equable temper were combined in his character with administrative energy and evangelizing zeal. He was particularly active in extending the area of conversion southwards into the rugged country of the Mixtecs. This was a region allocated for that purpose to the Dominicans, whose monasteries were included as from 1534 in the new diocese of Antequera (Oaxaca).

The conversion of Tlaxcala itself was virtually complete when Garcés arrived. A Franciscan monastery had been founded there as early as 1524 and the Tlaxcalans had from the first displayed a conspicuous eagerness to renounce their old religion. There does not seem to have been any friction between the Dominican bishop and the Franciscans, although the latent jealousy between the Orders was producing at that period some bad examples of unbrotherly back-biting; a Dominican, for instance, was prominent in denouncing Motolinía to the Audencia. Luckily for Garcés, the Indians of Tlaxcala remained comparatively immune from the oppression and harassment which reached their peak during Guzmán's Audiencia. They were not in encomienda but directly subject to the Crown, and the royal officials did not presume to tamper with the privileges which the Crown had granted to the former republic as a reward for its loyalty in the wars. Also the fear lurked in the back of their minds that the adherents of Cortés might join with the Tlaxcalan warriors in sweeping their government out of existence.

The previous rulers enjoyed a dignified status more or less similar to that of Crown vassals in Spain, as well as the hereditary services rendered to them by their own macehualtin. But it was the virtues and abilities of these common people which made an overwhelming impression on the bishop. Both as their pastor and as a humanist of strict intellectual honesty, he thought it his duty to vindicate the character of the much-maligned Indians in the highest possible quarter. So eventually his enthusiasm overflowed into a sonorous Latin letter to the Pope, Paul III, which is a remarkable paean of praise for a race which many of his compatriots professed to regard as sub-human.

The bishop reserved a special eulogy for the young. Indian boys, he told the Pope, were more attentive, diligent and obedient, kinder and more generous, than Spanish children of the same age. They were less tiresomely assertive, less quarrelsome, jealous and complaining. They absorbed the truths of the Catholic religion easily and joyfully, without a trace of the obstinacy and suspicion characteristic of Moors and Jews. They remembered everything they had been taught; in fact they learned the principles of all the mechanical and liberal arts with astonishing facility and speed. They easily mastered reading, writing, arithmetic and painting, while they became so rapidly accomplished in European music that the churches could soon dispense with non-Indian musicians. They were generally superior to Spanish children in the vigour and vivacity of their intelligence.

Even if the bishop was exaggerating, he found a way of establishing the point that Indian adults possessed the same mental and moral qualities as their progeny. It was foolish and scandalous, he concluded, that Spaniards should declare that people so obviously endowed with aptitudes for handiwork and the arts were not fully rational beings and incapable of grasping the Christian faith. So false a doctrine sprang from their cruelty and avarice and was instigated by Satan.

Bishop Garcés's letter was written early in 1537 and by then the lot of the Indians of Anáhuac had notably improved. Although it contained no novel message, it was nevertheless an extremely forceful restatement of what enlightened Europeans familiar with New Spain had been saying about the Indians ever since the Conquest. The views of Cortés, Pedro de Gante and others about the attainments and potentialities of the subject race were as well known at the Vatican as they were at the Spanish Court. The friars, too, had been giving practical expression to them for the last decade and more in their huge paternal labours for the protection of the Indians. Garcés, however, had consciously or unconsciously chosen the right moment for presenting his case, for his letter elicited an instant and completely favourable response. In a Bull dated June 9th of the same year Paul III categorically condemned all those who for selfish motives kept the Indians in subjection and treated them like brute beasts on the pretext that they were unfit for the Catholic faith. He himself was aware that these Indians were not only capable, as true human beings, of becoming Christians but were in fact also keenly anxious for conversion. Therefore he declared and determined with the full weight of his apostolic authority that although they might still be outside the Christian fold, they should not now or in future be deprived of their personal liberty or of their goods, but should be invited and attracted to the faith by preaching and good example. And all statements and actions to the contrary should be regarded as of no effect.

Zumárraga's attitude towards the Indians and their problems differed in no respect from that of Garcés. The two bishops worked closely together in opposing Guzmán, but Zumárraga in Mexico City bore the brunt of the furious conflict which broke out between the Audencia and the Church, and the reputation which he won in that struggle for fearlessness and integrity of purpose made him the dominant personality in New Spain until his death in 1548. He admirably fulfilled the trust placed in him by Charles V, for it was the King-Emperor who, struck by his force of character when he came across him as Prior of a monastery near Valladolid, had himself promoted his appointment.

Zumárraga was a Basque and his temperament, both fiery and unbending, was typical of his race. So was the austerity of his personal life, his intense religious fervour, his compassion for the oppressed and his brilliant organizing ability. He was also an intellectual steeped in the humanist culture of his age. Most unfortunately the only fragment of his reputation which has become firmly fixed in the Anglo-Saxon mind is the excessive zeal he is alleged to have shown in the destruction of Aztec monuments and manuscripts. The grounds for this accusation will be examined in due course, but Zumárraga was neither a bigot nor a vandal, and as a sixteenth-century churchman he may perhaps be pardoned for having taken a different view of the pre-Columbian civilization from that of a modern librarian or museum curator. Quite apart from these considerations, it is undeniable that the twenty years of his life in Mexico were devoted to defending the Indians and helping them to adapt themselves to their new circumstances.

The bishop—or rather bishop-elect, because he left in such a hurry that there was no time to consecrate him—reached Vera Cruz with Guzmán's oidores. On his way up to the capital, where he lodged at the Franciscan monastery, he received many attentions from the Indian notables. Having been officially nominated Protector of the Indians, a title originally assumed by Las Casas, he shewed at once that he was determined to take this function seriously. He proceeded to convoke a meeting of Indian lords and, using Pedro de Gante as interpreter, informed them that he had been charged by the king with the duty and authority to defend them from abuses. Moreover he invited them to register their complaints and began to collect a formidable volume of evidence against guilty Spaniards. He was flooded with depositions, but naturally found difficulty in distinguishing the false from the genuine.

As was to be expected, the Audiencia took alarm. The president accused Zumárraga of trying to usurp his own civil and judicial responsibilities, arguing that as he was so far only bishop-elect, he possessed no more authority in dealing with the Indians than any ordinary friar. He summarily ordered the Protector to desist from hearing complaints and to confine himself to catechizing. Zumárraga's answer was to remind Guzmán that his instructions were derived from the King in person and that he proposed to carry them out, if necessary at the cost of his life. He must have known that he was skating on thin ice, because his instructions were in fact imprecisely drafted and he had not been provided with inspectors or officers to enforce his judgments. If the president had not been a villain, there would have been some substance in his complaint that the bishop was encroaching on his powers. Nor was Guzmán a man to be scared by spiritual thunders alone. But Zumárraga had deliberately resolved to bring matters to a head. He was exasperated by the accounts of Spanish brutalities which were reaching him from all sides, reminiscent, as he afterwards reported to the King, of Diocletian's persecution of the Christians. Spaniards had crucified or hanged Indian lords who had failed to produce the gold required of them. The president and the iodores, not content with demanding the sisters and daughters of the chief men of Tlatelolco for their pleasure, had broken into a school for Indian girls set up by the friars at Texcoco and abducted the prettiest of the pupils.

The bishop's most vehement protests were ignored and Guzmán refused to see him. His house was beset by spies, while he himself was threatened with deportation. Indians visiting him were made liable to the gallows and Spaniards to the loss of their encomiendas. He tried to consult a lawyer, but none dared speak with him. When, thus isolated, he hit back at the Audiencia in his sermons, the oidores boycotted church services and circulated libellous pamphlets about himself and the Franciscans in general. Such was the situation when the bishop was further provoked by the scandalous affair at Huejotzingo. His reaction was to summon a council of his own Order, at which it was decided to stage the most solemn and public remonstrance with the Audiencia.

The occasion chosen was the pontifical high mass celebrated in Mexico City on Whit Sunday by the Bishop of Tlaxcala in the presence of Guzmán and the oidores. As the preacher, a certain Father Ortiz, began his prearranged homily Guzmán shouted at him to change the subject or leave the pulpit. On his attempting to continue a constable, instructed by the oidor Delgadillo and helped by followers of the agent Salazar, pulled him out of the pulpit and flung him on the floor of the church. The service dissolved in tremendous uproar and the bishop's representative or provisor, judging that those responsible for the outrage had automatically incurred excommunication, banned them from the mass until further notice. The oidores retaliated by exiling the provisor from New Spain and when he took sanctuary in the church, by cutting off supplies to him and all others inside. At that point Zumárraga, who had not been present at the Whit Sunday tumult, returned and patched up a compromise by which he granted absolution to the oidores in return for the burning of the libels and the performance of a trifling but nevertheless public penance.

During the truce which followed the somewhat tame ending to this confrontation the president and the bishop relieved themselves by composing long letters to the King in justification of their conduct. Zumárraga's despatch, a crushing indictment of the Audiencia's crimes, took a long time to reach Spain, for Guzmán, who was beginning to feel insecure, succeeded at first in effectively stopping the bishop's correspondence. Eventually the crucial document was smuggled down to Vera Cruz, concealed by a Basque sailor in an oil barrel and secretly delivered to the Council of the Indies. Despite Guzmán's censorship, rumours of the Audiencia's incompetence and tyranny were already filtering back to Spain, but Zumárraga's letter was vital in convincing the Council that the Audiencia would have to be superseded without delay. While it was wrestling with the problem Zumárraga's prestige in Mexico gradually grew and Guzmán's correspondingly declined. On hearing from friends in Spain that his replacement was imminent the president started to prepare, as the most promising means of restoring his position, a campaign of conquest in the west of Mexico, the region subsequently known as Nueva Galicia and now as the state of Jalisco. It was in his absence from the capital that Zumárraga had his final flaming dispute with the Audiencia. The issue was not ill-treatment of Indians but a direct invasion of the bishop's recognized sphere of authority.

The clash arose over the oidores' action in removing by force from the Franciscan monastery two clerics who were awaiting trial for misconduct by the bishop's court and subjecting them to torture in the public prison. Zumárraga and Garcés led a procession of clergy to the gaol to demand their release. Exchanges of abuse developed into a street battle between the bishop's partisans and followers of the oidores, who refused to surrender the men. Indeed they ordered one of them to be hanged and quartered and the other to be flogged and to have a foot cut off. This time Zumárraga not only again excommunicated the oidores but placed the whole city under an interdict. Services were suspended and the sacraments withheld. The Franciscans dismantled their monastery and decamped to Texcoco, taking with them the Indian children from Pedro de Gante's school.

The interdict was not long maintained, but by the time it was lifted the Council of the Indies had already appointed a new Audiencia. Nine months passed before the latter arrived in New Spain and in the interval Guzmán marched away towards Jalisco, leaving the discredited and excommunicated oidores to face the consequences of the Council's displeasure. Less than two years had sufficed for Zumárraga to triumph over the most tyrannical and incompetent government that colonial Mexico was ever to endure.

Chapter 7

UTOPIA IN MICHOACÁN

THE DISGRACEFUL FAILURE of the Audiencia forced the Council of the Indies to rethink the whole question of how to govern the intractable realm of New Spain. The solution adopted was to make it a Viceroyalty on the model of that already created for the Kingdom of Naples, at that time one of the most valuable dominions of the House of Hapsburg. Pending the choice of a Viceroy the Council appointed a new Audiencia with Sebastián Ramirez de Fuenleal as its president. He had previously combined the offices of bishop and president of the Audiencia in Santo Domingo. With him came a new batch of oidores of a very superior stamp to their predecessors. They set to work conscientiously to restore order and to tackle the problems already endemic in New Spain, such as slavery, forced labour and the survival or abolition of the encomienda.

One of the oidores was a sixty-year-old lawyer called Vasco de Quiroga, who in the remaining thirty-five years of his life (he died in 1565) was destined to gain the affection of the Indians as no other Spaniard succeeded in doing during the whole of the colonial era, and to acquire in his own day a prestige unequalled by anyone except Cortés. He is also the only outstanding Spaniard of colonial times to have retained the unreserved approval and admiration of Mexicans since their country achieved independence and it became the fashion, now luckily obsolete, systematically to denigrate historical figures of peninsular origin.

Don Vasco was projected into the New World at a time of life when only the toughest of old men managed to survive the Atlantic passage. For all his unimpeachable character and excellence as a jurist, it might have seemed unlikely that forty years spent in expounding Canon Law in such places as Valladolid and Granada would furnish the most suitable introduction to the crude and tumultuous conditions of New Spain. Nevertheless the Council of the Indies had picked the right man, although it could have had no inkling of the direction in which his hidden talents would lead him. With his shrewd

UTOPIA IN MICHOACÁN

judgment and slightly eccentric independence of mind, he was an instant success as an oidor, but it was not until he was enabled to concentrate his attention on one province, Michoacán, that he found full scope for his genius, a happy compound of humanist idealism, Christian charity and intense practical energy. After rescuing the Tarascans from the ruin inflicted on them by Nuño de Guzmán, he raised them in thirty years to a level of prosperity and security never attained by any other Indian people in the first century of Spanish rule.

The Spaniards were delighted with the beauty of Michoacán, the perfection of its climate and the fertility of its volcanic soil. Their early writers praised the abundance of its natural resources and the word "paradise" crops up regularly in their enthusiastic descriptions. They also quickly discovered that its mountains contained rich veins of ore. When he invaded the region, Guzmán was convinced that gold was to be had for the asking, although he was disappointed not to meet with an outward display of riches such as that which had dazzled the conquerors of Tenochtitlán. The Tarascans, or Purépecha as they called themselves, were a frugal people, not addicted to luxury and grandeur. Unfortunately the very absence of ostentation made him suspect that they were concealing their wealth, and they were made to suffer grievously in consequence.

The Tarascan kingdom occupied a vast area comprising not only modern Michoacán but also Guanajuato and large parts of Jalisco. Unlike most of the nations of New Spain, the Purépecha were essentially pacific and had no designs on their neighbours' territory. But when occasion demanded they were excellent warriors and especially skilful with the bow. They decisively defeated the Aztec army when the emperor Axayácatl was so ill-advised as to attack them. Apart from that feat of arms, and the undoubted fact that they had been settled in Michoacán from very early times, nothing certain is known of their origins or history. The only pictographic manuscripts recording their myths and traditions date from after the Conquest and are unreliable as guides to their historic past.

In their language and physical characteristics the Purépecha differed considerably from the neighbouring Nahuas and Otomis as well as from the numerous tribes in the north. The men were—and are—conspicuously tall and good-looking with a more European cast of countenance than is usual in Mexican

Indians. They seem to have preserved throughout their original migrations and long period of settlement in Michoacán a very strong degree of individuality, and their basic kinship with the surrounding peoples is only established by their possession of cultural habits common to all American Indians. In general they were culturally much less advanced than the Nahuas. It is curious that this intelligent and adaptable race should have remained so little affected by the influence of the classic civilization handed down from Teotihuacán through the Toltecs to the latter's successors in the Valley of Mexico. But the limit of the Aztec domain was also a sharply defined cultural frontier. Beyond it the Tarascans vegetated quietly in rustic seclusion. They achieved next to nothing in the fine arts and apparently had no other intellectual pursuits. Their massive architecture—still visible on the site of their capital Tzintzuntzán—was clumsy and uninspired. On the other hand their forthcoming and receptive nature, by contrast with the rather standoffish character of the Nahuas, was peculiarly susceptible to the right sort of approach from Europeans.

Having watched the downfall of the Aztec empire, the Tarascans came to the conclusion that it would be foolish to risk the destruction of their nation by resisting the Spaniards. Their king, Sintzicha Tanguaxan II, whom the Aztecs called Caltzontzin, accordingly offered his submission to Cortés, in the evident hope that he would be left in peace. But Cristóbal de Olíd, despatched by Cortés to make the king's acquaintance, abused his mission by his exactions and high-handed behaviour. Ironically enough, we hear of Tarascan chiefs subsequently accompanying Cortés on his Honduran expedition, the ostensible purpose of which was to punish the same Olíd.

In 1526 Fray Martín de la Coruña, one of the original twelve Franciscans, was chosen at the Tarascan king's request to undertake the conversion of Michoacán. Discarding the Franciscans' normal mild approach to their intended converts, he embarked at once on a furious campaign of temple-wrecking and idol-smashing, to which the Tarascans apparently submitted without protest. He founded a monastery at Tzintzuntzán, city of the humming-bird god, and in due course the monarch and his kinsmen were baptised, being known in future as Don Pedro, Don Pablo, Don Antonio, etc. So were many thousands of their subjects. Altogether Michoacán fared much better at that time

UTOPIA IN MICHOACÁN

than the parts of New Spain more immediately exposed to the depredations of corrupt royal officials and violent oidores. After the visit of Olíd few Spaniards penetrated into the province and the Tarascans were still largely left to themselves.

This immunity was shattered when Nuño de Guzmán decided to attempt the subjugation of the vast region to the north-west of Michoacán later known as Nueva Galicia. His motives for quitting Mexico City while still president of the Audiencia were twofold. In the first place he knew that he was in for trouble from Spain and wished to put as great a distance as possible between himself and the juez de residencia who would inevitably be sent to examine and indict him for maladministration. Secondly he calculated that his best chance of eventually avoiding the penalty for his misdeeds was to rehabilitate himself as an useful servant of the Crown by adding valuable territories to New Spain. If he succeeded he could reasonably hope to be retained as governor of the new province until it was pacified and settled, while his previous black record was conveniently forgotten.

His departure, at the head of a strong Spanish force and no less than fifteen thousand Indian carriers pitilessly impressed into service, bore a superficial resemblance to Cortés's Honduras adventure. It also happened to coincide with the Conquistador's return to Mexico as Marquess of the Valley of Oaxaca, full of glory and honour and restored to the King-Emperor's favour. Although it had been made clear to him that he could not expect any share in the government of New Spain and must content himself in future with enjoying the revenues of the enormous estates set aside for his maintenance, he would clearly continue to be a power in the land and the weight of his influence would be thrown against Guzmán. Díaz was careful to record that they were never on good terms.

In order to reach Nueva Galicia Guzmán had to pass through Michoacán. He came determined to suck the province dry by the same methods as he had employed with such ghastly success in Pánuco. In addition to his measureless rapacity he was evidently a sadist with a taste for atrocity for its own sake. The full effect of his ravages among the Tarascans is hard to estimate, but his vicious cruelty stunned and horrified a peaceful folk which had hitherto been only too desirous to welcome the Spaniards with open arms, acknowledging their overlordship but expecting to be treated decently in return. As excesses multiplied the Indians resorted to mass flight from their villages into wooded fastnesses where pursuit could easily be evaded. The few friars already at work in Michoacán were impotent to avert the terror and could only wait in despair for it to pass on to Jalisco.

The worst, or at least the most spectacular, of Guzmán's crimes was the murder of the Tarascan king. A naive but moving account of this episode is contained in a document* thought to have been compiled about 1538, probably by Fray Martín de la Coruña, for the first Viceroy, Don Antonio de Mendoza. Indeed its vivid style suggests that it is not so much a compilation as a direct rendering in Spanish of the actual words used by Tarascan eye-witnesses in describing to the friar scenes at which they had been present. The same manuscript—not printed until the nineteenth century—has a curious passage about the reactions of the natives when they saw their first Spaniard; for instance they at once assumed that it was the horses who were giving directions to the riders and telling them where to go.

Before Guzmán crossed their borders, the Purépecha observed a great comet passing over the sky. It was followed by a message ordering them to produce supplies for the expedition—four hundred suits of padded cotton armour, plenty of bows and arrows, four thousand loads of maize and "an infinity of hens" (i.e. turkeys). When the lords of the country, with the king at their head, came out to greet him, Guzmán pressed the ruler to leave his house and take up his quarters in the Spaniards' camp. Like Moctezuma in a similar plight, the wretched Caltzontzin knew he was cornered and had no choice but to comply. With an accurate presentiment of what was in store for him he sent word to warn his household that he thought he had to die. He told the older men to console his women, look after his children and see that the Spaniards were given all they needed; they must be given no excuse to blame him. On the next day Guzmán began to upbraid the king and his family, complaining that the supplies furnished were inadequate and alleging that eight thousand Tarascan warriors, with all their weapons and armour, had made their way to a place on the

* *Relación de las cerimonias y rictos y población y goberhaión de los Indios de la Provincia de Michoacán* (in *Crónicas de Michoacán*)

UTOPIA IN MICHOACÁN 189

expedition's route to Jalisco and were preparing an ambush for it. He tried to bully the king and his son, Don Pedro, into revealing the whereabouts of the real or imaginary royal treasure. He thrashed Don Pedro with the flat of his sword and had father and son confined in the latter's house.

Other Spaniards, including Guzmán's unsavoury interpreter Pilar, continued the questioning, threatening the king with having his feet burned (as Cuauhtémoc's were) unless he showed them his treasure. On his protesting that he had no more gold to offer, the Spaniards asked him how he preferred to die. They tied up Don Pedro and himself and put them to the torture, beating them in the sexual parts with a thin rod. While they were thus engaged Fray Martín, alerted by some unnamed Indian youths, burst in crucifix in hand and reproached the torturers. They answered that the princes were being punished for refusing information about the best road for the army's onward march. After the friar had returned to his monastery the prisoners were again taken before Guzmán, together with two more of the king's sons. He was furious at the friar's intervention but did not at once order the torture to be resumed. However he persisted in demanding gold, also a special levy of eight thousand men to serve and accompany the Spanish army (eight thousand seems to have been the Tarascan way of emphasizing any large number). The king retorted that if Guzmán wished the villages to be combed for men and gold, he had better carry out the business himself, for the villages now belonged to the Spaniards, but after further menaces he agreed to send the necessary orders to his lords.

The "eight thousand" were duly produced, but many managed to flee before they were distributed among the Spanish soldiers. The army then began its march towards Jalisco, carrying the king fettered in a hammock. He endured his final agony with amazing stoicism and dignity. His face, says the record, turned black and he could eat nothing. Charges old and new were rained upon him; he was urged to produce "the skins of Christians" which he was hiding and again accused of planning an ambush complete with pits to trap the horses. They tied his hands and poured water into his nostrils, asking if it was true that he possessed a great golden idol. He said no, but he thought there might be some gold left at Pátzcuaro, where he had a summer residence by the lake. But when a considerable treasure, including four hundred golden disks and shields, was unearthed on that spot, he somehow succeeded in arranging that only a small proportion of it finally reached Guzmán. The latter responded by again torturing Don Pedro and other members of Caltzontzin's family. But he got nothing out of them or out of the priests and elders whom he questioned at the same time. Thoroughly exasperated, he sentenced the king to be dragged at the tail of a horse and then burned. A Spaniard mounted the horse and a herald rode ahead shouting: "Look at this rascal who wanted to kill us. You lesser fry who are all rascals too, take warning from this example."

Still alive after his ordeal, the king was bound to a post and asked for the names of others involved in his alleged conspiracy against the Spaniards. He replied "I know nothing". Thereupon he was strangled; wood was heaped around him and set alight. Guzmán ordered his ashes to be thrown into a river, but his servants collected some of them and they were buried at Pátzcuaro and in another place. With those at Pátzcuaro were interred, according to custom, a golden shield and jewellery, together with hair and nails cut when he was a child and clothes worn by him in infancy. In the other place, which was kept secret, a woman was said to have been killed and buried with the ashes. It is interesting to find Fray Martín, or whoever the anonymous compiler was, confessing to this survival of pre-Columbian rituals.

Don Pedro narrowly escaped with his life. It seems that the accountant Albórnoz, who though a jealous intriguer was not a fool, wrote to warn Guzmán that Michoacán would be lost if he put the king's heir to death. Don Pedro and his relatives were taken as hostages when the army moved on. Even Guzmán was forced to admit, on arriving at the suspected danger spot, that his fears of an ambush were unjustified, for the eight thousand enemies failed to materialize, but the hostages were retained until two Franciscans following in the expedition's wake obtained their release. Don Pedro returned home and was later recognized as ruler (gobernador) of his people under the viceregal régime, but he bore the scars of torture for the rest of his days.

Although Guzmán, fortunately, never returned to Michoacán, little was done in the next few years to repair the damage caused by his incursion. The few Franciscans working in the province had to contend with an almost universal apathy and distrust of anything Spanish. But in 1534 Vasco de Quiroga, in the course of his duties as oidor, made a tour of inspection and decided that a special effort would have to be made to improve matters. He had already given proof of an extraordinary aptitude for understanding the Indians and their needs, and was consequently turning from purely administrative functions towards bold social experiments. The most original of these was his foundation known as the Hospital de Santa Fé, situated in hilly country overlooking the Valley of Mexico.

The Aztecs had a well developed hospital system of their own, but it was swept away at the Conquest, while their considerable medical skills degenerated into a mixture of herbalism and magic. The Spaniards must be given credit for promptly recognizing the very special need for organized care of the sick in a country where they had their own difficulties with the climate and diet and the Indians were fatally susceptible to European diseases. Cortés and Bishop Garcés both built hospitals at their own expense, one in the capital (the Hospital de Jesús) and the other at Perote on the way down to Vera Cruz. Infirmaries were established in all the principal monasteries, one of the earliest being at Uruapan in Michoacán. But Quiroga's conception of what a hospital should be was much grander and what is more he put it successfully to the test in two places, first near the capital and later on the shores of Lake Pátzcuaro, where the foundation was called Santa Fé de la Laguna. These establishments, which were run on exactly similar lines, were self-supporting agricultural colonies of many thousands of Indians practising an unique kind of Christian socialism. Each was the owner of its buildings, land and cattle and was originally financed by Don Vasco out of his personal fortune. Its produce was consumed on the spot or distributed to the needy. Moreover the communities were under no obligation to furnish labour or tribute to any Spanish authority or encomendero.

The Indians were organized in units of about forty persons called "families", each with its headman and consisting of about eight married couples with their children. A family occupied a group of houses surrounded by individual garden plots. The rest of the land was worked in common on a system closely resembling what the Indians had been accustomed to in their villages. All offices in the community were elective, no re-election being permitted. Disputes were settled internally and any member guilty of misconduct was simply expelled. As regards membership preference was given to young persons who had received some preliminary training from the friars. The hospital proper was the central feature of the communal scheme. Facing each other across a courtyard were the quarters for patients with contagious and non-contagious diseases respectively, the director's house and the dispensary occupying the other two sides. Other prominent buildings were the church, homes for old people and orphans and a variety of schools and workshops where instruction was given in religion, letters, music and all kinds of technical matters. The communities were encouraged to administer themselves with a minimum of European supervision. The spiritual director of the hospital was, however, a friar, and in the case of Sante Fé de Mexico we find this function exercised by Fray Alonso de Borja, a member of the family which produced two Borgia popes and one contemporary Saint, Francisco Borgia, third General of the Jesuit Order.

These institutions, which if he had known of them would have met with the vehement approval of Tolstoy, were not only realized in practice but prospered for forty years after their founder's death. They were not just theoretical conceptions liable to be blown away by the first adverse wind. In some respects they harked back to the organization of the rural calpulli of Aztec times, but the direct inspiration for Don Vasco's initiative in detail (e.g. the six-hour working day) as well as in broad outline, was undoubtedly derived from a contemporary European source, the *Utopia* of Thomas More. In the first quarter of the sixteenth century England was still a pillar of the Catholic Church and a leader in the current upsurge of Christian humanism. While Quiroga was establishing his first hospital, More was Lord Chancellor of England, and impending events which were to cast the English in the role of heretical pirates had not thrown their shadow across the Spanish colonial world. When he wrote *Utopia* More was fascinated by the discovery of America and the apparent resemblance between its supposedly simple societies and his own ideal commonwealth. Men like Zumárraga, whose copy of *Utopia* still exists, and Quiroga, participating as they did

Bartolome de las Casas

Vasco de Quiroga

in the intellectual movement of this era, were correspondingly attracted by More's ideals. In Quiroga's view, too, the Indians were perfect natural material for the social planner. Their abilities, he thought, were those of the golden age of primitive man, and their virtues those of the Christians in the early Church.

The first enterprise was carried through by Don Vasco's personal energy and influence as oidor. For his work in Michoacán he needed spiritual authority as well. In the mid-thirties of the century it was conveniently decided to create two new bishoprics, Oaxaca and Michoacán, and since the sixty-five-year-old lawyer had already set himself up as patron of the Tarascans and was campaigning strongly on their behalf, it seemed logical to make him their bishop as well. So he was rapidly ordained and consecrated by Zumárraga and proceeded to take charge of his diocese.

He embarked impatiently on a whole row of ambitious projects. His basic idea was to organize the Indian communities of Michoacán into one vast "hospital" system, with its largest unit centred on Pátzcuaro and in effect constituting a great extension of his foundation of Santa Fé de la Laguna. He deliberately chose the site in preference to Tzintzuntzán because the latter was too deeply steeped in the old religion and traditions. Originally he planned a sort of Indian agrocity which, along with its suburban villages, would group together seventy thousand people, hardly a megalomaniac conception when compared with the enormous urban complex created by the Aztecs in the Valley of Mexico, but far surpassing anything yet achieved by the Tarascans. At the heart of this conglomeration was to stand a huge, austere cathedral into which thirty thousand worshippers could be fitted. Don Vasco did not entirely fulfil either of his ideals and when it came to building it must be confessed that he overreached himself. At his death in 1565 the church was still unfinished. Its grandiose scale and design, providing for no less than five naves, became the perpetual target of criticism, from the Viceroys because the construction used up the labour of such quantities of Indians, from the friars because it eclipsed their monastery churches, and from the local Spaniards because the bishop was catering for the Indians and not for them. The Spaniards wanted the Cathedral situated at Valladolid (the present Morelia), a town for Europeans founded by the Viceroy Mendoza forty miles away on the model of Puebla. In the end they prevailed. The Cathedral was transferred to Valladolid and what was to have been the largest church in the world was reduced to quite modest proportions. Besides, so many Tarascans died in the terrible epidemics of the late seventies that it would never have been filled in later years, even if its architectural and other problems could have been solved. But it was still the Cathedral when Don Vasco died and was buried in it.

In the greater part of his immense diocese the bishop had a free hand to realize in practice his vision of a rural Utopia. Michoacán was so rich in natural resources that despite the ravages of disease it could hardly fail to prosper if its inhabitants could be shielded from exploitation and successfully encouraged to co-operate in making Utopia work. As regards the first requisite, the encomenderos in Michoacán were not sufficiently numerous or truculent to frustrate Quiroga's plans; nor indeed was he opposed in principle to the encomienda as a basis of the settlers' existence. The Tarascans, however, had to be convinced that there were substantial advantages to be gained under the new dispensation to compensate them for the loss of their liberty and for the outrages which they had suffered. The trouble was that they had lost heart and could see no incentive to rebuild their society. Don Vasco saw that it was not enough to give them, by way of restitution for their wrongs, a new religion, elementary safeguards against oppression and social benefits of the kind provided in the "hospitals". The Utopian communities also needed a sharp economic stimulus and opportunity of access to the culture and technique of the conquerors.

Quiroga's first concern was to transform agriculture by bringing in European plants and animals. This was of course already being done in Anáhuac, but in a haphazard manner and amid Indian complaints that the Spaniards' cattle were eating their crops and putting land out of cultivation. The bishop was determined to introduce the necessary changes in Michoacán in a planned and orderly fashion, which meant that he would personally have to decide who would grow what and where. He travelled ceaselessly from one end of his diocese to the other, surveying, organizing, exhorting and persuading. It was not as if he could rely on the services of agricultural experts to help instruct and train the Tarascans. Apart from a few friars and laymen whose names are unknown to us he was on his own. Also the difficulties of arranging for the import of regular supplies of seeds, animals and implements into his remote province must have been daunting. Everything had to come from Spain, or at the nearest from the Antilles, in small rickety ships and then cross three formidable ranges of mountains. But the astonishing fact is that by 1547, only twelve years after he had begun his work among the Tarascans, the revolution in their lives was so successfully advanced that he felt it safe to spend several years away from his diocese, attending the Council of Trent and in Spain dealing with a variety of Mexican affairs. His advice in all matters concerned with New Spain was eagerly sought, and he was himself no mean lobbyist for the interests of his diocese. In all he stayed in Europe for seven years, which was probably much longer than he or anyone expected. However, he undertook the Atlantic crossing once more at the age of eighty; in 1555 he was back in Michoacán and working as hard as ever.

Observers writing in the seventeenth century, a hundred years after Quiroga launched his rural revolution, depict Michoacán as a second Sicily or Vega of Granada. At Uruapan three crops of wheat were harvested in the year and the province as a whole exported grain to the rest of the viceroyalty. On some farms fourteen thousand head of cattle were branded yearly, together with large numbers of horses and mules. Besides cereals there was an abundant yield of native products —maize, chiles, beans, cotton, honey and wax. Since the province contained temperate and sub-tropical zones, both well wooded and watered, its fruits were amazingly diversified. The indigenous chirimoya, zapote, mamey and lime flourished alongside apples, pears, cherries, quinces and pomegranates; oranges, lemons, grapefruit and bananas; melons, pineapples, peaches and grapes. There were extensive and valuable plantations of sugar and cocoa. All visitors were astounded by the exuberant growth and by the care expended in its cultivation.

As agriculture expanded, country industries also multiplied. Don Vasco was active in promoting new ventures and in fostering the traditional Indian crafts, the quality of which he often improved by teaching the Tarascans the use of European techniques. He arranged that each community in his Utopia should practise the industry which he thought best suited to it, having regard to the peculiar skills of its inhabitants, its site, access to raw materials and other such factors. Once the principle of specialization was established, the communities were encouraged to exchange their products among each other and to offer their surpluses in external markets. Thus Michoacán became a source of vigorous commercial activity. As it has often been remarked, there is still a lively trade in the villages round Lake Pátzcuaro in the goods which Don Vasco decided that those villages should manufacture. No greater tribute to the success of the bishop's economic scheme can be imagined than that its profits are being gathered—frequently on an increasing scale—four hundred years after it was introduced.

Don Vasco calculated that after absorbing a strong dose of the right kind of European culture in their working lives the Tarascans would be able to stand on their own feet without too much European tutelage. His own relationship with his protégés was certainly paternal (he is known to this day as "Tata" Vasco), but his highly individual brand of paternalism differed from the typical Franciscan approach, which was based on a much less optimistic estimate of the Indians' capacity to resist colonial pressures. He believed that when the Indians were earning their keep and their social cohesion had been strengthened by his Utopian régime they would no longer need the friar perpetually at their elbow. The difference in the two attitudes probably accounts for the coolness which existed between him and the Franciscans in his diocese; they were uncharitable enough never to miss an opportunity of putting in a disparaging word about him to the colonial government. Don Vasco, however, was quite equal to handling Viceroys.

On the other hand he found the Augustinians very ready to co-operate. They thoroughly understood his ideas and in establishing their first monasteries in Michoacán applied them with enthusiasm. Their show-place, Tiripitío, dated from 1537. An Augustinian account of its foundation and early development shows clearly how much it owed to Don Vasco's inspiration. The Indians were assembled in a large village approached by broad paved roads and supplied by an aqueduct two leagues long with water which was channelled through streets lined with orange trees to fountains in the main plaza, the hospital and the monastery. The houses were uniformly low, but each had its bedroom, living-room, kitchen and small oratory. The principal buildings round the plaza were a great church adorned with pillared portico and wall paintings, the monastery itself, the hospital, the choir school and the open chapels where the children learned their "doctrine".

The hospital for Indian patients was so spacious that it seemed to have been designed for Spaniards of high rank. It had high rooms and long corridors, and a courtyard also shaded by orange trees. Plenty of clean linen was supplied, and the domestic tasks were performed for a week at a stretch by relays of eight to ten married women and their husbands. They did the cooking, swept the patients' rooms and made the beds. When not so employed they worked at a trade and the surplus of what they produced was sold for the hospital's benefit. Among these curious organizational details it is not mentioned who actually doctored the sick; it was presumably the friars themselves.

The village contained a great number of workshops (fábricas). Indeed it was regarded as the main school of craftsmanship in Michoacán. Among the trades taught and practised were carpentry and furniture-making, metal-working, weaving and tailoring. The natives were so skilful and adaptable that there was a great demand for them in other communities; many emigrated and were lost to Tiripitío.

As the most intellectual of the three Orders of friars, the Augustinians took special pride in their educational work. The Indian children were taught to read and write from the age of eight. Only the most gifted, however, went on to some form of secondary education. At Tiripitío that normally meant music. The students learned plain chant and "canto de órgano". Certain of them also became famous organists. One was so eminent and scientific, in the words of the chronicler of Tiripitío, Fray Diego de Basalenque, that he astounded a meeting of Spanish organists assembled for a competition in Mexico City. Fray Diego adds that he was acquainted with this man's son, one Matheo, when he was organist of Valladolid cathedral, but people said that he was not a patch on his father.

In 1540 the monastery was made a centre for higher studies, that is Theology and Arts (the classical languages and Hebrew). It was in no sense a University where Spanish and Indian students could mix on equal terms, but a small training college in which the Augustinians could renew and perfect their academic knowledge while living in the wilds. There was, however, one important addition to the curriculum, as the native language was also made a compulsory subject. The standard of erudition reached by the Augustinians of Michoacán can be judged by the attainments of Fray Diego himself, who knew Latin, Greek, Hebrew, Italian, Tarascan, Náhuatl and Matlatzinca, and composed twenty books of theology, philosophy, common law, history and linguistics. Obviously, therefore, there was no question of Tarascan youths who had just taken their first steps in literacy being fit to participate in the friars' advanced studies. Nevertheless Fray Diego mentions one notable exception to the rule that only Spanish friars were eligible for the courses and hints that there were others. That exception was none other than Caltzontzin's son Don Antonio, who set up house at Tiripitío in order to receive instruction. Having already become an accomplished Spanish speaker, he made himself extremely useful in teaching the friars Tarascan. It would be interesting to know if he made as much progress in the classics as the young Aztecs who were at the same time studying in Bishop Zumárraga's school at Tlatelolco. His son Pablo, who was eventually ordained priest, was no doubt proficient in Latin.

On the whole we must assume that very few Tarascans were given a chance to qualify for higher education. It is true that two colleges, both bearing the name of St Nicolas, were founded by Don Vasco at the same period at Pátzcuaro and Valladolid, but their purpose was primarily to educate Spanish boys for the priesthood, while the instruction of such Indians as were also admitted to these institutions was limited to "doctrine" and the Spanish language. (It will be recalled that in Anáhuac the friars were not even keen for their converts to learn Spanish.) These colleges were later amalgamated and became the joint ancestors of the present University of Michoacán.

It may be doubted whether Quiroga ever envisaged a more advanced evolution of his Purépecha on European lines. The old man was a consistently practical idealist and it was surely enough for him to have performed the surprising feat of grafting the Christian socialism of Thomas More on the rustic Tarascan stock. His experiment of creating a modest Utopia by combining elements of two cultures in a social and economic scheme had turned out a brilliant success. Why then endanger the whole structure of what he had built by attempting a further advance towards a very uncertain goal? As compared with the Aztecs, the Tarascans were a simple people. Don Vasco was deeply fond of them and appreciated their natural capacities, but like all Spaniards he was sceptical about the ability of any Indians to develop without long years of preparation, if at all, the moral and intellectual qualities which would fit them to assume leading positions in the civil and religious life of New Spain. Furthermore it would have been quite impracticable for him to promote any significant measure of interracialism, even if he had desired to do so, in the face of opposition from the colonists. It was therefore safer and more prudent to leave his commonwealth as he first conceived it. As shaped by him it survived his death by many years and gave the Tarascans a greater degree of prosperity and security from arbitrary treatment than was enjoyed anywhere else in the viceroyalty. Thanks to Don Vasco, Michoacán continued to bask in a kind of Arcadian calm.

Quiroga's record as a defender of the Indians invites comparison with that of Las Casas. The latter, operating on the widest of stages, now in Spain, now in the Indies, bearding Sovereigns and their Council, indefatigably protesting against violence and spoliation, awoke the conscience of Church and State and produced a reaction in the Indians' favour without which the work of men like Don Vasco could never have got started. Where Las Casas failed was in his practical endeavours; when he tried to found a model community in the Caribbean it collapsed lamentably; and even his heroic championship of the natives of his own diocese of Chiapas, at the same time as Quiroga was so signally succeeding in Michoacán, ended in frustration and defeat. He was the greater man of the two, but his flamboyant attitudes and capacity for sustained theatrical indignation alienated many people who sympathized with his purposes; Motolinía, for instance, regarded him as an irritating poseur who did not always live up to his principles, arriving at Tlaxcala with a train of thirty-seven porters carrying his personal possessions. Don Vasco, in the small world of Michoacán, obtained his results by tact, moderation, common sense and sheer hard work.

Part IV
THE VICEROYS AND THEIR WARDS

Chapter 8

LORDS OF TWO RACES

IN 1538 THE first Viceroy, Antonio de Mendoza, Count of Tendilla, presided over a series of splendid entertainments, the official purpose of which was to celebrate the recent conclusion of the ten-year Truce of Aigues-Mortes between the King-Emperor and the King of France. For New Spain, however, they marked the beginning of a new era of stable government, as well as the ostensible settlement of outstanding differences between the Viceroy and the King's most eminent vassal in the colony, Hernán Cortés, Marquess of the Valley of Oaxaca. From the local point of view the timing was more appropriate than if the celebrations had taken place shortly after Don Antonio's arrival in 1535, for it was now plain that his firm and experienced handling of Mexican affairs, following on the patient preparatory work of the second Audiencia, had once and for all put an end to anarchy and implanted in New Spain a branch of the orderly, centralized administration of Charles V's empire.

Indian ingenuity was called in to enliven the festivities, which are described with great gusto by Díaz. The pageantry was staged primarily in honour of Mendoza and Cortés and for the pleasure of Spanish "caballeros y conquistadores", but although Díaz does not specifically mention that the Indians were invited it is unlikely that the native aristocrats, for whom the Viceroy was always careful to show regard, were excluded from the guest list. At all events Indians were given a free hand with the first of the two grand set-pieces in the programme, under the general direction of an Italian who claimed to be a descendant of Roman patricians, and therefore skilled in the organization of triumphs.

One morning the main square (Zócalo) of Mexico City was seen to have been transformed overnight into a wild wood, thickly stocked with all kinds of trees and plants and looking entirely natural, with old rotten trunks covered with vegetation lying on the ground and festoons of moss hanging from the branches. It was also full of wild birds and animals—two little pumas and four little jaguars, deer, foxes and a multitude of smaller fry like rabbits and opossums, all discreetly fenced in until it was time for the hunt to begin. Two parties of Indians dressed as "savages" then sprang out from opposite corners of the wood and gave chase to the animals before engaging in a sham fight with each other. One can imagine such a display being mounted by an Indian who had at one time tended Moctezuma's famous parks and zoos. A more exotic colonial touch was provided by a procession of masked and richly adorned negroes on horseback, and the show ended with a battle between them and the "savages".

By the next morning the sylvan scene had been swept away and replaced by the turrets and battlements of the fortress of Rhodes, besieged by the Turks and defended by the Grand Master of the Knights of St John, who was represented by Cortés himself. Two squadrons of magnificently accoutred Turkish cavalry ambushed and carried off Christian shepherds and their flocks; these were duly rescued by a hundred Christian knights even more finely equipped, and the Turks were driven from the field. At one stage in the conflict four Christian ships entered the square under full sail, presumably on the canals which still gave access at that period to the centre of the city, and turned about three times amid salvos of artillery. For some unexplained reason their crews included a number of Indians dressed up as Dominican friars, "just as they come from Castile, plucking hens and some fishing". The point of the joke escapes us, but it apparently both amused the Spanish spectators and tickled the sense of humour of the Indians, who were for once encouraged to indulge their talent for mimicry and poke fun at their mentors. Evidently they had entered into the carnival spirit of the occasion. At the end of the day fighting bulls (toros bravos) were let loose in the plaza, a form of entertainment which has never failed to give pleasure to Mexicans of any origin from that day onwards.

Yet another day was devoted to racing and a tournament. The gentlemen riders had to gallop all the way to the Zócaló from the plaza of Tlatelolco, site of the great market of Aztec times. There was also, somewhat surprisingly, a ladies' race, the course being from the house of the treasurer Estrada, wherever that was (the owner being a Vicar of Bray who had precariously survived all changes of colonial government), to the Viceroy's palace in the Zócalo. Very valuable prizes were offered for both these events. In the jousting many lances were splintered, the most eminent casualty being the Marquess of the Valley, who was unhorsed and emerged with a limp. When these excitements were over the conquerors relaxed and romped about in fancy dress.

Prodigies of eating and drinking accompanied the celebrations. The ladies watching from the windows of the newly built Spanish houses on the square were served with cold snacks, sweets, wine, foaming cold chocolate made in the Aztec style and other spiced drinks from tables laid in the corridors. The highlights of the occasion were two grand formal banquets given for hundreds of guests by Cortés and the Viceroy respectively. The latter was the more lavish and lasted until two in the morning, growing rather less pompous towards the end when the jesters got drunk and had to be thrown out; and other inebriated persons, perhaps fortunately, cut off the flow of red and white wine through specially devised conduits. The tables were set in the courtyard and passages of the viceregal palace, which were arranged to resemble fruit-bearing orchards with branches twined overhead, birds flitting from tree to tree and water gushing from a replica of the fountain at Chapultepec. To the music of trumpets, harps, viols, flutes and pipes dishes succeeded each other in stupendous variety—whole sheep, boars' and deers' heads, turkeys, geese and ducks with silvered beaks—while huge pasties unexpectedly disgorged live quails, doves and rabbits. In the outer courtyard grooms and servants, mulattos and Indians feasted simultaneously on steers roasted whole, poultry and game. According to Díaz many uninvited Spaniards found their way into the banquets, and he implies that it was they who were responsible for the Marquess missing more than a hundred marks' worth of silver in the course of the evening. The Viceroy's majordomo, however, arranged with the Indian notables to post an Indian to keep watch over every valuable piece of plate on the tables, and to accompany every piece sent with gifts of food to individual houses. Thus Mendoza only lost a few salt-cellars, together with a quantity of knives and linen.

Not to be outshone by anything originating in the Valley of Mexico, the Tlaxcalans decided to present a spectacle of their own, also with the object of commemorating the Truce of

Aigues-Mortes. Doubtless it was the friars who suggested to them that instead of the Siege of Rhodes they should enact an imaginary but much more important event, the Siege and Taking of Jerusalem by the Christian armies of Charles V. This took the form of an enormous open air pantomime with probably thousands of performers, and the execution, if not the planning, was left entirely to the Tlaxcalan Indians. In a sense it was the indigenous reply to the Spanish initiative in the capital. The Tlaxcalans wished to prove that they could do as well or better than the Spaniards and their Culhúa rivals in the Valley.

An immense arena was reserved for the performance and its central feature was the walled city of Jerusalem. The participants were divided into three armies: the defending Moslems in the city itself, later to be reinforced by levies from "Galilee, Judaea, Samaria, Damascus and the whole of Syria" as well as "Moors and Jews with many munitions and supplies"; the army of Spain, "with a rearguard of Germany, Rome and Italians"; and the army of New Spain. That of Spain was grouped under the colours of Toledo, Aragon, Galicia, Granada, Vizcaya and Navarre. That of New Spain, under the royal and viceregal standards, consisted of Tlaxcalans and Mexicans, supported by contingents of Huaxtecs, Cempoalese and Mixtecs, "certain captaincies which were said to come from Peru and the islands of Santo Domingo and Cuba", and a rearguard formed of Tarascans and Guatemalans. Significantly enough, Spain and New Spain were placed on an equal footing as Christian powers under the same monarch, and the army of New Spain was composed entirely of native Indians with apparently no admixture of local Spaniards. The Tlaxcalans did their best to copy European arms and costumes for the Spanish army and to simulate the enemy they wore Moorish head-dresses, but as the Indians of New Spain they turned out in their pre-Columbian glory of plumes, painted shields and banners with personal and tribal devices. All the performers, we are told, were "lords and principals".

The infidels were commanded by the "Grand Soldan of Babylon and Tetrarch of Jerusalem", the Spaniards by Don Antonio de Pimentel, Count of Benavente, and the Indians by the Viceroy Mendoza. Other exalted personages, including the Pope, the Emperor and the Kings of France and Hungary, made their appearance at various stages of the pageant. The anonymous friar quoted by Motolinía, to whom we owe a detailed description of the performance, says that the Soldan was represented by Cortés himself ("que era el Marqués del Valle, Don Hernando Cortes"), that the Soldan's Captain-General was Pedro de Alvarado, Governor of Guatemala, and the principal commander on the Spanish side Andrés de Tapia, one of Cortés's most faithful henchmen. It is not in the least improbable that these three most eminent conquerors should have decided to lend their patronage to the proceedings in Tlaxcala, to which they were bound by such close ties of gratitude and affection.

The Christians were not allowed to win too easily. Two separate assaults by the forces of Old and New Spain were beaten off. In response to their commanders' appeals the Emperor brought up his reserves, but victory remained uncertain. The Pope and his Cardinals invoked divine intervention, whereupon Santiago on his white horse was seen to be leading the Spaniards, and Saint Hippolytus, on whose feast-day Spaniards and Tlaxcalans had stormed Tenochtitlán, put himself at the head of the Indian army, mounted on a black charger. Even so the final battle lasted until the Archangel Michael appeared and offered pardon to the Moors for having respected the holy places during their occupation of Jerusalem, provided that they submitted promptly and agreed to be converted. The spectacle ended with their doing homage to Pope and Emperor.

It was of course a very remarkable fiesta. Though stage-managed by friars, it gave spontaneous expression to Indian sentiments, or at least those prevailing in Tlaxcala. Politically these Indians appear to be moving towards a kind of Christian nationalism which proclaimed their loyalty to their Indian identity as well as to the King-Emperor. But they have also identified themselves proudly with causes and aims, such as the recovery of Jerusalem, which are perfectly alien to their own traditions. Twenty years after the Conquest they are already partially absorbed into their conquerors' cultural background and adopting their religious and historical aspirations as their own. It must be assumed that both participants and spectators had a general idea of what the scenes meant that they were acting and watching. What is certain is that they were inspired by the most genuine enthusiasm. In the past they had been accustomed to portray their own myths by means of dramatic mimes involving hundreds of performers and ecstatic audiences, and the friars were now adapting the old vehicle of symbolic expression to new teachings and ways of thought.

The Indians found in the Viceroy the focus which they needed for their loyalty to the Crown. Mendoza did not of course inherit the intense devotion which both the conquered Aztecs and the native peoples who had joined in conquering them felt for Cortés. His prestige derived from the nature of his office and the unquestioned authority with which he exercised it from the moment he landed. No Spaniard of anything approaching his rank and style had yet been seen in Mexico. The Indians, who were sensitive in such matters, quickly appreciated that their new ruler commanded the respect and obedience of his own countrymen in a degree which placed him in a category well above Cortés and his Conquistadores.

Indeed the Mendozas were the most illustrious of all Spanish grandees. They possessed no less than seventy titles of nobility, including the senior dukedom of the Infantado. During the fifteenth and sixteenth centuries they held every conceivable high position in Church and State. Iñigo Lopez de Mendoza, Marqués de Santillana, famous as statesman, general and poet under John II of Castile, left six sons. The most remarkable of these was the Viceroy's uncle Pedro Gonzalez de Mendoza, Cardinal Archbishop of Seville and Toledo, Primate of Spain, leader of the Castilian armies under John II and Henry IV, and so powerful as chief minister under Ferdinand and Isabella that he was known as the "third king". The climax of his career was the planning and execution of the Catholic Kings' triumphal campaign against the Moors of Granada. Although also a patron of literature and founder of a University, he was no ascetic like his successor, Cardinal Ximenes de Cisneros, and the austere Queen Isabella was obliged to legitimize his bastard sons. The Viceroy's father was a younger Iñigo Lopez de Mendoza, Ambassador of the Catholic Kings at the Papal Court, and one of his brothers, Diego Hurtado de Mendoza, served Charles V as his adviser on Italian affairs and personal representative at the Council of Trent. He too was a man of letters and towards the end of his life wrote a classic account of the desperate revolt of the Moriscos of Granada against Christian rule in 1568. Both nephews of the great Cardinal were steeped in the atmosphere of the court, men of the world trained in diplomacy and the higher administration. Moreover the careers of Don Antonio's uncle and of another brother, the Marqués de Mondéjar, had been closely concerned with the province recently wrested from the Moslems. It was taken for granted that his family's experience in governing conquered and converted infidels would stand him in good stead in ruling heathens who had undergone the same progress. Again it was correctly calculated that a magnate with no personal stake in New Spain would handle the settlers' problems with the strictest impartiality, and that his sheer eminence in the Spanish hierarchy would check their tendency to faction and indiscipline.

Mendoza's portrait in the Gallery of Viceroys at Chapultepec Castle presents a robust aristocrat in early middle age with the expression, both self-confident and wary, of a man accustomed to being obeyed and getting his own way. He has a strong mouth, a long fleshy nose and prominent, penetrating eyes. His appearance certainly suggests the calm and unhurried approach to public affairs which characterized his fourteen years tenure of office. He was in no rush to take up his appointment; indeed it was nearly five years before he declared himself satisfied with the salary offered (eight thousand ducats a year) and consented to set sail. By the time he arrived the second Audiencia under Fuenleal had largely succeeded in restoring respect for authority, clearing away the shameful abuses of the preceding period and taking the heat out of local enmities. But when he himself got to work his conduct of the administration was far from dilatory. The first of the sixty-one Viceroys who governed New Spain is rightly considered to have been the greatest, just as his friend and collaborator, Bishop Zumárraga, outclassed all his successors in the highest ecclesiastical office.

Don Antonio's adroitness in dealing with awkward personalities is well illustrated by his handling of Cortés and Nuño de Guzmán, the two men who were most likely to make difficulties for him. By 1540 he had got rid of them both with virtually no trouble, and by studiously avoiding a confrontation. Although the collapse of the first Audiencia coincided with Cortés's return to Mexico in 1530 and freed him from the indignities which he had suffered at its hands, it did not put an end to his differences with the government. Inevitably he was irritated by the supervision and restrictions which the second Audiencia, under orders from home, saw fit to impose on him.

The last ten years which he spent in Mexico were by no means idly employed. He moved restlessly about the country, exploiting his lands and mines, and above all fitting out on the isthmus and the coast of Michoacán ships to explore the trade routes across the Pacific and the western seaboard of North America. But the satisfaction he derived from those activities was marred by running disputes, first with the Audiencia and then with the Viceroy, about the delimitation of the vast domains of the Marquesado del Valle, and by his failure to obtain compensation for the material damage inflicted on his interests by Guzmán and his oidores. According to his own interpretation of the grants made to him by the Crown, he had been given full feudal jurisdiction over twenty-three thousand households of Indians. The Audiencia argued, however, that this figure was meant to refer to persons, not heads of families, and that his Indians ought to be held in encomienda like those of other Spaniards and not treated as peasants on a feudal estate in Europe. A compromise was eventually patched up by which the Marquess was permitted to hold the valuable lands centred on Cuernavaca on feudal terms, but even so he was harassed by inspectors who complained that he was overtaxing and overworking his Indians.

Meanwhile the Audiencia had no means of bringing Guzmán to book. In Nueva Galicia he had placed himself effectively out of range of its authority and was behaving as an independent ruler, snapping his fingers at the lawyer appointed to "take residence" on him in Jalisco and send him in custody to Mexico City. Cortés, as titular Captain-General under the Audiencia, was powerless to help, for the government had no standing army and a levy of encomenderos would clearly not relish a campaign against their fellow colonists in the West. It was even more irritating for the Marquess that Guzmán, in control of the coast of Jalisco, was in a good position to hamper his own attempts to establish a foothold on the peninsula of Lower California. In the hope of validating his claims, he complied with the Viceroy's polite request for his return from that region to Mexico City, only to find that far from proceeding sternly against Guzmán, Mendoza had summoned him too to the capital and was apparently treating him with every consideration, to the horror of the old Conquistadores who were longing for his downfall. He even invited him to stay at the palace and asked him to dinner.

Most probably Mendoza was anxious to form his own judgment of this adventurer, who despite his infamies had added a new province to the viceroyalty and was personable and well educated enough to be capable of making a good impression on first acquaintance. He was not, however, allowed to continue governing Nueva Galicia. After a suitable interval the Viceroy quietly sent him under guard to Spain, where he ended as a penniless and unsuccessful suitor for the royal indulgence.

Cortés's relations with the Viceroy remained formally correct after their grand public reconciliation. There were no open recriminations, but Cortés became convinced that his only chance of overcoming Mendoza's sly though suave evasions in the matter of his claims for compensation and restitution would be to plead them himself at Court. This decision exactly suited Mendoza's book, because he knew that his credit with the sovereign outweighed that of the Marquess. So Cortés left New Spain for the second time, never to return, forfeiting an honoured retirement in the country for which he felt an almost passionate attraction for a profitless pursuit of favours which the King no longer felt disposed to grant. It is pitiful that so great a man should have been so easily edged out and reduced to impotent begging in Spain when he could have been enjoying the fruits of his exploits on his own lands in Mexico. The truth is that in facing a man of Mendoza's cool superiority he lost the sure touch which had so seldom failed him in his duels with opponents of lesser calibre.

Mendoza applied the same detached judgment and unhurried method to the fundamental problems of New Spain. These were in essence the establishment of a workable system of civil government and the search for a better-defined relationship between the two races. The framers of Crown policy in the Council of the Indies were full of ideas on these subjects, which they embodied in volumes of detailed instructions to the Viceroy. Although their continuing concern for Indian welfare was tempered by a preoccupation with the royal need to obtain a steady and if possible increasing income from the Indies, one can only admire the conscientious persistence with which they struggled to understand the unfamiliar conditions of the new world and to devise fair solutions. Their performance in that respect compares most favourably with that of the British East India Company two centuries later. What, however, they often failed to grasp was the extent of the Viceroy's difficulties in carrying out their directives on the spot.

The apparatus at the Viceroy's disposal for administering a territory larger than the defunct Aztec empire was meagre in the extreme. Aztec power had rested on easily mobilizable armies, a numerous bureaucracy at the centre and a closely-knit system of control over the provinces. Although not starved of money and surrounded with pomp on ceremonial occasions, Mendoza possessed none of these resources. To enforce his decisions he had little more than moral authority, and for his information he was forced to depend largely on bishops and friars. No resident governors or senior officials were available to oversee the behaviour of colonists and Indians away from the capital, much less to watch the activities of a Nuño de Guzmán four hundred miles away in Jalisco. In theory one or more oidores should always have been on tour (the Viceroy was of course at the same time president of the Audiencia), but he had only two in all and both were needed to deal with business in Mexico City. He himself had to make do with a few secretaries, clerks and constables.

So far as local administration was concerned, the deficiencies were partly remedied in Mendoza's time by the establishment of the system known as corregimiento. This was one of the reforms thought out by the Council of the Indies and its introduction was entrusted to the second Audiencia. Initially it was applied to the government of Indians in the encomiendas granted by Guzmán and subsequently withdrawn by the Crown, but ultimately the Council's purpose was to substitute it for the encomienda over the whole country. The corregidor was a salaried Spanish official whose duty it was to assess and collect the tribute from a particular Indian community. He was also made responsible for supervising its social and moral behaviour and if there was no monastery in the district, for its religious education. In a large community he would be assisted by a deputy, a secretary, a constable and if necessary a priest. He was also charged with keeping an eye on neighbouring encomenderos.

The corregimiento was planned so as eventually to bring the whole Indian population under the control of Spanish officials, and it in fact came to provide New Spain with a fairly efficient form of civil government. It outlived the encomienda and survived in one form or another throughout the colonial period. But at first it was not a great success. There were not nearly enough Spaniards to go round and some of those appointed were unsuitable. An encomendero in one district often served as corregidor in another, and joined with other encomenderos in fleecing the Indians. At one stage Mendoza proposed to abolish the corregimiento altogether, not only because the corregidores were incompetent but chiefly because the encomenderos, whom he had no intention of antagonizing as a class, resented the spread of the rival institution. Luckily they were delighted by an unexpected royal decision, in flat reversal of the previous enactment on the subject, authorizing the son or widow of a deceased encomendero to inherit his grant of Indians instead of automatically forfeiting it to the Crown.

In Mendoza's day there must still have been many Indian villages, buried in the remote forests and sierras, which were untouched by the Spanish presence. The picture that emerges, however, is of a majority paying their tribute and labour service to an encomendero or corregidor, while if they were fortunate they had a monastery to help them. The Spaniards, a few thousand in number, lived mostly in their own towns, Mexico City, Puebla and Vera Cruz, to which were soon added Guadalajara in Jalisco, Antequera (Oaxaca) and Valladolid. These were municipalities (cabildos) on the peninsular model administered by their traditional officers, the alcaldes and regidores. Outside their narrow limits the country was still solidly Indian, apart from a handful of royal officers, encomenderos, overseers in mines and plantations, priests and friars. Subject to its tribute and labour obligations it was run by Indian officers. The Spanish cabildo of Mexico City, for instance, had no jurisdiction in the teeming Indian suburban settlements of San Juan Tenochtitlán and Santiago Tlatelolco which hemmed it in. They obeyed their own native authorities which were directly responsible to Viceroy and Audiencia. During the first thirty years of viceroyalty they were exempted from tribute in return for providing as much labour as was required for the city's public works.

The principal Indian officer in each township or large village was known as the gobernador and the institution (in bastard Náhuatl) as "gobernadoryotl". At first he tended to be a member of a tlatoani or princely family in the old empire. Thus, with one or two exceptions, Moctezuma's kinsmen governed in Tenochtitlán, Nezahualpilli's in Texcoco and Tetlepanquetzal's, who adopted the surname of Cortés, in Tlacopan (Tacuba). Other communities were likewise governed by lesser chieftains of the tlatoani class, assisted by a traditional council of advisers loosely referred to by the Spaniards as alcaldes and regidores. When the dynastic families died out, as they did rapidly in the recurrent epidemics, they began to be replaced by persons of humbler origin who might be brought in from a different region, or even by enterprising mestizos. But the office of gobernador continued to confer much prestige on the holder, together with opportunities of enriching himself. All Indian officers were eventually made elective, the electors being all men of consequence in their localities, and were subject to approval by the central government. The more important office-holders received their staffs of office from the hands of the Viceroy himself. At first these notables were remunerated in goods and services levied from their own people, just as they had been supported in pre-Conquest times, but as money came into general circulation, replacing payment in kind, they were put on fixed salaries, with the result that they gradually lost their status of nobles. On a lower level a variety of minor employees performed much the same municipal tasks as in the Aztec calpulli.

Indian gobernadores and alcaldes also sat as judges in civil and criminal suits between their compatriots, dealing with quite complicated litigation as well as simple police matters. Records were kept as previously in pictograms, and subsequently written in Náhuatl. Suits between Spaniards and Indians were heard by the corregidor, or in very important cases by a member of the Audiencia. The legalist tradition of Aztec society helped the native judges quickly to grasp the principles and procedures of Spanish law and to apply them in their own courts. It also enabled the Indians to become skilful pleaders before the Spanish tribunals, where they often successfully prevented encroachments on native rights.

It should not be difficult to imagine how the typical Indian town would have appeared to an observer about 1540. Let us suppose that it was the cabecera or administrative centre of a district and contained some ten thousand people, exclusive of the inhabitants of a dozen or so outlying hamlets dependent on it. It is divided into quarters (barrios), corresponding, as do the hamlets, to the former calpullis. This town may stand on its original pre-Conquest site; alternatively it has been removed from a less accessible area several miles away and rebuilt where it can more easily be supervised for civil and religious purposes. In that event the old town will have been left deserted, while the new one is laid out on a rectangular pattern, identifiable in dozens of existing villages, with one or more tree-planted plazas and broad streets lined with single storied houses of white-washed adobe, each with its garden behind it. But these dwellings do not differ substantially from the pre-Columbian model, and the planning of the older settlements is often very similar.

The most prominent feature of both old and new towns is a tall barrel-vaulted church visible for miles across the surrounding countryside. Stone and rubble from demolished pyramidal temples have probably been used in its construction. Next to it stands a two-storied stone cloister with rounded arches and classical columns, or even pointed arches and buttresses, and an elegant stone stairway ascends to the friars' cells on the upper floor. Perched on a scaffolding in one corner of the cloister, an Indian artist is putting the finishing touches to an intricate scheme of black and white wall paintings which he has copied from Renaissance motifs. Beyond the wall is the refectory, which still remains to be decorated, and above it is the library, for which the friars are anxiously awaiting a consignment of the Fathers and the Classics, the splendid products of German and Italian presses. The books have been carried by mules as far as Mexico City but have to complete the last fifty miles of their journey on the backs of Indian tlamemes. In the outbuildings behind the monastery a friar is giving an elementary writing lesson to a group of solemn-faced Indian youths. Others are supervising what is going on in the workshops and a big irrigated orchard newly stocked with European fruit-trees. To the west of the church and cloister stretches a vast courtyard or atrio enclosed by a low wall. A paved path leads from the church entrance to a richly carved stone cross of Indian workmanship in the centre of the courtyard and thence to the gateway. On this particular day there are few people in the atrio, but a few days ago it was thronged with Indians acting a series of elaborate tableaux from the Old Testament, and mass was said for them in the open chapel south of the church porch.

Outside the atrio is a much larger square where the tianguis or town market is in full swing. Here all the commodities of the region are displayed and bartered at stalls aligned in neat rows, as in the great market of Tlatelolco. The plaza is thick with purchasers and onlookers, and files of porters loaded with merchandise come trotting in from the adjoining streets. There is no clamour but a sustained murmur of voices as from a human beehive. Order is kept by market police under the direction of a native alcalde. The crowd parts to give passage to a youngish man of dignified appearance wearing white trousers of fine cotton and an embroidered tilmatli, or cloak, knotted at the shoulder. He is the gobernador of the town, the only surviving legitimate son of its former tlatoani. His father and uncles were killed in the war of the Conquest and his two brothers died of smallpox ten years afterwards. In his retinue can be seen an obvious mestizo boy, his sister's son by a Spaniard who has long since abandoned her. Although he is a devout Christian the gobernador has not, like many of his class, rushed to adopt Spanish habits and dress. He speaks only Náhuatl, is proud of his ancestry and married to the daughter of another tlatoani. He lives in one of the rare stone-built houses in the town, a roomy building with two inner patios.

Suddenly there is a commotion on one side of the square and people scatter hurriedly to avoid a small party of Spaniards on horseback returning from a hunt in the hills behind the town. The Indians have lost their fear of the horses but are scared by the hounds, so different from the fat little dogs which the Aztec lords used to consider such a delicacy. These Spaniards are the local encomendero, his majordomo and friends on the way back to the house which the encomendero, responding to a strong hint from the Viceroy that he might lose his encomienda if he spends so much time loafing around Mexico City, has hastily built himself outside the town. They are bringing a deer which they have killed as a present to the prior of the monastery, whom the encomendero wishes to appease after an awkward interview in which the prior has reproached him for driving his Indians too hard. He has not in fact maltreated them physically, but has exacted excessive quantities of product from them in the guise of tribute in order to sell it elsewhere at a profit, and he has appropriated their cultivable land to graze his imported sheep and goats. Meanwhile the gobernador has slipped quietly out of the square. He has no wish to come face to face with the encomendero with whom he is on bad terms because the Spaniard is continually grabbing for himself the tribute due from the Indians to their own lord. Knowing that the friars sympathize with him, he is wondering whether it would be worth trying to bring his grievances before the Viceroy.

This picture of rural Anáhuac could be completed in much fuller detail without becoming too fanciful. The imaginary tlatoani belonged to a class which was already on the way out. As the century progressed it was gradually superseded in the "gobernadoryotl" by persons from a more diverse background, notably those whom the friars' schooling had equipped for the new conditions of life. For the time, however, the tlatoque were generally respected by both Spaniards and Indians and favoured by the Viceroy. Some of them retained their wealth and even added to it by experimenting with Spanish-type agriculture, raising domestic animals and also taking advantage of the growing market among the Spaniards of the capital for Indian products. Some of the more exalted tlatoani families were granted encomiendas just as if they had been Spaniards. Among them were to be found children of Moctezuma: his son Don Pedro received Tula, his daughter Doña Leonor, married to the Spaniard Juan Paz, got Ecatepec and another daughter, Doña Isabel, who had two Spanish husbands before settling down with a third, Juan Cano, was given Tacuba. Don Pedro, who started life as Tlocahuepan Yohualicahuatzin, became the founder of a Spanish noble family, the Counts of Moctezuma and Tula, one of whose members was Viceroy of New Spain in 1700.

The fate of Don Carlos, tlatoani of Texcoco, stands out in sharp contrast to the painless absorption of Moctezuma's descendants by Spain. In 1539 this son of Nezahualpilli was arrested and accused of pagan practices, "idolatry and concubinage". Worse still, he was alleged to have incited his compatriots to reject Christian teachings. The case was referred to the Inquisition with Bishop Zumárraga himself acting as Inquisitor. After a lengthy trial and much deployment of evidence he was condemned to death as an obstinate heretic and handed over for execution to the civil power.

The scandal caused by this affair was heightened by the fact that the victim had hitherto figured as a particular favourite of the friars and of the government. Together with the rest of his family, he had been baptized by the first party of Franciscans. In 1536, when Mendoza and Zumárraga jointly sponsored the foundation of the Franciscan college at Tlatelolco for the education of young Indians (its history will be examined in a later chapter), Don Carlos was one of its original pupils, a clear sign that he was considered as reliable as he was intelligent. The Spanish surname which he adopted was that of Mendoza. Yet his conviction on a capital charge occurred in the very same year as he succeeded one of his brothers as tlatoani, which suggests that he long had concealed his addiction to paganism.

The Spanish authorities were wise enough to deal gently with lapses into idolatry unless they were repeated or involved human sacrifice. Indeed no less a person than the Inquisitor-General in Spain was of the opinion that Don Carlos had not deserved the extreme penalty. Why then did Zumárraga, who had always been distinguished by his humanity towards the Indians, react with such unusual severity? The only explanation is that he regarded the case of Don Carlos as exceptional. He was surely convinced by the evidence that the prince, while trusted by the Spaniards and receiving conspicuous benefits from them, had not only been a hardened idolator for many years but had been systematically working to turn his people against their new faith. In fact he had been the leader, and perhaps the effective leader, of an Indian underground. So profound and successful a deception was unpardonable. It amounted not to a series of casual lapses but to treasonable subversion.

All the same the actual nature of the tlatoani's offences hardly seems to have justified his indictment by the Holy Office. Concubinage was a very common Indian failing, especially in princely circles, which the authorities countered with routine penalties and penances. Occasional idolatry was a more serious matter but was also dealt with by unsensational methods. When the authorities searched Don Carlos's palace, they found idols, pictograms and other proofs of paganism. His son, a boy of ten, declared under questioning that his father had refused to bring him up as a Christian. Other witnesses testified that he consistently sought to frustrate the work of the friars, exhorting the Texcocans in secret to ignore Catholic doctrine and stick to their old ways. The prince denied these accusations and his wife, though complaining of his debaucheries, backed him up, claiming that she had never seen him worship idols. The defence, however, was brushed aside. It has been suggested that Don Carlos was framed by false evidence concocted by hostile Texcocans who wished to have him removed from his position of tlatoani in favour of yet another of his brothers, but it seems unlikely that so shrewd and upright a judge as Zumárraga could have been duped by that kind of intrigue. We must assume that he was satisfied that the accused was guilty of conspiracy, and that his activities had gone far enough as to prejudice the security of the government as well as the conversion of the Indians. He had made up his mind that Don Carlos, apart from having fooled the Spaniards over his real personality and sentiments, was a dangerous element who had to be removed at all costs. Hence the decision to make a public example of him. Whether or not the authorities took serious fright from their discoveries, the fact is that Don Carlos was the only prominent Indian of the period who tried to launch anything of a resistance movement in Anáhuac, and that it was scotched before it had a chance to develop. He may fairly be regarded as a genuine but lone martyr for the old religion. His native name, Ometochtli, was the same as that of the primeval god, "the Lord Rabbit", who presided over pulque, drunkenness and irrational enthusiasms.

More than twenty years afterwards, under the viceroyalty of Mendoza's successor, Luis de Velasco, another local potentate was indicted for a clandestine lapse into paganism. He was the elderly Zapotec prince Cosijopi, a nephew and former vassal of Moctezuma who had submitted voluntarily to Cortés and had been cosseted by the Spaniards for the last forty years. Outwardly a blameless Christian, he was eventually discovered celebrating the ancient rites in the company of two Zapotec high priests to whom he had given secret asylum in his palace. For his error in trying to have the best of both worlds Cosijopi was hauled before the Audiencia in Mexico City and punished by the confiscation of his very large estates in the region of Tehuantepec. He was then released, but died of chagrin on the way home. Unlike Don Carlos he was not suspected of inspiring a political reaction in favour of paganism.

Mendoza, on the other hand, faced a serious rebellion in the west, the so-called Mixtón war, which blazed up in the two years following Don Carlos's death. Conditions in the newly occupied province of Nueva Galicia were very different from those prevailing in Anáhuac. Jalisco itself had not formed part of Moctezuma's dominions but its inhabitants were of the same ethnic origin as the Aztecs, an agricultural people who had traded with the empire and were to some extent influenced by its culture. Further to the north the stark sierras of Nayarit and Sinaloa, the unending expanses of Zacatecas and beyond, harboured a succession of barbarous tribes which were proving stubbornly unamenable to Spanish rule and conversion to Christianity. So long as Nuño de Guzman controlled it, the province remained virtually independent of Mexico City. As might have been expected, his régime was extremely harsh and the settlers to whom he granted encomiendas on his own authority were the roughest kind of adventurers.

The basic cause of the revolt was certainly the brutalities of these men, but the story is that it was sparked off by certain Indian wizards who were one day performing incantations around a large empty gourd. When this was suddenly lifted into the air and swept away by a whirlwind, they announced that it was a sign from the gods that the Indians should rise and sweep away the Spaniards. However that may have been, the rebels did not move until Mendoza had ousted Guzmán. Then, led by chieftains from the frontier tribes, they launched a general attack.

Their first victims were friars already operating in the wilds, many of whom were tortured and killed and their missions burnt. They sent messengers round the villages calling on the people to repudiate the Christian god in favour of their own god Tecoroli. Accompanied by their dead ancestors whom he had resuscitated for the purpose, Tecoroli was about to appear among them and conquer Nueva Galicia. All those who followed him were promised eternal youth and as many wives as they wanted, but anyone professing himself satisfied with one wife only would not be allowed to live. Having finished with Jalisco, Tecoroli would go on to overrun Michoacán, Anáhuac and even Guatemala.

At first the colonists could do little to check the uprising. Blockaded in the provincial capital, Guadalajara, they begged the Viceroy to rescue them. To meet the threat Mendoza depended entirely on a scratch force of encomenderos, many of whom were not even veterans of the Conquest, and it was clear that if they were defeated there would be nothing to prevent rebellion, or at least chaos, spreading over the whole of New Spain. It was therefore fortunate for him that a small but disciplined army happened to be at hand under the command of the most ruthless of all Indian fighters, Pedro de Alvarado, a man who, in the words of a Dominican historian,* "had rather be feared than loved by all those subject to him, whether Indians or Spaniards".

Alvarado's career had had its ups and downs since he left Mexico in 1523 to occupy Guatemala, a highland country populated by tribes of Maya origin but held down by Aztec garrisons. Although the latter had submitted, his object was not attained without much hard fighting in the course of which Alvarado lost an eye, for the Maya would not tamely exchange one foreign domination for another. After founding a city for Spaniards, Santiago de los Caballeros, he left the province in 1526 for Spain, where he was officially confirmed in his conquests and appointed Governor and Captain-General of Guatemala. As we have seen, this did not save him from being imprisoned by the first Audiencia on a false charge while passing through Mexico on his way back to his province, which he did not reach until 1530. Instead of settling down he started to prepare a fleet for a trans-Pacific expedition to what were vaguely known as the Spice Islands or Moluccas, a region in which the Spanish Crown, always on the look-out

---

* Fray Antonio de Remesal, quoted by Garcia Icazbalceta, in *Opusculos y Biografias*.

for new sources of revenue, was taking an active interest. But before the armada was ready Alvarado became excited by the accounts which were reaching him of Pizarro's fantastic exploits in Peru. In particular he had heard that the province of Quito, the wealth of which was rumoured to rival that of conquered Cuzco itself, had not yet been subdued, and he calculated that he might have a good chance of forestalling Pizarro there if he acted promptly. Such was the attraction of Peru that he soon collected a fine array of five hundred Spaniards eager to take part in this foolhardy enterprise.

Alarmed that he was stripping his province of men and arms, the Audiencia in Mexico, whose formal authority extended to Guatemala, forbade him to proceed, warning him of the impropriety of his encroaching on Pizarro's jurisdiction. But Alvarado, headstrong as ever, refused to be deterred; he set sail and landed on the coast of Ecuador. As it happened, his expedition turned out a complete fiasco. Ignorant of Andean geography, unaware that the extremes of climate which he had to encounter were even deadlier than those of Mexico, he blundered through the coastal jungles and lost his way in the frozen mountains. His passage was marked by ferocious outrages against the Indians. When at last he found the right road it was only to realize that Pizarro's lieutenants, Sebastián de Benalcázar and Diego de Almagro, had got to Quito first. His own force had suffered such grievous losses on its march that he could not risk a battle between Spaniards. Accordingly he was obliged to conclude an agreement with Almagro by which, in return for an indemnity of 100,000 gold pesos, he handed over his ships, his men and what remained of their equipment and left Peru.

But Alvarado's impulsiveness was matched by his persistence. Convinced by a second short visit to Spain that he could repair his damaged reputation by persevering in his original plan of an expedition to the Spice Islands, he began to put together a new fleet and army. To the consternation of the Spaniards and Indians of Guatemala, who had been practically ruined by the previous venture, his preparations assumed an even grander scale. Díaz writes that neither the Peruvian indemnity, nor the gold from Guatemala's mines, nor the tribute from the province, nor the loans which he contracted, sufficed to cover his needs. Finally he left the harbour of Acajutla with twelve ships and five hundred and fifty men. His first port of call was on the coast of Jalisco, where he hoped to take on more soldiers and provisions.

At that juncture the Viceroy of New Spain developed an intense interest in Alvarado's plans. The staid Mendoza was infected with the same fever for voyages of discovery as Cortés, Alvarado and countless other contemporary Spaniards. He had already dispatched Vasquez de Coronado, the man whom he had appointed to replace Guzmán in Nueva Galicia, on a ludicrous search hundreds of miles beyond the Rio Grande for the seven cities of Cibola, each of which was supposed to surpass Aztec Tenochtitlán, and which was of course a pure product of the overheated Spanish imagination. But when he grasped the purpose of Alvarado's enterprise he conceived a more practical idea, which was to turn it into a joint expedition, to be partly equipped and financed by himself. He sent to invite Alvarado to visit him and discuss his proposal. The two men met at Tiripitio in Michoacán and agreed to cooperate; Alvarado and a relative of Mendoza called Villalobos, "a great cosmographer" (according to Díaz), were to be joint captains of the fleet.

This happy project was frustrated by the sudden outbreak of the Mixtón rebellion. At Puerto de la Navidad, where he had returned after his interview with the Viceroy, Alvarado received an urgent message from Cristobal de Oñate, acting Governor of Jalisco, calling for his help in the King's name. Oñate reported that he was hemmed in by Indians in some hills called the Peñoles de Nochistlan, adding that the fate of New Spain hung on the result of the impending battle. Without waiting to assemble his whole army, Alvarado hurried to the spot with a small detachment. Disregarding Oñate's advice, he attacked impetuously and was repulsed. In the retreat which followed he was marching on foot with the rearguard when a soldier riding close to him lost control of his horse. The animal fell and rolled on Alvarado, leaving him senseless and suffering from internal injuries. His soldiers carried him to Guadalajara where he died after a few days. Asked in which part of his body he felt pain, he replied: "In my soul; take me where it can be cured with the oil of penitence."*

---

* Mota Padilla, *Conquista de la Nueva Galicia*, quoted by Garcia Icazbalceta.

The dispatch of reinforcements by the Viceroy, together with the support given by Alvarado's army, ensured the collapse of the revolt, and apart from sporadic troubles in the Zapotec region New Spain was not again disturbed by native uprisings. Thus there was no longer any place in its society for Conquistadors of Alvarado's type with their insatiable restlessness and callous contempt for the Indians among whom they lived. In the Viceroyalty of the sixteenth century the way lay open for the bishop, the friar and the lawyer to work out, if they could, a balanced and harmonious relationship between the two races.

Chapter 9

THE LIMITS OF JUSTICE

TWENTY YEARS AFTER the Conquest the theory behind Spanish colonialism was growing more and not less liberal. The long fight waged by the Dominicans against the oppression of subject peoples, and against attempts to justify and systematize it, had been won by the Order and its sympathizers to the extent that the Spanish establishment had come down unreservedly on its side. Concern for the welfare of the Indian subjects of the Crown in New Spain and elsewhere was the official policy of Church and State. It had been increasingly observed in practice since the middle twenties, when the Dominican Loaisa became president of the Council of the Indies, and the appointment of Zumárraga as Protector of the Indians was a significant step in its application to New Spain. It was not until 1532, however, that the great jurist and theologian Francisco de Vitoria sought to redefine in strikingly radical terms the theory underlying the royal policy, thus preparing the way for a thorough reform of colonial legislation. It was felt that a new code was urgently needed to replace the tentative and outdated Laws of Burgos, which had been devised as far back as 1512 to remedy the appalling situation in the Antilles but had signally failed in their purpose.

Vitoria's principles were embodied in two Latin theses presented to the University of Salamanca. They dealt generally with the status of the newly discovered Indians of the New World and in particular with the circumstances in which Spaniards could have the right to make war on them. While admitting that such a right did exist, Vitoria insisted that it must be very severely limited. The Indians, he declared, were the natural owners of the lands in which they lived and of everything in them. The fact that they were heathens in no way disqualified them from such ownership and in itself gave the Spaniards no right to take possession of their lands and goods in the name of the King or of the Pope. Thus the Borgia Alexander VI had been entirely unjustified in decreeing that the western hemisphere should be arbitrarily divided between two Christian rulers, the kings of Spain and Portugal.

On the other hand Vitoria maintained that Spaniards had the right to settle peacefully in the Indies and trade there, so long as they did not maltreat the native inhabitants, and that they had not only the right but the duty, especially when it was entrusted to them by the Pope, to convert the Indians. But if the latter refused conversion, the Spaniards were still forbidden to attempt it by force. Only if the Indians wantonly attacked the peaceful Spanish traders, or used force to prevent the peaceful Spanish evangelizers from making themselves heard, were those Spaniards entitled to subdue them, seize their property and enslave them.

Since the subjection of the Antilles, Mexico and other regions of America was an accomplished fact when Vitoria propounded his theses, and the peculiarly savage conquest of Peru was in full swing, we are tempted to dismiss them as an academic exercise, and an hypocritical one at that. After all the lands in question had all been occupied by force and in a sense converted by force as well, and no jurist had the power to put the clock back. Moreover the hypothesis of the peaceful presence in the Indian lands of Spanish traders and evangelizers without any precise political relationship with the inhabitants was unrealistic to the point of absurdity. But Vitoria could convincingly reply that while he was of course well aware that a mere formulation of principles, however valuable in themselves, would never redress past errors and crimes, there was no practical reason why they should not provide a solid foundation for legislating with regard to the future.

The Crown for its part was determined to endow its Indian vassals in the whole of the American continent with a new and durable charter, and in the decade following the publication of Vitoria's theses the best legal and administrative talent in Spain was engaged in drawing it up, in accordance with the royal directions. The task was treated as one of primary importance, not only because the Crown's advisers were genuinely anxious, for religious and moral reasons, to safeguard Indian rights, but because they were convinced that the survival of the Spanish empire overseas depended on the establishment of the absolute authority of the Crown in all matters involving relationships between Spaniards and Indians. They had been disgusted by the misgovernment of New Spain under Nuño de Guzmán and more profoundly shocked by the seemingly uncontrollable anarchy prevailing in Peru. They also knew that unless peace and prosperity in the new realms were guaranteed by a workable regulation of inter-racial affairs, no profits were likely to accrue from them to the Crown.

The code was compiled by a special council convened at Valladolid, and subsequently transferred to Barcelona, under the presidency of Cardinal Loaisa. The inclusion among its members of the former president of the Audiencia of New Spain, Ramírez de Fuenleal, and of Juan de Salmerón, one of his former oidores, ensured that Mexican conditions and requirements were given proper weight. As the council's long and conscientious discussions were extended from year to year, rumours began to reach the Indies that its thinking was taking an ominously radical turn. Las Casas, the settlers' inveterate enemy, was known to be busy in its antechambers, and it was rightly assumed that his advice was being receptively listened to. When the New Laws were eventually promulgated in 1542, they realized the settlers' worst fears.

The Laws established unequivocally that Indians no less than Spaniards were free vassals of the Crown. It therefore followed that no more Indians should be enslaved, even as the result of war or rebellion, and that all those already held as slaves by Spaniards, whether by purchase or in any other fashion, should at once be released. The Audiencias were instructed to see that this provision was strictly enforced; it meant, among other things, that no slave labourers except negroes could any longer be employed in the mines. Private Spaniards were forbidden to impose any form of serfdom or forced labour on the Indians, and even the use of hired carriers was drastically limited.

All this was galling to the colonists, but what really dismayed them was the home government's evident intention, as revealed in the Laws, to do away with the whole encomienda system within a short space of years. As a first step the holding of Indians in encomienda by the Viceroy, his officials, clergy, monasteries and other institutions was prohibited altogether; all such existing encomiendas were to lapse immediately. Furthermore no new encomiendas were to be granted to any individuals whatsoever, and on the death of any person holding an encomienda it had to be forfeited to the Crown; it might not be passed on to his heirs. Indians from lapsed encomiendas would automatically become subject to a corregidor for all purposes of administration and justice. Those remaining in encomienda until the death or removal of the existing incumbent would have only one obligation towards him—to pay him the tribute fixed by the government. The encomendero would not be permitted to demand personal services in lieu of tribute in cash or kind. In other words the sole labour owed by the Indian to the encomendero was to be that expended in producing the necessary money or goods for the payment of his tribute.

The Laws did in fact throw out a few sops to the doomed encomenderos, and especially to the families of the original conquerors. The latter were given priority as regards the appointment of corregidores, and if they happened to have held no Indians in encomienda they were to be subsidized out of the general tribute revenue collected by the Crown's agents. Widows and children of deceased encomenderos were made eligible for royal money grants. But none of these palliatives compensated for the suppression of inherited rights to hold Indians, and that blow was considered all the more treacherous in that the right had been expressly conceded, after years of indecision, as recently as 1536. It was felt that the Crown was not playing fair with the loyal encomenderos without whom there could be no security nor indeed any Spanish settlement at all in New Spain. A loud howl of protest from the settlers greeted the Crown's special commissioner, Tello de Sandoval, when he arrived in Mexico with the object of helping the Viceroy to put the Laws into force. From the pitiful tone in which they voiced their grievances it might have been deduced that the Spaniards had suddenly become the underdogs, and the Indians the favoured element among His Catholic Majesty's subjects. Fortunately for Tello the worst he had to face in the peaceful and disciplined viceroyalty of New Spain was indignant remonstrance, whereas his colleague who went to Peru on a similar mission had his head cut off. In Nicaragua, too, the encomenderos took up arms.

The principal credit for ensuring that the crisis which followed was solved not by violence, but by argument and the avoidance or postponement of the more disagreeable issues, must be awarded to Mendoza, who handled the situation with magisterial calm. Supported by the heads of the Mendicant Orders, who could not be accused of lack of concern for Indian interests, he managed to convince Tello that it would be wise to hold up the application of those laws which most offended the settlers pending an appeal to the Council of the Indies. The Viceroy was in an awkward position. It was his duty, as guardian of the royal authority, to prevent the legislation from being frustrated by a successful "Obedezco pero no cumplo" attitude on the settlers' part. On the other hand it was equally essential not to alienate the settlers to the point of upsetting the smooth course of his viceroyalty. Hitherto he had adroitly reconciled conflicting interests in New Spain while squeezing out dissentient and unruly elements. Now it seemed that ten years of progress would be followed by another indefinite period of strife. In the event, however, his severely pragmatic approach found a way out of the dilemma.

Mendoza, Zumárraga and all those most deeply versed in Indian affairs saw no point in treating the encomenderos of New Spain as if they were public enemies. Even the local Dominicans showed much greater tolerance towards them than their superiors in the peninsula. The Council's hostility was founded partly on the burning prejudices of Las Casas, which had been developed elsewhere than in Anáhuac, partly on the past misconduct of the encomenderos there before and during Guzmán's Audiencia. But so far as Mexico was concerned, their behaviour had greatly improved during the period while the New Laws were being elaborated. For that improvement the purge carried out by the second Audiencia, the civilizing influence of viceregal rule and the wider diffusion of the monasteries all played their part. The friars, who were still quick to denounce abuses of the encomienda system, were the first to acknowledge that as a general rule the holders of Indians were treating them with greater humanity and common sense. Meanwhile the rival system of the corregimiento had made a slow start, chiefly because it was difficult to find the right men to staff it. Mendoza and his advisers saw no objection to the survival of the encomienda, at least for the time being, provided that it was subjected to effective checks. If the King was adamant about abolishing it, it must be brought to an end gradually and gently.

Delegates were sent to Spain in due course in order to deploy before the Council the traditional arguments in favour of the retention of the encomienda. With no encomenderos to watch over them the Indians, they maintained, would drop their new religion and become disaffected. They would refuse to work the Spaniards' lands and since they were by nature lazy and unenterprising, they would only cultivate as much of their own land as might suffice for themselves without bothering to produce a surplus; nor would they furnish the necessary labour to allow Spaniards to develop industry and trade. But no Spaniard could afford to keep a permanent stake in the country unless he had the right to draw on the service of Indians, whether the latter liked it or not. Moreover, if his tenure could not be passed on to his heir, it was hardly worth his even trying to establish himself. Thus for religious, military and economic reasons the "perpetual" encomienda was vital for the future of New Spain.

The royal advisers were not responsive to pleas based on the now discredited theme of the alleged congenital faults of the Indians. On the economic issue, however, they were highly sensitive, for it would never have done for the King to lose revenue because the colonists were both becoming ruined and failing to make the country pay. It was also hard to refute the argument that to deprive the settler of all security of tenure for his heirs would be to paralyse his initiative. So it was decided once again to allow the immediate heir to inherit, thus limiting the span of the encomienda to two generations at the most. This grudging reversion to the *status quo* did not satisfy the colonists, but at least it prevented an explosion.

The official policy of treating the encomienda as an outmoded system was in fact quite sound, and was borne out by the development of more flexible forms of land ownership and use by Spaniards. Much more fundamental for the economy, and also for the whole relationship between Spaniards and Indians, was the adjustment of the labour problem. The Crown stuck to the provision in the New Laws preventing individuals from demanding labour service in lieu of tribute. It hankered after a wage-earning labour force which would be free to hire itself to the best bidder. The settlers, for their part, contended that it was impossible to rely on voluntary labour. Some method of compulsion was inevitable, they argued, in a country where the natives had been accustomed in pre-Columbian times to the performance of obligatory communal labour for a variety of masters, and where such service had always been considered compatible with the status of free peasants. As for the colonial government, it needed to recruit an unending supply of labour for building and public works, especially in and around the capital, and could not dispense, in the Aztec tradition, with full powers for the purpose. The Viceroy, therefore, found himself obliged to seek the best practical compromise between the principles of the New Laws, the interests of the settlers and the requirements of his own administration.

As Mendoza frequently pointed out, it was not possible to put the New Laws into force immediately and in their entirety without disrupting the economy. Nevertheless, by availing himself of the discretion which he persuaded the Council of the Indies to allow him over the timing and extent of the reforms, he brought about many salutary changes. Officials and ecclesiastics were obliged to surrender their encomiendas, carrier service was strictly regulated as regards hours of journeys, size of loads and rates of pay, quantities of slaves were set at liberty. Of course anomalies and abuses did not disappear but it became much more difficult for individuals to behave as little tyrants within their own jurisdictions. The most intractable problem of all, that of the disposal of Indian labour, came to a head after 1545 because the supply of Indians, which had so far remained relatively plentiful, was suddenly reduced by deadly outbreaks of the disease known as matlazáhuatl (probably typhus) recurring for four years in succession. So devastating was this plague that when it was over the government was forced to assume direct control of virtually the whole labour market. Thenceforth the dwindling supply of workers had to be rationed between the diverse claims on labour. Those of the administration tended to be given priority; then came those of the corregimiento and encomienda lands and of a new but important category of properties, individual Spanish farms on the European model employing hired farm labourers. Most of the latter grew wheat for the Spaniards of Mexico City. In such conditions the Council's well-meaning aspiration to end coercion of Indian labour could clearly not be realized. Instead, compulsion organized on practical and comparatively humane lines became a necessary function of government, and labour did not become available without governmental approval.

The procedure for mustering huge drafts of Indians for communal service on public works was inherited directly from Aztec practice and had been adopted since the earliest period of Spanish rule. There was also a strong pre-Columbian flavour about the new arrangements for the apportionment (repartimiento) of agricultural labour. It involved a close understanding between the Spanish officials in charge of the operations and the Indian officers in the small towns and villages. The workers had to be assembled, marched to their places of work, provided with implements, paid, assured of their proper rest time and finally dispersed to their communities when their stint was finished. Each draft worked for a fixed number of days and was succeeded by others in rotation, so that a man would not be expected to perform more than a fixed number of days of obligatory service in any one year. However the system evolved in practice, it was essentially an attempt to provide a fair solution for a problem which grew more troublesome as further shrinkages of population occurred. Originating under Mendoza, it was extended and regularized by his successor, Luis de Velasco, who took over the government in 1550.

The second seven years (1542–9) of Mendoza's viceroyalty were thus bedevilled by frictions over the New Laws as much as by the destructive epidemics, but with his usual calm skill he kept the unrest to the minimum. His tactful tolerance was valued by the colonists, but also frequently abused. A bad example of the persistently offending encomendero was the agent Salazar. His record of seriously maltreating his Indians extends over a quarter of a century and he was never brought to heel. Like all royal officials (and it is surprising enough that he succeeded in maintaining his status as such), he was required to surrender his profitable encomienda at Tepetlaoztoc, a small town on the road from Texcoco to Tlaxcala. But unlike most of his colleagues who complied with the law, Salazar elected to flout it and Mendoza forbore from removing him by force. Such leniency appears excessive, but the Viceroy preferred a rather tortuous policy of attrition to head-on collisions with influential settlers. Salazar continued with impunity to exact excessive tributes and to annex Indian lands and buildings. He expelled the local Indian lord and diverted the village water supply for the benefit of his private textile mill. All these activities were entirely illegal but remained unchallenged because the Indians, in their fatalistic way, had made up their minds that no remonstrances of theirs were likely to prevail in Mexico City against so powerful a patronage. It was a situation which could doubtless be paralleled in many parts of New Spain. Nevertheless the machinery for the elimination of abuses was becoming more efficient. When, for instance, Salazar died his son inherited his encomienda, but the Indians plucked up courage and took their grievances to the Audiencia. Thence the case was referred to the Council of the Indies and eventually the oppressed villagers of obscure Tepetlaoztoc won their suit. The younger Salazar was compelled to quit the illegally occupied properties, to accept a lower tribute and to relinquish control of local labour. Cases of this kind grew frequent, for as soon as the Indians found that redress could be obtained by litigation, both communities and individuals resorted freely to the courts.

The enforcement of justice for the benefit of the Indians was strengthened under the Velasco régime by the dispatch of inspectors to tour the country districts and smell out abuses. These visitadores, as they were called, or corregidores on a special mission, acted as circuit judges with extensive powers. They could free slaves, fix tributes and deprive holders of their encomiendas. Not unnaturally their activities were intensely unpopular with the encomendero class; nor were they always welcome to higher authority when the inspectors were thought to be showing excessive zeal. Such was the case of one Diego Ramirez, whose proceedings against two rich encomenderos at Metztitlán, a former bastion of Aztec rule on the rugged fringes of the Huaxteca, produced another legal *cause célèbre* which zigzagged like that of Salazar between Mexico and Spain. Although Ramirez had armed himself with specific authority from the Council of the Indies to investigate Metztitlán, and notwithstanding a ruling by the Council that there could be no appeal from his decisions to the Audiencia, the latter insisted on sending a judge of their own to the spot to carry out an independent enquiry, with the result that he not only declared Ramirez's inspection to be *ultra vires* but had him arrested. This high Spanish official was then publicly exhibited to the Indians of the district as a prisoner strapped to his horse. Released from this humiliation by Velasco's orders, he promptly sentenced the two men to lose their encomiendas, only to have his judgment eventually set aside by the Council at home on the Audiencia's advice.

In the latter case, therefore, it was the encomenderos who triumphed all along the line. The sufferings of the visitador were an early example of how overseas Spaniards were tempted to react to fussy interference by officials arriving straight from Spain with doctrinaire prejudices and no sympathy with local realities. It is interesting, however, to find the Audiencia siding with the encomenderos, because its members were drawn from the same high legal bureaucracy as the visitador and might normally have been expected to back him up. But oidores and inspectors did not always see eye to eye, for the former were themselves by no means immune from the "visita". Even Mendoza was investigated by Tello de Sandoval but emerged without a shadow of blame. Indeed no feature of early colonial history is more typical than the inordinate trouble wasted by senior lawyers and administrators, by the Council's orders, in checking and censoring each other's actions. We find the learned oidor Vasco de Puga, who compiled the first Cedulario or collection of colonial laws, deposed, together with one of his colleagues, after ten years of office by the visitador Valderrama, but returning subsequently with a commission to examine and deliver into custody another—and extremely noxious—visitador named Muñoz.

The Audiencia was the local repository of all experience of the affairs of New Spain and assured continuity in the administration. Its members were required to serve for long periods in the country. Francisco de Ceynos spent twenty-three years there altogether in the course of two separate appointments, and Alonso de Zorita, author of a penetrating critique of Spanish rule, ten years at one stretch, like Vasco de Puga. In general they could be relied upon to exercise sound and balanced judgment, without undue partiality for the interests of either settlers or Indians, although an individual oidor would take his own distinctive line; Zorita, for instance, was outstandingly liberal and pro-Indian. The system of checks on settlers by officials and by officials on each other obviously rebounded to the Indians' benefit. So did the Audiencia's preoccupation with the problem of adjusting tributes and repartimientos to the steep decline in the population and accompanying changes in economic patterns. Quite apart from the need to pay respect to their new status as free Christian subjects of the Crown, on which their rights under the New Laws were based, the natives could no longer be looked upon as a mere mass of expendable human units and recklessly squandered as in the early years of Spanish domination. Now scarcity had immensely enhanced the value of every able-bodied and taxable Indian, and to overload him with work and tribute began to be viewed not just as incidental injustice but as an economic blunder. If the competing claims of agriculture, the mines and workshops, the carrier service and the numerous public corvées were in future to be satisfied, common sense dictated that Indian affairs should be handled with special solicitude. The new Viceroy was worried by the prospect of falling revenues, of a chronic shortage of foodstuffs and of Spaniards losing their means of livelihood because there were not enough Indians to support them. At one time he was actually recommending a fresh distribution of encomiendas, but his proposals met with no sympathy in Madrid.

Much to its credit the colonial government did not lose its head when faced with the nightmarish results of the epidemics. Throughout the sixteenth century the Indians continued to be fatally susceptible to the plagues introduced from Europe—smallpox, measles, typhus and other not exactly identifiable diseases. These became endemic and at unpredictable intervals they flared up to a truly horrifying pitch of mortality. The worst periods were 1545–8 and 1576–81. Before the real nature and extent of the outbreaks were properly evaluated the so-called "black legend" of colonial rule made the atrocities committed by the conquerors responsible for the depopulation of the country as well as for all other aspects of Indian suffering. In recent years, however, a close study of tribute records surviving from before and after the Conquest has enabled researchers to establish with reasonable confidence just how precipitous the decline was from the estimated pre-Conquest level of population. According to the best founded calculation Moctezuma's dominions contained upwards of twenty-five millions in 1519 and Anáhuac alone about eleven million. But by 1565 the figure for the heartland had dropped by between sixty and eighty per cent and there was a decrease of at least another thirty per cent by the end of the century.

It may be that the deductions drawn from necessarily incomplete tribute assessments have been too sweeping. One suspects that the decline was by no means uniform in all areas and was much less sharp in regions which were remote, prosperous and less well documented. Also the population of Mexico City continued to rise as the gaps were filled from the surrounding country. However that may be, the overall estimates must be accepted as approximately accurate in default of more comprehensive evidence. The story they tell shocks us no less than if we had had it presented to us in vivid detail by some great writer of the period, as were the Black Death and the Plague of London. But the Mexican plagues inspired no literary masterpiece, and only occasional references in contemporary chronicles and official records throw a human light on the dreadful statistics. The mestizo historian Muñoz Chimalpahin provides all too brief glimpses of the capital in the grip of the plague, of Spanish regidores and physicians visiting the stricken quarters, of the distribution of medicines, wine, fresh fruit and vegetables to the sick and of ceaseless religious processions imploring divine intervention. The colonial authorities did their best to organize relief as well as to ease the burden of the successive calamities on the survivors. For example, in 1553 a new hospital was built by royal order in the city at a cost of two thousand gold pesos, and four hundred were budgeted for its annual maintenance; three years later a further sum of two thousand pesos was contributed by the treasury and it was expressly specified that the purpose of this foundation was to serve "poor Indians". It was part of a great philanthropic tradition which originated with Cortés's Hospital de la Concepción and can be traced through the more ambitious achievements of Vasco de Quiroga to a host of smaller institutions, public, monastic and private, all devoted to the care of the sick and poor.

Such widespread exercise of charity in the face of recurrent disasters helped to overcome the feeling of helpless misery generated by the epidemics and to forge links of sympathy, however frail, between conquerors and conquered. All the same one may wonder that New Spain could have endured such losses without suffering complete social disintegration and economic ruin. The truth is that the Indians never surrendered to apathy and despair; they kept their innate social discipline intact from one catastrophe to another. While the Spaniards were no worse affected by the diseases than if they had encountered them in Europe, the native population was pinned at the low level to which it was reduced about 1600 until nearly a century later, when it gradually resumed a normal rate of growth. Probably the increase in the mestizo element helped in the long run to build up the necessary measure of immunity.

The loss of approximately five-sixths of the total population of New Spain in eighty years is a stark fact which we can only register without trying to point a moral or impute blame. At a distance of four centuries we cannot easily grasp what the continuing crisis meant in terms of human suffering, and the cool fatalism with which it came to be accepted as part of the natural order of things is equally hard for us to understand. However, from a purely political point of view, the situation did help the Viceroys to enforce the New Laws in their two important aspects, the protection of the surviving Indians and the assertion of the royal authority against any challenge from disaffected colonists.

Now that there were so many fewer Indians, it was easier for the government to administer them and at the same time to alleviate their burdens. Although there was no question of their ceasing to be the underdogs, the opportunities for their exploitation by individual Spaniards were increasingly circumscribed by law, even if the law was often evaded or ignored. Under a strict Viceroy—and most of the sixteenth century Viceroys were men of energy and integrity—it was difficult to get away with malpractices. The authorities were especially concerned with preventing the revival of slavery in any form. One of the forms which it was apt to take was the illegal impressment of Indians in the workshops called obrajes, mostly small private factories for the manufacture of woollen cloth which had sprung up in the wake of the new sheep farms. It was the only considerable industry which flourished in the century after the Conquest. These establishments had originally been staffed by slaves or criminals condemned for minor offences. When the supply of slaves and prisoners ran short, free Indians began to be employed under contract with wages and hours fixed by law. In practice, however, the contracts were commonly disregarded by Spanish employers, who locked their workers into factories patrolled by negro guards, treating them no differently from the criminals they had replaced. In a memorandum written in 1589 for the benefit of his successor, the Viceroy Marqués de Villamanrique roundly denounces such behaviour. He mentions that employers were already resorting to what was in future years to become the classic method among owners of haciendas for turning their Indian peons into serfs, that is by encouraging them to contract debts which they could never redeem. Thus, says Villamanrique, they spent the rest of their lives in prison, without rest or pay. He goes on to describe the licensing system which he has introduced to control the abuse; he will not allow obrajes to be set up in Indian towns; they must be confined to the Spanish municipalities where the authorities can keep a watch on them; lists must be kept of all free Indians employed in them and regularly checked by a corregidor; wages must be paid in the presence of officials, and "other things directed towards the liberty of the Indians".*

A similar strain of rather fussy solicitude for the Indians runs through the viceregal pronouncements of this period. As regards the effectiveness of the official policy, Father Motolinía, with thirty years of experience behind him, was quite sure that it had justified itself by results. In 1555, while again living in his favourite Tlaxcala, he was moved to address a long letter to the King-Emperor himself in order to refute the wildly outrageous propaganda which Las Casas was still directing against the whole principle of Spanish overlordship in America, to say nothing of the excesses, real or alleged, of the overlords. The old friar was infuriated by what he regarded as the obtuseness and dishonesty of the Bishop of Chiapas in persisting in his denunciation of a state of affairs which had long ceased to prevail in New Spain and had indeed only prevailed there locally and for short periods. In any case he considered that Las Casas's acquaintance with viceregal Mexico was as superficial as his sweeping indignation was wide of the mark. His exaggerated attacks on the reformed encomenderos were pointless, and his impugnment of the vigour with which the authorities were applying the New Laws lacked all reasonable foundation. In Motolinía's eyes, too, he was guilty of even

* Text in *Historia Documental de Mexico*, Vol 1, University of Mexico, 1964.

graver calumny in casting doubt, if only by implication, on the purpose and success of the Mendicants' mission in New Spain. For a man who had devoted his whole career to creating a commonwealth in which Spaniards and Indians could live and work peaceably together, and had stood up to the Indians' real oppressors at great personal risk, it was particularly galling to find that roving trouble-maker Las Casas insinuating that for all those years he had been doing little better than condone the oppressors' acts.

But in his scathing counterblast to Las Casas the gentle Motolinía showed that he could match him in invective. He was astonished, he wrote, that Charles V had been able to put up for so long with such a boring, restless, importunate and obstreperous litigant in a religious habit, a man so badly brought up, so brazen, so abusive and so noxious. Zealous as he was in seeking out the bad while passing by the good, and in collecting piles of evidence, most of it spurious, against his fellow-Spaniards, Las Casas had never bothered to learn an Indian language to help him substantiate his accusations. He would not even pay the numerous Indians who carried his bundles of nonsense around New Spain, as everyone was now obliged to do by the regulations. As for the changes themselves, if one were to tot up all the most atrocious crimes committed in the whole of New Spain since its foundation, they would not be found to exceed those punished by law during a similar period in the city of Seville alone. Chiapas, on the other hand, had been "destroyed both temporally and spiritually" since Las Casas had been made its bishop. Worse still, he had resigned that bishopric without proper cause, and would be lucky to escape a charge of having abandoned to the wolves the souls entrusted to his care, and of having run away like a hireling and no true shepherd. In fact his conduct would be more correctly termed apostasy than resignation.

Motolinía goes on for page after page in this vein. The intensity of his indignation reveals how deep an aversion Las Casas was capable of inspiring even in the best type of Spaniard overseas. At home, when awakening the conscience of the Court and needling the government to reshape its colonial policies in accordance with humanity and justice, he was an incomparable power for good. In America, however, his incredible tactlessness and inability to recognize that reform is best achieved by compromise alienated his natural allies, such as the friars who had been working for decades among the Indians, besides irritating the normal run of colonists to the point of frenzy. Motolinía feared that his indiscriminate attacks on the encomenderos would upset the delicate balance of interests maintained by the early Viceroys. He was acting as if the dreadful conditions which he had encountered in the Santo Domingo of 1515 had been perpetuated in the New Spain of 1555. Since that was manifestly not the case, he was ignoring with a kind of perverse dishonesty, the changes for the better which he had himself promoted over so many years. At best he was wasting his ammunition on the wrong target for, as Motolinía pointed out, the greater part of the Indian population was now directly subject to the Crown and no longer held in encomienda. The remaining encomiendas existed only on sufferance. The Marqués del Valle, Don Sebastian Ramirez, president of the second Audiencia, and the Viceroy Mendoza had all governed excellently "the republic of Spaniards and Indians" and the Viceroy Velasco was continuing to do so. The Indians were moderately taxed, justly treated and spiritually well cared for under the existing dispensation and to deny the truth of this was a libel on the King's Councils and officers. To be sure, greedy and ill-intentioned persons were still to be found among the Spaniards of New Spain, but many more were merciful and generous in their dealings with the Indians, and it was ludicrous to lump them all together as rapacious brutes.

Having lived in Mexico since 1524, Motolinía was better qualified than most observers to judge whether the Spaniards in general had undergone a change of heart, or had at last realized that their true interest lay in handling their Indians gently. His character and record demand that his testimony be accepted. In the same letter to the King he remarked that the Indian peasant, for his part, had developed a very keen sense of what his rights were, as well as confidence that they would be upheld. Not only was the tribute at which he was assessed lower than that paid by a farm labourer in old Spain, but in no circumstances would he allow himself to be pushed into paying one farthing more. Again, no encomendero would dare to overcharge him by as much as a single cacao bean, because he knew that neither his confessor nor the magistrate would let him get away with it. The old oidor Ceynos, who arrived in the country six years after Motolinía and was still there and in office thirty-five years later, tells much the same story, adding that suits brought against encomenderos for bullying and tricking Indians, which used to occupy most of the Audiencia's time, had become very rare. Obviously malpractices did not suddenly stop short, but they were pared down till they became an exception rather than a habit. A typical example mentioned by the oidor Zorita, preoccupied as he was with the seamy side of Spanish domination, recalls the racket pursued by the hero of Gogol's "Dead Souls", who bought up dead Russian serfs and resold them at a profit. In New Spain a dishonest encomendero would inflate his tribute lists by failing to strike off the dead and infirm, and would continue to extract payments in their names.

At the same period encomenderos were bringing lawsuits against Crown officials and, ironically enough, native lords for filching their Indians and seizing the latter's lands. It is intriguing to find Bernal Díaz winning a case of this sort in his old age, after he had been permanently settled in Guatemala for about thirty years. His fighting days ended with Cortés's Honduran venture, from which he returned penniless and in rags to embark, like many of his kind, on a long struggle to obtain and hang on to sufficient encomiendas to support him in the leisured and dignified style which he considered to be worthy of an original conquistador. In that phase of his life he figures as the classic example of the rootless adventurer, eternally discontented with what he had and petitioning the authorities for more and more lucrative grants of Indians. There were no more treasures to be won from the Indies, but a man could still hope for a few well-stocked tributary villages.

For some reason Díaz did not wish to live in Anáhuac, the scene of his heroic exploits and sufferings. Perhaps he thought it was too near the seat of the central government. He plumped instead for the swampy and exuberant lowlands of the isthmus, where Spaniards were founding the town of Espiritu Santo by the mouth of the Coatzacoalcos river. There Cortés presented him with two villages in encomienda, and as a reward for his services in the subsequent conquest of Chiapas he received a second valuable grant of four hundred households in the neighbourhood of Chamula, a beautiful highland region of rocky peaks and thick pine forests. With two homes, one tropical and one semi-Alpine, Díaz should have been able to look forward to a life of affluent ease, but the authorities were capricious: what they gave with one hand they removed with the other. He soon lost enchanting Chamula, and when he got back from Honduras he found that half of his isthmus Indians had been taken from him. He was thus obliged to resume his hunt for encomiendas virtually from scratch.

He first tried for the region of Mexico City, but got nowhere. Then the government ruling in the interregnum between Cortés and the first Audiencia relented and granted him three further villages in the isthmus area. These, however, failed to satisfy him, and he bombarded the two successive Audiencias with one petition after another. The second sought to fob him off by appointing him visitador for Coatzacoalcos and Tabasco, but the career of an itinerant official evidently held no attraction for him. To his repeated requests for more Indians, first the Audiencia and then the Viceroy politely replied that they could do nothing for him without authority from Spain. Nothing daunted, Díaz crossed the Atlantic twice, in 1540 and again in 1550, to help plead the encomenderos' cause; he was particularly insistent on their keeping the right to bequeath their grants to their heirs. His efforts on his own behalf were successful in that the necessary authority to help him was sent to Mendoza and to Alvarado in Guatemala. Although the Viceroy remained obdurate and Alvarado was killed in the Mixtón rebellion, the latter's successor eventually produced three good Guatemalan villages for Díaz. But far from accepting them with gratitude, he was still protesting loudly against the inadequacy of the grant in letters addressed to the King in 1552 and 1553.

In these begging letters Díaz affects a querulous tone foreign to his usual manly style; he portrays himself as suffering penury and "weighed down" by children and grandchildren to whom he has nothing to bequeath. But this was a literary convention resorted to by practically all aspirants to encomiendas and other bounties. Out of the 1385 persons whose names are inscribed in a register of petitioners opened by Mendoza only a bare twenty refrained from crying extreme hardship. When the Mexican capital was full of Spaniards building themselves palaces and flaunting their newly acquired wealth in extravagant entertainments, such pleas did not ring true, and the authorities could afford to ignore most of them. Both in Mexico and Guatemala, however, they genuinely tried to give a measure of preferment to old Conquistadores, and despite his assertions to the contrary Díaz was undoubtedly one of the better favoured claimants. Married to the daughter of a rich and prominent settler, he was made a regidor of the city of Santiago de Guatemala and a legal document drawn in his old age describes him as exhibiting "much splendour and abundance of arms and horses and retainers, a very fine gentleman and servant of His Majesty". In other words he lived in lavish and thoroughly patriarchal style among the Indians who brought him a fat income.

It is not known exactly when he died, but it was probably at the beginning of 1584, and he would have been about ninety. His *True History of the Conquest of New Spain* was finished in 1568. It is strange that so great a writer as W. H. Prescott should have dismissed this splendid epic of human triumphs and disasters as a mixture of vanity and naiveté lacking literary merit. In reality Díaz possessed a wonderful flair for selective observation and a prodigious talent for description and character-drawing. His history is a subtle work of art—however artless he himself may have thought it—with an uncanny power of transplanting the reader through time and space into the Anáhuac of the Conquest and of convincing him of the essential veracity of the narrative. It is a masterpiece of the first order, whether it is regarded as a monument of the golden century of Spanish literature or the earliest work of genius written on American soil. The exceptional freshness of his memory enabled him to describe with astonishing vividness and accuracy events which had occurred thirty or forty years before he started to write. He only falters when the supply of dramatic reversals of fortune begins to run out. Perhaps he had difficulty in deciding at what point to bring his book to an end. It might have been more effective for him to cut his narrative short at the death of Cuauhtémoc and the departure of Cortés from Mexico in semi-disgrace than to extend it as he did into the early years of the viceroyalty. But his treatment of the aftermath of the Conquest is sketchy. He jumps from one topic to another without ever getting down to the task which he appears, from his frequent references to the theme, to have had very much in mind, namely that of preparing a full-scale *apologia* for the acts of the Conquistadors and for their presence among the Indians of the New World.

Intellectually he was not equipped for such an attempt. Nevertheless his text reveals a deep preoccupation with the arguments for and against the "perpetual" encomienda and with the general debate about the ethics of the Spanish treatment of Indians in which he personally had taken part in 1550 before the Council of the Indies at Valladolid, in the company of such formidable controversialists as Las Casas and Vasco de Quiroga. The latter, incidentally, shared Díaz's views and it was he who, as good lawyer as well as saintly bishop, put the encomenderos' case to the Council. Against the familiar denunciations of Las Casas they maintained that in "perpetual" encomienda the Indians would be better treated and instructed (the word used is "industriados") in the faith; that if they fell ill they would be tended like the settler's children and part of their tribute would be remitted. The settlers, if granted security of tenure from one generation to another, would devote proper care to growing crops and vines and to breeding cattle. Quarrels and lawsuits about Indians would cease; there would be no need for visitadores; peace and concord would prevail among the old soldiers if there were no longer any excuse for presidents of Audiencias and governors to remove their Indians and bestow them on their own relatives. Díaz's stubborn hope that the old Conquistadores, if not the later arrivals, would be permitted to found local dynasties supported by the same Indian communities was doomed to disappointment, for the government was determined to let the encomienda die as an institution, but that hope was founded on the conviction that the system he was fighting for was workable and in the best interests of both races in New Spain. Indeed he himself was making it work in Guatemala, where the conditions were essentially the same as in Anáhuac.

To illustrate his belief Díaz devotes one all-too-brief chapter to an impressionistic description of Indian life under Spanish tutelage, as it might be observed in the small towns and idyllic countryside of the Guatemala highlands. Although he is pleading a case, his picture is not over-idealized. He begins, like other contemporary writers, by stressing the real fervour with which the conquered have embraced their conquerors' religion.

THE LIMITS OF JUSTICE   245

The churches with their richly adorned altars, the magnificent silver plate and embroidered vestments, the services with their elaborate music, both choral and instrumental, the solemn processions on feast days, all bear witness to the ease and completeness with which the Indians have assimilated the thousand-year heritage of the Catholic church. However, while praising their devotion to the friars, he takes a side-swipe at the Spanish secular clergy, a race for whom he seems to have felt a particular aversion. Once the natives have experienced their avarice and malpractices, he writes, they will have nothing more to do with them, and will insist on having Franciscans and Dominicans for their parish priests. He ends his paragraph with the words "Oh how much there is to say on this matter, but it must stay in the ink-pot!" In former days Díaz had been brought face to face with the grimmer manifestations of pre-Columbian savagery. Twice, he records, he was rescued at the last moment from the clutch of Mexican warriors intent on dragging him to the sacrificial stone. He and his contemporaries who were living among the Indians in the fifties and sixties of the century interpreted their conversion and consequent mildness as a kind of miracle which in itself provided sufficient justification of the Conquest. Indeed they recognized that these peaceful and kindly people had developed a better idea of what Christianity was really about than many of their would-be mentors.

In another striking passage Díaz reminds his readers that the Indians under Spanish rule were not merely a nation of docile drudges, but had to a large extent remained responsible for internal government and the administration of justice within their own communities. Each year, he says, they elect their municipal officers, who meet twice weekly in the town hall to hear both civil and criminal cases and to impose sentences for debt and minor offences, while murders and other serious charges are referred by them to the Audiencia, or if that is impracticable to the Indian gobernador. When the municipal councils meet, say in Tlaxcala or Texcoco, Cholula, Huejotzingo, Tepeaca and other large towns (here Díaz's imagination strays from Guatemala to Anáhuac itself), the gobernadores and mayores walk in procession escorted by mace-bearers with gilded maces, just like the Viceroy. At their assizes they pronounce judgment with as much decision and authority as Spaniards; they take pride in their work and carefully study the laws of the realm.

Continuing, Díaz gives a fascinating sketch of those Indian lords who had adopted Spanish traits. He claims that all such lords are rich; they own horses with fine saddles and trappings, and when they ride out through the towns and take their pleasure in the country they are attended by pages and servants. In some places they go tilting and fighting bulls, especially on the feasts of Corpus Christi, of St John and St James and of the Assumption. Many face the strongest bulls and are excellent horsemen—more particularly at a village called Chiapa de los Indios.

Díaz does not say how these upper class Indians managed to live in such style, whether in Anáhuac, Chiapas or Guatemala, but clearly those who survived the wars and epidemics were well provided for and had a reasonable chance of keeping their status and property intact. The resources which assured their affluence came from lands owned by them directly or exploited for their support by Indian villages under their jurisdiction, in the same way as Spanish encomenderos were supported by their communities. As the century progressed, the population declined and was regrouped and encomiendas fell in, much land simply became vacant and private owners occupied it. Most of the latter were Spaniards, who acquired the land by viceregal grant, by direct and legal purchase or by pressure and intimidation. They were more enterprising and less scrupulous than either the encomenderos or the survivors from the Indian tlatoque and noble families. Thus Indian lands, both private and communal, were always in danger of being encroached upon, especially if they were fertile and conveniently situated. However there was plenty to go round, and even Indians took advantage of the existing opportunities for getting hold of landed property. Some of them in turn intermarried with whites and mestizos and were absorbed into the hacendado class which grew up after the turn of the century.

Díaz is full of enthusiasm for the speed and facility with which the Indians learned European crafts and trades. Although he does not say so, this was the more admirable because the early Spanish immigrants cannot have included a large percentage of artisans capable of acting as their instructors. Nevertheless the first generation of Spanish-trained native craftsmen were already proficient in a wide range of trades, producing silks and embroideries, lace, woollen cloth and European garments, hats, leather goods including gloves, shoes and saddlery, iron tools, swords, exquisite jewellery and gold and silver work of European design. The technical revolution which plucked them out of the Stone Age took a decade or two at the most, and subsequently there was nothing that a Spaniard made that an Indian could not make too. Since native craftsmanship was fully approved of and encouraged, for obvious economic reasons, by the government, it created a large class of ingenious and independent Indian workmen earning a good living from their special skills, for there was a high demand for their products from the extravagant and competitive Creole society. These artisans formed the most stable element in the Indian community. With their ability to bargain freely for the price of their labour, their condition was greatly superior to that of the peasants, bound as they were to the soil and subject to the corvée, although they too were learning to plough with oxen and plant new trees and crops. The artisans fared no worse, and occasionally better, than the tolteca of the preceding age whose talents they inherited. Díaz, Motolinía and others were right in pointing to them as a happy and flourishing feature of colonial life, but it was one which perhaps owed more to the innate Indian genius than to alien inspiration.

Old Conquistadores of the type of Díaz, who had fought alongside Indians against Indians and had afterwards settled among them, claimed to understand their minds and feelings and to sympathize with their needs. They were genuinely indignant with critics who insisted that their wards were not receiving a square deal, and they were apt to resent the liberalism of Crown policy because it seemed calculated to upset their own position without necessarily furthering Indian interests. The friars, whose whole mission was to the Indians, saw things from a rather different point of view, but reached a roughly similar conclusion. Their own record was clean; they had brought into being a whole new Christian people, protected it successfully against oppression and taught it the useful arts. As a result it was no worse and probably better off than most peasant peoples in Europe in respect of the burdens which it had to bear. With no illusions about the faults of their own countrymen, the friars did not accept Las Casa's sweeping condemnation of the whole colonial system, the "Black Legend" according to which the Indians were sunk in total misery. While quick to denounce outrages, they were quite prepared to tolerate the encomienda so long as the encomenderos behaved themselves and were subjected to proper controls. Few of them would have dismissed Díaz's sketch as a distortion of reality.

The civil lawyers responsible for carrying out Crown policy looked at Indian problems from yet another angle. These were the men who staffed the Audiencia, heard the interminable court cases, carried out the arduous visitas and drew up the tribute assessments. As the Spanish empire spread through the American continent the lawyer-administrators multiplied until they formed a select overseas civil service. As graduates of the Spanish law schools, they had received much the same humanist education as the friars, and like the friars, once they had started on a career in the Indies, they were in it for their working lives. Nerve-wracking journeys in harsh climates took them from one Audiencia to another on a succession of exhausting and even dangerous duties, as they wrangled with violent colonists or investigated the conduct of members of their own profession in the capacity of jueces de residencia. Punctilious, highly conscious of the dignity of their office and persons, obstinate and uncompromising in controversy, not always responsive to common sense or inclined to charity, they were nevertheless distinguished by their integrity and incredible industry. The visitador Ramirez, whose misadventures at Metztitlán have already been mentioned, was a typical representative of his class. In the oidor Alonso de Zorita we find the scrupulousness of a royal official tempered by an unusual generosity of heart.

When Zorita reached Mexico he had already spent eight strenuous years in the Indies. Beginning as an oidor in Santo Domingo, he was then ordered to undertake a difficult mission as juez de residencia in Nueva Granada (Colombia), where the settlers, in league with a corrupt Audiencia, were resisting the application of the New Laws. There he met with every conceivable obstruction and was finally obliged to quit Nueva Granada in a hurry, narrowly escaping arrest by the colonists and death at the hands of the wild forest Indians, who ambushed the boats carrying him and his party down the Magdalena river to the coast. Nevertheless his ordeal stirred the Council of the Indies into sending out a new juez with wider powers, who reduced the province to order, and Zorita was judged to have acted bravely and correctly. He had scarcely returned to Santo Domingo when he was appointed an oidor in Guatemala, where he spent three useful years supervising the execution of the New Laws under the guidance of a sympathetic president of the Audiencia. At that period the royal policy of curtailing the powers of the encomenderos was being strictly enforced and Zorita, a keen upholder of Indian rights, encountered much opposition in the course of his tours of inspection. However, he appears to have been on good terms with Bernal Díaz and to have respected him for his honesty and moderation. At any rate the old man allowed him to read his unfinished History.

In 1556 Zorita was transferred to New Spain, where Velasco was Viceroy. The Mexican Audiencia's time was largely consumed by the complicated task of reassessing the tributes, the collection of which had fallen into confusion as a result of the prolonged epidemics of the late forties. It was necessary to find out how many assessable Indians were left, how much they were capable of paying and whether the encomenderos were getting too great a share of the tributes. All these questions demanded urgent investigation, but the answers were not easy to come by. Indians were hard to count; at the approach of royal officials they were apt to melt away into the hills, while lists furnished by encomenderos or by their own gobernadores were more than often faked. Fewer Indians meant less tribute, and the Viceroy was under instructions not to overtax the survivors, but at the same time the Crown, always short of money at home, was pressing for larger revenues from overseas. There was really no way out of the dilemma, although the revenue might be boosted marginally by cancelling the exemptions enjoyed by certain Indian communities on account of their special services to the Crown, and by cutting down the size and number of encomiendas.

Both these expedients were adopted during the sixties, when the taxation system was thoroughly overhauled and tightened up. But while the authorities took immense trouble to get the assessments right, to spread the burden as equitably as possible and to prevent the falsification of lists and other abuses, the inevitable result of the fiscal reform was to squeeze the tributaries more harshly than before. Under the old system inherited from the Aztec past the Indians had paid their tribute in kind from the produce of lands worked in common for that purpose; now the individual, not the community, became the tributary and he had to pay part of his tribute in cash, although maize was also acceptable. The average individual contribution paid by a peasant was one silver peso plus about a bushel of maize. It must be remembered that a money economy had only been introduced into New Spain after 1535, when the first colonial mint was set up and the currency standardized, but the circulation of the coinage among the poorer Indians remained restricted.

These changes were lengthily debated by Velasco with his oidores and by correspondence with the Council of the Indies. Zorita was not in sympathy with them and fought hard against the tendency to increase and regularize the load on the Indians. He wanted a more humane and flexible system, less susceptible to abuse and more in keeping with native tradition, and he was full of ideas as to how one could be worked out for the benefit of the Indians and with no injury to the real interests of the Crown, or even of the encomenderos whom he disliked as a class. He was particularly opposed to a uniform tax in money, insisting that except in towns where money could easily be earned tribute should be raised in the forms of the typical produce grown in the region, while assessments should take account of the relevant factors such as population and fertility. When the total assessment for a given district had been made by Spanish inspectors, after consultation with Indian leaders, it should be left to the latter to apportion deliveries of produce among individuals according to their capacity to pay. The officials, oidores and others concerned with assessments should confine themselves to that work and not undertake judicial functions, and their recommendations should be endorsed by the Audiencia and frequently reviewed. Zorita also held strong views about the need to simplify judicial procedure for the Indians and to reduce their obligations for forced labour.

Although he was much esteemed by the Viceroy and his views were upheld by the heads of three Orders of friars, Zorita felt that the current was against him. After two years service he was sufficiently disillusioned to ask permission to return to Spain on grounds of ill-health. It was not granted, but his spirits revived when he became absorbed in a quixotic project for pacifying the Chichimecs beyond the settled frontier. The northward expansion of silver mining had provoked incessant clashes with these nomads, and their attacks on the silver trains were countered by slaughter and slave-raiding. In conjunction with an elderly friar named Fray Jacinto de San Francisco, whose first contact with Mexico had been in 1518 as a member of Grijalva's almost forgotten venture, Zorita conceived a scheme for taming the Chichimecs by methods of kindness and persuasion such as had been employed by Las Casas in dealing with the recalcitrant Indians of a small province in Guatemala—indeed the only real success scored by Las Casas in that kind of endeavour.

They planned an expedition which, although protected by soldiers, would scrupulously avoid aggression, in the hope that its leaders would manage to convince the tribesmen of the advantage of settling in towns and taking up agriculture under the tutelage of royal officials and friars. Encomiendas would not be permitted and no trouble would be required for a number of years. In a letter to King Philip II, Zorita proposed that he himself should be appointed Governor of the existing province of Nueva Galicia, huge enough as it was, with *carte blanche* to extend it indefinitely into tribal territory. The future security of the mines; and the addition of a vast new settled area to New Spain, would amply compensate the Crown for the initial expense involved.

Not unnaturally this was too much for the Council of the Indies to swallow, and the project was turned down. Apart from the immodesty of Zorita's personal claims, the Council could hardly be blamed for thinking that the approach used by a Vasco de Quiroga or a Las Casas to the village folk in Michoacán and Guatemala was not likely to produce the right results among the ferocious nomads. So frontier warfare continued as usual until the government gradually settled the territory by bringing in agricultural Indians from the south. As for Zorita, he again sought leave to resign his post, and this time he was allowed to retire to Spain. The rest of his life he devoted to writing books, including a compilation of laws relating to the Indies and a painstaking history of the conquest and conversion of New Spain drawn from contemporary sources. A much more original and interesting work is his *Brief and Summary Relation of the Lords of New Spain*. Under this somewhat misleading title Zorita described in straightforward language the condition of the Indians, as he viewed it, under Spanish rule, compared it with their condition before the Conquest and set out his own ideas, for consideration by the King, for reforming the administration and preventing injustice. The book takes the form of a series of answers to a questionnaire circulated in 1553 by the Council of the Indies to all Audiencias and designed to elicit the necessary information for working out a fair and uniform tributary system. As Zorita explained, he had left the Audiencia of Guatemala too early to contribute to its official reply and the report from Mexico had already been despatched before he reached his new post.

The general run of Spanish officials serving in Mexico were strict and rather cranky legalists conscientiously performing their duties, often at the cost of considerable hardships. They had no hesitation in slapping down the settlers when royal policy so required, but felt scant sympathy, either cultural or humanitarian, towards the Crown's native subjects. Zorita, however, developed an intense interest in Indian life and the Indian past. It is unlikely that he learned Náhuatl, but from what he reveals in his history and the *Relation* he sought out the company of those who were most deeply versed in Indian antiquities, including Sahagún and Motolinía. He quotes at length from a collection of maxims called "huehuetlatolli" (Speeches of the elders) made by a third Franciscan expert, Fray Andres de Olmos. He picked up a wide knowledge of the history and social system of the Aztecs, and some of this was clearly derived at first hand from Indian sources.

But Zorita was carried away by enthusiasm for his studies and by his profound compassion. The picture he paints of the Aztec world is that of a nation basking in peaceful harmony under its "natural lords", of a Golden Age, both simple and sophisticated, in which benevolent aristocrats dispensed justice to contented macehualtin and all classes shared in a common prosperity. In his eagerness to make his contrast between past happiness and present miseries as sharp as possible he purposely ignores the perpetual warfare, the horrific religion and the tight compulsions of a hierarchical society. Nevertheless anyone who had seen Anáhuac in its prime would have recognized the truth behind his exaggerations. Curiously enough, he cherished the romantic notion that pre-Columbian Mexico owed its contentment and good order to the enlightened rule of its "natural lords", by which he meant the whole Indian upper class from the three supreme tlatoque downwards. He insisted that the evils which later oppressed the Indians, and continued to perplex the Viceroys, could all have been avoided if the control of Indian affairs had only been left in the hands of the traditional leaders. This was certainly an arguable thesis, but we now know that Aztec society was a much more complex affair than Zorita suspected, and that the upper class was more like an aristocracy of service than a benign feudal nobility. Where he went wrong was in his idealization of the role of the "natural lords" after the Conquest.

> When New Spain was conquered by the Spaniards [he wrote] this mode of government of the natives was retained and continued for some years. Moctezuma alone lost his kingdom and dominion, which were vested in the Crown of Castile. Some of his towns were given in encomienda to Spaniards. All the other lords of provinces, both those who were subject to him and those who were independent, including the rulers of Texcoco and Tacuba, possessed, ruled and governed their lands, but they did so as representatives of Your Majesty or of encomenderos. These lords did not have as much land or as many vassals as they once had, but the people brought them tribute of produce and other things before the Conquest, and they were obeyed, feared and respected. The towns they retained also brought them tribute to give to Your Majesty and the encomenderos. Each ruler appointed persons to collect this tribute; and Your Majesty's officials in the Crown towns and the encomenderos in other towns received the tribute from the ruler. Thus the ancient dignity of the rulers was preserved . . . Under the old system of government the whole land was at peace. Spaniards and Indians alike were content, and more tribute was paid with less hardship, because government was in the hands of the natural lords . . . The natural lords cherish and support their vassals, for they love them as their own, as their inheritance from their forebears . . . They seek to ease their vassals' burdens, treat them like their own children, defend and protect them. Of such lords but a very few remain.

Zorita's imaginative account of an ideal Aztec commonwealth outliving the Conquest, with the "natural lords" still in the ascendant, did not of course square with the facts. It depicted things as they should have been, in his eyes, rather than as they were in that turbulent period. He may have thought that the very simplicity of his thesis would incline the king and his Council to accept it and to introduce the equally simple reforms which he proposed. He bitterly condemned the government's mistake in allowing the authority of the "natural lords" to be eroded by corrupt officials, grasping encomenderos, dishonest mestizos and native upstarts, to the detriment of all social harmony and with the result that the common people were reduced to penury and could not meet the demands made on them. But he believed that it was not too late to stop the rot and revive the old order.

The essential reform would be to entrust the collection of tribute, the drafting of labour and the organization of all services performed by natives for Spaniards solely to the Indian leaders. The latter, including the gobernadores and all other Indian officials, would have to be carefully selected, if possible from the families of the former lords, and proper provision would have to be made for their maintenance in suitable style and dignity. Once well provided for, and protected against intimidation and intrigue, they would have no incentive either to cheat the Spaniards of their due or to grind down their own people. The middlemen who at present bullied and defrauded the Indians would be eliminated, and the Indians would have no need to resort to ruinous litigation in vain attempts to assert their rights.

Zorita professed complete confidence that his reform would redress the abuses which were causing so much misery among the Indians, but his insistence on the necessity for regular checks and inspections by oidores suggests that he was not too sure that Indian lords would prove trustworthy in practice. His idea was that oidores not engaged on judicial business in the capital should spend all their time on tour, reviewing assessments, making themselves familiar with local conditions or conducting a "residencia", which meant that they would be enquiring formally into the affairs of a town or province and hearing in public grievances against persons in authority, whether Spaniards or Indians. This method of inspection, he

THE LIMITS OF JUSTICE

thought, was preferable to the occasional "visita", which was intended to be a secret procedure and was often carried out by an official who did not know the country.

The style of the *Brief Relation* was easy and persuasive. New Spain, it suggested, was ripe for the millennium if only His Majesty would give the right orders. It did not throw doubt, in the manner of Las Casas and for religious or philosophical reasons, on the right of Spaniards to rule over Indians, but showed the Spaniards the way to make their subjects contented with no sacrifice on their part. But like so many other memorials on American affairs, it was drowned in the mass of paper flowing into the Council of the Indies and remained, if not unread, certainly unheeded by higher authority. It did not appear in print until 1840, when a first edition was prepared from a defective copy, and the original manuscript was dug out of the royal library at Madrid as late as 1909. However, even if it did eventually reach King or Council, it had already become a historical curiosity, outdated by the violent and tragic events of 1564–7 which engulfed Viceroys, oidores and Creoles and were in full swing before Zorita actually left New Spain.

In 1564 Luis de Velasco died at his post. He was as fond of his Indians as Zorita and his concern for them during the fifteen years of his viceroyalty is attested by a series of judgments upholding their rights against Creoles. The vigour which he displayed on their behalf does not indeed bear out Zorita's marked pessimism about their plight. But shortly before his death the Viceroy was to all intents and purposes superseded by the visitador Jerónimo de Valderrama, who came out with a mandate to tighten the screw on the tributaries. A harsh bureaucrat, he proceeded to increase Indian assessments. He dismissed two oiodores, Puga and Villanueva, who disagreed with his policy, and no doubt would have got rid of Zorita too had he not already resigned.

The untimely irruption of the visitador, and the Viceroy's subsequent death, had an unsettling effect on the Creoles, resentful as they were of Velasco's squeeze on the encomenderos. Disaffection crystallized round Martín Cortés, the second Marqués del Valle, and two rich Creoles, the brothers Alonso de Avila and Gil González de Benavides. Don Martín, Hernán Cortés's legitimate heir, had spent his early youth at the

Spanish court and campaigned with King Philip in France. In 1562 he decided to return to Mexico and make good his titles to the enormous properties of the marquisate, which contained at the time more than sixty thousand tribute-paying Indians. In spite of the Viceroy's suggestion that the Cortés fief was much too large and that some of its valuable encomiendas should be forfeited, Don Martín's claims were confirmed by the King. He was a weak man, utterly different in character from his father, but pretentious and impressionable, and the semi-regal state which his riches enabled him to affect in New Spain went to his head. He behaved with studied insolence to Velasco and listened readily to the complaints from encomenderos whose position was threatened by the curtailment of their grants.

Creole opinion was by no means unanimously inclined towards a conspiracy, but the strong group of malcontents led by Alonso de Avila believed that the moment was ripe for overthrowing the rule of Madrid and the viceregal government with its awkward scruples about Indians and its coolness towards American-born Spaniards. The visitador was apparently intent on harassing the Indians instead of themselves and the three remaining oidores who constituted the government had no armed force to suppress a really determined coup. Above all, Don Martín seemed to be an excellent candidate for the crown of an independent New Spain.

If the uprising had taken place, it might initially have succeeded. Whether the majority of Creoles and Spaniards in the country, to say nothing of the Indians, would have acquiesced in it is another question. Nor would Philip II have tamely accepted so tremendous a rebuff, for all the difficulties of mounting an expedition across the Atlantic. In the event, however, the rebellion, timed for December 1565, never broke out. Martín Cortés was not cast for the role of a George Washington. He took fright at the last moment and refused to commit himself, with the result that the other conspirators' nerve began to fail, many sympathizers withdrew their support and the plot was inevitably denounced to the oidores. Wisely enough the latter, who included the old and experienced Ceynos, did not act in a hurry. They waited until Valderrama had returned to Spain, the props of the conspiracy had further rotted and they themselves had amassed all the evidence they

Monastery Church at Huejotzingo. 16th century

Monastery Church at Tecamachalco. 16th century

Monastery Church at Acolman. 16th century

needed. Finally, on July 16th, 1562, they struck. The magnificent Don Martín was arrested. So were his two brothers Luis, the illegitimate son of a Spanish woman, and the mestizo son of Doña Marina, also called Martín, a Knight of Santiago and husband of a noble Spanish lady. So were Avila, his brother and all the leaders of the plot. No one offered the slightest resistance.

The Avila brothers were promptly put to death. Pending the arrival of the new Viceroy, Gaston de Peralta, Marqués de Falces, no further capital punishment was inflicted, but several conspirators and suspects were kept in prison while preparations were made to try the Cortés brothers. When he reached Mexico Peralta was all for leniency and reconciliation; he commuted to banishment a suspended death sentence passed on Luis Cortés; then he dispatched the Marqués del Valle and certain other incriminated persons to Spain with orders to present themselves to the Council of the Indies. He reported that good order prevailed in the colony and recommended that further proceedings against Creoles should be dropped. All Mexico expected an amnesty. The Viceroy's advice did not, however, prevail. Exactly how it came to be rejected is obscure, because the accounts of the drama which have come down to us reflect the Creole point of view and are violently prejudiced against the oidores. But it is clear that these three lawyers, understandably proud of having mastered a very serious threat to the royal supremacy in New Spain, were furious with Peralta for handling traitors so softly. They were convinced that the Creoles deserved a much sharper lesson. So in their own reports to Spain they sought to discredit the Viceroy and demanded sterner measures. According to the story current in Creole circles, they contrived that the Viceroy's dispatches should miss their ship at Vera Cruz, so that the Audiencia's case was the only one to be presented to the King. Whether this tale was true or not, Philip's reaction was to appoint a new trio of judges, under the presidency of Alonso Muñoz, to take over the government of the colony, with authority over the existing Audiencia. The Viceroy was recalled to Madrid.

The new rulers could not have been worse chosen. In the over-heated atmosphere of Mexico City Muñoz entirely lost his mental balance and unleashed a reign of terror reminiscent of the worst judicial butcheries of the age of the Tudors and the

Valois. Scores of Creoles were beheaded, quartered and garotted: many were subjected to the rack and water tortures, and it is related that the half-Indian Martín Cortés, the bastard, endured his ordeal with exceptional stoicism worthy of a Cuauhtémoc. The ferocity displayed by the royal agents was especially horrifying because it was so uncharacteristic of a viceregal government which, by contemporary standards, had always treated both whites and Indians with unusual mildness. Although their tormentors were backed by the minimum of armed force, the Creoles tamely submitted to being crushed. More than two centuries were to go by before successful revolutions in British America and in France emboldened them to break loose—and even then with reluctance—from the Spanish monarchy.

Meanwhile the cries of despair which reached the King from Mexico convinced him that he had made a ghastly mistake. His remedy was not to send back Peralta, but to restore to office Puga and Villanueva, the oidores dismissed three years previously by the visitador Valderrama, with instructions to arrest Muñoz and his colleague and deport them from New Spain. The reinstated pair dutifully recrossed the ocean and carried out the royal commands, thus putting an end to the carnage. The wheel had turned full circle, and New Spain was again governed by the same Audiencia as in the good old days of Viceroy Velasco. In due course a new Viceroy, Martín Enriquez de Almansa, made his appearance. He was a proconsul of the same stamp as Mendoza and Velasco, tolerant, prudent and determined to bring peace to strife-torn Mexico. Like Mendoza, he went on to govern Peru after a long spell in New Spain.

The lesson of the lurid events of 1564–7 was that only a firm and experienced Viceroy, enjoying full discretion and unhampered by interfering officials from Spain put in to supervise him, was competent to control discordant tendencies in the colony. He was the sole qualified and impartial judge of how the interests of Creoles and Indians, the claims of the Church, the exigencies of the home government and the pretentions of its local agents, the lawyer-officials, could be balanced and reconciled. When his hand was removed from the tiller, the caravel veered erratically off course. The Creoles entertained extravagant dreams of separatism and the lawyers, acting no longer as the Viceroy's subordinates, indulged in an orgy of vindictive repression. The Church was powerless to check the cruelties perpetuated by Spaniards against men of their own race while the Indians, impassive spectators of the conflict, could only pray that when their masters had ceased to cut each other's throats, the principles of colonial rule upheld by a Zorita might eventually prevail.

The Indians watched, but kept their emotions to themselves. References to the conspiracy by native writers are rare and laconic. One comes from a Xiuhámatl or *Book of the Years*. Such chronicles were summary records of events which were regularly compiled by official scribes before the Conquest and were kept up by individuals writing in Náhuatl for many decades afterwards. The entry reads: "9 Rabbit. 1566 (the year is given in both the Mexican and the European calendars). On the 16th July, Tuesday, the Marquess, Alonso Dávila and his younger brother were taken and imprisoned. And Alonso Dávila and his younger brother, Don Pedro González, died on 3rd of August. Those imprisoned numbered nineteen."

The execution is also mentioned in the diary of a certain Juan Bautista, a minor Indian official employed as a tribute collector. He was an entertaining character who formed his record of the sixties not in the dry, clipped style of the Aztec chronicles but in a lively, personal and almost journalistic vein. At his best he sounds like an Indian Samuel Pepys, but for this occasion he abandons his usual chatty manner for something more solemn. This is all he says:

> Today Saturday, the 3rd of August 1566, Alonso Dávila and his elder [*sic*] brother, Gil Gonzalez Dávila, were beheaded. Precisely as the Ave Maria sounded they were killed. It was two days before the Feast of Saint Dominic. And their heads stayed for six days fixed to the pole of the scaffold, and on Friday, at the first light, they came to take them down; they went to bury their bodies at Saint Augustine's, on the eve of the Feast of Saint Lawrence.

The Indians did not waste epitaphs on rebellious encomenderos.

Part V

THE SEARCH FOR FUSION

Chapter 10

THE FRUSTRATIONS OF LEARNING

IN HIS AUTHORITATIVE study of the Indians of the Valley of Mexico under Spanish rule, the American scholar Charles Gibson says: "The most evident changes in Indian society took place during the first forty or fifty years [after the Conquest]. This was the time when Indian peoples, or some of them, met the Spanish influence part way and reached positive degrees of cultural accord" (*The Aztecs under Spanish Rule*).

The first steps towards a synthesis of the two cultures were taken while Cortés was still master of Anáhuac. It was then that the principal survivors from the native ruling class were being baptized, that Pedro de Gante was beginning to educate their children and that the Twelve Franciscans were planning their programme of mass conversion. Despite political difficulties the movement gathered pace in the twenties and thirties and reached its highest point during the viceroyalties of Mendoza and Velasco. To quote Gibson again:

> in many ways the mid-sixteenth century was the period of greatest harmony in Indian-Spanish relations. The immediate stresses of the post-Conquest period had ended, and a new generation of Indian leaders, schooled by friars and not yet disillusioned by Spanish exploitation, had come into being. Spaniards of the middle sixteenth century showed more respect for Indian civilization, and Indian leaders more respect for Spanish civilization, than at any other time.

To assert that in the early years Indian receptivity was matched by Spanish open-mindedness implies no insensitivity towards the tragedies and horrors of the Conquest. As soon as the flames had died down and the ruins were being cleared away, both sides were ready for a rapprochement. The Conquest coincided with the flowering of liberal and humanist attitudes in Spain. These were widely diffused among the

Mendicant Orders and the lawyer class which became respectively responsible for the religious and civil government of New Spain before the establishment of the viceroyalty. Pedro de Gante, the Twelve, Vasco de Quiroga, Zumárraga, Garcés, Sahagún, Motolinía and many other personalities who devoted their lives to New Spain were conspicuous examples of an intellect which managed to combine the deep learning of the Renaissance with a fervent sense of Christian mission and the strictest principles of their calling with an imaginative and flexible approach to Mexican problems. These men recognized that the Indian genius was ready to be released from its neolithic straitjacket and, if properly cultivated and protected during the period of its adaptation to European modes of thought and expression, was capable of reaching great heights. They were eager to communicate to the Indians a share of the ferment in their own minds, a measure of their own extraordinary intellectual energy.

Unlike those fiery spirits, the plain soldiers who formed the majority of the Conquistadores had hardly emerged from their mediaeval shell. However, the social order which they had left behind them in Spain was not utterly different from that which they found among the Aztecs. Both were strictly hierarchical. Even the complex Aztec religious organization presented a grotesque parallel with the Catholic Church. In Anáhuac as in mediaeval Europe the economy was based on serf agriculture, with the macehualtin performing the same role as the European peasants (except that the macehual enjoyed more liberties and his rights were more scrupulously respected). As the social ladder ascended, the tolteca corresponded to the European guild craftsmen and the pochteca to the merchant associations. As regards the upper class, no one conversant with the highest grades of feudalism would see anything unfamiliar in the Aztec division into the tlatoque or minor sovereigns, the tetecuhtin or nobility and the pipiltin or gentry. The Spanish soldiers, however humble their origin at home, liked to regard themselves as hidalgos in New Spain, and were at first ready enough to consort on equal terms with the members of the tecuhtli class, whom they termed "grandes Senores" or "Señores naturales", once the latter had been baptized and had accepted the King-Emperor as their sovereign. As for the Indians in general, they saw little strange in the structure of native society, shorn of its obvious exoticisms. The idea that they were an inferior or only semi-human race, by reason of their brown skin or essential otherness, was a legacy from Caribbean experience. In New Spain, though discouraged by the Spanish élite, it survived in the diluted form of a vague but obstinate prejudice against the subject race and a convenient excuse for excluding Indians from offices and advantages.

The ordinary Spaniard felt no aversion for the Indians so long as they had abandoned the cruel and ugly practices of their religion. He was, however, apt to despise them for their meekness and apparent lack of spirit, and such contempt stimulated the worst instincts of bullying brutes like Nuño de Guzmán. The typical Spanish attitude was not callous but lazy; the settler could indeed afford to patronize in a kindly way the people who supported him by the product of their labour. But the cultural advancement of the Indian did not interest him, and in the second and third generations, when he had ceased to be a Spaniard and become a Creole with a thoroughly colonial outlook, he was all the more unsympathetic to the development of a meaningful association between the two races on the basis of equality on any social level. It was left for the mestizo, whose roots were embedded in the past of both continents, slowly to build the bridges which were not completed until modern times. All progress towards a close "cultural accord" that was achieved in the sixteenth century stemmed from a small group of peninsular Spaniards and petered out when the supply of such men was not replenished from the homeland. The atmosphere of increasing bigotry and conformity which characterized the reign of Philip II cast a chill which withered the bold initiatives of the preceding decades.

If those initiatives eventually proved abortive, there is no doubt that they started under the most promising auspices. Their authors were surprised and delighted by the rapid changes in Indian life brought about by the Conquest and the conversion. While the people's habits and outlook remained fundamentally Indian, they also acquired in many respects a pemanently Hispanic tinge. The revolution in their religious belief was especially significant and it would be wrong to assume that it simply cloaked a basic adherence to paganism.

The Indians' acceptance of Christianity was sincere and in general wholehearted, though they imparted to it a peculiar colour of their own. As Jacques Soustelle observes of their modern descendants, their "religion is not that of their ancestors covered over with a superficial gloss, any more than it is the Christianity of Europe. It is an original synthesis" (*The Daily Life of the Aztecs*).

European influence modified the Indians' life throughout without transforming it. It widened their moral and material horizons, affecting to a greater or lesser degree how they behaved and reacted, how they worked and played, how they sowed, planted, ate, dressed and spoke. At the popular level two currents of civilization joined and were blended. It was a process which the friars, as the chief agents of the change, tried carefully to control, for they wanted their converts to be Christian Indians, not imitation Europeans. Wherever they had their own way in shaping society, they were insistent that it should retain its indigenous character.

While the Indian masses were acquiring a veneer and in some cases, particularly in the larger towns, more than a veneer of Spanish culture, the more intelligent and active of the friars were already preoccupied by two problems. The first was to decide how far they could and should go in introducing the Indians to the higher studies of Europe; the second was that of planning their own voyages of exploration into the historical and intellectual past of the civilization which lay broken around them. The problems were largely interconnected, and the Mendicant scholars, mostly young men steeped in the classical and Christian learning of their epoch, flung themselves into both tasks with uninhibited energy and curiosity. It did not take them long to conclude that it was their duty to go the whole way in instructing young Indians in European humanism, and that their pupils would be capable of absorbing it. At the same time, as soon as they had surveyed the wreckage of the pre-Columbian world and advanced their own study of Náhuatl, they grasped that they were investigating not barbarism but a strange, antique and bewilderingly complex civilization. They found that the Aztecs had inherited a long intellectual tradition, the origins of which they themselves were unable to account for, and despite their lack of an alphabet, a very considerable literature. This discovery confirmed the leading spirits among the friars in their conviction that the Indians were ripe for higher education, and encouraged them to pursue their own work of research into the native culture. At a very early stage they established that the latter contained valuable elements worthy of preservation, and that the Náhuatl language should be fostered both as a link with the past and as a vehicle by which future generations of Indians should make their first approach to European learning. For instance they should go straight from Náhuatl to Latin, the key to the civilized state, without passing through Spanish. And they must also be taught to assimilate alien ideas and feelings through the medium of their own tongues.

By a bitter paradox, the work of salvage and intellectual enquiry undertaken by friars brought up in the European tradition was accompanied by the widespread but luckily not the wholesale destruction of the documents which, as soon as they were trained to interpret them, gave those friars an exact and comprehensive insight into the pre-Columbian culture. Zumárraga, perhaps the most Erasmian of them all in his zeal for Indian education, has been castigated by scores of critics for ordering the burning of Aztec pictographic books, with the result that his reputation as a book-burner has stuck to him while his achievements as a defender of the Indians and a promoter of intellectual activity are passed over. Admittedly the attempt by his nineteenth-century biographer, Garcia Icazbalceta, to acquit the bishop of this charge will not hold water against evidence of contemporaries and near-contemporaries. It is true that both he and other Mendicant missionaries did deliberately destroy codices, and many more vanished in the fires which consumed the temple libraries where they were mainly stored. But Zumárraga was not a vandal or philistine dedicated to the destruction of native manuscripts as such, nor were these destroyed with the systematic thoroughness of which he is frequently accused. A missionary was guided by the rough rule that any object—a temple building, a piece of sculpture, a mural or a pictographic book—which he might suspect to be a dangerous adjunct to idolatry ought to be destroyed, but the application of the rule was left largely to his discretion. It seems that the bishop, in his anxiety to stamp out paganism for good and all, was stricter than the majority of friars in his diocese.

Even so he and his fellow bishops felt as late as 1537 that they were obliged to seek special permission from Charles V to pull down the teocallis which were still standing in Texcoco and other places. The fate of the Texcocan royal archives, the largest accumulation of books in Anáhuac, was probably typical of that of other collections. It was not, as has been alleged, destroyed by Zumárraga in one huge bonfire, but according to the mestizo historians Ixtlilxóchitl and Pomar some of the books were burnt when the Tlaxcalans plundered the palace, others by order of the friars and others, which had been appropriated by certain Texcocan notables, by their owners, for fear that Zumárraga might track them down in their possession and they might be condemned for idolatry, like the unfortunate tlatoani Don Carlos. Ixtlilxóchitl, however, goes on to say that his ancestors saved books from these calamities and that he used them as material for his own history.

Luckily other personalities as forceful as Zumárraga set a higher value on Indian antiquities and were worried that they were disappearing so rapidly and irretrievably. Prominent among these were Ramirez de Fuenleal, president of the second Audiencia, and Fray Martín de Valencia, leader of the Twelve and himself a determined wrecker of idols. In 1533, according to the Franciscan historian Mendieta, they jointly commissioned Fray Andrés de Olmos, of the same Order, to study native antiquities and to prepare a book which should serve as a kind of official record of the Mexican past.

Olmos was chosen because he was "learned and discreet" and the best linguist in New Spain, where he had arrived with Zumárraga in 1528. He spoke Náhuatl perfectly, apart from mastering Totonac, Tepehua and Huaxteca. After consulting as many manuscripts as he could find in the possession of Mexican notables, and questioning the older men, he compiled a "very copious" book, but it was never printed, and both the original and various copies were sent to Spain, where they vanished without trace in his own lifetime. Later, however, he made a summary which was used by Mendieta. He incidentally founded seven monasteries. But his chief importance lies in the fact that he was the first to devote himself systematically to the marriage of the Latin alphabet with the Náhuatl language, a triumph of phonetics and dictionary-making. Like Motolinía,

THE FRUSTRATIONS OF LEARNING 269

who was simultaneously engaged on the same task, he realized how much easier it would be to teach the Indians if they could be instructed in their own tongue. Only Náhuatl, however, lent itself to this purpose, for the more obscure and difficult Indian languages, being much richer than either Náhuatl or the European languages in both vowels and consonants, could not easily be rendered in Latin letters. But fortunately Náhuatl was the *lingua franca* of New Spain; it was not hard to pronounce and it was sufficiently clear, concise and flexible for the conveyance of information and ideas. A modern Náhuatl scholar has claimed that Aristotle and Hegel could be translated into it without losing a single nuance.

Long before Olmos had perfected his technique of instruction in Náhuatl, Pedro de Gante was teaching boys to read, write and sing at his school housed in the Franciscan monastery of Mexico City. This early teaching was of course elementary, but the methods used in all the monastery schools at the time must have been very similar. They were at all events singularly successful. In the early thirties Latin was being taught directly from Náhuatl at San Francisco and Fuenleal was planning to form the best pupils in this advanced group into a separate college for higher education. In two years, he wrote to the Queen, he hoped to have fifty Indians who knew Latin and were also capable of teaching it themselves. He was not disappointed, for the famous College of Santa Cruz de Tlatelolco was duly inaugurated on 6th January, 1536, the Feast of the Epiphany.

Clearly the authorities attached very real importance to this development in the life of the colony. The site chosen for the college was in itself significant; on it had formerly stood the grand teocalli of Tlatelolco, scene of bloody combats between Aztecs and Spaniards during the siege of Tenochtitlán, towering above the teeming market which Bernal Díaz so greatly admired, just as the skyscraper containing the Mexican Ministry for Foreign Affairs now dominates the ruins of the temple and the simple friars' church of the sixteenth century. The Franciscans, headed by the Provincial of the Order, Fray García de Cisneros, went in procession all the way from the city to Tlatelolco, where the newly arrived Viceroy Mendoza, the outgoing president of the Audiencia, Fuenleal, and Bishop Zumárraga, together with other dignitaries and a vast crowd, were awaiting them. The proceedings comprised a mass, two sermons and a banquet offered by the bishop in the refectory of the small monastery which adjoined the modest building of the college.

The college opened with sixty pupils and was expanded, like Eton, to seventy in the following year. They were picked not merely as proficient Latinists but as the sons of the Indian aristocracy. Zumárraga would have liked the numbers to grow to three hundred, and it seems that they were in fact increased as the years went by through the selection of boys of ten to twelve years of age from all the principal townships, but the eventual figure reached is not known. The régime was suitably monastic and austere; the boys heard mass daily, ate together in a refectory and slept in one long chamber. Each had by his bed—or rather mat and blanket in the Indian fashion—a chest in which he kept his clothes and books. He wore a sort of soutane called a "hopa".

The teaching staff set a frighteningly high standard of scholarship. It included Sahagún, Olmos, Fray Arnaldo de Basaccio (an Italian) and Fray Juan de Fochez (a Frenchman). The curriculum consisted of reading, writing, music, Latin, rhetoric, logic, philosophy and (another example of contemporary broad-mindedness) native medicine. Basaccio, Sahagún and Olmos were the Latin teachers and the philosophy master was Fray Juan de Gaona, an outstandingly brilliant product of the University of Paris. In time the studies were increasingly conducted by Indian masters who had graduated from the college.

The ownership of the college was soon transferred from the Franciscans to the Crown, which allotted the tribute from various villages to its support. So long as it enjoyed royal and ecclesiastical sponsorship, and the quality of its teaching was assured by the academic standing of its professors, it prospered exceedingly and its pupils began to make their mark both as scholars and as men of the world. These graduates were natural choices for the "gobernadoryotl"; the best Latinist of them all, one Antonio Valeriano, governed the Indian community of Mexico-Tenochtitlán for twenty years. The son of a pilli, he married a niece of Moctezuma and was the shining example of the educated Indian, who, in the words of Fuenleal, "brought advantage to the Spaniards", while Don Carlos

Ometochtili, who paid with his life for a relapse into paganism, provided the anti-Indian faction among the colonists with a stick with which to belabour the college. A whole group of young Mexicans, equally at home in Latin, Spanish and Náhuatl, aided Sahagún and other friars in their researches into the past of Anáhuac and collaborated in translating European books. Thus Francisco Bautista de Contreras, gobernador of Xochimilco, helped to turn the "Imitation of Christ" of Thomas á Kempis into Náhuatl, and Pablo Nazareo, who became Rector of the college and married another of Moctezuma's nieces, was celebrated as philosopher and poet and translated the Gospels and the Epistles.

Some graduates produced original works, especially of history. Francisco Acaxitli, gobernador of Tlalmanalco, wrote a contemporary account of Viceroy Mendoza's campaign against the frontier Chichimecs. Of the composers of chronicles, Ixtlilxóchitl, Tezozomoc and Chimalpahin all studied at the college. An unusual example of cultural fusion is the so-called Badianus Herbal, a collection of recipes for the cure of diseases written in Náhuatl by Martin de la Cruz, a native doctor from Xochimilco, and translated into Latin by another Xochimilcan and pupil at Tlatelolco, Juan Badiano. Its style reflects that of Pliny's *Natural History*, which is known to have figured in the college library's remarkably rich stock of classical authors. The manuscript, beautifully illustrated, is dated 1552 and was dedicated to Don Francisco de Mendoza, son of the Viceroy.

Within ten years of its foundation Tlatelolco was turning out a plentiful supply of trained scholars and potential leaders of the Indian people, whereas the Royal and Pontifical University of Mexico, planned by Zumárraga for the education of Spaniards and Creoles, was not inaugurated until 1551, three years after the bishop's death. Indeed the college was working so smoothly that the Franciscans unwisely decided that the responsibility for its administration could in future safely be left to its former alumni. So the Indians were allowed to elect their own Rector and governing body, who in turn appointed the teachers. But the new system proved a disastrous failure, and the mismanagement by the Indians of their own affairs of course played into the hands of the institution's Spanish critics. They omitted even to keep the buildings in good order, and although Velasco supported the college and provided it with new funds, it had become so ruinous by 1560 that the pupils could no longer be maintained as boarders, with adverse effects on discipline and the educational programme.

Moreover opposition to the college's aims was growing. Zumárraga's successor, Archbishop Montufar, was less than lukewarm about higher education for Indians. He was a Dominican, and despite his Order's record of enthusiasm for Indian emancipation, it fell short of educating the natives as humanists. The basic reason for this reluctance was that the Dominicans did not want Indians as friars or priests. They feared that their newly acquired culture might prove to be skin-deep; they also suspected them of levity in religion and (not within reason) in morals. Knowledge of Aristotle and the Church Fathers did not altogether quell their addiction to girls and pulque. One argument used by the Dominicans in support of their point of view was more frank than reputable, namely that if the Indians became too good Latinists they would detect how ignorant some of the Spanish clerics really were.

The Dominicans' apprehensions were nevertheless based on a sincere if incorrect and pessimistic assessment of the Indian character: the objections of the colonists, most stridently voiced by a clerk named Jerónimo Lopez, sprang from selfish cynicism and prejudice. During the forties Lopez repeatedly importuned the Crown with warnings that knowledge of Latin and the "sciences" would lead to heresy and sedition among the Indians. So long as Mendoza and Zumárraga controlled Mexican affairs, the home government paid little heed to these complaints, but the climate of opinion changed rapidly for the worse in the succeeding years both in the colony and in Spain. Then, in 1555, the bishops of New Spain met in council and, in deference to the Dominican view, resolved that Indians, mestizos and negroes might not be ordained priests. This decision was a shattering blow to the prospects of the college and effectively frustrated the advancement of young Indians to positions of trust and responsibility. In an age when the Church offered the widest opportunities for advancement, they found themselves peremptorily barred from entering it. Nor were they allowed to practise that other influential profession, the law, although the Aztec tradition of legalism should have amply qualified them for that career. They were not permitted to bear arms and were excluded from the government, the higher ranks of which were filled from Spain and the lower positions from among the Creoles. All that was reserved for ambitious Indians was municipal office in their own towns, which was little more than honorific, while for the more intelligent practically the sole outlet for their new erudition was to act as assistants to the Spanish scholars who were burrowing into the culture of their ancestors. So narrow a sphere of activity was quite insufficient to sustain their interest or their self-respect.

Sahagún, who watched the college rise and fall, had no doubt that the original policy was right. Writing more than forty years after its foundation, he condemned his own compatriots for first sneering at its ideals and then trying to stultify them as they were being realized. Directly refuting Jerónimo Lopez, he claimed that the college had vastly contributed to the introduction and maintenance of the Catholic faith. He placed the blame for its decadence mainly on the slipshod behaviour of its Indian governors, partly on the incapacity of a Spanish steward, and partly on the failure of the friars to repair the damage before it was too late. In fact they resumed control in 1570 and undertook a reform in which Sahagún himself took part. It did not, however, arrest the decline, and it was further accentuated by the terrible plague of 1576, which carried off most of the students. The Jesuit Acosta, a keen apologist for the Indians, made much the same comment as Sahagún on the decay of the attempt to give them a humanist education:

> The Mexicans used to bring up their sons with much order and attention, and if the same heed were now paid to educating the boys, no doubt Indian Christianity would greatly flourish. Some zealous persons started the process, and the King and his Council openly supported it, but it is no longer a business that concerns anyone; it makes very little progress and creates no enthusiasm.*

He was quite right; the Crown and its agents had lost interest, the Creoles were actively hostile and the friars preferred their own studies to educating others.

* *Historia Natural y Moral de las Indias*

We have a last rather pathetic glimpse of Tlatelolco in 1584, when the pupils made Latin speeches and staged a little comedy in honour of a visiting dignitary. But they found it necessary to excuse themselves for spouting their Latin like magpies and parrots, and for their general lack of ability. Finally a tall Indian, dressed as a Spaniard and speaking Spanish, mimicked a colonist making a fuss about having to support an institution which merely turned out Indians as drunken and ill-mannered as the rest of their race. But he was interrupted by a teacher, who protested that the pupils were all good boys and keen scholars, and attacked the spectators for never opening their mouths without slanging the poor Indians and objecting if they ever reached a higher station in life than load-carriers.

Thus this bold attempt to create an Indian élite of mixed culture, faithful to the new order but linked to the old by family and tribal traditions, capable of holding its own with Spaniard and Creoles and fulfilling a necessary function in colonial society, collapsed for a variety of reasons including, it must be confessed, a certain lack of stamina and purpose among the chosen Indians themselves. It was, perhaps, too much to ask of them to digest in so short a time the mass of unfamiliar knowledge and ideas which was suddenly thrust on them, and then consciously to direct their abilities towards championing the interests of their own people. The first generation of young Mexicans trained by the friars was brought up in the shadow of the Conquest; the second and last wilted under the restriction of its opportunities, and was frustrated by pressure and neglect.

Nevertheless in mid-century, before the attitudes of Church and State had hardened, the joint endeavours of Spaniards and Indians rediscovered and recorded the precious culture of Anáhuac. Above all, they established that a rich literature in Náhuatl had flourished before the Conquest. They even succeeded in reviving it temporarily by giving it fresh material to work upon, and with an alphabet to shape that material with a clarity and precision which the old mixture of pictograms and ideograms could never attain. As a method of transmitting ideas, the latter was of course inadequate, but for lack of a better word it must be regarded as a true form of "literacy", especially as it complemented the use of the trained memory for the preservation of long and complicated texts. To judge

THE FRUSTRATIONS OF LEARNING 275

only by the sheer bulk of the documents produced at the height of the Aztec civilization, pictographic writing supplied a very real practical need and a great many people must surely have been able to interpret the pictograms. Crude as their books may have been, the Aztecs were a literate people.

It is not clear to what extent the primitive Aztecs learned the art of book-making from the peoples already settled in and around the Valley of Mexico. We must assume that their more civilized predecessors already knew how to prepare paper from the inner bark of the wild fig tree, or from maguey fibre, and to set up the pages so that they folded handily like little screens. Sahagún's Aztec informants passed on to him a curious story about the fourth ruler of Tenochtitlán, Itzcóatl (1427–1440), who was said to have burnt all the books written before his reign in the area under his control (which did not of course include Nezahualcóyotl's Texcoco). He was the king who finally smashed the Tepanec power in the valley and replaced it by Aztec overlordship. He may therefore have taken the opportunity of doing away with the documents in which the culture of the Tepanecs (apparently a non-Nahua tribe) was enshrined and to start afresh. However that may be, the Aztecs made and collected books in vast quantities, and they especially prized those which commemorated their tribal traditions and exploits. But their literary production had lasted less than a century when it was choked off in its prime by the Spanish invasion.

The libraries of Anáhuac had been disintegrating for ten years before either of the two principal rescuers of their remnants, Olmos and Sahagún, arrived in New Spain, and as we have already seen, the former was not directed to start his research until 1533. By then the greater part of the manuscripts had already been consigned to the fire or the rubbish-heap. Moreover the Audiencia's interest in Mexican antiquities was historical, not literary. But as the enquiries progressed, sufficient texts of all kinds came to light for the friars engaged on the task to appreciate the variety and merit of the Náhuatl literature of pre-Conquest times. Unfortunately much of what they uncovered has since perished, because many of the books which they themselves compiled, or encouraged their Indian helpers to compile, and which contained collections of ancient texts, never found their way into print and have disappeared between the sixteenth century and now. The actual process of discovery was of course inseparably bound up with the friar's endeavours to give the Náhuatl language a new lease of life and to adapt it for the dissemination of Christian and humanist knowledge. In doing so they managed to sponsor a whole new corpus of Náhuatl writing.

From the moment that they mastered the indispensable Latin alphabet, the post-Conquest Indians felt a strong impulse to use it for expressing themselves in their own language. In this they needed no stimulus from their teachers. So long as their urge was fostered or even tolerated, and the monastery schools continued to turn out literate Indians, the volume of such writings multiplied. The difficulty is to form even a vague estimate of how great it had become by its peak period, coinciding roughly with the third quarter of the century. If Indians had not only been encouraged to indulge their talent for writing, but had also been helped to get their works printed, we should be much better informed today. The truth is that although the first press was set up in Mexico City as early as 1535, and seven separate printers can be identified as having practised there before 1600, no Indian author is known to have had his own book printed by any one of them during that period. To be sure, a great many texts made their appearance in Náhuatl, as well as in other Indian languages (one friar had a "doctrine" published in Spanish, Náhuatl and Otomi), but as a general rule these were composed or edited by Spaniards and Creoles, and if any Indian writers made original contributions towards them, they remained anonymous.

Consequently books written in Náhuatl by Indians and mestizos stayed in manuscript until the lucky few that escaped destruction were rescued by nineteenth-century editors. However, we may reasonably suppose that for each manuscript which has turned up, complete or fragmentary, after three centuries, dozens more must have perished. Those that survived did so by accident. While Mexico was still New Spain the Náhuatl writings mouldered gently away, ignored and unread, in the obscure corners of monastery libraries, with no enemies except mice, dust and indifference. Then three storms burst successively over Mexico, the struggle for independence, the civil wars of the eighteen-fifties and sixties and, finally the Revolution of 1910–20. From the cultural point of view all

THE FRUSTRATIONS OF LEARNING 277

these were devastating, but the second was the worst. In the course of the furious conflict between clericals and liberals, in which the latter, led by Benito Juarez, eventually triumphed, the monasteries were dissolved and sacked from top to bottom. Their great collections of manuscripts and printed books, a store of priceless historical and literary value as yet unsifted by scholars, were pitched into the soldiers' camp-fires.

At the present time the few manuscripts which escaped destruction are to be found scattered between libraries in Mexico, the United States and Europe. A single volume may contain a seemingly haphazard jumble of unrelated texts, annals, sagas, poems, calendars, translations of classical authors and all kinds of religious material. Their only common characteristic is that they are all in Náhuatl. The splendid anthology known as *Cantares Mexicanos*, the main source of our knowledge of pre-Conquest poetry, is bound up with such oddments as a life of Saint Bartholomew and an ingenious adaptation of Aesop's fables in which Mexican animals have been substituted for European. No attempt has been made to separate writings of permanent value from those of purely ephemeral interest.

Transcriptions of ancient texts into alphabetical Náhuatl are frequently found in the same manuscripts as original post-Conquest works. The output of the former was probably very considerable and, to judge from existing fragments, of superb quality. But the friars who commissioned them were not necessarily interested in preserving them for posterity. Once they had studied them and used them, if they felt so inclined, as source material for their own books, they might easily discard them. Hence their chances of survival were not promising. Original works, on the other hand, stood a higher chance of preservation, as shown by the number of histories and narratives from the sixteenth century that are still intact.

The friars, too, were nervous about perpetuating any pre-Conquest texts that smacked of idolatry. Here their scholarly curiosity clashed with their religious scruples. It cost even Sahagún, with his passion for uncovering the Aztec past and his ambition to leave behind him an exact record of the old civilization, a great effort to incorporate in his work the invaluable collection which he made of hymns to the great gods of Anáhuac. These, inherited from the pre-Aztec era and handed down by the priestly caste throughout centuries of migration and tribal upheavals, are the earliest examples we possess, thanks to Sahagún, of native literature. In his preface to the collection he cannot repress a shudder as he warns his readers that the high-flown, hieratic language of the hymns is full of hidden meanings and beset with the snares of the devil. He knew that it would have been obvious to those versed in the old religion that the flowers in which Teteoimman, Mother of the Gods, known as Itzapapálotl or "Obsidian Butterfly", took delight were not simply those which cover the Mexican uplands in the rainy season, but also symbolized the flower of the warriors claimed by the goddess in sacrifice.

Nevertheless Sahagún went ahead and preserved the Aztec hymns. At the same time he was editing a *Psalmodia*, or collection of Náhuatl poems by native writers on Christian themes, and appointed to be sung by Indians on feast days. This type of composition, which was designed for a massed choir with the appropriate music and dancing, of course followed the pre-Columbian model. At first it was eagerly promoted by the friars and as usual Pedro de Gante was the pioneer. The Franciscan historian Mendieta mentions two other members of his Order, Luis de Fuensalida and Francisco Jiménez, who were equally adept at devising Náhuatl texts and setting them to music—"un canto llano muy gracioso" (*Historia Ecclesiastica Indiana*).

But most of the poems and scenarios were the work of the Indians themselves. By contrast with the ancient hymns, the language of the Christian poems is straightforward and even popular, but often full of beauty and very real fervour. The best examples are not those from the *Psalmodia*, which are frankly dull, but the Christian element of the *Cantares Mexicanos*, in which pre-Conquest poems—pre-Conquest poems adapted (sometimes with scant disguise) for Christian use—and purely Christian pieces all find a place. In the latter biblical stories and allusions are interwoven with the vivid images of Anáhuac. The same exotic birds and flowers, the jade and the emeralds, are brought into the service of the new faith. One Francisco Plácido, an Indian from Azcapotzalco, composed a hymn for Christmas 1553, in which the angels celebrating the birth of Jesus appear in the guise of the legendary quechol birds of Tlalocan, the lush and flowery paradise of the pre-Columbian after-world which is already depicted in fresco at Teotihuacán.

THE FRUSTRATIONS OF LEARNING 279

The three Kings greet Jesus "as a jewel, as a quetzal", and Herod's child victims are compared to torn plumage, or to a broken necklace of fine jade.

Something has already been said in Chapter II about the numerous forms of Náhuatl poetry current at the courts of Texcoco and Tenochtitlán. If the right conditions had prevailed under the viceroyalty, one can imagine it blossoming afresh, developing in new directions and providing scope for the free expression of personal thoughts and emotions, perhaps by absorbing secular European influences. But the opportunity lapsed when an Indian élite of mixed, but predominantly native, culture failed to establish itself. Moreover the authorities grew increasingly apprehensive of the danger of pagan habits of mind creeping back under the cloak of literature, whether popular or imaginative. An ordinance issued by Mendoza in 1546 already banned emblems, banners, masks and chants recalling the Indian past, and imposed the penalty of a hundred lashes on anyone who tried to introduce them into Christian festivals. The Church Council of 1555, repeating that prohibition, ordered the texts of all hymns and songs by Indian authors to be censored. From then on, although nothing could extinguish the spontaneous Indian taste for song and artistic display, their celebrations lost their poetic and intellectual content, degenerating rapidly into picturesque folklore.

It may seem puzzling that when the Indians had become less numerous and more docile, and a serious relapse into the old ways was no longer imaginable, the authorities should have turned so sour. But as time wore on, the open-minded conception of the part which educated Indians might play in the development of New Spain gave way to the defensive and intolerant attitudes emanating from the Madrid of Philip II. The atmosphere was no longer conducive to the Indians' being helped to work out a higher culture of their own, drawing equally on the pre-Columbian and European traditions. Unless they became to all intents Europeans, they were discouraged from possessing any culture at all. Yet the former object had been thought perfectly feasible by the humanists who planned Indian education in the twenties and thirties, but who did not perhaps think out the possible implications of their projects.

Sahagún's long life illustrates the growing frustrations of

those who persisted in pursuing the ideals of Zumárraga and his circle. Born Bernardino Ribeira about 1500, he assumed, as was customary, the name of his birthplace on joining the Franciscan Order. He came to Mexico in 1529 and died there in 1590. At first he resided at various monasteries, and from that of Tlalmanalco he climbed both the volcanos, Popocatépetl and Ixtaccíhuatl. But as a graduate of Salamanca and an excellent Latinist, he was soon enrolled in the team which, even before the foundation of Tlatelolco, was experimenting with a classical education for young Aztecs. He continued to teach at the College until the instruction was rashly turned over to Indian masters.

The year 1547 found him living in the up-country monastery at Tepepulco, about fifty miles north-west of the capital. This place, now only a small village on the fringe of an industrial settlement which has been christened Ciudad Sahagún, was by no means a backwater in the mid-sixteenth century, but a populous Indian township where Cortés had maintained one of his many palaces in the palmy days of the marquisate and where the Franciscans had recently pulled down a colossal temple of Huitzilopochtli. There, according to the most likely as well as the most attractive hypothesis, Fray Bernardino received his commission from the Provincial of his Order to undertake the work that ended up, after many vicissitudes, as his *Historia General de las Cosas de Nueva España*. Whichever of the two originated the idea, it was conceived on the broadest scale and, in the words of Angel Maria Garibay, as an "encyclopaedia of the culture of the Náhuas of Tenochtitlán". But its peculiarity lay in that it was designed to be written in Náhuatl and so far as possible in the words of the Indians themselves. The Náhuas were to be invited to distil the essence of their own culture, with the Spanish friar acting as director and editor of the enterprise. In all possibility the project had been maturing for many years in Sahagún's mind and he had already collected much material before it was formally authorized.

According to Sahagún's own account, however, it was at Tepepulco that he first systematically tried out the method which he was to employ throughout his enquiries. What he did was to get hold of the leading Indian nobleman in the town, an old man who went by the name of Diego de Mendoza, "of great distinction and ability and well versed in matters pertaining to the court, warfare and statecraft and also to idolatry". Mendoza in turn introduced to the friar a group of ten or twelve of his own contemporaries, all equally knowledgeable about life in pre-hispanic Mexico and ready to volunteer information about all facets of the old culture. In questioning them and recording their replies Sahagún was helped by four young Indians who had been his pupils at Tlatelolco. The old men were encouraged to produce pictographic documents in support of their statements, and these were duly transcribed by the scholars into written Náhuatl.

This process, Sahagún says, lasted for two years. Among the material he gathered were the hymns already mentioned and a large selection of "huehuetlatolli"—precepts of the elders— or in modern terms detailed manuals of the rules of social behaviour to which well-bred Aztecs were expected to conform. His colleague, Olmos, had already assembled a similar list and his manuscript, dated the 1st January, 1547, is still extant. Perhaps Sahagún derived his technique of recording them from the other friar.

At the close of this period Sahagún was ordered back to Tlatelolco, where he continued his work and built up a much larger store of material. Again he made use of a team of elders chosen for him by the local Indian gobernador, as well as of four or five graduates of the College. They were all trilingual and included the native Rector, one Martín Jacobita. Later he was once more transferred, this time to the monastery of San Francisco in the capital, where he recruited a third set of coadjutors and clerks, the most remarkable of whom was Antonio Valeriano, a native of Azcapotzalco and gobernador of Tenochtitlán itself. He always took the greatest pains to have his work vetted by the best qualified Indians and with their help he expanded and revised it for another three years. Finally he divided it into twelve books, complete with prologues, annexes and a dictionary.

The vast scope of the *General History* is best appreciated by setting out briefly the subject-matter of its component books. Book I deals with the gods formerly worshipped by the inhabitants of New Spain, Book II with the "calendar, feasts and ceremonies, sacrifices and solemnities" of the Aztec religion; the text of the hymns being appended to it. Book III recounts myths of the origin of the gods. Most of it is taken up with the detailed history of Quetzalcóatl as the folk-hero of the Toltecs, while a long and valuable annex outlines Mexican belief about the after-life, the education imparted in the telpochcalli and the calmécac and the hierarchical structure of the priesthood. Book IV is all about the astrology and divination which filled so large a place in Mexican life, and Book V, descending a little down the scale, lists the omens derived from the behaviour of birds, animals and insects; if, for instance, you see a rabbit enter your house, you will probably be burgled (Sahagún adds as an afterthought that Mexican rabbits are like Spanish ones, but less good to eat). There are two chapters on ghosts and an appendix of various taboos and superstitions.

Returning to a higher plane, Book VI purports to treat of the "Rhetoric, Moral Philosophy and Theology of the Mexican people". In fact it begins with specimens of the language used in invoking the gods and Sahagún then brings in all the material extracted from the huehuetlatolli. The book is of the highest interest from both the linguistic and sociological points of view. It concludes with lists of proverbs, riddles and "delicate metaphors". Book VII sketches Mexican ideas of astronomy and gives a short account of the calendrical system. Book VIII turns to politics. It summarizes the history of Anáhuac down to 1560 and explains the governmental, military and legal systems of the Aztecs, with many sidelights on the life of the ruling class. Book IX, on the other hand, tackles trade and gives an admirable description of the activities of merchants and craftsmen.

Book X is rather a hotch-potch, but it completes the information about the various social classes of Mexicans, their customs and daily habits, their diet, their physique, the diseases they suffered from and their medicine. It ends with a long ethnological section on the non-Nahua peoples. Book XI, the Natural History of Anáhuac, is perhaps the most attractive of them all, with its colourful descriptions of living creatures, of trees, flowers and waters, of stones and metals. One can hardly imagine a more intriguing blend of facts of the deepest scientific and utilitarian value with the humorous fantasy of the Aztecs' approach to the natural world around them.

The twelfth and final Book contains, as is fitting, the story of the conquest of Tenochtitlán, beginning with the omens that foreshadowed the coming of the Spaniards and ending with the surrender of Cuauhtémoc amid scenes of desolation. Composed at Sahagún's invitation by unknown Indians, or conceivably by one man, it is stylistically the finest piece of Náhuatl prose in existence; even in translation it imposes by its fluency and precision, as well as by its emotional and dramatic strength. Especially effective are the passages that describe the horrors of the Tóxcatl massacre, and the extremes of suffering and humiliation to which the Aztec people was reduced during the final stages of the siege. While the detail is agonizingly realistic, the language is markedly polished and sophisticated.

The experts are divided on the question of the dates at which the different parts of the *Historia General* were completed, but Sahagún quite clearly states in the prologue to Book XII that although the final versions of the latter's text, in Náhuatl and Spanish, were finished under his direction as late as 1585, when he was a very old man, the original Náhuatl text was prepared more than thirty years before. In 1555 there were still men living who had witnessed the Conquest and might have been capable of writing or dictating first-hand accounts of it. Nevertheless the language of Book XII sounds too fresh to have been squeezed solely out of the memories of persons in advanced middle age. It looks as if the writer or writers had largely relied on earlier descriptions recorded very soon after the Conquest. Indeed one of these still exists in the shape of a manuscript dated 1528 in the Bibliothéque Nationale at Paris. This devoted twelve pages to the overthrow of Tenochtitlán, and the language is even more direct and poignant than that of the text prepared for Sahagún. Apart from his mastery of the Latin script, the earlier writer belongs to the old culture as yet untinged by the influence of the friars. Yet there is an essential similarity between the Indian style of 1528 and that of 1555. Plenty of Spaniards were writing in Náhuatl between those years: their output of educational and edifying works was extremely prolific, but no Spaniard could have written creatively in the native language. He could never have absorbed the Indian spirit even to the extent of producing a convincing pastiche of their forms of expression.

Sahagún was not satisfied with the original Náhuatl of Book XII because the style was too rough (tosco) and as for the content, some facts had been wrongly put and others wrongly suppressed. So he had it rewritten with greater attention to both elegance and truth. Finally he had it transcribed in three parallel columns, the old Náhuatl text, the new one and a Spanish version of the latter. Unfortunately this product of his editorial zeal has disappeared. The Náhuatl text of Book XII which has come down to us is to be found in the bilingual manuscript called the Codex of Florence, which happens to be the only complete version—or as complete as we are likely to get—of the *General History*. Two manuscripts in Madrid, however, contain incomplete Náhuatl versions, and scholars regard their language as purer and more correct than that of the Florence Codex.

In 1569 he submitted a fair copy of the whole book for examination by his superiors, and immediately found himself in trouble. So far successive Provincials, or heads of the Franciscan Order in New Spain, had sympathized with his aims. They may not have shared his intensely scientific interest in ethnology and linguistics, but they knew that if a missionary friar wanted to know what was going on in the minds of the Indians in his care he must have soaked himself in their past and have trained himself to use their language as a clue to their most intimate thoughts and feelings. Sahagún compares him to a doctor who has to discover all the relevant facts about his patient's condition before he can prescribe a remedy. As for his work on the Náhuatl language, he saw himself as wielding a huge net in which he hauled its words and phrases out of the depths, exposing their secret and metaphorical meanings to the light of truth. But the members of his Order, headed by their new Provincial, Fray Alonso de Escalona, were no longer attracted by his ideals. They would not accept his encyclopaedia of Nahua culture as an indispensable part of every friar's equipment in dealing with Indians. They even obstructed his work in the most niggling fashion, objecting to his hiring clerks for copying his manuscripts on the ground that it infringed his vow of poverty. He was ordered to dismiss his helpers and write everything himself, despite his failing eyesight and shaky hand.

Undeterred by his mean treatment, he composed a Spanish summary of his work and had it conveyed to Spain by two sympathizers, the former Provincial Fray Miguel Navarro and his fellow-writer Jerónimo de Mendieta. At his request they took it direct to the President of the Council of the Indies, who received it with approval. When he heard that he had been thus by-passed Escalona was furious. As a punishment for what he regarded as a gesture of rebellion, he confiscated all Sahagún's papers and dispersed them throughout the province, thus making it impossible for him to work on them. By that time the Franciscans on both sides of the Atlantic were taking sides vehemently for or against Sahagún. The pendulum again swung in his favour when his friend Navarro was appointed Commissary-General of the Order with powers overriding those of the Provincials. He got his papers returned to him and was able to complete the Spanish text of the *General History* without further interruption. That was in 1577, thirty years after he had started to shape the Náhuatl original. He was only just in time, for after a few months the Viceroy, Enriquez, was sharply instructed by King Philip to impound all copies of the book and remit them to Spain for further scrutiny by the Council. The Viceroy was also warned not to allow anyone within his jurisdiction to write, in any language, about the Indian religion and ancient way of life.

In Mexico the royal officials were inclined to take a more relaxed view of the matter than the bureaucrats in Spain. For the former, and for the Creoles, there was nothing strange in the existence of books in Náhuatl. Religious books in that language had been circulating in print for a long time, and it was in current use for official, legal and business purposes. In the easy-going society of the colony, which took the Indian background for granted, no one seriously imagined that there was any danger of the natives being roused or corrupted just because a learned friar, who had lived among them for fifty years, had compiled with their help a full account of their antiquities and ancestral customs. To King Philip's Spanish advisers, however, Sahagún's History appeared not as a monument of scholarship, nor as an aid to confirming the Indians in their new faith, but in the guise of a perverse attempt to perpetuate the memory of a repulsive pagan world. In the era of the Spanish crusade against the Turk and the Lutheran, of the battle of Lepanto and the bloody struggle with the heretics of the Netherlands, the slightest hint of an objective survey of heathenism was inadmissible. Even the expressions of horror with which Sahagún accompanied his description of Aztec rites could not palliate his irresponsibility in presuming to describe them at all. The effect of some of his chapters must have been hair-raising for readers who had no first-hand knowledge of Mexican realities and were trying to catch him out anyway; it was perhaps inevitable that they should suspect that the most sinister under-currents continued to flow beneath the smooth surface of colonial life, belying the optimistic assessments of Viceroys and friars with local experience.

Needless to say, the royal prohibition was not fully enforced. Even Sahagún ventured, a few years later, to polish up his last section, the story of the Conquest as told by Indians. Subsequently plenty of information about Indan culture and religion was relayed to Spanish readers by white and mestizo writers. But the order sent to the Viceroy was aimed primarily at the *General History*, and it killed it stone dead. All Sahagún's hopes that it would finally be published and sanctioned for general use by clerics and other educated persons were utterly dashed. It not only failed to get printed but remained, so far as the world was concerned, a non-book for the next two hundred years. The Spanish censors did their job only too efficiently, for of all Sahagún's papers confiscated under the royal edict none survived except the manuscripts in Madrid and Florence already mentioned, which came to light in the late eighteenth century, and part of a summary in the Vatican Library. We do not know if Sahagún managed to keep a full copy for himself: presumably he understood that his opponents' aim was to let his work disappear without trace. He spent the last years of his life at Tlatelolco, but was taken to die, at the age of ninety, among the Franciscans in Mexico City.

Chapter 11

TOWARDS A NATION

ROYAL NARROW-MINDEDNESS and Creole indifference ruined the Indians' prospects of continued cultural advancement, which had shone so brilliantly under the first two Viceroys. With the decay of Tlatlolco they lost the access to higher education which had formerly been reserved to them, and they never were made eligible for the excellent schooling in the humanities provided by the Royal and Pontifical University of Mexico City for students of European origin. New Spain in the seventeenth century was full of learned men, but apart from a few exceptional mestizos they were all Creoles or migrants from the Peninsula. The Indians had dropped out of the running.

The result was that the native race no longer produced leaders. They died out not because they were violently eliminated but because the class from which they would naturally have been recruited was allowed to stagnate without training or opportunities. By virtue of their high birth and an admixture of Spanish blood a handful of individuals succeeded in crossing the racial line and were virtually transformed into Creoles, but in general the descendants of the Indian lords gradually lost their social status and with it what remained of their former wealth. Lacking culture and the influence stemming from it, they were no longer able to defend their inherited possessions against Creole landgrabbers, the forerunners of the hacendado class which dominated colonial society for the remainder of its existence. Nor were they permitted to retain the new lands which many of them had acquired in the confusion following the Conquest, or in the wake of the first great epidemics. The lords slid back into the mass of the population and stood no better chance of reasserting themselves than the sons of the macehualtin. Men of rank disappeared from the Indian communities and persons of the village headman type succeeded in their place to the office of gobernador in the native townships, once the perquisite of the nobility or of graduates from Tlatelolco. Ixtlilxóchitl, the most prominent of the mestizo writers, complained sourly that in the reign of Philip III even the princes of Texcoco had no shelter left but God and the King's clemency.

Another sad consequence of the neglect of Indian education was that the Nahuas were ceasing to employ their own language as a means of literary expression. In its spoken form Náhuatl remained the *lingua franca* of New Spain throughout colonial times and was only gradually superseded by Spanish in the mouths of the people: it is still alive to this day. It was also admitted as the second language of the courts and of the administration. Thus it continued to be used for keeping some legal, official and business records, and there was always a demand for native clerks capable of expressing themselves fluently in it on paper for all practical purposes. But its voice was not heard in poetry and imaginative prose, since the Indians no longer felt any incentive or inspiration for creative writing. In fact the literary revival of the language stimulated by the friars was a short-lived, though remarkable, effort which had exhausted itself before the sixteenth century was over, and much the greater part of the production of both original works and alphabetical versions of pre-Conquest writings took place in the fifty years between 1530 and 1580.

The Jesuits, who arrived in Mexico in the early seventies, at first behaved as if they intended to give a fresh impulse to the flagging cause of Indian education. With that end in view they founded three colleges, one in the capital, a second at Pátzcuaro and the third and most important at Tepotzotlán, a village lying near the road from Mexico City to Querétaro and a few miles from Cuauhtitlán, a large Indian township and once a flourishing centre of Nahua culture. But the original purpose of these foundations was rapidly lost sight of, and Tepotzotlán became not a college for Indians but a seminary for budding Jesuits, and since Indians were barred from the priesthood the seminarists were necessarily Creoles.

To do the Jesuits justice, they took particular trouble to master the local languages, and were soon writing books in polished Náhuatl. Their most distinguished scholar, Father Horacio Carochi, was a Florentine, and it is a strange irony that such excellence in the language of the Nahuas should have been attained by an Italian when they themselves were at the best capable of drafting a simple will or translating a court

Monastery Church at Actopan. 16th century

Monastery Church at Tepeaca. 16th century

order. The Jesuits steeped themselves in the culture, past and present, of the Indians among whom they lived, but in Mexico they did little to help the Indians to develop and adapt that culture to colonial conditions, along the lines laid down by the earlier friars. The era of active evangelism and of restless social experiment, in which the energy of the Renaissance had been given free rein, was over, and practical humanism, exercised for the benefit of people, gave place in the monasteries of New Spain to scholarship and the amassing of knowledge for its own sake, or to the mere accumulation of material wealth. In the eighteenth century Jesuit Tepotzotlán was as famous for the riches of its library as for the splendour of the Churrigueresque decoration of its church. But the books were scattered on the dissolution of the Order in 1767, while the remnant subsequently preserved in the capital was destroyed in the anti-religious troubles which convulsed Mexico in the nineteen-twenties.

To discourage Indian enlightenment eventually became the deliberate policy of both State and Church in the colony. The new attitude was perfectly typified by Pedro Moya de Contreras, who succeeded to the Archbishopric of Mexico in 1573, filled concurrently the office of Viceroy from 1582 to 1586 and on his return to Spain was made President of the Council of the Indies. His conviction, so recorded by Mendieta, was that it was a mistake to teach the Indians Latin, rhetoric, philosophy or indeed any other science; they should be compelled to concentrate on craftsmanship, for which they had a natural bent. In other words the Christian Indian's only proper vocation was that of a skilful but obedient drudge, and his voice must count for nothing in the land.

We may well ask why Archbishop Moya should have arrived at a conclusion so diametrically opposed to the optimistic estimate of Indian capabilities held in the days of Zumárraga and other brilliant figures of the early age of New Spain. We may be sure that it did not just stem from dull racial bigotry. Experience had shown that young Nahuas could master the studies pursued at any contemporary Spanish university, and plenty of living examples were at hand to prove it. Moya was certainly acquainted with many literate and learned Indians. He was not, however, a friar, but a member of the secular clergy, and as such he had not inherited the idealism of the

Franciscans. Without disputing the genuineness and depth of an Indian's intellectual attainments, he was entitled to question whether these were likely to lead the Indian anywhere, and whether he could usefully fit into the life of New Spain. He decided, not without reason, that the Franciscan experiment had been a total failure. It was high time to abandon the absurd attempt to create a race of paragons combining the best elements of the two cultures.

Even the friars were forced to agree, after considerable heart-searchings, that it would be unwise to allow educated Indians to become friars and priests. It was not that they were lacking in devotion or incapable of grasping Christian theology. Intellectually they were up to the mark, but they did seem to be deficient in the necessary authority and energy. There was a disturbing moral fecklessness about them. That, added to the colonists' distaste that Christianity should be dispensed to Indians or Europeans by the sons of horrific idolators, was enough to exclude Indians from the wide field of opportunities offered by the Church. Furthermore, the government of New Spain was so constituted as to give them no hope of preferment in civil life outside the restricted sphere of their own communities. It would have been unthinkable to give them places in the closely knit Spanish bureaucracy which it was hard enough even for Creoles to penetrate.

In the circumstances the attitude of Moya and his contemporaries was logical enough. It is intriguing, if unprofitable, to speculate whether they would have been able to sustain it had Tlatelolco fulfilled the hopes of its founders and turned out men of such abilities and character that they could have surmounted the barriers of jealousy and prejudice and gained acceptance by Europeans as equals or near-equals. In all probability the obstacles were too formidable. It was too much to expect that the conquered race could so soon have produced an élite capable not only of assimilating European culture, while not forgetting their own, but also of recovering, under the colonial system, a share of the authority formerly wielded by the hierarchies of the Aztec empire. Yet this aim was not considered unrealistic by the men who started to school the Indians after the Conquest.

The truth is that, quite apart from the more brutal pressures to which they were subjected, the Nahuas were not ready, even at a distance of three decades from the Conquest, to dispense with the tutelage of the friars. Much less were they fit to compete on their own merits for status in the strange and uncomfortable colonial world of hostile settlers and sceptical Viceroys. The shock of the Conquest, the brusque removal of the props upon which their civilization was supported, fatally deprived them of their self-confidence and left them groping confusedly in the harsh new environment. In Aztec times the members of the ruling castes—administrative, military and priestly—had been carefully trained in the habit of authority. They exercised it confidently within their particular spheres and in the fulfilment of well defined functions. When the elaborate edifice of their society was shattered, the military establishment survived to some extent so long as the Spaniards needed Indian warriors to subdue other Indians. As soon as they were disbanded, the martial spirit of the Nahuas vanished with them. Remnants of the civil hierarchy lingered on while the descendants of local princes were still permitted to wield a measure of authority in their traditional territories. The priesthood, however, crumbled immediately, and the speed and completeness with which it abdicated its role is a very significant feature of the total collapse of the old order in Anáhuac.

Though not all-powerful, the priests (tlamacazque) were immensely influential, for the reason that the whole of Indian life revolved around the service of the gods. They were the interpreters of the highly complicated symbolism which underlay the outward forms of the Nahua religion, the guardians of the cultural tradition inherited from the classical age, the repositories of astronomical and other recondite knowledge and the superintendents of public education and morality. But when their system was forcibly broken up, their cosmos too dissolved into the void. Their gods failed them, and suddenly they saw no more purpose or meaning in life. Nor did there seem to be any point in trying to preserve the old beliefs and disciplines through some kind of underground movement inspired by a tough fanaticism. Such a spirit was notably absent. What prevailed was apathy and a sense of helplessness and resignation to the inevitable.

Some light is thrown on the state of mind of these former keepers of the Nahua conscience by a manuscript discovered fifty years ago in the Vatican library. Entitled *Colloquies and Christian Doctrine with which the Twelve Friars of St Francis sent by*

Pope Hadrian VI and the Emperor Charles V converted the Indians of New Spain, it purports to be the record of a debate between the original twelve Franciscans and a group of Indian lords and priests held shortly before the arrival of the former in Mexico City. The text, unfortunately incomplete, is in both Spanish and Náhuatl. Sahagún contributed a preface explaining that it was derived from notes taken at the time but not written up until 1564, when his native collaborators turned it into literary Náhuatl. As such it is a striking example of the cultural fusion which the old friar was trying so strenuously to promote.

The book was frankly designed as propaganda showing how the friars persuaded the Mexicans to repudiate paganism. However, it is clearly not a mere product of clerical invention. In all likelihood it is a literary version of discussions which actually took place, more probably in unharmed Texcoco, where the population was swelled by fugitive members of the Aztec establishment, than in the ravaged region of Tenochtitlán. It is entirely in line with the character of the Twelve that they should have wished to challenge representatives of the old religion to a debate, although as early as 1524 the exchanges would necessarily have been conducted through interpreters. What stands out in the *Colloquies* is the dignity and pathos with which the Indians present their *apologia*. Moreover they make their own philosophic view of reality, and of the relationship between gods and men, sound peculiarly reasonable and attractive, while toning down the enormities which were practised in order to propitiate those gods.

They indignantly refuted the friars' attack on their religion as false and repugnant.

> Our fathers and ancestors [they replied] who came to live in this land, told us something quite different. They taught us to believe in the gods, to accord them due honour and service; that is why we eat dirt before the gods, draw blood from our bodies, make offerings, burn incense and render human sacrifice. Their doctrine was that the gods gave us our life through their grace and merits. It is the gods who provide us with our sustenance, all that we eat and drink; maize, seeds, beans, herbs and sage. From them we beg water, the rain that causes things to grow on earth. Could there ever have been a time when they were not honoured

and invoked with dances and worship? They have established their seats and thrones throughout the whole world, and have granted to men kingdoms, lordships, honour and fame. Who are we now to discard the teaching and tradition of our elders, of the Chichimecs, the Toltecs, the Culhúa and the Tepanecs? It lives in our hearts, it is present at our birth, in our growth, in our upbringing. It is the voice of our feelings, the source of our own prayers.

Whether they were relying on notes taken forty years earlier or on their own imagination, the Indians of Tlatelolco who wrote the Náhuatl text of this eloquent swan-song did their best to mirror their grandfathers' state of mind. Consciously or unconsciously they gave it the rhythm of a psalm. When it came to printing the *Colloquies*, a licence was duly granted in 1583, but like other works which treated the Mexican past with understanding and sympathy, and invested it with glamour, they were in fact never published. Either the licence was rescinded or other means were found of suppressing the book.

But for all their eloquence the Indian spokesmen had already conceded defeat. It was not so much the military disaster that mattered for it was recognized that Cortés could not have overcome Tenochtitlán if he had not been joined by Tlaxcala and Texcoco. They knew that the whole vast fabric of Nahua society, intellectual and moral, cosmology and all, had been irreparably ruined. They could also see that their doctrine had already been repudiated by the Nahua people, who had turned their backs on them and were eagerly awaiting to hear what the friars had to tell them. They themselves were left high and dry, the prophets of a world order which had suddenly lost its credibility.

In the circumstances no adaptation or compromise could be expected of them. Those Indian lords who were useful to the government and enjoyed privileges and favours from it in return, rapidly assumed a veneer of Spanish manners. They wore European clothing, furnished their houses in European style, mounted horses, carried swords and guns and even sported Castilian coats of arms. They tried to make the best of both worlds, hanging on to their hereditary possessions and vassals while intermarrying with Spaniards and turning themselves gradually into Creole landowners. In the long term they sacrificed their Indian identity in order to preserve their status and material well-being. This gradual process involved their assimilation or disappearance, and can be traced in numerous family histories down to late colonial times. It was otherwise with the men who provided the intellectual mainspring of pre-Conquest society, those "whose duty", in the words of the *Colloquies*, "it was to observe the course and appointed order of the heavens, and how the night is divided, those who watch and those who teach, those who turn the pages of the codices". They were unassimilable, and faded silently into oblivion.

In neither case did the friars, when working out their conception of the future place of the Indian in New Spain, bother much with the survivors from the higher stratum of the old society. They were content if these conformed with the outward observance of Christianity and caused no scandal by relapsing into the old ways like Don Carlos of Texcoco. There was nothing to be made of people whose stuffing had been so thoroughly knocked out of them. The new Nahua élite would have to be formed from the new generation. The friars planned to draw it chiefly, but not exclusively, from the children of the upper class, while the mass of the people, once converted, was so far as possible segregated from unsettling influences and controlled by strict paternal discipline. They proceeded from the assumption that the kingdom of New Spain must necessarily be built on a foundation of thousands of self-subsistent and largely self-governing peasant communities. Apart from their obligation to provide the King with the revenues and labour required to make his overseas realm a profitable concern, and to furnish sustenance for the purely Spanish towns, these Indians ought to be left alone. Their traditional life should be modified only by the substitution of Christianity for their ancestral beliefs and by the introduction of such novelties from Europe as would make their economy more prosperous. Their society was to be basically egalitarian, because the native lords entitled to live parasitically off peasant tribute would be phased out with the passage of time, and the development of a middle class was not envisaged at all.

The ideal of a separate or semi-separate Indian commonwealth as the foundation of New Spain was too Utopian to prevail for long, even in those provinces, like Vasco de Quiroga's Michoacán, where it obtained its best results in practice. In the country as a whole the friars' experiment in static paternalism broke down after a few decades. Monasteries might proliferate, but there were never enough friars to guide and protect their wards against change. Nor did the Mendicant Orders succeed in preserving the very special prestige which had made them a virtually independent Estate in the early years of the colony. Both government and Church became jealous of their influence and gave preference to the secular clergy. Inevitably, too, the friars shed their dynamism. Their once burning sense of mission cooled into the comfortable acceptance of a leisured and civilized existence varied by a little teaching and the management of monastic lands. This loss of élan was an important factor in encouraging the spread of the hacienda system at the expense of the Indian communities. Especially in the more fertile and accessible districts, Creoles encroached on Indian lands and gradually reduced their former communal owners to the status of landowners' serfs.

Admittedly this was by no means a uniform development. In many regions the Indians remained unmolested, with their lands and institutions intact. The diary of an enterprising Spanish friar, Francisco de Azofrin, who footslogged his way round Mexico between 1763 and 1766, is full of references to the "repúblicas de Indios" which he found living their own lives free from official or private pressures and where he was invariably made welcome. Incidentally his chosen method of travel was regarded as decidedly eccentric in the eighteenth century. The whole rugged province of Oaxaca, he reported, was "possessed by Indians", while further north, where the landscape was more accommodating and the economy richer, the Creoles had taken over with their haciendas, mines and towns of the Spanish model, and towns governed by Indians were comparatively rare. In general society had become more fluid, with the mestizos, an element which had not entered into the idealists' calculations, constantly on the increase.

The enthusiasts who launched Tlatelolco believed that the new Indian leaders whom they hoped to train would be imbued with the best elements in the two cultures and that they would come to rival their Spanish opposite numbers in attainments and general ability. Although they were not visionaries but men accustomed to deal in realities, their aims were no doubt unreal and quixotic—more so than appeared at the time. It was wrong to expect that a race of Nahua paragons would so easily emerge from a shock-stricken human environment, or that Spaniards and Creoles would ever put up with their pretentions to equality. In retrospect all that we can say is that their attempt to bring about a racial balance at the top was doomed to failure.

Eventually the cultural bridge was built at popular level, as Hispanic influence seeped steadily into the Nahua mass. Of the new habits which the Indians acquired, not all were beneficial, and one of the most harmful, in the eyes of contemporary observers, was the use of alcohol. Social drinking in the European fashion was not practised in pre-Conquest Anáhuac; indeed it was stringently forbidden by the Aztec rulers and fiercely punished. Anyone found drunk in public was liable to be strangled or clubbed to death. Only one kind of alcoholic drink was known to the Nahuas, that is octli (now called pulque), the fermented sap of the maguey cactus, but it did not need much of this powerful liquor to befuddle those who were rash enough to indulge in it illicitly. The sole exception to the strict ban on the social drinking of octli was made in the favour of old people, who were allowed to resort to it on certain festivals and family occasions, but it appeared that it also figured in religious rites in honour of the rustic deities known as the Four Hundred Rabbits. One suspects that there must have been much clandestine brewing which the rulers were powerless to prevent. At all events they had no illusions about the natural tendency of Mexicans of every class to drink to excess if the prohibitions were relaxed. Unlike the sober Iberians, their instinct was to get dead drunk or not drink at all.

In the light of the Aztec emperors' warnings against alcoholism as a source of vice and crime, it is unnecessary to attribute its spread after the Conquest to the miseries of colonial rule. For some unexplained reason the addiction was innate and was only waiting for an opportunity to get out of hand. The Spaniards tried to check it, but as they did not regard drinking as a crime in itself, their attempts at restraint were less wholehearted and effective than the Aztec regulations. Moreover, with the advent of European economics, the manufacture and sale of pulque became good business. Pulquerías abounded and lands formerly under maize were increasingly turned over to maguey plantations.

Before leaving the subject of drunkenness one is tempted to add a word about the consumption by Indians of intoxicating and hallucinatory mushrooms, interest in which has become almost obsessional in some quarters. Much use was made in pre-Columbian Mexico of a whole range of narcotic and intoxicating plants for religious and medicinal purposes, but in strictly controlled conditions. It may also have been considered less reprehensible to induce excitement or stupor by this means than by drinking alcohol. In contrast to the banning of pulque at banquets, there is an almost light-hearted description in Sahagún of the effects produced by the little black mushrooms which were eaten, together with honey, as a kind of *hors d'oeuvre* at the feast traditionally offered by a merchant (pochtecatl) to his friends and superiors in society as soon as he felt rich enough to afford it. Such effects on the pochteca and their guests were, we are told, quite unpredictable. Some danced, some sang, some sat and wept quietly. Others had extraordinary visions, which might be delightful or extremely disagreeable, but which provided much food for speculation when they sobered up. But this sort of behaviour was only tolerated in exceptional circumstances, and after the Conquest drug-taking was not regarded, like alcoholism, as a social problem.

Hispanicization was a gradual process and apart from the conversion itself the Spaniards did not force the pace. It was not their purpose to turn Indians into imitation Spaniards. They preferred that a clear racial line should be drawn between conquerors and conquered, that the latter should continue to live like Indians and not ape Spanish manners. In the early colonial period the official policy that they should all be instructed in the Spanish language was not seriously put into effect, and it was anyhow nullified by the policy of the friars who contended that there was no need for the majority of them to learn Spanish at all. The main channels through which the Indians absorbed alien social influences were religious and economic.

The outward observances of Christianity—presence at Mass, participation in the sacraments and the performance of duties of one kind or another—did not make an Indian think and act like a Spaniard. Over the years, however, they did help him to forget many of the premises upon which his former existence had been based and slowly to change his attitudes and habits in the direction of Europe. The Christianity which he learned from the friars was confined to the essentials: doctrine and ethic were extremely simple and uncomplicated as compared with the unwieldy mass of myths and legends, rites and precepts constituting the pre-Columbian religion, which could never be grasped in its entirety by an ordinary individual and whose involved and esoteric symbolism could only be appreciated by select members of the priesthood. The Christianity of Anáhuac owed its unique flavour to the ingenuity and imagination with which the missionaries remodelled the old festivals and used their colour, dancing and music for new purposes, but they left no room for doubt among their converts that service was no longer being paid to the multitude of gods whose idols had been smashed into fragments. These had been swept away for good, and faded swiftly from folk memory even when the Christian God or Saint inherited useful attributes from the former deity. When the Augustinians penetrated the wild country of the Ocuiltecs in the mountains behind Malinalco, and after some tense moments succeeded in displacing the image of the local cave-god in favour of Nuestro Señor de Chalma, the Ocuiltecs recognized that the break was complete. There was no question of merely perpetuating the old cult under a new name, but equally there was no objection from the Augustinians' point of view to Nuestro Señor taking over the healing powers attributed to the cave-god and thus attracting the tens of thousands of pilgrims who still visit the shrine.

Much the same revolution occurred in Mexico as in the Mediterranean world of the fourth and fifth centuries A.D., but it was accomplished in an incomparably shorter time. There was a radical change of religion, but various features of the old cults were retained. Over the whole of New Spain, and beyond the frontiers of the former Aztec realm, the introduction of Christianity had a simplifying and unifying effect, with polytheism reduced to a veneration of the saints differing little from that practised in southern Europe. The unifying function is no better illustrated than by the development of the cult of the Virgin of Guadalupe.

Many people outside Mexico are familiar with the story of

Juan Diego, the middle-aged Indian to whom the Virgin appeared on the hill of Tepeyac, the town which stood at the end of the northern causeway from Tenochtitlán, while he was walking to Tlatelolco from his home at Cuauhtitlán. She commanded Juan Diego to seek out Bishop Zumárraga and say that she desired him to build a church in her honour on the spot of her appearance. Twice he tried and failed to obtain an audience from the Bishop, and when he was eventually received he was ordered to produce proof of the Virgin's wishes. In his predicament he was granted a third vision. This time he was directed to climb to the top of the hill, pick the roses which he would find there, wrap them in his cloak and display them to the Bishop. He duly gathered the roses, which he found miraculously growing among the waterless rocks, but when he unfolded his cape (tilma) to show them to Zumárraga, there was seen to be imprinted on it the likeness of the Virgin which is now preserved in the great Basilica of Guadalupe at Tepeyac.

The third appearance was said to have taken place on 12th December, 1531, and two years later a small chapel was built to house the picture. About the middle of the century the romantic legend was put on record in Náhuatl, but it was not published till 1649, when the then Vicar of Guadalupe added an introduction and a list of miracles worked by the image, also in excellent Náhuatl, and gave the book to the press. By that time La Guadalupana was well on the way to becoming the patron saint of New Spain and the symbol of nascent Mexican nationalism. But at first the cult encountered stiff opposition, and was fiercely denounced by prominent Franciscans. This may seem surprising, especially if it is accepted that Zumárraga, himself a Franciscan, was responsible for perpetrating a pious fraud recalling the Holy Shroud of Milan and the Holy Face of Lucca, and for borrowing the name of Guadalupe from a famous shrine in Spain. Whatever the source of the story, the Franciscan critics declared roundly, with a rationalism worthy of the French Philosophes, that the picture had been painted by an Indian. Moreover it threatened to revive the worship of the mother-goddess Tonantzin, one of many aspects of the all-purpose goddess Coatlicue, whose temple had formerly stood at Tepeyac. They advised strongly that the new cult should be suppressed. However, in the ensuing controversy Zumárraga's successor, Archbishop Montúfar, came to the Virgin's rescue, and the Franciscans' fears of an emotional reaction in favour of the old religion proved groundless. The "dark Virgin" came to be revered by all Mexicans, whites as well as Indians, not as a member of the now shadowy Aztec pantheon but as the Christian Mother of God and special patroness of their country.

The family life of the Nahuas was affected to some extent by the conversion. The Church was particularly fussy in its insistence that its converts must be properly married, or remarried with Christian rites, and strictly observe Christian marriage rules for the rest of their lives. Spaniards pretended to believe that Indians had exceptionally strong sexual appetites and that this natural inclination to "luxury" needed to be strongly repressed. The only substance for this view was the polygamy indulged in by the richer members of the upper class. The latter could not understand the Spanish attitude towards what they considered not so much as an outlet for "luxury" as a sensible economic arrangement for absorbing surplus women into large households. Nor did they see why, provided that they married one legal wife in the Christian fashion, they should not continue to support a quantity of women of undefined status. It required much pressure to compel them to dissolve their seraglios. The macehualtín, on the other hand, presented no such problem, because they were in the main already monogamous. The only trouble was that many of them had never bothered to go through the elaborate and picturesque native marriage rites but had simply settled down for life with a partner without any formal sanction or ceremony. These needed convincing that Christian marriage would confer superior social status on those who entered into it, and opened the door to many benefits which the friars were ready to dispense to the non-recalcitrant.

Nevertheless it was frequently hard to sort out which of the women with whom a man was associated was the one who should be properly wedded to him. A typical and ludicrous case was reported from Michoacán. Two Indians, Pedro and Maria, were married by a friar in church, but Pedro soon grew tired of his wife and took up with another girl. Having done this, he decided that he wanted to marry her. So he calmly went back to the friar, saying that he had been formerly married to the girl in the native fashion before he married Maria. The friar hastily declared Pedro's church wedding invalid, married him off to the girl and even found a new husband for Maria. So far so good, but the volatile Pedro became equally tired of his new wife and wishing to go back to the first, sought out the friar once again and confessed that he had told a lie. He besought the friar to straighten things out. Quite confused, and behaving more and more uncanonically, the friar proceeded to divorce both couples and remarried Pedro to Maria. We leave him scratching his head over the difficulty of bringing together Maria's ephemeral husband and Pedro's discarded girl.

Similar situations must have often cropped up before the Indians grasped what was expected of them. From the beginning they seem to have welcomed with enthusiasm the Spanish custom of compradrazgo (godfathership), by which a child's godparents are linked in a peculiarly close and lasting relationship not only to the child but to its real parents. Compadres are more like blood-brothers, and the term is used universally as an intimate and friendly form of address.

In general the changes brought about by the Conquest tended to strengthen an Indian's direct family ties at the expense of his allegiance to wider groups such as the calpulli, which was essentially a group of families living in close association. He retained his strong sense of communal loyalty, but with the instant disappearance of educational institutions such as the calmecac and the telpochcalli and their substitution by the monastery school, his social training acquired a European tinge. Hispanicization was also assisted by the levelling process which Indian society underwent during the sixteenth century, and which was accelerated by the rapid shrinkage of the population as a whole. Although the upper stratum of the Señores Naturales put up a tough fight for survival, the junior nobles or pipiltin could not afford the struggle and were easily reduced to the status of commoners. At the other end of the scale the two classes roughly corresponding to serfs and slaves in the Aztec period vanished completely. Such telescoping of the classes into a more or less uniform society undoubtedly favoured the absorption of influences from the other civilization.

On the economic side such influences were most active in the towns. An independent artisan, say a leather-worker or silversmith producing high quality goods of European style for the

Creole market, would end by becoming something of a European himself and having more in common with his counterpart in Seville or Córdoba than with a pre-Conquest craftsman. His attachment to the old communal life would weaken when he made a good living by his individual efforts in semi-European surroundings. Indians who hovered half-way between the two societies could make money if they showed initiative: for example they successfully exploited the retail trade for supplying Creole needs for Indian products, despite the official policy, not very conscientiously adhered to and anyway unworkable, of keeping the Creole and Indian economies as separate as possible. Nevertheless they did not start to build up into a distinct Indian or Indian-mestizo middle class, while the former privileged merchant caste, the pochteca, was dissolved after the Conquest.

Another category of natives with one foot in each world were the minor employees of the administration—interpreters, clerks, constables and such-like—and the higher servants, stewards and overseers of Spanish and Creole masters. These were more or less familiar with Castilian ways and could manage at least a smattering of written and spoken Spanish. Such was that Juan Bautista already mentioned as a tribute collector and the keeper of a diary in Náhuatl, which unfortunately covers only five consecutive years, 1569–74. He is one of the examples revealed to us of the city-bred Indian of early colonial times, lively, inquisitive and almost professionally *au courant* with what was going on in Mexico-Tenochtitlán. The diary ranges from ultra-laconic entries from which we learn the contemporary price of a chicken or a bunch of bananas, or that "paper of Castille", i.e. writing-paper, has become insufferably scarce and expensive, to descriptions of current events—bullfights, tournaments, Indian fiestas, crimes and punishments, natural phenomena, epidemics, social, personal and religious occasions (including a stirring sermon by Sahagún). Here is an extract from his piece about a riot in the city in which the rather solemn, repetitive style of the Náhuatl gives way to racy and straightforward reportage worthy of a modern newsman.

> There was a great uproar. The Gobernador plucked up courage and without waiting for orders dashed into the mob.

He, Peter the Penitent, shouldering his staff of office, tried to restrain and separate the rioters, pushing them to one side or the other. But they flung themselves on him, mishandled him and crowded round with intent to kill him. They nearly pulled his shirt off, so he was stuck there half-naked. However they left him in peace when Juan Cano came to his aid, drew his sword and told the mob to be quiet. If it had not been for him, they would have killed the governor. When the shouting began everyone rushed to the roof-tops to have a look. The Castilians gathered on one of them, and a group ran off from there to see what was happening at the palace. More and more people flocked to the spot. The stall-holders from the San Hipolito market left their stalls and ran to see what was up; so did people from their houses, indeed everybody, old men, old women, children, everybody living in the city. Such was the crush that they burst through the parapet of the upper house (the one that had flowers planted along the edge). At that moment a Spaniard constable came on the scene, drew his sword and ran after the people. Spanish spectators also drew their swords and attacked them. But the women made a hole in the wall of the left-hand courtyard and they were carried bodily through it. The men charged roughly through it, tearing their clothes in the process; many were hurt and some seriously.*

The Gobernador who tried to stop the riot and had so narrow an escape was presumably the chief Indian municipal officer, but we have no idea why Juan Bautista called him "Peter the Penitent". His vivid reporting of the incident gives us an all-too-rare glimpse through Indian spectacles of the turbulent Mexico City of the time of the Avila conspiracy. It is a pity that we know so little about him. He had certainly received an adequate education, for he wrote a clear and up-to-date Náhuatl and his very occasional use of a Spanish phrase suggests that he also was at home in that language. He can be pictured as a man of humble origin, the product of a friars' school, who had secured himself a comfortable niche in colonial society and come to terms with it. No doubt there were many like him.

* Bautista's manuscript is quoted by Angel Maria Garibay, *Historia de la Literatura Náhuatl*

In the larger towns where the natives lived alongside Spaniards and a fast-growing, rootless mass of mestizos, mulattos and more complicated products of cross-breeding, opportunities for advancement and enrichment through personal initiative were not lacking, though no Indian outside the decaying tlatoque class could hope to climb beyond the lower rungs of the social ladder. In the countryside, however, the villagers led a static existence. They seldom left their communities except when recruited for forced labour. The only really mobile Indians were those who adopted the typically Spanish occupation of arrieros, drivers of the mules and packhorses which were replacing the traditional human carriers for the long-distance transport of goods. Changes in agriculture, the introduction of stockbreeding and the diffusion of new techniques brought greater variety to the rural scene and produced a very gradual shift towards Europeanization, but this was at first confined to the minimum required from the efficient farmer or rural craftsman. When preparing to sow wheat the peasant employed a plough, but for planting maize he continued to use the ancestral coa or digging stick. In deference to his European masters he wore trousers—but a very Mexican form of that garment which has still not yet been entirely superseded by blue jeans—and eventually adopted the straw hat to which the urban worker as well as the peasant still clings. But he spoke only his own language, and his horizon was bounded by the next range of hills.

Yet it is in the rural backwaters that the most significant examples of early fusion between the two cultures are to be found. There the process developed swiftly and strikingly in the artistic rather than in the economic and social field. As a general statement it is true that New Spain was a Spanish superstructure set on Indian foundations. As regards the arts, however, Rodney Gallop, in his perceptive book *Mexican Mosaic*, was right to claim that these

> are the product not of Spanish influence on an Indian foundation but of Indian influence on a Spanish foundation. In other words, the Spaniards substituted their own for the pre-existing Indian arts, and the Indians stamped them in turn with their unmistakable cachet. Nowhere is this more obvious than in the field of architecture . . . and in ornament

especially the Indian masons influenced its evolution as much or more than the Spanish or Italian architects who worked in the New World.

Proof of this assertion is afforded by the innumerable sixteenth-century monuments of Anáhuac. According to an eminent Mexican authority, Pedro Rojas, 272 major or minor edifices were built within the century in New Spain as a whole. This creative outburst can only be compared with what happened in the Europe of the early Middle Ages when "the whole earth was clothed anew in a white mantle of churches". The friar-architects of New Spain were not professionals but gifted improvisers. They experimented with a variety of architectural and decorative styles, some of which were already centuries out of date in the Old World, and succeeded in evolving from them a uniform and harmonious pattern singularly suited to Mexican requirements and the Mexican landscape. Romanesque, gothic, mudejar, contemporary plateresque and classical renaissance were all pressed into service, while the underlying simplicity of design which governed the use of these styles was complemented and in some cases overlaid by the exuberant ornament derived by Indian craftsmen from a mixture of tradition and fantasy.

In pre-Columbian days the artistic genius of the Nahuas and other Indian peoples had been overwhelmingly concentrated on the construction and adornment of their temples. It was therefore logical that these energies should have been transferred to the monasteries which replaced the wrecked teocallis. Few religious structures of a non-monastic character were erected during the sixteenth century and these, such as the primitive cathedral of Mexico City, were undistinguished architecturally and destined to be swept away in the succeeding age of the baroque. Similarly the houses of the early colonists, though frequently laid out on a lavish scale, possessed little artistic merit. Of the surviving examples, the so-called palace of Cortés at Cuernavaca is essentially a modest mediaeval manor house. The residence of the conquistador Montejo at Mérida in Yucatán (outside the former Aztec realm) has a charming plateresque portal, but neither of these buildings can be regarded as the mixed product of Spanish and Indian talent.

But hybridism in the arts, as manifested in the monasteries, became a more conspicuous feature of the Mexican scene than the small degree of hybridism of behaviour which we have already noticed. The Nahuas may have been reluctant to adopt Spanish customs but they responded quickly to the artistic stimulus resulting from the virtually total erasure of the finer products of the old culture. They had not yet finished reducing the Aztec monuments, with all their wealth of ornamental sculpture, to a mass of shapeless rubble before they were executing fresh designs, under the friars' sponsorship, for the decoration of the monastic ensembles. The urge to recreate and reshape took immediate effect.

The churches themselves were often constructed on the former temple platforms and with stone from the teocallis. They also owe their simple grandeur and solidity as much to the excellence of Indian masons as to the imagination of Spanish architects, few of whom had been trained as such. Basically, however, they are European in inspiration and design, a special form of late gothic evolved for Mexican conditions. While they bear the stamp of the Tudor age, they were never, as John McAndrew observes, mere replicas of churches in Spain, or indeed in any European country. Taken together with their subsidiary buildings, they are more typically and originally Mexican than the baroque and churrigueresque monuments which too often monopolize the admiration of visitors.

The largest of these massive structures measures about two hundred feet in length and seventy in width. A standard church —not many vary from the norm—consists of a huge, austere nave without aisles or transepts. It is tall, barrel-vaulted, thick-walled and well buttressed on the exterior. For the Indians the vault was a wonderful innovation; at first they could not understand why the blocks composing them failed to collapse when left without scaffolding.

The stark interiors were relieved by attractive patterns of rib-vaulting over the chancel, the choir-gallery at the west end and sometimes the nave as well. "There is no more handsome or dramatic display," says McAndrew, "of the successful transplanting of mediaeval artistic forms to the New World than these thoroughly gothic interiors" (*The Open Air Churches of Sixteenth Century Mexico*). A marked complexity of style characterizes the windows and portals which break up the solemn exteriors. Mediaeval rose windows adorn churches in the States of Morelos and Hidalgo, and in the wild depths of Huaxteca. Doorways may be in a plain or romantic version of romanesque, plateresque or severely classical in the Italian manner, but in many cases a bizarre mixture of styles occurs on the same façade, and there is no stylistic unity between the portal and the window above. Often, too, Indian sculptors have been given licence to introduce motifs of their own into the decoration, and when these are combined, as frequently happens, with mudejar or the late form of Portuguese gothic which reflects Hindu influence, the results are almost freakish.

The Indian carvers became adept at reproducing non-Indian models, but they infused into their work a subtle indigenous quality, and many ornamental details are purely Mesoamerican, as in certain floral designs, or when the conventional sign representing speech, familiar from Aztec manuscripts, issues from the mouth of a human figure. A Mexican expert, José Moreno Villa, labelled this composite style with the name "tequitqui", a Náhuatl word meaning "person who pays tribute". The term thus applies to works of art produced by the subject race for its alien masters and is the rough equivalent of "mudejar", that is the work of conquered Moslems in Spain for their Christian overlords.

The temptation for the tequitqui artists was to cover large surfaces with thickly woven designs, a natural tendency which could conflict with the requirements of Christian iconography. But when given a chance, they indulged it to the full. Countless examples of their work can be studied throughout New Spain, from sophisticated Anáhuac to rustic Michoacán, notably on the chapels for Indians opening on the monastery courtyards and on the smaller processional chapels standing at the corners of these vast "atrios". The richest and most spectacular sequence of sculptured ornament is that of the open chapel of Franciscan Tlalmanalco, a village lying on the western slopes of Ixtaccíhuatl. Fray Martín de Valencia, leader of the Twelve, was buried there, and the writer Chimalpahín was the local tlatoani.

Here the chapel was planned on a grand scale, and the Indian genius has frankly taken charge of the decorative scheme. Arches and pilasters are a mass of intricate carving, floral reliefs mingling with the busts and heads of human figures, monkey-like grotesques, skulls and animal forms. The basic conception is more plateresque than anything else, but the idiom of its execution is compulsively Indian. Indeed pre-Conquest Tlalmanalco was famous for its stone-carvers, and some idea of the high quality of their work may be derived from the remnants of Aztec sculpture now gathered in the Museum of Anthropology at Mexico City.

Another curious illustration of cultural fusion in the artistic field is the almost disconcerting affinity between certain outstanding pieces of Aztec sculpture and the sculptured crosses erected in the centre of the monastery courtyards. The former are compact masses of symbolism carefully intended to portray the whole relationship between gods and men. Such is the great statue of the goddess Coatlicue in the same museum, which before it reveals its significance looks merely blockish and even repulsive to European eyes. The latter convey a more simple message. They are profusely decorated, if not smothered, with carvings in relief of the symbols of the Passion, such as the Crown of Thorns, the Nails and the Blood. One particularly elaborate example includes the column of the Flagellation, with the cock that crowed for St Peter perched on its capital and with a sceptre and a ladder on either side of it. Below it come a Nail and a gush of Blood between a hammer and pliers, and further below a Host and Chalice between a scourge and a spear. The figure of Christ is hardly ever represented in its entirety but by a bearded face or mask. On one cross in Michoacán the Indians actually substituted for the Holy Face an obsidian mirror surrounded by a Crown of Thorns, thus combining an especially sacred symbol of the old religion with one of the new. Fleurs de Lys are twined round the letters INRI at the head of the crosses or sprout from the ends of the arms. There is much variety in the grouping of symbols. The inevitable Aztec skull may appear at the foot of the cross, and occasionally there is a touch, as it were, of light relief as when, at Cuauhtitlán, the heads of the local encomendero (the ill-fated Alonso de Avila) and of the guardian of the monastery are realistically sculpted on each arm. In two other examples it is the encomendero and his opposite number, the local Indian lord, who are represented.

The Spaniards much admired the facility with which the Nahuas learned to paint in the European manner. They learned so easily that they promptly abandoned their own muralist technique and conventions which they had inherited from the depths of the classical age, retaining their traditional style only in the codices which they continued to produce for many years after the Conquest. In the decoration of the monasteries, however, they had enormous scope for practising an art for which they possessed an inborn talent. The Conquest resulted in the complete obliteration of the miles of colourful frescoes which had adorned the teocallis and the dwellings of important men, but the Indians, who had a horror of leaving surfaces undecorated, seem to have been highly stimulated by the challenge which was offered them of giving visible expression to the content of their new faith. They painted churches, cloisters and open chapels; walls, staircases, ceilings and even whole vaults, in short whatever spaces they were allowed or encouraged to fill. Motolinía, an enthusiastic sponsor of Indian artists, recalls how in 1539 the Tlaxcalans painted the outside of a large chapel in four days. On one surface they depicted the labours of the first three days of the creation, and on another those of the three following days. Also represented were the tree of Jesse, St Francis, the Pope with princes of the Church and the Emperor with the grandees of his realms.

All over New Spain native painters were displaying the same ant-like activity. Very many of their murals have disappeared, defaced in civil wars or hidden under coats of whitewash, but in recent years much has been done to rediscover, preserve and restore them, particularly in the impressive groups of Augustinian houses within easy distance from Mexico City. Painting is usually in black on a white ground, bright colours being used more sparingly. Although far the greater part of the compositions were executed by Indians, both the Christian iconography and the endless decorative friezes with their typical Renaissance motifs are almost totally European, being taken from books and collections of prints imported from the Hapsburgs' European dominions, the Iberian countries, Italy, Germany and notably Flanders. A few itinerant masters from those lands may have been invited to work in the larger monasteries. The Indians were enjoined to copy the models faithfully and were not permitted to indulge in anything like the fantasy which breaks through in their sculpture. Thus their work is more remarkable for its volume than its quality and the indigenous accent, with a few exceptions, is very faint. Only occasionally are scenes of local interest portrayed, such as Cortés prostrating himself before the friars in the presence of three Indian lords, the martyrdom of Indian child converts by recalcitrant pagans and the likenesses of the Twelve at Huejotzingo. But although the Indo-Spanish mural painting has a limited aesthetic value, it remains a splendid monument of collective energy and a significant example of spontaneous Indian response to an exotic stimulus. It was also a short-lived phenomenon which hardly outlasted the sixteenth century. The baroque era that followed produced a flourishing school of painters of retables and panel pictures of Spanish or Flemish inspiration, but these were the creations of individuals, mostly Creoles and mestizos, and not of a widespread movement of popular origin.

We have seen that by 1600 the forces working for harmony between the two races and for the fusion of what was best in the two cultures had spent themselves like rivers running into the desert. The ideals which had been pursued with such enthusiasm and intensity of purpose while New Spain was being founded had lost their potency or seemed no longer relevant in the prevailing atmosphere of unadventurous repose.

Picking our way through the wreckage of frustrated hopes and abortive enterprises, we have to ask why the period should not simply be written off as a dismal failure, beginning with the tragic extinction of a civilization and ending in the colonial exploitation of a subjected people, up to four-fifths of whom had been swept away by deadly and uncontrollable diseases imported by the exploiters. Was it not a record of failure in terms of government and human relations, of cultural progress and material betterment?

The opposite thesis is well presented by the French scholar, Robert Ricard, who (in *La Conquista Espirituelde Mexico*) writes as follows:

> the sixteenth century is the period of fundamental importance in the history and formation of post-Hispanic Mexico. During that time the encounter between civilizations which so delights ethnologists took the most vigorous form; native American elements and contributions from Spain were juxtaposed, fused and amalgamated. From their union arose

the personality of Mexico as it is today; it contains the germ of the country's development in later eras.

Few Mexicans would now quarrel with that assessment, but it is perhaps hard to understand why.

It is true that the co-existence and parallel development under the Crown of two racial communities, each with its properly defined status and functions but one subordinate to the other's authority while retaining its rights and dignities, had proved an unworkable concept. What is surprising is the persistence with which it was upheld in the early period by the Spanish government and the religious Orders alike. Broadly speaking, colonial policy was swayed by two competing and contradictory pressures. The first was a straightforward urge to exploit the transatlantic territories for the purpose of satisfying the material needs of the Hapsburg empire. The second, and more powerful, was a deeply felt sense of religious duty which enjoined the conversion of native peoples and the equitable treatment of the converted. It sprang from an ardent sense of mission which was part of the mediaeval Spanish inheritance and was enhanced by the bold ideas of Renaissance thinkers which had been imbibed by so many of the leading figures in New Spain. Thus the government at home and its agents, the first Viceroys, were acutely sensitive to the need to resolve the contradictions of policy for the benefit of the indigenous population. They worried over this problem to an extent almost inconceivable for the rulers of a society which had hardly emerged from its mediaeval shell. Confronted with utterly novel situations, they tried to deal with them by painstaking bureaucratic methods and a flood of enactments, ordinances and instructions of every kind which, though frequently self-defeating, testify to their very real preoccupation with making New Spain a justly governed, prosperous and contented Christian Kingdom. Hence their irritation when they met with obstruction and disobedience from encomenderos and unscrupulous adventurers, and their unsympathetic attitude, throughout most of the century, to Creoles in general.

If any other European seafaring power in the Tudor age had blundered upon Mexico and undertaken its conquest, it is, to put it mildly, less than likely that the Indians would have received better treatment from those conquerors than they did from the Spaniards. Much more probably, after the horrors of conquest, they would have had to endure the sufferings of colonial rule without the advantage of any of its redeeming or palliative features. At the worst they could have been systematically wiped out, like their cousins further to the north. If it is rightly assumed that the Aztec empire and civilization were bound to be discovered and destroyed sooner or later in the century, it was fortunate that the death blow was inflicted by Spaniards. To judge only by the stormy controversies that fill the archives of the time, no other conquerors could have searched their consciences for so long and so thoroughly.

But with the accession of Philip II idealism in colonial affairs, so far as Mexico was concerned, was already waning. In the peninsula the bureaucracy hardened; it became less involved and less imaginative, and in New Spain itself the very intractability of the difficulties with which the government had to struggle spread a spirit of disillusion. There can have been little joy for a Viceroy in administering a country where the native population was so regularly decimated, and the Creoles were full of obstinate grudges. Yet the government did not lose its grip. Despite a disastrous shortage of labourers and tributaries, and an inevitable decrease of land under cultivation, the agricultural economy of Mexico was improved and diversified, mining was developed and the demands of the treasury at Madrid satisfied. Discipline, order and peace were maintained. Meanwhile the Creole society of Mexico City flourished in careless affluence, and the capital astonished contemporary visitors with its stately buildings and the broad, clear avenues which contrasted favourably with the poky constrictions of European cities. In 1605 Bernardo Balbuena celebrated its marvels in a rhetorical but lively epic entitled "Grandeza de Mexico", heaping fulsome praise on the elegance of its ladies, the beauty of the horses and the learning of the "heroic and eminent professors" of the seven liberal arts.

Such magnificence was attained by forgetting the precepts of the founders of New Spain. Position and affluence were firmly reserved for those of European descent and denied to the Indians by the most rigid barriers of privilege. In cultural matters Indians were refused both assimilation to the whites and development along their own lines. So Mexico settled down in a fixed colonial pattern which lasted until it was broken by the movement for national independence in the early nineteenth century.

In spite of the exclusion of the Indians from advancement there is much to be said in favour of the last two centuries of the colonial period. They exhibited a strong and attractive character of their own. Living as they did in conditions of unusual tranquillity and freedom from external disturbance, the Creoles evolved their peculiar culture and a way of life which sparkled with gold and gems as in Moctezuma's heyday. The cities and villages of Mexico are full of great monuments of their baroque and post-baroque architecture, and the sun flashes from the polychrome tiles of their domes. The styles, transplanted from Europe, are virtually untouched by indigenous influences; nevertheless, in numerous country churches, Indian sculptors and decorators have run riot with startling effect.

The age also produced outstanding writers, including the classical dramatist Juan Ruiz de Alarcon, born at Taxco, and the brilliant nun-poetess Juana Inés de la Cruz. However, the study of the Indian past, which had formerly been pursued with such dedication in the monasteries of New Spain, became the province of a few specialists. In his enormous *Monarquia Indiana*, first published in 1614, the Franciscan Fray Juan de Torquemada tried to bring together the researches of his sixteenth-century predecessors, incorporating in his work whole chunks of the writings of Mendieta and other friars. A much more original figure was the polymath Carlos Siguenza y Góngora, who occupied the chair of Mathematics at the Royal and Pontifical University towards the end of the seventeenth century. This erudite Creole, trained by the Jesuits of Tepotzotlán, revived the study of Indian antiquities at a time when such curiosity was regarded as distinctly eccentric. He made a large collection of pictographic manuscripts and composed a history of pre-Columbian Mexico which is unfortunately no longer extant. During the following century Mexico began to attract the attention of foreign historians, but the latter's descriptions were apt to be fanciful and unduly coloured by fashionable "philosophic" ideas. On the other hand the *Historia Antigua de Mexico* of the Creole Jesuit Francisco Xavier Clavijero, which he wrote in exile after the expulsion of his Order from New Spain, is a model of contemporary scholarship, reflecting his thorough acquaintance with the literary sources and, what is of still greater interest, a deep pride in the origins of the Mexican nation. He wrote as a patriot, the citizen of a lost fatherland, now the joint patrimony of Creoles, Indians and mestizos, whose glories he had undertaken to interpret to the world.

The nascent nationalism which led to Mexican independence in 1821 owed much to the steady improvement in material well-being which continued throughout the eighteenth century. As from 1650 the population ceased to shrink: all three categories of Mexicans gradually multiplied while the general level of prosperity rose significantly. Mexico surpassed all other overseas territories of the Spanish Crown in riches and contentment. Foreign travellers, from the naive Spanish friar Azofrín to the sophisticated Alexander von Humboldt, were vastly impressed by the evidences of material progress which they saw around them as well as by those of intellectual activity based on the foundation by the colonial government of new scientific and artistic institutions. New Spain was not only keeping pace with European countries but moving faster than many of them. Indeed the colony, outwardly so stable and smiling, had become an anachronism, for Mexico was now intellectually, economically and demographically fit to be a nation on its own.

The successful revolution in the British-American colonies showed the Creoles the way, but such was their innate respect for traditional monarchy that it was only when the latter's authority collapsed under the strain of the French revolutionary and Napoleonic Wars that they eventually, and half reluctantly, made their bid to take the government into their hands. In the destructive campaigns of independence and the accompanying popular tumults most of the colonial progress went by the board. Nevertheless the stage was now set for the processes of fusion which had been initiated in the sixteenth century under such promising auspices but later stultified and forced, as it were, underground, to emerge and gather strength. Independence for the first time brought to the fore men of mixed blood and some whose origins were more Indian than Creole, and in 1855, when the liberal reformers were swept into power, their leader was Benito Juarez, a pure Zapotec Indian.

Fifty years later a series of violent revolutionary upheavals confirmed the results of the slow biological change which had been taking place under the surface. The pendulum swung so far that Mexico's national mystique was for a time based purely on an appeal to the pre-Columbian past, and the achievements of the colonial era were officially denigrated. More recently, however, a just balance has been restored. Vasca de Quiroga and Sahagún are recognized as national heroes along with Nezahualcóyotl and Cuauhtémoc. National unity has at last been won through racial fusion and harmony between the two cultures and traditions. The vision of the sixteenth-century pioneers has been well and truly justified.

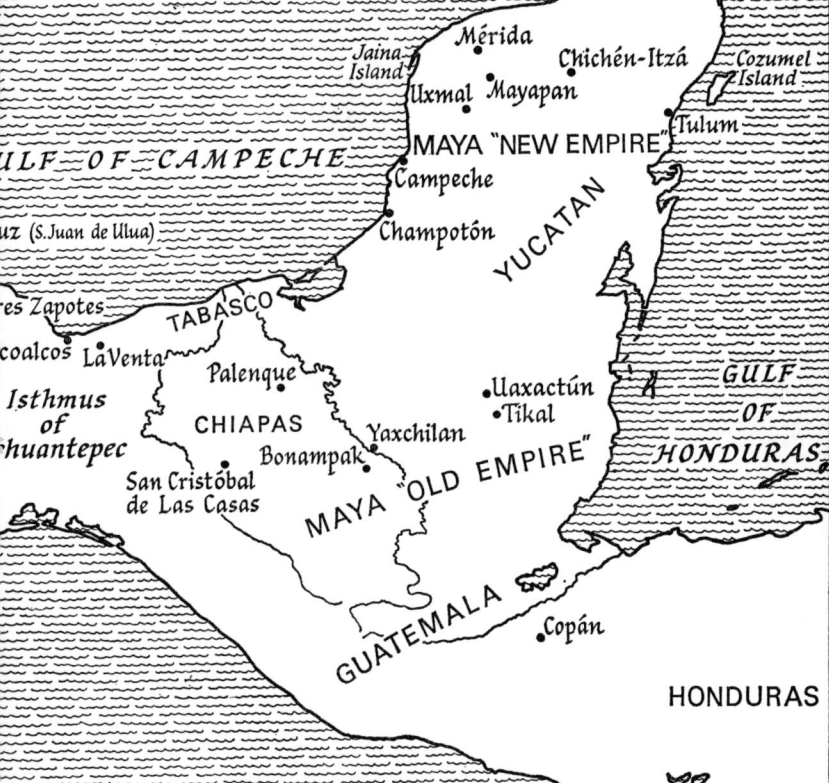

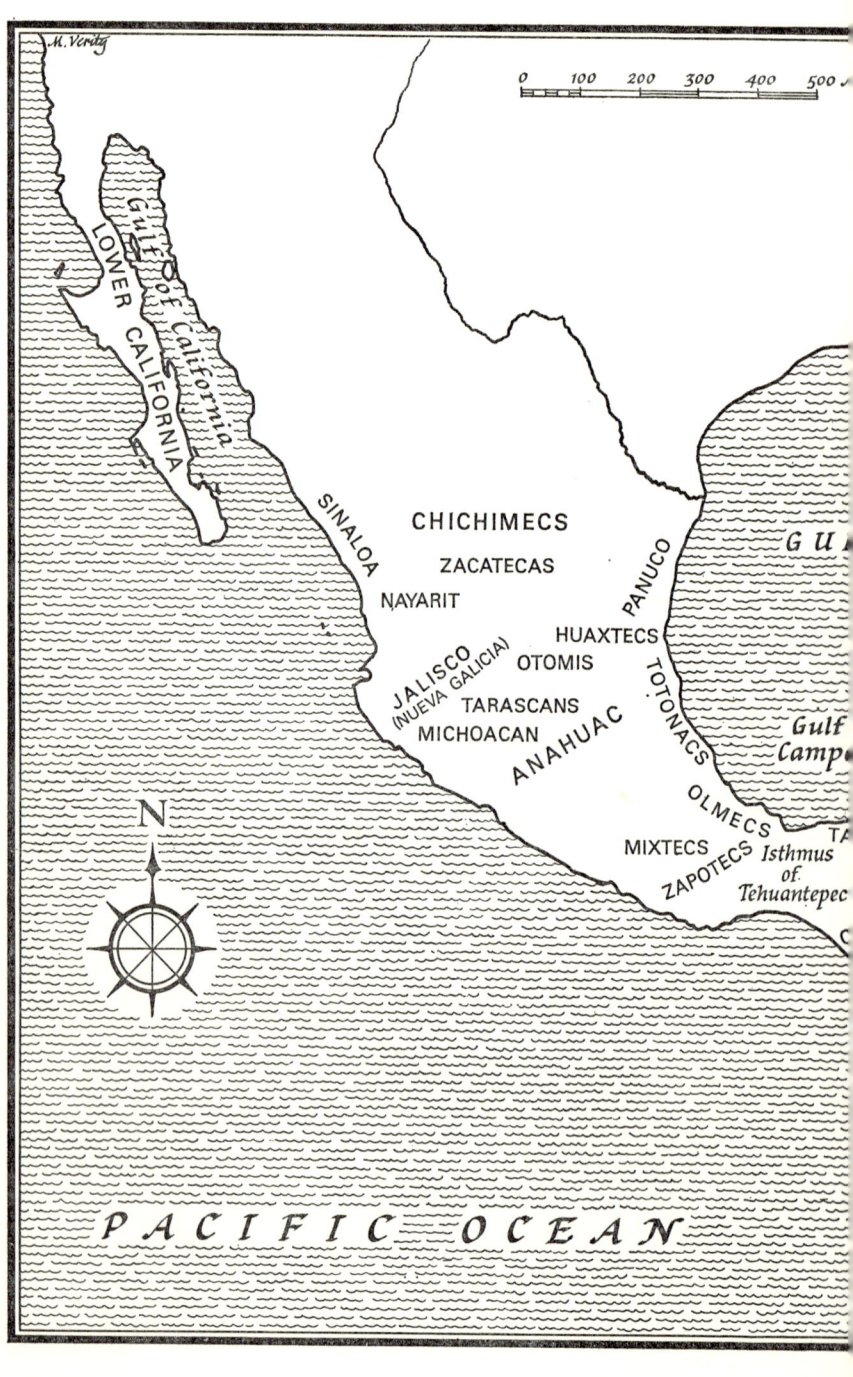

GLOSSARY

alcalde—mayor and judge of a Spanish Municipality or Indian town
amatl—wild fig tree, the bark of which the Aztecs used for making paper
arriero—muleteer
atrio—courtyard of a monastery
audiencia—high court and council of state, presided over by the Viceroy or by its own president
cabecera—Indian town, administrative centre of a district
cabildo—municipal council
calmecac—Aztec seminary, school for higher education
calpullec—chief or elder of a calpulli
calpulli—territorial or clan unit, parish
calpixqui (plural calpixque)—tax collector, steward or overseer. Uei calpixqui—Chief Minister in Aztec Empire
chichimec—frontier tribesman
chinampa—floating garden
chirimoya—tropical fruit, custard apple
Cihuacóatl—"serpent woman", highest dignitary of the Aztec Empire under the Emperor
coa—agricultural implement, digging stick
coatepantli—"snake-hedge", wall of sacred precinct in Tenochtitlán
compadre—godfather
corregidor—Senior Spanish official in charge of a district
corregimiento—Office of Corregidor
cuicatl—song, poem
encomendero—holder of an encomienda
encomienda—grant of tribute-paying Indians
gobernador—senior official of an Indian community
gobernadoryotl—office of gobernador
hacendado—Creole landowner
hacienda—private landed estate
halach uinic—Maya high chieftain
huehuetlatolli—"precepts of the elders", rules of Aztec social behaviour
juez de residencia—judge acting as inspector general

GLOSSARY

macehual (plural macehualtin)—commoner, peasant
maguey—agave cactus, producing pulque and fibres
mamey—tropical fruit
matlazahuatl—infectious disease, probably typhus
maxtlatl—breach-cloth
mestizo—person of mixed white and Indian blood
mudejar—art executed by Moslems in Spain for their Christian masters
nacom—Maya military commander
nahuatlato—interpreter
obraje—workshop, small factory
octli—liquor of the maguey, later called pulque
oidor—member of an Audiencia, judge
petlacalcatl—"granary-keeper", Aztec High Steward
peyotl—root with narcotic qualities
pilli (plural pipiltin)—lesser nobleman
pochtecatl (plural pochteca)—merchant
pulque—see octli
quetzal—tropical bird with gorgeous plumage
regidor—member of a municipal council
repartimiento—allotment of labour
tecuhtli (plural tetecuhtin)—higher nobleman
telpochcalli—college for young men
temazcalli—steam bath
tenochtli—prickly pear
teotl—god
teocalli—pyramidal temple
tequitqui—post-Conquest art style combining European motifs with Indian influence
tianguis—Indian market
tlacatecatl—Aztec Commander-in-Chief
tlacochcalcatl—Aztec "Adjutant-General"
tlacotli—slave
tlalmaitl—serf
tlamacazqui—priest
tlatoani (plural tlatoque)—sovereign, prince. Uei tlatoani—the Aztec Emperor
tlatocan—Aztec council of state
tochtli—rabbit
toltecatl (plural tolteca)—craftsman
tzompantli—skull-rack

visita—official inspection
visitador—official inspector
xochiyaoyotl—"flowery war"
yauhtli—hashish
zapote—tropical fruit
zocalo—the main square of colonial Mexico City

BIBLIOGRAPHY

Acosta, José de (1540–1600), *Historia Natural y Moral de las Indias*, ed. Edmundo O'Gorman, Mexico City: Fondo de Cultura Economico, 1962.

Aiton, A. S., *Antonio de Mendoza, First Viceroy of New Spain*, Durham, North Carolina: Duke University, 1927.

Ajofrin, Francisco de, *Diario del Viaje que hice a la America Septentrional (1763)*, Mexico City: Instituto Cultural Hispano-Mexicano, 1964.

Anonymous Conqueror (16th century), *Narrative of Some Things of New Spain and the Great City of Temestitán*, New York: Cortés Society, 1917.

Benitez, Fernando, *The Century after Cortés*, Chicago and London: University of Chicago, 1965.

Bernal, Ignacio, *Mexico before Cortés: Art, History, Legend*, New York: Doubleday, 1963.

Cameron, Roderick, *Viceroyalties of the West*, Weidenfeld and Nicolson, 1968.

Caso, Alfonso, *El Pueblo del Sol*, Mexico City: Fondo de Cultura Económica, 1953.

——, *La Religión de los Aztecas*, Mexico City: Enciclopedia Ilustrada Mexicana, 1936.

Cervantes de Salazar, Francisco (16th century), *Crónica de la Nueva España*, Madrid: Hispanic Society of America, 1914.

Cheetham, Sir Nicolas, *A History of Mexico*, Hart-Davis, 1970.

Clavijero, Francisco Javier (18th century), *Historia Antigua de Mexico* (4 vols), Mexico City: Editorial Porrúa, 1945.

Collis, Maurice, *Cortés and Montezuma*, Faber and Faber, 1954.

Cook, Sherburne F., and Woodrow, Borah, *The Indian Population of Central Mexico, 1531–1610*, Berkeley: University of California, 1960.

Cortés, Hernán (1455–1547), *Letters (Five Despatches to Charles V)*, translated and edited by F. A. McNutt (2 vols), New York: Putnam, 1908.

Diaz del Castillo, Bernal (1492–1581?), *Historia Verdadera de la Conquista de la Nueva España* (2 vols), Mexico City: Editorial Porrúa, 1960.

Dorantes de Carranza, Baltazar (late 16th century), *Sumaria Relación de las Cosas de la Nueva España*, Mexico City: Museo Nacional, 1938.

Duran, Diego (1540–88), *Historia de las Indias de Nueva España y Islas de Tierra Firme*, ed. José F. Ramirez (2 vols), Mexico City: Mexico City, 1867–80.

Fernandez, Justino, and O'Gorman, Edmundo, *Santo Tomas More y la Utopia de Tomas More en La Nueva España*, Mexico City: Alcancia, 1937.

Gallop, Rodney, *Mexican Mosaic*, Faber and Faber, 1939.

Garcia Icazbalceta, Joaquin, *Fray Juan de Zumarraga, Primer Obispo y Arzobispo de Mexico*, Buenos Aires: Espasa Calpe, 1952.

——, *Opusculos y Biografias*, Mexico City: University of Mexico, 1942.

Garibay, Angel Maria, *Historia de la Literatura Náhuatl* (2 vols), Mexico City: Editorial Porrúa, 1953.

Gibson, Charles, *The Aztecs under Spanish Rule*, Oxford University Press, 1964.

Gomez de Orozco, Federico (ed.), *Crónicas de Michoacán*, Mexico City: University of Mexico, 1940.

Hanke, Lewis, *The Spanish Struggle for Justice in the Conquest of America*, Philadelphia: University of Pennsylvania, 1949.

Ixtlilxóchitl, Fernando de Alva (1568–1648), *Obras Historicas*, ed. Alfredo Chavero (2 vols), Mexico City: Secretaria de Fomento, 1891–2.

——, *Decima Tercia Relación de la Venida de los Españoles y Principio de la Ley Evangelica*, Mexico City: Editorial Robredo, 1938.

Kirkpatrick, F. A., *The Spanish Conquistadores*, A. & C. Black, 1946.

McAndrew, John, *The Open Air Churches of Sixteenth Century Mexico*, Cambridge, Mass.: Harvard University, 1965.

Madariaga, Salvador de, *Hernán Cortés, Conqueror of Mexico*, Hodder and Stoughton, 1942.

——, *The Rise of the Spanish American Empire*, Hollis and Carter, 1947.

Marett, Sir Robert, *Archaeological Tours from Mexico City*, Mexico City: Ediciones Tolteca, 1964.

Martinez del Rio, Pablo, *Los Origenes Americanos*, Mexico City: Paginas del Siglo XX, 1943.

BIBLIOGRAPHY

Mendieta, Jeronimo de (1525–1604), *Historia Ecclesiastica Indiana*, ed. Chavez Hayhoe (3 vols), Mexico City, 1945.
Motolinía, Toribio de Benavente (?–1565), *Historia de los Indios de la Nueva España*, trans. F. B. Steck, Washington, D.C.: Academy of American Franciscan History, 1951.
——, *Memoriales*, ed. Luis Garcia Pimentel, Mexico City, 1903.
——, *Carta al Emperador, Refutación a Las Casas sobre la Colonización Española*, Mexico City: Editorial Jus, 1949.
Muñoz Camargo, Diego (late 16th century), *Historia de Tlaxcala*, Mexico City, 1947.
Nicholson, Irene, *Firefly in the Night: A Study of Ancient Mexican Poetry and Symbolism*, Faber and Faber, 1959.
Oviedo y Valdes, Gonzalo Fernandez de (1478–1557), *Historia General y Natural de la Indias* (4 vols), Madrid, 1951–5.
Parkes, H. B., *History of Mexico*, Eyre and Spottiswoode, 1962.
Parry, J. H., *The Spanish Theory of Empire in the Sixteenth Century*, Cambridge University Press, 1940.
Pomar, Juan Bautista (late 16th century), *Relación de Texcoco*, ed. Chavez Hayhoe, Mexico City, 1941.
Prescott, W. H., *History of the Conquest of Mexico*, many editions.
Ricard, Robert, *La Conquista Espiritual de Mexico*, Mexico City: Editorial Jus, 1947.
Rivet, Paul, *Maya Cities*, Elek Books, 1960.
Rojas, Pedro, *Historia General del Arte Mexicano, Epoca Colonial*, Mexico City: Editorial Hermes, 1963.
Sahagún, Bernardino de (1499–1590), *Historia General de las Cosas de Nueva España*, ed. Miguel Acosta Saignes (3 vols), Mexico City: Editorial Nueva España, 1946.
Simpson, L. B., *The Encomienda in New Spain*, Berkeley: University of California, 1950.
Soustelle, Jacques, *The Daily Life of the Aztecs*, Pelican Books, 1964.
Tezozomoc, Hernando Alvarado (end of 16th century), *Crónica Mexicana*, Mexico City: Editorial Leyenda, 1944.
——, *Crónica Mexicayotl*, Mexico City: University of Mexico, 1949.
Thompson, J. Eric, *The Rise and Fall of Maya Civilization*, Norman (Oklahoma), 1954.
Torquemada, Juan de (1565–1624), *Monarquia Indiana*, ed. Chavez Hayhoe (3 vols), Mexico City, 1943.
Toussaint, Manuel, *Arte Colonial en Mexico*, Mexico City: University of Mexico, 1948.

Vaillant, George C., *Aztecs of Mexico*, New York: Doubleday, Doran, 1941.
White, John Manchip, *Cortés and the Downfall of the Aztec Empire*, Hamish Hamilton, 1971.
Zavala, Silvio, *La Utopia de Tomas More en la Nueva España otros estudios*, Mexico City: Editorial Robredo, 1937.
Zorita, Alonso de (1512–85), *The Lords of New Spain* (*Breve y Sumaria Relación de los Senores de la Nueva España*; abridged and translated by Benjamin Keen), Phoenix House, 1965.

INDEX
Compiled by H. E. Crowe

Acamapichtli, Aztec king 43
Acaxitli, Francisco 271
Aguila, Jerónimo de 89, 90, 151
Ahuaxpitzactzin (Don Carlos) 120
Ahuitzotl, Aztec Emperor 44, 58, 91
Alarcon, Juan Ruiz de, dramatist 313
Albórnoz, accountant 169, 190
Alcalá de Henares, university of 134, 135
Alexander VI, Borgia Pope, Bulls of 80
Almagro, Diego de 222
Almansa, Martin Enriquez de, Viceroy 258
Altamarino, Diego, friar 168
Alva, Don Fernando de, *see* Ixtlilxótchitl
Alvarado, Pedro de 88, 98, 104, 114, 117, 121, 174, 207, 221, 222, 223, 242
Anáhuac 22–45 *passim*, 57, 72, 73, 74, 90, 93, 95, 108, 112–24 *passim*, 129, 138, 145, 146, 164, 165, 168, 172, 198, 217, 219, 220, 221, 229, 243, 245, 246, 264, 271, 278, 282, 291, 296, 307
  agriculture in 194
  Christianity in 298
  culture of 64, 69
  government 49
  libraries and records 274–5
  life in 53–4
  post-Conquest monuments 305
  plagues 174
  population 235–6
  religious and cultural unity 116
Antilles, Spanish 159, 160, 172, 195, 225, 226
Aquiyauhtzin of Huejotzingo, poet 74
Arawaks 82
Audiencia 148, 171, 173, 176, 177, 180, 181, 209, 210, 220, 227, 229, 234, 242, 244, 248, 249, 252, 268

Augustinians 133, 135, 144
Auwera, Johan van, Franciscan friar 138, 139, 164
Avila, Alonso de, Creole 255, 256, 257, 303
Axayacatl, Aztec Emperor 44, 51, 54, 109, 114, 185
Azcapotzalco 41, 42, 43, 278, 281
Aztecs *passim*
  accompany Cortés to Spain 171
  and alcoholism 296
  ceremonial sacrifices 113
  church 53, 61, 64
  civic behaviour of 65
  culture 103, 275
  empire, growth of 37–78
  and Europeans 97
  goldsmiths 69
  government of 49
  hospital system 191
  human sacrifices 58, 59, 60
  intellectual tradition 266
  judicial system 49, 50, 55
  literary culture 72
  losses in battle 124
  loyalties 122
  military power and administration 50, 51, 52, 92
  organizing ability 45
  paintings of 68, 69
  political weakness of 106
  power of 63, 64
  priests 57
  primitive techniques 46
  pyramid 38
  religious system 47
  ruling class 48
  sculpture of 68
  slavery 55, 60
  social system 47, 48, 53, 63
  temples 66–7
  trading 46
  tribal god 40
  warriors 52
  writers 32

Badiano, Juan 271
Balboa 81

INDEX

Balbuena, Bernardo 312
Basaccio, Fray Arncaldo de 270
Basalenque, Fray Diego de 197–8
Bautista, Juan 259, 302–3
Benalcázar, Sebastian de 222
Benavente, Toribio de (Motolinía), Franciscan 126, 140
   See also Motolinía
Benavides, Gil Gonzalez de 255
Bonampak murals 29, 68
Borja, Fray Alonso de 192
Brothers of the Common Life 137
Burgos, Laws of 82, 225
Burgundy, Dukes of 136, 137

Cacama, King of Texcoco 92, 111, 112, 119
Calatrava, Knights of 52
Campeche 25, 165
Caribs 82
Caro, Juan 217
Carochio, Father Horacio, Jesuit scholar 288
Cempoala/Cempoalans 98, 99, 101, 104, 108
Ceynos, Francisco de, oidor 234, 241, 256
Chalchihuitlicue, water-goddess 57
Chalco 53, 74, 122, 162
Chamula 241, 242
Champótón 84, 85
Chapultepec 41, 65, 205, 209
Charles V, King-Emperor 67, 94, 99, 101, 113, 135, 136, 137, 138, 139, 149, 166, 179, 203, 206, 238, 239, 242, 268, 292
Chiapas 21, 25, 148, 199, 239, 241, 246
Chichicuepan of Chalco, poet, 74
Chichén-Itzá 26, 35, 67
Chichimecatecuhtli 121
Chichimecs 40, 64, 133, 148, 172, 251, 271, 293
   dynasty 48, 69
   habits 37
   kings of Texcoco 38
   of Tenayuca 43
Chimalpahin, Muñoz, historian 236, 271, 307
Chirinos, inspector 169, 173
Cholula, city 34, 44, 58, 64, 68, 107, 109, 117, 121, 245
   Aztec ally 105
   culture of 31
   excavations at 22
   massacre at 106–8
Cisneros, Cardinal, Ximenes de 134
Cisneros, Fray García de, Franciscan 269
Citlaltepetl volcano 40, 85
Clavijero, Francisco Xavier, Jesuit, quoted 71, 313–14
Coatlicue, goddess 299, 308
Coatzacoalcos 85, 128, 241, 242
Cohuanococh, King of Texcoco 120, 164, 166
Colima 128
Columbus, Christopher, lands in Bahamas 79, 80, 161
Contreras, Francisco Bautista de 271
Contreras, Pedro Moya de, Archbishop and Viceroy, 289–90
Copán 28
Coronado, Vasquez de 223
Cortés, Hernan, leader of expedition, later Governor and Captain-General, lands at Vera Cruz 43, 88; and Aztec religion 53; army of reinforced by Tlaxcalans 59; despatches treasure to Madrid 69; arrival at Tenochtitlán 87, 88; mistaken for Quetzalcoatl 88, 90, 92, 93; and Aguila 89, 90; receives Doña Marina as gift 89, 90; receives adornments of Quetzalcoatl 93–4; nickname of 98; presentation of girls 99; action against Aztecs 99, 100; influences Totonacs and Tlaxcalans 59, 101, 102, 103; writes to King 101; Aztecs visit 102; and conversion 103; prepares to confront Aztecs 105, 106; and Cholula 107; in Tenochtitlán 110–11; treatment of opposition 112; calls for allegiance to Charles V 112; introduces Aztecs to Christianity 112; battles with Aztecs 117; retires to Tlaxcala 117; victory at Otumba 117; political activities 118; at Texcoco 118; takes Tenochtitlán 122–4; rebuilds city 125, 126; leniency to defeated 125; appointed Governor and Captain-General of New Spain 127; prestige of 127; opposes slavery 127; con-

INDEX

version of Indians 128, 140;
relinquishes power 159, 160;
defence of encomiendas 161–2;
protection of Indians 162; Honduras expedition 163–8, 241;
has Aztec notables hanged 165,
166; welcomed back to Mexico
168; authority suspended 168;
leaves for Spain 171; encomiendas of 176; views on Indians
179; returns to Mexico 184,
186, 187; new title of 187, 203;
hospital of 191; at festivities
203–7; Viceroy and 209; work
of 210; leaves New Spain 211;
property of 256, 305; also 32,
35, 67, 85, 86, 140, 141, 220,
236, 242, 263, 280, 293
Cortés, Luis 257
Cortés, Martin 255, 256, 258
Coruña, Fray Martín de la 186,
188, 190
Cosijopi, Zapotec Prince 219–20
Council of the Indies 173, 174, 177,
182, 183, 184, 211, 225, 229,
231, 233, 244, 248–9, 250, 251,
253, 285, 289
Council of Trent 148, 195, 208
Coyoacán 125, 138, 162
Cozumel, Grijalva at 84
Coxtemexi 166
Creoles 156, 255, 258, 271, 272,
273, 285, 287, 288, 290, 293,
295, 302, 310, 312, 314, 393
Cruz, Sor Juana Inés de la, poetess
313
Cruz, Martin de la, Indian writer
271
Cuba 81, 83
Cuitlalpitoc, Aztec noble 88, 92
Cuauchloitactin, Don Juan, Texcocan noble, 141
Cuauhcóatl 41
Cuauhpopoca, Aztec governor 110,
111
Cuauhtémoc, Aztec Emperor 90,
122, 123, 128, 140, 166, 189,
243, 258, 283
 defeated by Cortés 118
 hanged by Cortés 165
 national hero 315
Cuauhtitlan 53, 288, 299, 308
Cuernavaca 52, 210, 305
Cueva, Francisco de la 104
Cuicuilco pyramid 22

Cuicuitzcatl, Texcocan Prince 120
Cuitláhuac, Aztec Emperor 90, 109,
111, 114, 117, 118
Culhuacán 34, 41, 42, 43, 85
Culhuas 41, 43, 85, 89, 293
Cuzco 222

Daciano, Fray Jacobo 157
Darien (Tierra Firme) 89
Dekkers, Johan, Flemish friar 138,
139, 164
Delgadillo, oidor 173, 181
Deventer 137
Díaz del Castillo, Bernal, historian
of the Conquest 64, 66, 67, 83,
86, 92, 97–8, 104, 111, 118, 121,
122, 140, 159, 171, 187, 241,
242, 248, 269
 on Alvarado venture 222–3
 appeals for Indian labour 242
 appointed regidor 243
 condemns Cortés 166
 on Doña Marina 90
 on festivities 203–5
 and Grijalva's entry into Pánuco
85
 on Indians under Spanish rule
245–6
 on siege conditions 124
 writes to King of Spain 242
Diaz, Juan, Spanish priest 136
Diego, Juan, Indian peasant 299
Dominican Order of Friars 82, 133,
135, 144, 148, 160, 175, 177,
245, 272
Don Antonio, Tarascan Prince 198
Don Pedro, Tarascan Prince 189,
190

Eagle-Knights, military order 52, 74
Ecatepec 217
Ecuador 222
El Tajín, architecture of 32
Encomenderos (landholders) 150,
151, 228, 229, 230, 242
 See also Encomiendas
Encomiendas 150, 153, 159, 160,
170, 240, 251
 conditions of labour 162–3
 differences over 160, 161, 162
 and new laws 227–8
 given as rewards 241
 See also Encomenderos
Erasmus 137, 161
Escalona, Fray Alonso de 284, 285

INDEX

Estrada, treasurer of administration 169
   temporary governor 170, 177

Ferdinand, King of Spain 79, 127, 133-4, 208
Flanders 137
Florence 286
Fochez, Fray Juan de 270
Fonseca, Bishop 170
Franciscan Order of Friars 106, 133, 134, 135, 140, 142, 144, 147, 148, 175, 177, 183, 190, 196, 218, 245, 263, 264, 269, 271, 284, 285, 286, 290, 299
Friars 133, 188, 217, 247, 267, 293, 294
   approved by King and Pope 135, 136, 138, 139, 140
   architects 305
   authority of 154, 155
   and conversion 266
   denounce malpractices 173
   encomienda system and conversion 162, 229
   flaw in experiment 155
   linguistic ability 147, 148-55
   mission system 148, 150
   and Nahuatl literature 275, 276, 277
   oppose Indian priesthood 290
   reinforcements 142
   stage-manage pageant 207
   struggle for Indians 175
   view of Indians 179
   work breaks down 295
Fuenleal, Sebastien Ramirez de, president of second Audiencia 184, 209, 227, 240, 268, 269
Fuensalida, Luis de, Franciscan 278

Gama, Vasco de 80
Gante, Fray Pedro de (Peter of Ghent) 42, 136, 137, 142, 143, 147, 164, 175, 179, 183, 263, 264, 269, 278
Gaona, Fray Juan de 157, 270
Garcés, Fray Julian, Bishop of Tlaxcala 177, 191, 198, 264
Garay, Francisco de 171
Góngora, Carlos de Siguenza y 313
Granada 67, 79, 80, 103, 127, 134, 184
Grijalva, Juan de, leader of expedition 84, 85, 86, 88

Grijalva river 19
Guadalajara, colonists at 221
Guadalupe 199
Guanajuato 185
Guatemala 21, 25, 44, 128, 148, 174, 221, 222, 241, 242, 243, 244, 245, 246, 249
Guerrero, Gonzalo 21, 89
Guzmán, Beltrán Nuño de, President of the Council 171, 172, 174, 185, 209, 210, 211, 229, 265
   accuses Zumárraga 180, 181
   assumes authority in New Spain 172
   misrule of 227
   murders Tarascan king 188
   opposed by Bishops 179
   prestige declines 182
   sent to Spain 211
   and Tarascans 188-9
   treatment of Indians 172, 173, 176, 190, 191

Hadrian VI, Pope 135, 137, 138, 139, 292
Haiti 80
Hapsburg, House of 136, 137, 149, 184, 309, 311
Havana 84, 168
Hernandez de Cordóba, Francisco 83, 84, 85, 89
Hidalgo, state 34, 38, 101
Hispaniola, Spanish settlers in 80, 81
Holy Face of Lucca 299
Holy Shroud of Milan 299
Honduras 25, 83, 163, 164
   expedition of Cortés to 164-8
Honduras, Gulf of 129, 165
Hospital de Jésus 191
Hospital de la Concepción 236
Hospital de Santa Fé 191
Huaquechollan 121
Huaxteca 44, 58, 233, 268
Huaxtecs 37, 39, 148
Huejotla 121
Huejotzingo, city 44, 58, 74, 101, 105, 118, 139, 142, 176, 181, 245, 310
Huemac, Toltec ruler 36
Huitzilopochtli, tribal sun-god of Aztecs 40, 41, 52, 57, 58, 60, 66, 93, 111, 113, 125, 280
Humboldt, Alexander von 314

INDEX 331

Indians, Mexican, *passim*
administrative employees 302
aristocracy 270
and Christianity 145, 153, 266, 297-8
Church and state protect 82
civil advancement 156
college 271, 290, 293
concubinage of 219
conversion of 128, 140
notables 141
and Cortés, support for 32, 33, 90, 118, 159, 168, 171
craftsmen 301-2
culture 156, 281
  royal orders against writing on 285
  prospects of ruined 279, 287
discipline of 237
education 142, 197, 267
  neglect and objection to 272, 286, 288, 289
and encomiendas 160-2
and European crafts and trades 143, 195, 246-7, 266
freedom of 227-8
and Guzman, life under 171-6, 188
Hispanic habits acquired 296
history prohibited 279, 285-6
hospitals for 197
hymns and songs censored 279
idolatry 145, 218, 219
polygamy of 152, 300
population decrease 301
preferment denied 290
priesthood denied 272, 288
professional practice refused 272-273
refute attack on their own religion 292-3
revolt and kill friars 220-21
scholars 270, 271
sexuality of 152
social training 301
and Spaniards, life under 244-5
  Crown protects 161
  intermarriage 293
and technological innovations 56
town life of 214-17
transport methods 46
upper class 246
villages for 176-7
welfare of 225, 226
writers 86

Inquisition 148
Isabel, Doña, Moctezuma's daughter 217
Isabella, Queen of Spain 79, 80, 133, 134, 208
Itzapapá'lotl (Obsidian butterfly) 278
Itzcoatl, Aztec Emperor 44, 119, 275
Ixtaccíhuatl volcano 22, 280, 307
Ixtapalapa 66
Ixtlilxóchitl (Don Fernando de Alva), chronicler 38, 58, 70, 71-2, 92, 119, 122, 124, 140, 165-6, 167, 268, 271, 287-8
Ixtlilxóchitl, Texcocan Prince 136, 138, 139, 167

Jacobita, Martin, Indian writer 281
Jaguar Knights, military order 52
Jaina Island 29
Jalisco 148, 182, 185, 189, 210, 220, 221, 223
Jamaica 81, 171
Jesuits 288-9
Jiménez, Francisco, friar 278
John II, King of Castile 208
Juarez, Benito 277, 314
Julianillo (Julián), Indian interpreter 84, 85

Kempis, Thomas à 271
Kukulcán, Maya name for Quetzalcóatl 35

Landa, Fray Diego de, Bishop of Yucatán 27
La Quemada 37
Las Casas, Bartolomé de, Bishop of Chiapas 82, 106, 149, 177, 180, 199, 200, 229, 238, 239, 244, 251, 255
  condemns colonial system 247-8
  settlers' enemy 227
  treatment of Indians 239, 240
La Venta 20, 21
Lawrence, D. H. 145
León, Luis Ponce de, special commissioner 81, 163, 164, 168, 170
Leonor, Doña, Moctezuma's daughter 217
Loaisa, Garcia de, General of the Dominicans 170, 177, 222

President of Council of the Indies 225
Lopez, Jeronimo 272, 273
Louvain, University of 137
Lower California 210
Low Countries, culture of 137

Madariaga, Salvador, quoted 82, 91, 92, 111
Madrid 256, 286, 312
Malinalco 52, 298
Marina, Doña 89, 98, 99, 107, 167, 257
Matienzo, oidor 173
Matlatzinca 43, 52; language 38
Maximilian, Emperor 41
Maxixcatzin 101, 105
Mayapán 35, 36
Maya/Mayas 21, 24, 26, 32, 35, 39, 221
  architects and architecture 28, 66
  barbarism of 45
  calendars 25, 26
  cities 64
  craftsmanship 36
  culture, renaissance of 26, 27, 29
  habits, style and customs 29
  New Empire of 26, 35
  Old Empire of 25, 26, 27, 29, 30
  oppose Spaniards 83
  ruler-priests 56
Mendieta, Jerónimo de, Franciscan historian 147, 175, 268, 278, 284, 313
Medina del Campo 67
Melchorejo (Melchor), Indian interpreter 84, 85
Mendoza, Antonio de, Count of Tendilla, first Viceroy of New Spain 156, 188, 194, 203, 205, 206, 209, 218, 231, 232, 234, 242, 258, 263, 269, 271, 272, 279; dispute Guzmán 210–11; and Cortés 211; and encomiendas 217, 229, 230; and Nueva Galicia revolt 220, 221–4
Mendoza, Diego Hurtado de 208
Mendoza, Diego de, Indian nobleman 280–81
Mendoza family 208
Mendoza, Inigo Lopez de, Marqués of Santillana, father of Viceroy 208
Mendoza, Pedro Gonzalez de 208
Mendicant Friars, Order of 127, 133, 149, 150, 153, 154, 159, 264, 295
  attitude to Indians 153, 155, 156
  and Indian labour 155
  spiritual and intellectual activity 134
  theocracy 148
Mercedarian friars 135
Mesoamerica 13, 17, 21, 42
  culture and civilization 20, 44, 45, 72
  development of 22
  gods of 57
  religion and sacrifices 58
  society 46
  warfare 52
Mestizos 156–8, 272, 295, 304, 310, 314
Metztitlán 233, 248
Mexica (Aztecs) 40
Mexico 13, 40, 47, 101, 164, 243, 251, 313, 314
  pre-Conquest 13–78
Mexico City 22, 34, 38, 42, 138, 142, 145, 157, 158, 175, 197, 203, 217, 220, 242, 276, 288, 303, 312
  See also Tenochtitlán
Mexico, Gulf of 18–19, 22, 39, 44, 45, 81, 84, 85
Mexico, Valley of 21–63 *passim*, 101, 105, 108, 118, 120, 122, 140, 148, 162, 191, 203, 275
Michoacán state 38, 39, 40, 157, 164, 184–200 *passim*, 210, 221, 223, 251, 294, 300, 307
Mije 168
Mixcóatl, Toltec chieftain 34
Mixtecs 30, 44, 46, 72, 118, 177
Mixtón rebellion 220, 223, 242
Mochuihquecholtzomatzin, Don Francisco, Texcocan noble 141
Moctezuma I, Ilhuicamina, Aztec Emperor (1440–69) 44, 47, 65, 70, 85, 89, 91
Moctezuma II, Xocoyotzin Aztec, Emperor (1502–19), palace of 67; harem of 69, 70; greets Grijalva 85; belief about Cortés 91; demoralized by Cortés 91; devoted to religion 91; and Cortés' arrival 95; attitude to Spain 96, 97; and Totonacs 100; invites Spaniards to capital 105; plan fails 106, 107;

INDEX

Cortés' prisoner 108, 110; refuses Christianity 109; hands over power to Charles V 112, 113, 114; demands Spaniards leave Anahuac 114; communicates with Narvaez 114, 115; killed 117; treasure demanded by Charles V 128; sons of go to Spain 171
Monasteries 148, 150–51, 153, 155, 157, 177, 295, 305–6
Mondejar, Marqués de 209
Monte Alban 21, 30, 31, 64
Montúfar, Archbishop 157, 272, 299
More, Thomas 161, 192, 193, 199
Morelia 193
Morelos state 21, 31, 34, 38, 148
Motagua river 25
Motenehuatzin of Tlaxcala, poet 74
Motolinía (Toribio de Benavente) friar, quoted 39, 126, 140, 152, 153, 157, 173, 174, 176, 177, 199, 207, 238, 239, 240, 241, 247, 252, 264, 268–9, 309
Muñoz, Alonso, visitador 234, 257, 258

Nahúa/Nahúas 31, 32, 37, 38, 39, 40, 45, 47, 54, 64, 103, 185, 186, 289–91, 294, 300, 305, 306, 309
Náhuatl, language 23, 33, 38, 53, 72, 73, 90, 98, 137, 143, 146, 147, 158, 266, 267, 269, 276, 279, 283, 288
Narvaez, Pánfilo de, 45, 114
Navarro, Fray Miguel, 284, 285
Nayarit 220
Nazareo, Pablo, Indian writer 271
New Laws 227, 248, 249
New Spain 312
  art in 305–10
  becomes viceroyalty 180
  cultural growth 314
  government after Cortés 169
  history of 270–7
  independence of 314
  population 237
  status in 312–13
  two cultures in 304
Nezahualcóyotl, philosopher-king of Texcoco 48, 74, 119, 141, 275
  designs embankment 29
  family 70

national hero 315
  reputation of 69, 70
  rule and succession 70, 71
Nezahualpilli, King of Texcoco 69, 70, 74, 87, 91, 119, 120, 212, 218
Noche Triste 115, 117, 120
Nombre de Dios, colony at 81
Nueva Galicia 182, 187, 211, 220–221, 251
Nueva Granada (Colombia) 248

Oaxaca 21, 24, 40, 59, 157, 193, 295
Oaxtepec 70
Oaxyecac, mines of 174
Observants, Order of Franciscans 134, 135
Ocuiltecs 298
Oidores 182, 183, 234
Olmec/Olmecs 19, 22, 23, 25, 29, 32, 56, 101
  archaic civilization of 19
  ceramics and sculpture of 20–21
  craftsmen 20
  culture 19, 21
  expansion 21
  lands 20
Olíd, Cristobal de, 164, 167, 187
Olmán 19
Olmedo, Bartolomé de, friar 94, 99, 107, 113, 135–6
Olmos, Fray Andrés, de 147, 252, 268, 269, 270, 275, 281
Ometecuhtli (Lord of Duality) 57
Ometochtli, Don Carlos, tlatoani of Texcoco 218–19, 268, 271, 294
Oñate, Cristobal de 223
Orteguilla, page to Moctezuma 114
Ortiz, Father 181
Otomi/Otomis 37, 38, 39, 44, 59, 101, 145, 148, 185
Otumba 125, 162
Ovando, Nicolás de 92

Pablo, Don, Tarascan Prince, 157
Padilla, Mota, quoted 23n.
Paganism 145, 155, 217–20, 292
Palenque 28
Pánuco, river 19, 85, 128, 171, 187
Patzcuaro 189, 190, 191, 193, 196
  college at 288
Paul III, Pope 155–6, 178–9
Paz, Juan 217
Peralta, Gaston de, Marqués de Falces, Viceroy 257

INDEX

Perote 191
Petén 25, 27, 28
Philip II, King of Spain 137, 149, 160, 251, 256, 257, 279, 265, 285, 312
Philip III, king of Spain 288
Pinotl, chief of the calpixque 92
Placido, Francisco, Indian hymn-writer 278
Pliny 271
Poets, Aztec 74
Ponce de León, Juan, *see* León, Ponce de
Popocatepetl volcano 22, 280
Pomar, historian 268
Prescott, W. H. 72, 243
Puebla, state 22, 38, 101
Puebla de los Angeles 177
Puerto, Don Nicolas del, first Indian Bishop 157
Puerta de la Navidad 223
Puerto Rico 81
Puga, Vasco de 234, 258
Purépecha (Tarascans) 39, 185, 198

Querétaro 288
Quetzalcóatl, Toltec Tlamacazqui, God or high priest 32, 33, 34, 35, 57, 58, 60, 66, 73, 93, 95, 96, 97, 101, 107, 281
  adornments of 93-4
  cult adopted by Toltecs 34
  Cortés mistaken for 88, 90, 92
  temple of 23, 31
Quintalbor 96
Quintana Roo 25
Quiroga, Vasco de 195, 236, 244, 251, 264, 294
  becomes Bishop of Michoacan 158, 192, 193, 195
  death of 193
  and encomenderos 244
  and Franciscans 196
  defends Indians 199
  founds hospital 191, 192
  national hero 315
  organizes Indians 191
  prestige of 184, 185, 191, 200
  transforms agriculture 194-5
Quito 222

Ramirez, Diego, visitador 233, 248
Remesal, Fray Antonio de, historian, quoted 221

Repartimiento (encomienda) 82, 83
Ricaud, Robert, quoted 310-11
Rojas, Pedro 305
Royal and Pontifical University of Mexico 271, 287, 313

Sahagún, Fray Bernardino de, Franciscan writer, quoted 33, 34, 36, 37, 39, 60, 73, 86, 88, 92, 93, 95, 96, 106, 145, 150, 252, 264, 271, 273, 275, 277-9, 280-1, 284, 286, 292, 297, 315
St. Nicolas college, Pátzcuaro 198
St. Nicolas college, Valladolid 198
Salamanca 67, 135, 225, 280
Salazar, agent 169, 173, 175, 181, 232-3
Salmerón, Juan de 227
Sandoval, Gonzalo de 164
San Francisco, Fray Jacinto de 251
San Juan de Ulúa 90
San José de los Naturales, school at 142
Santa Cruz de Tlatelolco, college of 269, 270, 271
Santa Fé de la Laguna 191, 193
Santa Fé de Mexico 192
Santiago de los Caballeros 221
Santiago de Guatemala 243
Santiago, Knights of 52
Santo Domingo 80, 240, 248, 249
Sinaloa 220
Sintzicha Tanguaxan (Calzontzin), Tarascan King 157, 186, 188, 190
Slavery 55, 60, 82, 127, 172
Soustelle, Jacques, quoted 266
Spaniards/Spanish acquire land 246
  in Anahuac 214-17
  and Aztec religion 113
  behaviour in Cortés' absence 168, 169
  colonial policy of 161
  conquest in Mexico 13, 26, 32, 35, 38
  education of 197, 198, 271
  given girls as gifts 104
  import plagues to Mexico 65
  and Mexican civilization 103
  officials, strictness of 252
  soldiers 264
  in Tlaxcala 116
  and treasure 128, 149
  See also Spanish Crown

INDEX 335

Spanish Crown, appoints Audiencia 171
 and Cortés 163
 and encomiendas 160, 161
 and Indians 161, 178, 230
 opposes slavery 172
 and settlers and Indians 82
Spice Islands (Moluccas) 221, 222

Tabasco, river 85
Tabasco, state 19, 21, 242
Tacuba, ruler of 44, 89, 125, 164, 217
Tapia, Andrés de 113
Tarascan/Tarascans (Purépecha) 39, 44, 51, 164, 185–7, 193–5, 198–9
Taxco 313
Tecocoltzin, Don Fernando, Texcocan Prince 120
Tecoroli, Indian god 221
Tehuantepec 21, 148
Tello de Sandoval, special commissioner 228, 229, 234
Temilotzin, Aztec Commander-in-Chief 164, 166
Tenayuca 38, 42, 43, 66
Tenochtitlán, Aztec capital city 22, 28, 42–58 (*passim*), 62–118 (*passim*), 214, 269, 275, 280–90 (*passim*)
 annihilation of 68, 124, 138
 assault on 121–3
 Náhuatl poetry on 279
 rebuilding 125–6, 174
 See also Mexico City
Tentitl, Aztec noble 88, 92, 94, 96
Teotihuacán 21, 22, 23, 24, 27, 29, 31, 32, 36, 38, 53, 63, 64, 101, 186, 278
Tepanecs of Azcapotzalco 41, 43, 119, 275, 293
Tepeaca, 121, 173, 245
Tepehua 268
Tepepulco monastery 280
Tepeyac, hill of 299
Tepetlaoztoc 232, 233
Tepotzotlán, college at 288, 289, 313
Tequitqui artists 307
Teteoimman, mother of the gods 278
Tetlahuehuezquititzin, Don Pedro, Texcocan noble 141

Tetlepanquetzal, King of Tlacopan 164, 165, 214
Texcoco, sub-kingdom 41, 42, 47, 48, 58, 59, 64, 70, 71, 72, 74, 87, 90, 92, 118, 119, 122, 123–5, 136, 141, 158, 162, 168, 181, 183, 212, 232, 245, 288, 292, 293
 archives destroyed 268
 culture 72
 Indian community 138
 King of 44, 50, 125, 164
 monastery 142
 Náhuatl poetry 279
Texcotzingo 70
Tezcatlipoca, Toltec war-god 34, 52, 57, 59, 93
Tezozomoc, Don Hernando Alvarado, chronicler, quoted 87, 88, 92, 271
Tezozomoc, Tepanec ruler 43, 44, 69
Tierra Firme 81, 89
Tikal 25
Tiripitío 196, 197, 198, 223
Tizoc, Aztec Emperor 44
Tlacochuatzin, Doña Maria, Prince Ixtlilxóchitl's mother 141
Tlacopán, sub-kingdom 44, 47, 48, 58, 214
Tlalmanalco 280, 307, 308
Tlaloc, god of rain and agriculture 24, 57, 58, 59, 60, 66, 93, 113
Tlacotzin (Don Juan Velazquez) 125, 126
Tlatelolco, city and college 53–4, 64, 66–8, 181, 204, 216, 269, 271, 274, 281, 286, 287, 290, 293, 295–6
Tlatilco 21, 22
Tlaxcala/Tlaxcalans 35, 38, 58, 74, 90, 100, 101, 105, 108, 109, 119, 121, 122, 123, 136, 140, 166, 168, 170, 207, 232, 238, 245, 268, 293, 309
 Aztecs and 44–5
 allied to Spaniards 58, 59, 79
 conversion of 104, 177
 festivities at 205–7
 fight with Cortés 117
 losses 124
 monastery 142
 rebuff Cortés 101
 and Spaniards 107
 warriors 106

336 INDEX

Tlaxcala, Bishop of 177, 181
Tlocahuepan Yohualicahuatzin (Don Pedro), son of Moctezuma 217
Tloque Nahuaque, god 74
Toltecs 31, 32, 33, 34, 35, 36, 37, 38, 43, 47, 55, 63, 64, 67, 93, 186, 282, 293
Toluca 38, 52
Tonantzin, mother-goddess 299
Tonatiuh, sun-god 57, 98
Topiltzin, son of Mixcóatl 34–6
Tordesillas, Treaty 80
Torquemada, Fray Juan de, Franciscan writer 313
Totonacs 32, 40, 49, 98–100, 268
Tovar, Juan de, 158
Tres Zapotes 20, 21
Tula 34, 35, 36, 39, 58, 92, 112, 217
Tulúm, Mayan town 84
Turécato (Tarécuato), Don Juan de 157
Twelve, The 139, 142, 292
Tzintzuntzán 186, 193

Uaxactún 25
Uruápan 191, 195
Usumacinta river 25
Utopia (More) 192, 194, 199
Uxmal 26, 35, 67

Vaillant, Dr. George, quoted 58
Valadés, Diego de, Franciscan mestizo writer 158
Valderrama, Jerónimo de, visitador 234, 255, 258
Valencia, Fray Martín de, leader of The Twelve 139, 140, 144, 174, 268, 307
Valeriano, Antonio, gobernador 270, 281
Valle, Marquesado del 210, 240, 255, 257
Valladolid 179, 184, 193, 194, 197, 227, 244
Velasco, Luis de, second Viceroy 219, 232, 233–5, 240, 249, 258, 263, 271
Velázquez, Diego, Governor of Cuba 83–4, 114, 159, 164
Vera Cruz 21, 32, 38, 43, 88, 92, 114, 140, 168, 171, 180, 191, 257
Villa, José Moreno 307
Villalobos 223
Villamanrique, Marqués de, Viceroy 238
Villanueva, oidor 258
Virgin of Guadalupe, story of 298–299, 300
Vitoria, Francisco de 149, 225, 226
Vives, Luis 161

White, J. Manchip, quoted 91

Xicoténcatl, Tlaxcalan magistrate 104, 117
Xicoténcatl, son of Tlaxcalan magistrate 104, 117, 121
Xilonen, harvest goddess 59
Ximenes de Cisneros, Archbishop, 134
Xipe Totec, festivity god 59
Xiuhámatl 259
Xiuhtecutli, Lord of Fire 57
Xochicalco 31, 32, 33, 34
Xochimilco 271
Xolotl, Chichimec chieftain, 38, 48

Yohyontzin of Texcoco, poet 74
Yucatán 25, 26, 28, 29, 34, 35, 36, 81, 82, 83, 85, 89, 148

Zacatecas 37, 220
Zapotec 21, 24, 29, 30, 44, 147, 168, 219, 220
Zorita, Alonso de, oidor 234, 241, 248–55
Zuazo, lawyer 167
Zumarraga, Fray Juan de, Bishop and Archbishop of Mexico 177, 179–80, 182–3, 192, 193, 198, 209, 218–19, 225, 229, 264, 267–9, 271, 272, 280, 285, 299